DATE DUE

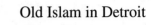

Old Islam in Detroit

Old Islam in Detroit

Rediscovering the Muslim American Past

SALLY HOWELL

OXFORD
UNIVERSITY PRESS

Oxford University Press is a department of the University of
Oxford. It furthers the University's objective of excellence in research,
scholarship, and education by publishing worldwide.

Oxford   New York
Auckland   Cape Town   Dar es Salaam   Hong Kong   Karachi
Kuala Lumpur   Madrid   Melbourne   Mexico City   Nairobi
New Delhi   Shanghai   Taipei   Toronto

With offices in
Argentina   Austria   Brazil   Chile   Czech Republic   France   Greece
Guatemala   Hungary   Italy   Japan   Poland   Portugal   Singapore
South Korea   Switzerland   Thailand   Turkey   Ukraine   Vietnam

Oxford is a registered trademark of Oxford University Press
in the UK and certain other countries.

Published in the United States of America by
Oxford University Press
198 Madison Avenue, New York, NY 10016

© Oxford University Press 2014

Library of Congress Cataloging-in-Publication Data
Howell, Sally.
Old Islam in Detroit: rediscovering the muslim American past / Sally Howell.
   pages cm
Includes bibliographical references and index.
ISBN 978–0–19–937200–3 (hard cover: alk. paper)—ISBN 978–0–19–937201–0 (updf)—
ISBN 978–0–19–937202–7 (epub)   1. Muslims—Michigan—Detroit.
2. Arab Americans—Michigan—Detroit.   I. Title.
BP67.U62M54 2014
297.09774'34—dc23
2013050459

9 8 7 6 5 4 3 2 1
Printed in the United States of America
on acid-free paper

CONTENTS

ACKNOWLEDGMENTS

Dozens of people welcomed me into their homes, mosques, and businesses during the nine years I worked on this project. They shared their memories; they let me borrow treasured photographs and papers; and they were willing to reflect deeply on the past and how it relates to the contemporary practice of Islam in Detroit. Without their trust and patience, this project would not have gone forward, and their openness to my curiosity was not without risks. I carried out my research during a period of deep geopolitical crisis, when US mosques and their leaders faced intense public and governmental scrutiny. As I have listened and re-listened to their voices on tape, transcribed their words, and pondered our conversations, I have come to find all of this testimony moving and precious. It has helped me make sense of larger narratives of Muslim American history in ways only personal contact and sharing can do. The voices of Detroit's old and new Muslims do not appear as often in this text as I would like, but the knowledge they shared with me informs every page, and I am profoundly grateful to everyone who agreed to sit for an interview. Their names appear in the bibliography on pages 331–347.

As my research progressed, I came to rely on the special assistance and friendship of several members of the Detroit Muslim community who, almost without fail, were willing to answer my repeated inquiries, put me in touch with other sources, guide me through their own understanding and practice of Islam, show me around Detroit, and make me feel welcome in their homes and mosques. In particular, Hajj Chuck Alawan, Hajj Eide Alawan, Hajj Akil Fahd, and Hajj Dawud Walid are so close to this project that they deserve special recognition, even part ownership. Others who were of immeasurable help to me, I am sad to say, did not live to see this project completed. They include Abdullah Berry, Gladys Ecie, Hussien El Haje, Imam Vehbi Ismail, and Hussein Makled. *Allah yarhamhum.*

My project has entailed reconstructing a history for which there existed no accessible archive. Fortunately, many of the people I met and spoke with had papers and other materials they were willing to share, not just with me, but with posterity. The following individuals and families have donated papers from their personal collections to the Bentley Historical Library on the campus of the University of Michigan: Liela Abass, the Abraham family, Chuck Alawan, Raad Alawan, Helen Atwel, the Bazzy family, Victor Begg, Joseph Caurdy, Adnan Chirri, Allie Fayz, the Karoub family, Julia Haragely, Hussein Makled, and Mohammed Mardini. I drew heavily from these collections, and I thank these individuals for their generous gifts to the University of Michigan. Additional photographs and documents were provided to me by Ihsan Bagby, Kamel Bazzi, Abdullah Berry, Schrifia Aossey Chahine, Robert Dannin, Miriam Eastman, Shedrick El-Amin, Akil Fahd, Tahira Hassanein Khalid, and Haitaima Sharieff. I also benefited from the support of several avid research assistants and translators, including Nader Seif, Kamel Bazzi, Saja Alshamary, Ryan Ferris, and Rebecca Karam, to whom I am grateful.

Anyone who delves into the history of Islam and Muslim communities in the United States will quickly realize that archival holdings on these populations are few and far between. The Bentley Historical Library, through the work of Ken Scheffel and Len Coombs, has shown remarkable foresight in recognizing the significance of these populations. I thank both Ken and Len for their tireless efforts as collectors and curators of Muslim American history, work they began in the 1990s. One of the great joys of creating this book has been watching the relationship between these archivists, local Muslims, and the Bentley grow into a stable collaboration that will continue to generate and preserve historical knowledge of Islam in North America.

Many academic colleagues and advisors also contributed to my efforts. I thank the members of my dissertation committee, Scott Kurashige, Amaney Jamal, Nadine Naber, and Evelyn Alsultany for their careful attention, timely criticism, and lived example. Karen Leonard and Edward Curtis IV commented extensively on an earlier draft of this manuscript. I hope they feel that their time was well spent (and can see their positive influence) when they read this version. The anonymous reviewers for Oxford University Press, and my colleague Pam Pennock, also provided much appreciated feedback. I presented material from this book at several workshops where I received generous support and criticism. These events include the Luce Workshop on Islam in America organized by Amaney Jamal at Princeton University; the Islam in/and America workshop organized by Zareena Grewal, Rosemary Corbett, and Juliane Hammer at George Mason University; and the Mashriq/Mahjar Conference organized by Akram Khater, Andrew Arsan, and John Karam at North Carolina State University. I also received helpful suggestions from audiences at the Islamic Association of Greater Detroit, the Muslim Center of Detroit, and the ISNA Diversity Forum at the Islamic Center of America, where I debuted much of this material.

I am also grateful to the acquisitions editor at Oxford University Press, Cynthia Read, who has been supportive of this project from our first encounter. Likewise the entire OUP team, Stuart Roberts, Alyssa Bender, Molly Morrison, and Marcela Maxfield, has been a pleasure to work with at every stage. I am eager as well to acknowledge my collaborators on the Building Islam in Detroit project, with whom I first visited many of Detroit's mosques: Omar Baghdadi, Yusuf Begg, Mucahit Bilici, Akil Fahd, Mufaddal Kapadia, Mara Leichtman, Kate McClellan, Elshafei Mohammed, and Andrew Shryock. Their intellectual curiosity and ability to engage creatively with Detroit's Muslims was invigorating and made the early stages of my research in the city exciting. Yelena Godina, who designed the project's website and exhibition (which can still be viewed at http://biid.lsa.umich.edu/) was an indispensable help in the public cultural work that has been part of this project from its earliest stages.

Funding for my research in its many stages was provided by a Rackham Predoctoral Fellowship and the Susan Lipschutz Award at the University of Michigan. The Rackham Graduate School, the Islamic Studies Initiative, and the Duderstadt Center, all at the University of Michigan, provided additional support to the Building Islam in Detroit project, which also supported my work. The Center for Arab American Studies and the Department of Social Sciences at the University of Michigan-Dearborn offered much-needed support for the final stages.

Finally, I would like to thank Andrew Shryock and Eleanor Howell-Shryock for their support and sustenance. Andrew's intellectual contributions to my work run deep. He has been a great partner in life, taking me places I never would have ventured on my own and following me into the depths of my own research on Arab and Muslim Detroit in ways that go far beyond the call of duty. These experiences have enriched our lives, and it is a tremendous joy to share them with someone so insightful, honest, critical, and filled with humor and warmth. Eleanor left for college in the same week I mailed off this manuscript. She was at my side during

Muslim holiday feasts in Detroit and during our stays in Bedouin villages in Jordan. She has visited more mosques in greater Detroit than most local Muslims ever will, and she adapted cheerfully to a house turned upside down by deadlines, speaking engagements, and endless research obligations. We have had so many adventures together. So many discoveries. I thank you both.

LIST OF FIGURES

Old Islam in Detroit

CHAPTER 1 | Introduction

DETROIT, MICHIGAN, HAS BEEN home to sizeable Muslim communities for over a hundred years. Today, there are at least seventy mosques in the city and its suburbs, including several of the nation's largest, oldest, and most influential congregations. Efforts to build the city's first mosques began before World War I, and subsequent campaigns to control, reform, and sometimes replace these institutions have played a central role in shaping Muslim American identity. The ability of Muslims to embrace American models of citizenship and the willingness of non-Muslims to incorporate Islam in the American mainstream are plainly visible in this history, as are dramatic shifts (positive and negative) in the status of the city's Muslim populations. There have been, over the last century, many variants of Islam in Detroit. Tracing the development, interaction, alteration, coexistence, and disappearance of these traditions reveals important trends in the Muslim American past, and it suggests new possibilities, both political and religious, for the future of Islam in North America.

While these observations might seem unsurprising to historians of other American religious communities, they represent a new and potentially transformative focus for the history of Islam in America. Until very recently, the study of early twentieth-century Muslim immigrants has downplayed their ability to build viable institutions and establish the social infrastructure needed to sustain Islam in the New World. Scholars interested in this early period of Muslim American history have tended to focus on the Nation of Islam (NOI), the Moorish Science Temple (MST), the Ahmadiyya, and other heterodox movements that were embraced by blacks during the period of the Great Migration. These movements frequently encouraged their adherents to remain separate from immigrant

Muslims and from converts who based their practice of Islam on the Qur'an and Sunna (the living example of the Prophet Muhammad). Scholarship that traces the historical development of these communities has likewise produced segregated accounts. My own analysis runs counter to this trend, shifting attention to early Muslim Americans who recognized one another as fellow believers and worked across ethnoracial and sectarian differences to strengthen Islam in America. This community-building effort was commonplace long before most scholars of Islam in America thought it was happening (or even possible).

Drawing on untapped archival sources, on interviews with older Muslims who are personally connected to Detroit's past, and on early accounts of the region's mosques and Muslims that appeared in the local (Arabic and English) press, I chart the history of mosque development, pan-Muslim alliances, and Muslim identity formation. My goal is to prompt a systematic reconsideration of prevailing accounts of Muslim communities in North America prior to the 1970s. This project can succeed only if close attention is given to cities like Detroit, Cleveland, New York, and Chicago, each of which boasts ethnically diverse, temporally deep, and institutionally complex Muslim populations. Nowhere is documentary evidence of old Muslim American institutions richer than in Detroit, where new arrivals from Europe, Asia, Africa, and the American South converged to build the nation's first mosque in 1921; launch the NOI in 1930; develop immigrant Muslim enclaves in the 1930s that still exist today; establish a network of Muslim institutions to teach and sustain the faith; and create a vibrant Muslim American consciousness that, by the 1950s, had given rise to prominent local and national organizations that could accommodate several distinct Islamic traditions.

Detroit's early Muslims navigated turbulent periods of xenophobia, racism (anti-black and anti-Asian), Orientalist stereotyping, anti-Muslim prejudice, economic depression, and war. Yet by the mid-twentieth century, immigrant Muslims and their children had established prominent mosques whose leaders were on easy terms with American patriotism, upward mobility, modernism, and ecumenicalism. These same leaders participated in transnational Muslim political movements that frequently stood them in opposition to American Cold War policies, both domestic and foreign. As national organizations emerged in the 1950s to address the mounting concerns of Muslim Americans, activists in Detroit figured prominently as spiritual, social, and political exemplars, and the city itself was seen as a harbinger of successful Muslim incorporation in American society—a view shared by Muslims and non-Muslims alike. The Civil

Rights Movement, especially the more radical black nationalism inspired by Malcolm X, encouraged thousands of blacks in Detroit to join the NOI in the 1960s and 1970s, and eventually to explore the teachings, lifestyles, and traditions of a more universal Islam based on the Qur'an and Sunna.

By the late 1970s, new immigrants from South Asia and the Middle East and new black converts to Islam were rapidly becoming the majority of US Muslims. In Detroit, as elsewhere, these new American Muslims came to view the city's established Muslim institutions as undesirable, representative of an older, Americanized Islam that now looked alien, assimilationist, accommodationist, and increasingly unorthodox. This shift in perspective coincided with developments among Muslims over-seas, as their religious values once located most immediately in communal ritual, a shared social life, and (for rank-and-file Muslims) a comparatively unlettered relationship to the Qur'an and religious learning—in short, a tradition-oriented, *old* Islam—gave way to a more educated, activist, reform-oriented, and objectified understanding of the faith. This *new* Islam was articulated through clearly delineated intellectual and political move-ments that stressed the primacy of scriptural interpretation as a guide for everyday life and revivalist modes of religious authority and practice. The culture wars and doctrinal debates that coincided with these shifts gradu-ally overwhelmed America's older Muslim communities. Institutions and customs whose evolution could be traced to the late nineteenth century were denigrated, forgotten, rejected, and intentionally obscured. By the early 1980s, old Islam in Detroit had largely been displaced by something new, and the Muslims who were identified with this past had been pushed to the margins of the community's institutional and cultural life.

The large, highly visible Muslim populations of contemporary Detroit (and many other American cities) cannot be explained without refer-ence to Muslim institutions and personages of the early twentieth cen-tury. Yet it is precisely this early period of Muslim history that is largely unknown to the American public and to Muslim Americans themselves, who struggle to comprehend their status as a minority community often seen as quintessentially foreign by members of the larger society. The con-ditions that led Muslim Americans in the 1970s to re-evaluate their early history are re-emerging today as a new generation of Muslims faces heavy pressure (external and self-applied) to "Americanize" Islam while simul-taneously contending with new immigrants, new converts, new forms of politicized Islam, and new configurations of American foreign policy in Muslim-majority regions of the world. In the pages that follow, I lay groundwork for a new interpretation of the Muslim American past that makes sense of the tactical amnesias, persistent discontinuities, and narrative breaks that have kept crucial aspects of the history of Islam in America from being remembered and effectively understood.

A Complicated Celebration

The American Moslem Society (AMS) is the oldest mosque in greater Detroit and one of the oldest in North America. It celebrated its seventieth anniversary on May 15, 2009, with a large banquet at the Greenfield Manor in Dearborn, Michigan. Tickets for the event sold out quickly. Roughly one thousand members and friends of the mosque attended. The mosque had not held a formal banquet on this scale in decades, and their board of directors—mostly young professionals new to mosque governance—took the event very seriously. Although it is the oldest mosque in the Detroit area, the AMS—also known simply as Masjid Dearborn (the Dearborn Mosque)[1]—is today a congregation composed mostly of immigrants, the majority of whom came to the United States from Yemen after 1990.[2] The Muslims who built the AMS in the 1930s, developing and sustaining it during its first forty years, were largely of Syrian and Lebanese origin. Voted out of office in an ideological coup that took place in 1976, the founding congregation is not, for the most part, on friendly terms with the current AMS leadership. Most of the original members of the AMS and their families now worship in a breakaway mosque, which they established in 1982.

In celebrating the seventieth anniversary of the AMS, the banquet organizers faced a major dilemma: how to acknowledge the group's early history without drawing attention to the sharp, still painful rift between the mosque's past and present. This discontinuity was not simply a matter of demographic shifts in the immigrant status or national origins of the mosque's membership; also at stake were changing ideas about Islam, how it should be practiced in the United States, and what it means to be an American Muslim. These questions have proven especially vexing for Masjid Dearborn, and for Muslim congregations nationally, in the aftermath of the 9/11 attacks, when Muslims have been widely perceived as culturally alien and Islam has been portrayed as a (false) religion antithetical to American values.[3] The choreography of the anniversary celebration was intended to convey an upbeat sense of the group's confidence, religious devotion, and Americanization, which meant that much of the mosque's history would be off topic, politically vexing, and in poor taste.

The keynote speaker for the evening, Dr. Jamal Badawi, a professor of management and of Islamic Studies at Saint Mary's University in Halifax, Nova Scotia, had been asked to speak about American mosques and their varied strategies for survival as minority religious institutions. In his prepared notes, Dr. Badawi explored three ways of interacting with the larger, non-Muslim society: "isolation," "assimilation," and "positive integration." It was clear that Dr. Badawi, an unapologetic integrationist, had expected his Dearborn audience, filled with Yemeni immigrants, to display strong isolationist tendencies. Yet his journey to the podium led him past table after table of public officials (including several Muslim elected officials), and his speech followed the congratulatory remarks of Michigan governor Jennifer Granholm, US senator Debbie Stabenow, Wayne County executive Robert Ficano, Dearborn mayor Jack O'Reilly, and others members of the political elite, most of whom greeted the gathering in Arabic and quoted from the Qur'an for good measure. As Dr. Badawi looked back and forth between his notes and the crowd, he admitted that his talk now seemed inappropriate. Perhaps he had more to learn from Masjid Dearborn than the other way round. Nonetheless, he forged ahead.[4]

Isolationism, Dr. Badawi cautioned, is un-Islamic. It encourages fearmongering and misinformation among Muslims, cuts them off from the mainstream, and kindles distrust between Muslims and other Americans. Assimilation is equally harmful. It compels Muslims to reject their cultural identity and, ultimately, to abandon their faith. Positive integration, however, occurs when Muslims are allowed—and are able and willing—to maintain their cultural and religious distinctiveness, all the while participating in the larger society as full citizens. During the last seventy years, members of the AMS had traveled down all three of these paths, but most of Dr. Badawi's listeners that evening—Muslim and non-Muslim alike—would have agreed that "the straight path" leads to positive integration.

In the Detroit metropolitan area, where Muslims can trace their history back to the late nineteenth century, it is easy to conclude, as Dr. Badawi did, that Muslims have achieved successful integration. The Muslim community there is large (roughly 200,000), highly diverse, socially active, and politically engaged, which explains why so many public officials attended the AMS anniversary celebration.[5] In addition to members of the secular establishment, imams and lay leaders from over three dozen local mosques were on hand, proof that the event was important to the Muslim community as a whole. Leaders came not only from local Arab mosques (Iraqi, Lebanese, Syrian, Egyptian, Palestinian, and Yemeni), but also from Bangladeshi, Indian, Pakistani, black American, Nigerian, and Iranian mosques. Sunni and Shi'a, conservative and liberal, urban and suburban, the crowd included interfaith activists, civil rights advocates, representatives of Muslim and Arab service organizations in Detroit, and several hundred members of the AMS itself.

In the period following the 9/11 attacks, Detroit's Muslims have found it increasingly important to assert and make public sense of their presence in the United States. The AMS is the third mosque in the city to celebrate its past with a gala banquet in recent years and to have produced a video recounting the development of their congregation over time. A much younger mosque, the Islamic Center of America (ICA, established in 1962), made extensive use of interviews with its founders, old photographs, and home movies to reconstruct its past in rich detail in both a DVD and a commemorative book.[6] The AMS, lacking access to such resources (which belong to the people who left the mosque, en masse, in 1977), produced a brief video that made a simple point: if not for the small group of Lebanese Muslims who dug the basement foundation of the AMS with picks and shovels in 1938, perhaps none of the infrastructure of Detroit's Muslim community would exist today. Aside from this claim (which members of other local mosques might dispute), we learn very little about the mosque's founders or its long history. At the video's conclusion, the narrator stops a young man leaving the mosque after prayer and asks him: "If you could say one thing to that small group of Muslims, what would it be?" The young man replies, "I would say thank you. Of course it is by the grace of God that this place was established, but it was their effort that made this place possible, so I thank them very much. I wish they were here to see this place today, all the improvements, and all of the people that are coming here."[7]

Congressman John Dingell (then eighty-three years old), who was given a lifetime achievement award at the banquet, was a teenager when the founders of the AMS began work on the mosque. He assumed the audience would include several living founders and hundreds of their children and grandchildren. He wanted to hear their voices and thank them for their contributions to Detroit history. When accepting his award, he asked the founders to stand and be recognized. His entreaty was met with an awkward silence. No one stood. Unlike Dingell, many in the audience were aware that the Dearborn Mosque of today bears almost no resemblance to the AMS of the past. Many of today's members would argue that the small congregation of the past was oriented, rather shamelessly, toward assimilation and, beyond bricks and mortar, had contributed little to the practice of Islam in Detroit. This perspective on the mosque's past is used as a motivating tool by its current leaders, a warning of what the future could hold if today's members let down their guard.

In a generous attempt to mend this divide, the banquet organizers recognized two men as founders of their institution. The first, Hussein El Haje, was indeed among the original members of the AMS in 1938. He dug out the mosque's basement during his first summer in the United States. He sent his children to Sunday school at the mosque. And he left in 1977 with the other Syrians and Lebanese who felt the mosque had become isolationist, misogynistic, and anti-American. But El Haje, now well over ninety years old, had recently begun worshiping once again at the AMS, taking pride in praying with a congregation that sometimes exceeds two thousand worshipers. He wept tears of joy when he was recognized at the banquet. The second founder acknowledged that evening, Abdo Alasry, is a much younger man. A Yemeni immigrant who arrived in Detroit in 1966, he was among the newcomers who began worshiping at the mosque in the 1970s and who eventually took over the institution, making sure that it was open for all five of the daily prayers, insisting that women who enter the building wear an appropriate *hijab* (head covering) and pray in a space apart from that of male worshipers, banning dances and movie nights, and replacing Sunday morning services with a Friday congregational prayer. Alasry was the first Yemeni president of the mosque's board. A subdued and modest person, he took the stage briefly and without emotional display.

The message the board of directors sent with this pairing was clear. El Haje and his generation built the building; they are a living link to a remote past that will soon be gone forever.[8] By contrast, Alasry and his generation saved the mosque; they represent the present and the future of Islam in Detroit. With the inclusion of El Haje, Congressman Dingell had his surviving founder. El Haje appeared on the program because he had accepted the new order at the AMS, not because he represented the mosque's older heritage in the present. "The new mosque they got, it is beautiful," he told me. "It is beautiful to see a thousand people praying together. But sometimes they say things about our community [the founding Syrian-Lebanese congregation], and I don't like that."[9]

This way of dealing with the past is typical not only of the AMS but of Muslim organizations throughout Detroit and in the United States more generally. Despite a century of accumulated arrivals, heartfelt conversions, and the establishment of mosques and Muslim congregations; despite decades of teaching and preaching Islam among Americans, combating stereotypes, struggling to reshape American foreign policies in the Muslim world, and resisting racism at home, the history of the Muslim

American community prior to the 1960s remains oddly problematic. The difficulties faced at the AMS in the 1970s, when new immigrants displaced Muslim families who had been in America for three generations, have occurred repeatedly across North America.[10] They have been traumatic for all parties, who have often disagreed bitterly about the fundamentals of Islamic practice, the nature of American citizenship, and the function of the mosque in everyday life. These contests have also occurred—often in the same mosques—between new converts to Islam and those who are already Muslims.

My intention here is not to single out new immigrants or Muslim converts as the cause of this disharmony, but to point out that this pattern is pervasive in mosques and other Muslim American institutions in which immigrants and converts are the majority. This demographic reality has created a cultural environment in which older populations of Muslims, who are likely to have moved on to new suburbs, new parts of the country, and new voluntary associations, no longer identify strongly with the institutions they or their families helped establish. Without this connection to the older mosques, they are in no position to speak for these institutions or their histories. In many cases, members of these older communities—"legacy Muslims," we might call them—do not identify with newer Muslim populations and their concerns; some do not identify as Muslim at all. Meanwhile, the inheritors of the older mosques, who have much in common with the mosque's founders, whose fervent hope was to secure the future of Islam in the United States, are estranged from the history of their own institutions. Unaware (or dismissive) of the patterns that once shaped the practice of Islam among Americans, they are unable to see themselves as part of a history that is much deeper, and more diverse, than they realize.

Analytical Frames for the Study of Old American Islam

In his groundbreaking work on the history of Islam in America, Kambiz GhaneaBassiri argues that "nowhere are the contours of American Islamic history better seen than in varying Muslims' experiences of community and institution building in the United States."[11] He is also quick to point out that producing a history of Muslim Americans is difficult because for many periods, and in many locations, Muslim "organizations proved ephemeral and left scant records."[12] Even in a city like Detroit, where early twentieth-century Muslims experienced their greatest successes at institution building, very few archival materials documenting their efforts are available. Many early twentieth-century migrants were illiterate, highly mobile, unfamiliar with American voluntary associational procedures, or otherwise unconcerned with producing and maintaining institutional records. Yet even when textual records and the memories of living mosque founders are available, as they are for the AMS, the history of these institutions nonetheless poses a challenge for current leaders and historians alike. The ideological and political shifts that have taken place within the Muslim community over the last century impose significant constraints on what we can know and what questions we will ask about the history of Islam in the United States.

Before discussing larger historiographical frames, it is important to establish a few demographic facts that make American Muslims especially resistant to any analysis that attempts to represent them as a unified cultural community or a single political constituency. Islam in the United States is, depending on one's point of view, a pan-ethnic, diasporic, multiracial, polycultural, or highly sectarian religious tradition. The diversity of cultural, linguistic, and national backgrounds found among Muslims in the United States today is not duplicated in any Muslim-majority country, except in Saudi Arabia during the *hajj* (the annual pilgrimage to Mecca). The American Muslim population can be subdivided into black Americans (20 percent), South Asians (32 percent), and Arabs (37 percent), with smaller populations of Europeans, Hispanics, Africans, and culturally mixed people (11 percent).[13] Some of these Muslims trace their American roots back for centuries; others are still waiting for green cards. Some are descendants of the Prophet Muhammad; others are learning to say the *shahada* (the confession of faith) for the first time. Some are deeply religious and organize their daily lives around prayer, fasting, and religious study; others are Muslim in name only and pay little attention to the teachings and obligations of the faith. In short, Muslims in the United States do not belong to one diaspora, one racial category, or one religious tradition; they are attached to many. As immigrants (65 percent of Muslim American adults are foreign born), they face simultaneous pressures to assimilate to American cultural norms and to resist assimilation. As converts (20 percent of the adult Muslim population once belonged to another faith, or no faith), they face simultaneous pressures to adopt identifiably Muslim practices and to reject practices that are considered merely cultural or improperly Islamic.[14] There is not a single American or Muslim cultural setting to which all Muslim Americans adapt, whether they are immigrants, converts, or the American-born children of either.[15]

There are, however, general patterns of sociocultural adaptation that emerged among American Muslims prior to the 1970s that seem, in retrospect, highly distinctive. Many of these patterns are resurfacing today in ways that might help us understand how the tendency of contemporary Muslims to overlook (or simply not to know about) key aspects of the history of Islam in the United States is related to ongoing attempts to assert a distinctly Muslim sense of national belonging. Among the most pronounced of these old/new patterns is an intense longing for pan-Muslim unity, which is closely related to a contradictory desire for solidarity along racial, ethnic, and linguistic lines—or, increasingly, along lines of doctrine and everyday religious practice—that divide the Muslim community internally. A second trend is the persistent allure of "modernity" and a wary stance toward the political advantages of being modern. The third old/new pattern is an enthusiastic embrace of American citizenship and an equally vigorous critique of its inaccessibility to Muslims. Often the full range of these contradictory positions can exist within the same individual or institution. Sometimes, one set of possibilities decisively overwhelms and delegitimizes the others. To understand how these shifts influence historical consciousness, it is worth situating them within well-established traditions of historical writing about Muslims and other American religious minorities.

Minoritization and pluralism: Despite the "separation of church and state," which is enshrined in the First Amendment to the US Constitution, the United States has been governed as a de-facto Protestant nation for most of its history. The disestablishment of religion, originally undertaken in the context of a Christian majority, gave rise to an open market of religious affiliation.[16] Without state sanction and funding, American religious communities, congregations, and denominations were free (and indeed forced) to rely on popular support. They had to compete with each other and be responsive to changing social and political conditions in order to survive. Disestablishment is widely taken to account for the vibrancy of religion in the United States, and it produces religious structures and institutions that actively promote cultural pluralism.[17] Of course, not all religious traditions are created equal in this framework. As Tracy Fessenden reminds us, "at various points in American history, Muslims, Catholics or Mormons could be construed as enemies of republican institutions, Jews as a racial or economic threat, and Native American ritual practice as an affront to environmental or drug policy, all without apparent violence to cherished notions of religious freedom."[18]

Cultural pluralism, immigration, and the invention of distinctively American religious traditions—three projects to which Muslim Americans have contributed—have challenged Protestant hegemony in the United States since the nation's earliest days. Muslims have struggled with their position as a religious minority in several ways. The first Muslims in North America were African slaves who, as human chattels, were forbidden to organize institutions for the practice of their faith. Nor could they marry endogamously, as free religious minorities (Jews and Roman Catholics) did. This prevented the creation and spread of Muslim families among the enslaved. GhaneaBassiri argues that "Islam did not shape a distinct Muslim community in colonial and antebellum America but rather was a way through which Muslims made sense of their new experiences and encounters and formed new individual and communal relations," especially by "finding common ground" with other enslaved Americans.[19] Yet when Muslims were free to organize among themselves in the late nineteenth century, most were new immigrants to the United States—Syrians, Turks, Indians, Albanians, Bosnians—not former slaves from the Deep South. Linguistic, doctrinal, and cultural diversity were obstacles to interaction among these recently arrived and physically dispersed Muslims. Only in the early twentieth century did "common ground" emerge, as immigrant Muslims settled across the northeastern and midwestern states. Building a shared religious infrastructure was difficult for these populations. They were numerically small; their members were frequently denied US citizenship; they faced economic instability; and the construction and upkeep of mosques was, in their home countries, the work of ruling elites.

The early American Muslims were "religious outsiders," a status that, as Lawrence Moore suggests, does not inevitably disempower minorities; instead, it can sharpen their attention to the dynamics of ethno-religious solidarity, buffer them from the religious (and secular) mainstream, and enlist them in struggles for recognition that mirror the fight to win racial, gender, and other forms of social equality.[20] This process is dialogical. Religious outsiders who adopt hegemonic Protestant styles—of textual exegesis, congregationalism, volunteerism, denominationalism, ecumenicalism, and a personal faith based on sincerity and individual choice—often find themselves more accepted, more readily incorporated, than groups who reject these forms.[21] Although driven by strong assimilationist impulses, these adaptive transitions produce reciprocal change. As claims for recognition are expressed in languages and institutional contexts that are increasingly shared, the religious landscape itself adjusts to include minority traditions, a process that has culminated in the belief—widespread today but unthinkable a century ago—that the United States is a Judeo-Christian society in which Catholics, Jews, and Protestants have roughly equal access to the cultural mainstream.

In the case of Muslim Americans, this process has not been fully recip-rocal or inclusive, nor has it been a linear process historically. In the early twentieth century, many blacks, who were outsiders already due to rac-ist laws and customs, embraced Islam and syncretic movements like the NOI because these identifications offered them a firm step away from the religious mainstream rather than toward it. For immigrants and their chil-dren, the movement from religious (or racial) outsider to insider status has been blocked in different ways. The relative invisibility of most American Muslims in the first half of the twentieth century, which eased their incor-poration in many ways, has been reversed in recent decades and replaced by a negative hypervisibility, which is conducive only to certain types of incorporation.[22] For the most part, negative visibility has resulted in "dis-ciplinary inclusion," a political process that selectively incorporates Arab/Muslim citizens and their institutions by subjecting them to a kind of cul-tural rehabilitation that clears them of "enemy" associations.[23]

A second obstacle to incorporation is broadly similar in effect, but it operates at points internal to Muslim communities. As members of one Muslim American generation, ethnic community, or congregation embrace Protestant-inflected styles of worship, institutional governance, or the lan-guage of American religious pluralism, they do so under the critical gaze of Muslim communities and congregations who are not (yet) willing to take such steps, which they often reject outright as "compromises." In many cases, these critics are newly arrived immigrants, enthusiastic converts, or Muslims who observe American Islam from abroad. They are likely to assume that American religious styles (read as Christianity, weak reli-giosity, or secularism) will attenuate the relationship between American Muslims and the *umma*, the global community of Islam.[24] Meanwhile, many non-Muslim Americans believe that precisely because American Muslims are connected to a global umma—and because so many Muslims are immigrants who seem unnaturally "devout"—their claims to American identity are questionable; indeed, they are thought to represent a threat to national security. Views of the latter sort can even be found among American Muslims themselves, who often criticize newly arrived Muslim immigrants in terms many non-Muslim Americans would immediately recognize as nativist.

Peter Mandaville has described the project of institutionalizing Muslim American communities and connecting them to the global umma as a kind of "translocality," a mode of interaction "which pertains not to how peoples and cultures exist *in* places, but rather how they move *through* them," disrupting "traditional constructions of political identity" and giving "rise to novel forms of political space."[25] The American mosque is *translocal.* It is a space in which commitments to alternative homelands and to Islam (as an outsider religion) can be renewed and reinvigorated in ways that enable Muslims to imagine the United States as a Muslim homeland, as a religious and political field in which Muslim identities can be reinforced and not incessantly threatened. Once this recognition is possible, Muslims can invest in a politics of accommodation that (re)defines American nationhood and citizenship in ways intended specifically to include Islam. The American mosque is not the only translocal political space in which Muslim American identity takes shape, but it is an important and vital one.[26]

American mosques are also *transcommunal* spaces. They bring together, in a common institutional form (and frequently in the same institution), members of different diasporic and ethnoracial populations, each of which identifies differently with the American mainstream and cultivates its own historical understandings of Islam. The mosque is a context in which Muslims can observe, criticize, and emulate each other's institutional accomplishments, collaborating on the renewal of Islamic ritual practice, worshiping together, and teaching Islam to one another and to non-Muslim Americans. As Muslims encounter each other in American mosques, they (re)define the Muslim umma as culturally and religiously plural, not in the abstract, but in the everyday. In this way, the twinned political forces of translocality and trancommunalism combine in Detroit's mosques to enable local Muslims to assert and overcome their status as "religious outsiders." As I argue throughout this study, the processes that connect American Muslims to Muslims abroad are systematically related to the processes that, over time, make Islam compatible with American culture and intelligible to non-Muslim Americans. Because they are pragmatic, uneven, reversible, and oriented toward the political demands of the present, these processes have proven strongly resistant to historical analysis.

Orientalism in black and white: A more global framework in which Muslim American difference is commonly analyzed is that of Orientalist knowledge production. The uneven encounter between the West, defined as secular, and a Middle Eastern or Muslim world, defined as religious (and intolerantly so), is based ultimately on "an economy of representation in which the modern is prized over—and placed over—the non-modern."[27] These understandings of religiosity and secularism are firmly grounded, rhetorically and historically, in the colonial encounter between Europe and the Muslim world.[28] Debates about the status of Muslims in the West—about who is an insider, about relations between the colonized and the colonizer, about whose traditions are modern, and about the character-istics and rights of people defined as (non-)European—are conducted in a politically charged idiom that varies greatly across national contexts. These debates are actively pursued in the Muslim world as well, and they have greatly influenced modernist Islam, whose essential Other is the once Christian, now avowedly secular West.[29]

Timothy Marr has argued that nineteenth-century American under-standings of Islam differed from those of European Orientalism because the former were divorced from the experience of direct colonial encoun-ter. "Early Americans," he writes, "employed the difference of Islam to both frame and extend the boundaries of their own cultural enterprises," such as the abolition of slavery, the temperance movement, and efforts to exclude Mormons from US citizenship. Islam, in this tradition, stood for two related but oppositional sets of values.[30] On one hand, as Edward Said carefully illustrated, Muslims were thought to be culturally primi-tive and despotic, both repressive and repressed. On the other, the Muslim world was associated with extreme courtesy, chivalry, hospitality, spiritual purity, and sensual pleasure—in short, the qualities of the "noble savage."[31] For much of the nineteenth century, Americans used Islam and the Orient as "mobile signs" that attracted or repelled depending on how they were deployed.[32] The presence in the United States of tens of thousands of real people with Muslim beliefs or ancestry did nothing to disrupt this mindset. Instead, the handful of enslaved Muslims who became celebrities in the United States in the eighteenth and nineteenth centuries, men such as Job Ben Solomon (c. 1701–c. 1773) or Abdul Rahman Ibrahima (1762–1829), were treated as exceptional characters whose religious identities could be used to justify and criticize racial slavery simultaneously.[33]

In the early twentieth century, Detroit's Muslims were frequently depicted in local media as lethargic, inscrutable, polygamists, oppressors of Middle Eastern Christians, and unfit for US citizenship. "Their faces are blank with the mask of the Orient," wrote one journalist, assuring readers that the Syrian immigrant "gives as little and takes as much as he can."[34] But it is also true that the Orient was popular as a source of com-mercial kitsch, especially in the 1920s. Identification with the Muslim/Oriental Other was encouraged in popular films, pulp fiction, and ornate department-store displays.[35] In Detroit, a Syrian Christian family openly embraced this identification by launching the first middle-class Middle

Eastern restaurant, dubbing it The Sheik after the Valentino film of the same name that was an international sensation in 1921.

One did not need to be Muslim, or even from the Middle East, to embrace the likeness of this non-white Other. Eager to shed the negative associations of Negritude, many southern black migrants to Detroit appropriated the clothing, religious trappings, names, and identities of the Muslim Orient, using them to create the new religious movements that sprang up during the Great Migration. Two of the most influential of these movements, the MST and the NOI, channeled the Orientalist sensibilities of black migrants into a powerful rejection of anti-black racism and an exploration of pan-Africanism and black separatism. These movements looked beyond philological, imperial, and commercial Orientalism to construct religious worldviews that encouraged African Americans to explore and eventually convert to more universal variants of Islam.[36]

As American political and economic interventions in the Muslim world intensified during the second half of the twentieth century, domestic images of the Muslim Other became more consistently negative. In all forms of mass media, Muslims and Arabs were portrayed as violent, misogynistic, anti-Semitic, and eventually anti-American.[37] These hostile images legitimized and fueled the political intimidation of Muslim Americans, especially those who were critical of Israel or US foreign policy in the Middle East. In the post-9/11 period, the War on Terror institutionalized these antagonistic tendencies, selectively curtailing the rights of Muslims in the United States and encouraging Americanization under duress.[38]

As an artifact of geopolitics, the Orientalist framework does not capture important aspects of the Muslim American experience, nor does it address the vexed role Orientalist discourses have played in mosque politics. The Muslim world has undergone many internal struggles in response to European colonialism, nation building, and Cold War interventionism. These encounters have generated a wide array of alternative modernities, some secular and nationalist, others religious and global in orientation. Writing of Lebanese Shi'a (who are currently the largest Muslim community in greater Detroit), Lara Deeb describes a new religious sensibility that emerged alongside the Hizbullah-led resistance to the Israeli occupation of South Lebanon. This liberation struggle combined piety and progressivism to create an "enchanted modern."[39] Its "dual emphasis" is placed on "material and spiritual progress," both of which are needed to fashion a "viable alternative to the perceived emptiness of modernity as manifested in the West."[40] The enchanted modern confronts Western materialism and secularism, but it also confronts the failings of Muslim traditionalism, insisting on spiritual progress through piety and a renewed personal commitment to Islam and its everyday practice.

The "enchanted modern" came to Detroit with Lebanese Shi'i immigrants in the 1980s, but it is only one of the dozens of alternative Muslim modernities that have thrived, and withered away, in the city since the early 1900s. Attempts to build mosques, for instance, are often driven by explicitly modernizing impulses, with the ironic result that Orientalist tropes (accusations of backwardness, inferiority, misogyny, fanaticism, or ignorance) figure prominently in the identity debates that flare up within the Muslim community. Both immigrants *and* the American-born, new converts *and* those brought up as Muslims employ them. Because these tropes pervade the familiar binaries that underlie (and so often distort) Muslim American identity formation—black/white, immigrant/native, orthodox/heterodox, assimilated/oppositional, and authentic/inauthentic—they will inevitably be part of Muslim American historiography.

Common Assumptions about Old Islam in the United States

In the post-9/11 era, a new generation of scholars has taken up the historical study of Islam in the United States. Their work is distinct not only for its sustained engagement with the domestic and geopolitical conditions that shape Muslim identities but also for its ability to upend common assumptions about how Islam and America, as grand ideas and grassroots projects, have interacted over time. Edward Curtis IV and Jocelyn Cesari have recently edited major encyclopedias and sourcebooks on Muslim Americans.[41] Two well-crafted, synthetic histories of Islam in the United States were published while I was carrying out the research for this study: the artfully concise *Muslims in America*, by Edward Curtis, appeared in 2009, and a nuanced, large-scale study by Kambiz GhaneaBassiri, *A History of Islam in America*, followed in 2010. Meanwhile, smaller studies appearing in edited volumes and academic journals are more abundant than ever, and the older, pre-9/11 tradition of research that treats Muslim Americans as members of specific ethnoracial minorities (as Arabs, South Asians, Albanians, or African Americans) is still vibrant.

The speed with which information about Muslims in America is now being produced is amazing, and it is not without its troubling dimensions. Common assumptions have become even more common, the recycling of ideas and evidence is rife, and longstanding gaps in the literature remain unfilled. The conditions that make accelerated historical data collection possible—most obviously, the unprecedented release of public and private funds to study Muslims in the aftermath of the 9/11 attacks, and the availability of new digital and on-line sources—have not transformed the categories into which historical data is organized. Instead, they have given new clarity to these frameworks.

In 2003, when I began to collect information about Detroit's older mosques, I found that the raw materials I needed to assemble a schematic history of Islam in the city were frequently missing. Moreover, when institutional records or old news accounts were available, they often contradicted existing accounts, written and oral, of how the city's first Muslim institutions were established, when, and by whom. Inconsistent and absent data gave my research the feel of challenging detective work that most historians enjoy. What I found perplexing, however, was the systematic misfit between the new data I was uncovering and the explanatory frameworks into which I could fit them. Period newspaper accounts; incorporation records; and personal interviews conducted with the oldest living mosque founders, their children, and their grandchildren—all of these sources seemed to illustrate one point: that Detroit's early Muslims were committed to establishing Islam as an American religious tradition through the construction of viable mosque communities. By contrast, the available academic histories, interviews with second-generation activists, and the narratives of today's Muslim leaders asserted something else: Detroit's early mosques were failed institutions and not really mosques at all.

My research showed clearly that post-1965 Muslim immigration to Detroit, and thus the large and robust Muslim communities found in the city today, was made possible by the political and economic incorporation of Muslims who came to the city and established successful mosques there, well before the 1950s. Yet the extant scholarship, and much of local oral history, on Muslim Americans downplayed the accomplishments of earlier generations. Indeed, many local Muslims had completely forgotten or had never known about Islamic institutions established in the first half of the twentieth century. Because most of Detroit's adult Muslims are foreign-born or first-generation Muslims, this ignorance of the past is understandable. But even local Muslims who remembered the old mosques, who grew up praying in them, who taught Sunday school in them, who were married and attended their parents' funerals in them—even these people frequently described the old mosques as second-rate social clubs, as flawed endeavors not worth commemorating. New immigrants who never attended the old mosques assured me that today's institutions might also go bad if Muslims were not vigilant. Time and again, I was encouraged to focus on Detroit's newest mosques. Innovative, invested in regular activities intended to sustain community involvement over the long run, better financed, more likely to be controlled by college-educated professionals, and structured soundly on proper Islamic belief and practice, the newest mosques were deemed worthy of public attention and scholarly treatment.

My interlocutors were unaware of the extent to which Detroit's new mosques replicated, sometimes in precise detail, features crucial to the success (and eventual disintegration) of Detroit's first mosques. The steps early Muslims took to Americanize Islamic practice, to render it compatible with everyday life in the United States, have obvious analogies in the present, but few people wanted to see early experiments in pan-ethnic worship, the inclusion of women in institutional life, and the creation of new social activities for youth as part of a collective history worth knowing about or learning from today. Most interesting to me was the fact that many of the old mosques that are now seen as failed and flawed were originally built as reform projects, as new institutions that would improve the reputation of Muslims in America and make a more authentically Islamic lifestyle possible for Muslims in Detroit.

As I gathered information on early mosques in Detroit, I saw that the dominant characterizations of early Islam in America coalesce around a handful of themes, familiar to lay people, spiritual leaders, and scholars alike. During my visits to Muslim communities in other American cities, I have encountered similar ideas. A short list would include the following motifs.

Religious ignorance: It is widely assumed today that the religious education (and often the personal piety) of Detroit's early Muslim leaders was inadequate to sustain Islam as a minority faith in the United States. "One of the basic problems faced by the community members is how to learn their religion," Wasfi argued in 1971. "The lack of education of the pioneers and their ignorance of their religion prevented them from teaching their children."[42] Yvonne Haddad has long made a related point about the early immigrants nationwide, who, she argues, "were generally too busy with basic economic survival to make much attempt to promote Islam on a community level," a claim that would make Muslims a truly distinctive migrant population if true.[43] This trope is so pervasive that the imams who led congregations in Detroit prior to the 1950s were later referred to as "lay leaders" rather than imams or shaykhs, while those who took over from them in the 1950s and afterwards were described as "religious scholars."[44]

The efforts of early Muslim leaders to reach out to non-Muslims and to educate them about Islam are similarly dismissed today as half-hearted, or as assimilationist apologetics.

So-called mosques: The city's early mosques, it is now commonly believed, were not really mosques at all. The Arabic word *nadi* (club) was indeed used to refer to both of Dearborn's first Arab mosques. The Progressive Arabian Hashmie Society (est. 1937), for example, was known in Arabic as *al-Nadi al-Hashimi*. Sometimes the term nadi is used affectionately to indicate that these mosques played important social as well as religious functions. They hosted sock hops, weddings, union meetings, political protests, and fundraisers in addition to Sunday school, funerals, and communal prayers. The term is also used dismissively to suggest that the city's so-called mosques were not spaces in which good Muslims would be comfortable worshiping. In some cases, it is the eclectic usage of modified buildings that triggers critique. "The Virginia Park mosque," one leader told me, "was really just an old house where missionaries could stay. They used to sell *zabiha* (ritually slaughtered meat) out of the basement. We never thought of it as a masjid." In other cases, the ubiquitous presence of women in these institutions—women who adhered to mid-twentieth-century American understandings of fashion and modesty—is evidence for their status as clubs rather than mosques.[45] Finally, rumors abound about scandalous behavior, such as gambling and belly dancing at mosque fundraisers, or the consumption of alcohol at weddings and other events.

Ethnic isolationism: I am often told that Detroit's early Muslim communities, and the mosques they established, were not simply segregated along ethnoracial lines but existed in nearly complete isolation from one another. The claim surfaces repeatedly in scholarly discourse. Elkholy, for example, asserted that Arab Muslims in Dearborn had "no connection whatsoever" with other Muslim populations in the city in the late 1950s or at any time prior to this period. His observations have been sited widely ever since, and they are assumed to refer accurately to ethnic relations among the city's Muslims in general.[46] Many of my interviewees echoed this assertion while simultaneously sharing fond memories of early Muslim leaders from different ethnic and sectarian backgrounds. Extensive evidence of early twentieth-century efforts to establish universal, pan-ethnic mosques is dismissed or used instead to illustrate the failure of the Muslim pioneers to complete these ventures. The idea of ethnic isolation is also important because it is used, ironically, to blame immigrant Muslims for not having "corrected" the early teachings of the NOI by educating its leaders about the Qur'an and Sunna. This claim is especially egregious because it manages to both misrepresent the diligent efforts Muslim leaders did make along those lines *and* to disregard the capacity of the NOI to function as an autonomous religious movement with strong isolationist tendencies of its own.[47] Claims of rigorous ethnoracial separatism in the past are also used to explain contemporary divisions between blacks and immigrant Muslims and to account for the rapid growth in mosque construction that began in Detroit in the 1980s (when every new ethnic, racial, sectarian, or national group felt empowered to invest in its own house of worship).

Sunni-Shi'i (dis)harmony: Tensions between Sunni and Shi'i Muslims in Detroit are frequently attributed to the presence of newly arrived immigrants or outsiders, while sectarian relations in the past are typically remembered as peaceful. "The Sunni and the Shi'a...I never knew one from another. We kids grew up as sisters and brothers. We never knew Sunni/Shi'a till this last bunch come from the old country and they parted us."[48] This same claim is made in reference to people who arrived in the 1920s, in 1939, in the 1960s, in 1982, and continues right into the present. While this trope may seem like an inversion of the others, idealizing the past as it seems to do, it can also be read as an indirect critique of the indifferent sectarianism (and thus casual religiosity) of earlier Muslim communities. Claims to greater tolerance in the past are complicated by the fact that Sunni and Shi'i Muslims already had separate mosques in greater Detroit by the late 1930s, that doctrinal disputes between the two factions contributed to the demise of the city's first mosque in 1921, and that Detroit's principal clerics were all known to serve followings that were predominately Sunni or Shi'a (even if they willingly officiated at the weddings and funerals of families known to be of the other faction and frequently joined these families together in marriage).[49]

Political apathy: Earlier Muslim communities are described today as having been politically apathetic. To quote Elkholy again, "It is said that the [1948] Palestine War in which the Arab countries were defeated awakened the nationalistic sentiments of the Arab-Americans in general and especially of the Moslems."[50] The explicit assumption is that, before this date, American Muslims had no interest in politics. For other scholars and community leaders this awakening is said to have occurred after the 1948 partition of India, after Malcolm X rose to prominence as a representative of Black Power, after the 1967 Arab Israeli war, after religion was banned outright in Albania in 1967, after the 1979 revolution in Iran, after the start of the Lebanese civil war in 1975, after the attacks of September 11, 2001, and so on.[51] Similarly, Detroit's Muslims are described as having been uninvolved in the American political process. These tropes reflect a genuine ignorance of the lives of early twentieth-century Muslim Americans—who were active in electoral politics, the labor movement, and civil rights struggles—but they also illustrate the extent to which Muslim Americans still imagine their political commitments to be constructed in reaction to American geopolitical interests, violent events overseas, and moments of crisis involving Muslims in the United States.

The True Islamic Way

The empirical evidence I marshal against these common stereotypes is the subject matter of this book, and I reserve detailed case studies for upcoming chapters. I should emphasize at the outset, however, that I do not want to engage in a relentless debunking exercise in which I show that Muslims do not know their own past. In fact, I want to argue an almost opposite case: American Muslims do know and understand their past, and they know it in very particular ways. The common tropes I want to disturb and rehistoricize in this study are important to Muslims. They belong to a hegemonic moral project. Progressive in intent, they locate error in the recent past, truth in the original teachings of the Prophet Muhammad, and correction in the present and future. In this respect, they are a fluid combination of revivalist and modernist tendencies.

Once I began to think of these tropes as a moralizing discourse about the history of Islam in Detroit, I began to see a second explanation for their success. These tropes reflect a pervasive turn toward new forms of religiosity made throughout the twentieth century by Muslims in the Arab world, Iran, South and Southeast Asia, Africa, and in various Muslim diaspora populations, including those of the United States. Gregory Starrett, in his account of how this process unfolded in Egypt, describes "a growing consciousness on the part of Muslims that Islam is a coherent system of practices and belief, rather than merely an unexamined way of life."[52] What religious reformers viewed as the "traditional" Islam of the past was supplanted by a new, "functionalized" Islam, Starrett's name for a modernist interpretive style (typically linked to social progress and nation building) that was closely associated with the spread of popular literacy and higher education across the Middle East.[53] This "objectified Islam," as Eickelman and Piscatori describe it, represents a shift from an earlier religious experience based on traditions of communal practice to one that emphasizes individualized textual exegesis. The objectification process reflects both the "systematization" of religious tradition (such as religious instruction in public schools) and a self-conscious attention to how religion is taught and put into practice.[54] This political and social transition, which is by no means unidirectional, unilateral, or universal, has brought change to many Muslim traditions. It offers an explicit critique of the notion (popular in "the West") that Islam and modernity somehow stand in opposition to one another. My argument is that the shift toward reformist, objectified Islam has had tremendous effects on the history-making practices of Muslim Americans and that these effects have not yet been adequately analyzed or understood.

Another way of interpreting this new sensibility is to consider how it has been combined with ambient scholarly approaches to Islam in America as a marginalized and minoritized religious tradition. For example, historians who work in the antebellum period on enslaved Muslims have done exhaustive research and have constructed—from the scantest of evidence—thoughtful and compelling narratives about individual Muslims who practiced their faith under harsh conditions, the influence these Muslims had on the aesthetic and religious practices of other enslaved peoples, their contribution to American traditions of social hierarchy, and their purported role in the later revival of Islam among American blacks.[55] For the most part, these scholars avoid judging the efforts of enslaved Muslims on a scale of orthodoxy, authenticity, or efficacy. Similarly, a great deal of effort has gone into documenting and making sense of movements like the NOI and the MST. While much of the earlier work on these movements was judgmental, describing them as social and political responses to anti-black racism rather than as authentic American or Muslim religious movements, more recent scholarship has used the lens of syncretism to incorporate these communities more sympathetically within the Islamic fold.[56]

Once we leap from African American history and religious studies to the history of Islam among twentieth-century immigrant populations, this generosity of spirit quickly evaporates. Instead, the sentiment Yvonne Haddad captures in the following quote quickly becomes hegemonic.

The earliest immigrants to found mosques before the Second World War and, for the most part, their children and grandchildren appear to have fitted comfortably into America. They tried both to fit into the new culture and interpret it in new ways that tended to emphasize the respect Islam had for Jesus and his mother Mary and to quote verses from the Qur'an emphasizing the commonalities between the two faiths. To the immigrants who have come since 1960, however, this kind of accommodation seems too high a price to pay. They are critical of their coreligionists who appear to have diluted the importance of Islamic traditions, rituals, and distinguishing characteristics, going so far as to refer to the mosque as "our church," to the Qur'an as "our bible," and to the imam as "our minister."

The more recent immigrants are neither poor nor uneducated; on the contrary, they represent the best-educated elite of the Muslim world who see themselves as helping develop America's leadership in medicine, technology, and education. They have been influenced by a different socialization process, and while they appreciate, enjoy, and have helped create America's technology, they want no part in what they see as its concomitant social and spiritual problems. Confident that Islam has a solution to America's ills, they have no patience for the kinds of accommodations they see as compromising the true Islamic way.[57]

As Haddad suggests here, the new migrants expressed a will to power over older American Muslim populations. The newcomers were quick to criticize their predecessors, whom they faulted for their presumed embrace of American religious values. Two of the first monographs to focus on Muslims in the United States were written by Abdo Elkholy and Atif Wasfi, an (al-Azhar University trained) Egyptian and a Lebanese national, who received their PhDs from American universities based on research they conducted in Dearborn, Michigan, and Toledo, Ohio, in the 1950s and 1960s.[58] These sociologists provided synoptic histories of Detroit's Arab Muslim enclaves as background for their research findings, which focused on measures of religiosity and assimilation among American Muslims. In the absence of other sources, their work has been treated as a sort of eyewitness account of Dearborn's mosques at midcentury, which technically it is. Their sketches of the city's past have also been accepted at face value, and dutifully reproduced for over forty years, even though several of their claims are inaccurate. Linda Walbridge, who produced the third monograph about Dearborn's Muslim enclaves a generation later, was the first scholar to note that Elkholy gets many historical details wrong and that his perspective was biased. "What is most significant about Elkholy's account," she argues, "is that he tells the story of the community from a Sunni perspective. His history of the community is only one history. And one might even go so far as to say it is a dead history."[59] By "dead history" she means that Elkholy's focus on the Sunni congregation of the AMS (the same congregation whose seventieth anniversary is described earlier) led him to overlook the religious and institutional revival that overtook the local Shi'i community in the same period. By contrast, the AMS would not experience its revival until the 1970s, when, from Walbridge's Shi'i-centric perspective, the Lebanese American Sunnis were defeated and their history snuffed out by immigrant Yemeni fundamentalists. This reading is no less problematic.

Wasfi and Elkholy were part of the larger cohort of Middle Eastern immigrants and foreign students who arrived in the United States between the 1950s and 1970s. As Haddad suggests, they were highly judgmental of the way Islam was practiced in the United States. Their bias was not simply a Sunni one; it was generational as well. References to the indifferent Islam practiced in "churches," with "ministers" who sometimes abandoned their "pulpits" for the entire summer, and with "clubs" led as much by women as by men, were consistent with the assessments made by would-be Muslim leaders who sought to overturn the existing order and lead American Islam in a new direction.[60] Narratives about the failings of the early American mosques were important to the post-1965 immigrant cohort because many of the scholars and activists among them sought not simply to promote Islam in the United States or keep it alive among future generations, but also to bring about an international Islamic revival. "They strongly believed that the key to reviving Islamic civilization was the intellectual revival of the ummah … [yet the] freedom for rethinking the Islamic civilizational project and to indulge in serious rejuvenation of the stagnant Islamic sciences was not available in the Muslim world."[61] Thus immigrant intellectuals—men like Fazlur Rahman, Ismail Farooqi, Seyyed Hossein Nasr, and Taha Jabir Al-Alwani—inspired a generation of young student activists with their alternative reading of modernity. It was these student activists at first, and then a broader coalition of new immigrants, who set about reinstitutionalizing Islam in the United States in the 1960s and 1970s, building mosques and new organizations, like the Muslim Student Association, that eventually superseded those of earlier Muslim Americans.

The ambition of these Muslim intellectuals went well beyond condemning the Islamic centers and Muslim practices they encountered in the United States and encouraging a newly invigorated, Qur'an-based Islamic practice. These men migrated from rapidly decolonizing states that were of critical importance to American Cold Warriors. Some of them shared anti-imperialist agendas and were part of Islamist religious/political movements that represented the United States, and the West more generally, as *dar al-kufr*, the abode of infidels, a land antithetical to long-term Islamic cohabitation and compatibility. As they sought to establish roots in this country, they were compelled to reconcile their perspective with the record of earlier migrants who instead imagined the United States as *dar al-Islam*, a place in which Islam could be (and obviously was being) practiced freely.[62] Living and working in cities and on college campuses that generally did not have Muslim communities with deep historical roots, they were not concerned with Islam's past in the United States and were quick to simplify the experiences of their predecessors. Their critique of old Islam in Detroit (and elsewhere) was thus intensely political, in addition to being rooted in a specific set of spiritual and ideological commitments.

Ironically, many African American Muslims also came to embrace this way of thinking about the past. Sherman Jackson, for example, writing much more recently, argues that Islam is today viewed as a transplant religion that arrived in the United States in the post-1965 era. "Prior to 1965," he says, "Islam in America was dominated by an indigenous black presence," by which he does not mean the Sunni practices and beliefs of many black and immigrant Muslims, or the Shiʻi traditions maintained in Detroit and elsewhere by thousands of Lebanese Americans, but (rather remarkably) the traditions of syncretic movements like the NOI and the MST.[63] In Jackson's narrative, these "heterodox" Muslims were also overshadowed and robbed of their religious authority "following the settling of critical masses of Muslims from the Muslim world" and the accompanying shift "to the sources, authorities, and interpretive methodologies of historical Islam."[64] He goes on to argue that the underlying anti-Western political sentiments of both the new migrants and American blacks encouraged them to work together in the 1960s and 1970s. But this alliance was short lived due to a "mutually contradictory relationship to American whiteness."[65] Rather than inquire into the dynamic push and pull that marked the relationship between Sunni blacks, blacks in the NOI or MST, and non-black Muslims well before 1965, Jackson's treatment winds up privileging the NOI, and the black Sunni community that grew out of it after 1975, as the authentic, "indigenous" voice of American Islam. As a result, the "orthodox" Sunni and Shiʻi Muslims, black and non-black, who lived in the United States in the first three quarters of the twentieth century are little more than footnotes in his history of American Islam.[66] Beyond Jackson's work, this dynamic of privileging the history of the NOI over the experiences of other Muslim Americans has meant that very few studies have explored the early history of Sunni Islam among blacks or the history of non-black Muslims in anywhere near the depth of scholarship the NOI has received.[67]

When taking this larger literature into consideration, it is clear that the partisan perspective I encountered when documenting Detroit's past is not simply the work of local Muslim leaders in Detroit. It reflects instead a convergent sensibility shared by mid-twentieth-century scholars like Wasfi and Elkholy, post-1965 migrant activists and scholars, and contemporary African American Muslim activists and scholars. It has been useful to the new generation of religious leaders and institution builders who came to prominence in Detroit, as elsewhere, beginning in the 1970s. For these actors, the failings of Detroit's early Muslim communities took on an almost mythological relevance in the post-1965 period, as new immigration and the mass conversion of the NOI to mainstream Islam significantly altered the demographics of the Muslim American population. Those eager to build a new type of Muslim American identity first had to come to terms with a past that seemed unfamiliar and inadequate. Their critique of the Islam they encountered in Detroit and across North America—a unique, locally adapted Muslim habitus I call *old Islam*—was superimposed on the histories of these well-established, highly Americanized communities. As a more Qur'an-centered, self-consciously pious, and schematically modern Islam came to predominate in Detroit (and globally), the Islam still practiced in the city by older American Muslims and their children came to represent all that Detroit's new Muslim leaders wanted to overcome.

Itineraries

Each chapter of this book shows how forces of translocality and transcommunalism have influenced both the establishment of American mosques and the way Muslims in Detroit understand the challenges they face as minority populations living in the United States. In Chapter 2, "The Lost History of America's First Mosque," I consider Detroit's first Muslim immigrants, why they settled in the city, and how they practiced Islam. I explore interethnic relations among these early Muslims and their campaign to build the first mosque in the United States, the Moslem Mosque in Highland Park (established in 1921). This mosque was meant to stand as a unifying symbol of Islam in the United States, to educate Americans about the growing Muslim presence in their midst, to link Detroit's Muslims to those overseas, and to create a site of pilgrimage for Muslims living throughout the American hinterland. Despite these lofty ambitions, and perhaps because of them, the first American mosque was also the first to fail. I parse out the motives for the mosque's construction, the reasons for its demise, and the significance of this failure for the building efforts that would follow.

Chapter 3, "They are Orientals and Love the East," considers how American understandings of race, especially as tied to citizenship rights in the 1920s, influenced the prospects of different Muslim populations in Detroit. The second attempt to build a communal mosque in the city, named the Universal Islamic Society, was an explicitly anticolonial campaign organized in the name of pan-Islamism, a movement dedicated to the dismantling of European colonies in India, Africa, and the Arab world. This agenda overlapped with pan-Africanism, a sociopolitical movement that quickly became entangled with Islam in Detroit, giving rise to the NOI. In Chapter 4, "Dearborn's First Mosques," I explore the new Muslim American identities that took shape during the Great Depression. Reduced in size and sorted into ethnoracial enclaves, Detroit's Muslims in the 1930s embraced life in America as their certain future. Arabic-speaking Muslim families faced a new impetus to organize: the need to provide religious education and a distinctive ethno-religious social space for their American-born children. The mosques they built in this period, which effectively recognized Sunni and Shi'i differences, were creative spaces in which Muslim American institutional practices—many of which survive today—were first negotiated and stabilized.

Chapter 5, "Doctors of the Soul," focuses on the impact of the Cold War on Muslim institutions in Detroit. In the 1950s and 1960s, Detroit rose to prominence as the center of Muslim life in the United States. Eager to make their institutions vital, Detroiters imported well-educated clerics from overseas; helped organize the Federation of Islamic Associations of the United States and Canada (FIA); developed an active English-language Muslim press; built prominent, modern mosques; revitalized Islamic education for American-born children; and welcomed the visits, attention, and resources of foreign Muslim leaders. This period also saw painful disagreements over the adaptive steps Detroit's mosques had taken to remain relevant. The encounter between new and old models of American Islam was especially intense in two influential Detroit mosques: the ICA and the Albanian Islamic Center, where the older, more Americanized models of Muslim practice temporarily prevailed against all criticism. This outcome reinforced the authority of Detroit's clerics as leaders of American Islam in a transnational political sphere dominated by Cold War interests.

In Chapter 6, "Homegrown Muslim Leaders," I analyze the paradigm shifts that reconfigured American Islam in the 1960s and 1970s as transnational Muslim movements gained sway and the Civil Rights and Black

Power Movements became dominant among African Americans. I observe these changes from the perspective of two American-born Muslim leaders, one Arab and one black, and the ethnically distinct mosques they served. In many ways, the AMS and Masjid al-Mu'mineen were prototypical American mosques. Yet their religious authenticity and the authority of their imams became increasingly suspect to new immigrants and foreign Muslims living and studying in Detroit, and to radicalized black Muslims. In both mosques, new models of Islamic practice ultimately prevailed against the old. In Chapter 7, "Raising the Bar," I track the movement of Imam Warith Deen Mohammed and his followers from the NOI into Sunni Islam in the 1970s, and the reception these new believers received in the black mosques and Muslim movements of the period. I also examine the repercussions of the Islamic Revolution in Iran for Muslim institutions and identities in the United States. These transitions are presented from the vantage point of individuals and institutions already familiar from earlier chapters. Dominant models of Muslim American history, as they are understood today, coalesced during this period. Promulgated by the leaders of Detroit's many new mosques, and nationally by the Muslim Student Association and the Islamic Society of North America, this historical sensibility presupposed a past in which old Islam in Detroit (as elsewhere the United States) stood for assimilation, secularism, political passivity, and religious ignorance.

I conclude in Chapter 8, "Everything Old is New Again," by drawing parallels between the early 1980s and the post-9/11 period, when the possibility of reimaging Muslim American history has become urgent and necessary once more. Both eras are linked systematically to even earlier ones. By examining these links, I want to suggest that popular attitudes about old Islam (and lack of reliable knowledge about it) are constantly feeding into the discourses about American Islam that are prevalent among non-Muslims, a synergy driven by deeply held assumptions about supposed incompatibilities between America and Islam as ideas, lifeworlds, and contexts of political belonging. The ability to historicize these assumptions and describe how they shift and repeat themselves over time will, I argue, help Muslims and non-Muslims realize the extent to which their identities are connected and mutually reinforced within a complex array of Americanizing projects.

Finally, by focusing on interethnic relations among Detroit's early Muslims and ongoing contests between new immigrants and the native born, especially as they worked together to (re)invent the institution of the American mosque, I show how differences internal to the Muslim community, some of which Muslims came to respect and others they sought to overcome, have given American Islam some of its most distinctive and durable contours. These contours have become highly visible since the renewed immigration of the post-1965 era, and they have taken on new political urgency since 2001, but they have not yet been fundamentally transformed.

CHAPTER 2 | The Lost History of America's "First Mosque"

AMERICA'S FIRST MOSQUE WAS constructed in 1893 on "Cairo Street" at the Columbian Exhibition in Chicago. A close replica of the Mosque of Sultan Qayt Bey in Cairo, Egypt, it was built to display Islam for American audiences. The Muslim workers and performers at the Exhibition, including a well-trained imam, were encouraged to remain in their "native costumes" by the fair's organizers. But it was on their own initiative, and to the apparent delight of the public, that when the *adhan* (call to prayer) was made from the mosque's minaret five times a day, the visiting Muslims would duly gather inside and perform their obligations.[1]

> The exquisite and picturesque little mosque—it is the prototype of the purest bit of Eastern architecture in Stamboul—these thoroughly genuine people, this sacred service—not as a necessary part of the oriental exhibit, but as an essential, indispensable part of the life of the natives themselves—this combination of the genuine and the picturesque is to me the keynote of the Great Exposition.[2]

At the Exhibition's close, the mosque was torn down. The performers and staff of the "Cairo Street" exhibit, who had been imported to the United States as objects of spectacle in a hierarchical display of the world's "civilizations," returned to their more prosaic lives in Egypt, Morocco, and Palestine, where the ritual of prayer would draw little comment.

The second mosque to be built in the United States was completed in 1921, in Highland Park, Michigan. Built by Muslim immigrants as a place of worship, this mosque, like the one on "Cairo Street," was intended to represent Islam to American viewers. But the Muslims of Highland Park hoped to create a very different impression of their faith. The Islam practiced in the Highland Park mosque would not be exotic, foreign, or a thing of spectacle. It would be an American faith not unlike those found in churches and synagogues.

While histories of Islam in the Americas often begin with the arrival of Morisco conscripts who sailed with Portuguese and Spanish conquistadors, or with the Atlantic trade in African slaves, I argue that the history of today's Muslim American communities effectively begins in the twenty-eight years that separated the construction of the "Cairo Street" and Highland Park mosques. The "Islam brought by the enslaved West Africans," Diouf observes, "has not survived. It has left traces; it has contributed to the culture and history of the continents; but its conscious practice is no more. For Islam to endure, it had to grow...through transmission to the children...and through conversion of the unbelievers."[3] The performers at the Columbian Exhibition, who were free to come and go, were able to influence the development of American Islam in ways Muslim slaves could not. When they returned to their homes in the Levant, they told fanciful tales of their sojourn in America, tales of "progress and opportunity." Their testimony added fuel to the "emigration fever" that was already burning in many regions of the Ottoman Empire.[4] By the first decades of the twentieth century, Muslim immigrants from Ottoman domains began congregating in small mill towns, urban industrial centers, and on remote homesteads across North America, wherever work or trade could be found. These Muslim communities were small and dispersed, but unlike earlier slave populations, they were free to practice their faith in the New World. Many of them decided to stay.

At the time, Islam was strange to most Americans, and Muslims were new to the United States. Immigrants and converts would have to build viable Muslim institutions if they wanted Islam to survive in a predominantly Christian society. In cities like Detroit, Muslims faced serious constraints as they set about creating infrastructure for the practice and reproduction of Islam, an agenda that required and would generate a distinctively Muslim American consciousness. In this chapter, I explore the earliest attempts to articulate this consciousness and give it both an institutional and an architectural form.

Life for the Early Muslim Immigrants: Making Room for Islam

The Muslim immigrants who settled in the United States in the late nineteenth and early twentieth centuries came from a surprising array of

European, Ottoman, formerly Ottoman, and British colonial domains. They began arriving in the 1890s, but their numbers were small compared to the better-known European migrations of the same period. These pioneer American Muslims were a highly mobile group until the 1930s, moving from one city or work site to the next, seeking higher pay, better living conditions, marriage partners, and the company of others who shared their native languages and religious traditions.

Most of the early immigrants did not envision settling permanently in the United States. Their transience made it difficult for them to establish effective organizations, but by the early 1900s, Muslim associations had begun to appear in cities like New York, Chicago, and Detroit, and in smaller communities in the Midwest and Great Plains states. These immigrants needed a place to observe communal prayer. They needed fellow Muslims to wash and pray over their dead in keeping with Islamic custom. And they were eager to hear news of the families and friends they had left behind, information that was available only among informal networks of fellow immigrants from their home regions. These reasons for association were as social as they were religious. They were also political. Many of the early Islamic associations began as ethnic clubs or nationalist organizations. Gradually, as Muslims gathered in specific cities and towns, in the shadows of factories and the settlements beside railroad terminals, they began to build the infrastructure of a collective Muslim American life.

In 1906, for instance, a Yugoslav mutual aid society was established in Chicago under the name Khairat ul-Umma.[5] A group of Polish, Lithuanian, and Russian Muslims followed suit by forming the American Mohammedan Society in New York in 1907. After meeting in rented rooms for decades, the society bought three buildings in 1931, making it the "first corporate body to purchase property in New York City with the express purpose of practicing Islam."[6] In 1922, the Buffalo Moslem Welfare Society was inaugurated by a multiethnic group of immigrants in Buffalo, New York. In 1924, a congregation of Grenadians, Arabs, and Indian seafarers established a small mosque on State Street in Brooklyn.[7] Arabic-speaking Muslims had also begun to settle in rural communities and near working factories on the East Coast and across the Midwest. They established mutual aid societies in the first decades of the twentieth century in places like Sioux Falls, South Dakota, and Newcastle, Pennsylvania. Syrians founded the Bader Elmoneer Society of Michigan City (Indiana) in 1914, and in 1924 they incorporated this society as the Asser El Jadeed Temple (the New Generation Temple). They purchased their first building to be used as a mosque in 1935.[8] In Cedar Rapids,

Iowa, the mosque known today as the "Mother Mosque of America" was first organized as the Rose of Fraternity Lodge in 1925. By 1929 this congregation had begun construction of a purpose-built mosque, which was finally completed in 1934, after the worst of the Great Depression had passed.[9] Elsewhere, the Syrian Mohammaden Lodge opened in Worchester, Massachusetts, in 1918.[10]

Detroit's "Syrian colony" was part of this national trend. By 1897, a small population of Syrian peddlers had settled in the city.[11] The earliest Syrians were Christian, but by 1908 Muslims had also begun moving into the area, congregating with other Arabic speakers. Several of Detroit's older graveyards attest to the presence of Turkish, Kurdish, Afghan, and Albanian Muslims as well, again in the very early years of the twentieth century.[12] Muslims were but a small part of a much larger influx of immigrants who arrived in Detroit between 1889 and 1923. Their numbers swelled in earnest after 1914, when Henry Ford, greedy for men to keep his new factories in operation, began offering a five-dollar workday. The village of Highland Park, site of the world's first standardized, integrated assembly line, had a population of just over 4,000 in 1910, and 47,000 by 1920. Detroit's population more than doubled during this same decade, jumping from 465,000 to 993,000.[13]

This remarkable population boom was fueled not only by the arrival of new immigrant workers but also by the internal northward migration of blacks and whites seeking economic opportunity and an escape from Jim Crow conditions in the South.[14] Highland Park, like Detroit, was what might today be described as a "fast city," a town with cachet that seemed to spring up overnight. Money could be made there quickly, and those with ingenuity found they could often do better for themselves outside Ford's factory, building the city itself, laying out its streets and sidewalks, financing its model housing stock, feeding and furnishing the workers and middle-class families who were rushing into the new metropolis. In Detroit and Highland Park, there would be no immigrant ghetto, no overcrowded tenement houses. Highland Park offered those who could afford it (and were not excluded along racial lines) a domestic Eden where immigrant and American-born residents could own their own homes; raise vegetables in their back yards; and stroll around the neighborhood visiting one another's grocery stores, coffee houses, and churches. Neighborhoods close to the Ford factory also included modern, frequently mixed-race apartment houses.[15] Highland Park incorporated as a city in 1920 to avoid being absorbed by Detroit, which encompassed the small village during World War I.[16]

A sizeable population of Syrian Muslims had settled in Highland Park when Ford's factory was still under construction, and these Syrians attracted more Syrians once the assembly line began to churn out Model-T automobiles. Arabic-speaking Muslims came from two regions of today's Lebanon. Those from the Bekaa Valley were mostly Sunni; those from the southern villages of Tibneen and Bint Ijbayl and the surrounding countryside were predominantly Shi'a. Both were tightly knit communities. Unlike the Turks and Kurds who preceded them in Detroit, or the Indians whose numbers grew steadily after 1916, many of the Syrian immigrants were women and children.[17] Most Syrian Muslim families in the Detroit area in 1914 lived in or near Highland Park, but the overwhelming majority of Muslim immigrants at the time were men whose wives and children (if they had any) did not come with them to Detroit.[18] Many of these "bachelors" lived not in Highland Park but in the immigrant settlements closer to downtown Detroit.

It is difficult to estimate the Muslim population of Detroit at the time. Immigration statistics are unreliable, given that many Turks and Kurds claim to have identified as Armenians when they entered the United States.[19] American prejudice against Turks was strong at the time, and it was continually stoked by sensational media accounts of the Armenian Crisis, which had begun in the 1890s (see Chapter 3). Likewise, Albanian and Syrian arrivals were part of a migration flow that was majority Christian. While historians have long claimed that Muslims made up 10 percent of the Syrian immigration, there is no way to verify this estimate.[20] Bilge argues that there were about five thousand Ottoman Sunni Muslims in Detroit by 1914, and the *Detroit Free Press* cited this figure again in 1916, but the number is thought to have grown significantly during and after World War I, as famine, military conscription, and social chaos beset Greater Syria and the (formerly) Ottoman domains. Figures for the overall Muslim populations that circulated in the press in the 1920s varied significantly, but tended to hover between seven and sixteen thousand.[21]

While Muslim immigrants acknowledged that they had many things in common, they saw themselves primarily through the lens of national and cultural origins. They tended to live in ethnically distinct enclaves and to establish ethnically distinct associations. A combination of legal restrictions, both at points of immigrant departure and arrival, gave rise to a gender imbalance that had significant consequences for the religious and institutional life of the Muslim community. Immigrants with spouses and children were more likely to stay in the United States and invest in mosques, where their children could be raised as Muslims and exposed to religious education. Those without American-based families were likely to think of themselves as sojourners, a self-perception that nurtured their commitment to nationalist causes overseas, facilitated eventual return to their home countries, and discouraged investment in mosque-building projects, even among those who did remain in the United States.

An unknown percentage of immigrant men married non-Muslim American women. Scholars have tended to emphasize that these men ceased to practice Islam, practiced a hybridized version of Islamic tradition, or eventually became Christians.[22] While all of these patterns existed in Detroit, a large number of Muslim families in the city today trace their ancestry to Muslim immigrant men who married local, non-Muslim women. Exogamy did not automatically entail a weakening or loss of Islamic identification among migrants. To the contrary, many of the most active builders of early Muslim institutions in Detroit belonged to mixed households, and convert spouses contributed unique skills to the early Muslim establishment in the city.[23] Indeed, these individuals figure prominently in the chapters that follow.

Turkish and Kurdish Muslim enclaves were made up almost entirely of men, often young men who, like the Syrians, were mostly peasants who had left the Ottoman Empire around the turn of the century to avoid conscription, political turmoil, and overall conditions of neglect in the countryside. Many went abroad to make money, hoping to return once they were too old to be drafted. Uncertain about the conditions they would find in the United States, and not intending to stay, these men rarely brought women with them.[24] Indian immigrants were a different matter. Excluded by the Asiatic Barred Zone Act of 1917 and denied the right to naturalize in 1923,[25] Indian Muslims continued to arrive in the United States through undocumented channels. Bangladeshi Muslims made up a large percentage of British maritime workers between 1900 and 1925, and many jumped ship or found other means of entering port cities like New York, Boston, and New Orleans.[26] Scores of Bangladeshi workers, mostly from the rural Sylhet district, made their way to Detroit during and after World War I.[27] Acir Udin Maeh, who arrived in the city in 1916, expecting to be the only Indian there, was surprised to meet another man from his village shortly after his arrival.[28]

The Ford Motor Company also brought dozens of Indians from more privileged backgrounds to work in its factories in Detroit in the 1920s as part of a training program in industrial production. The intention was to prepare these "students" to work as supervisors in the company's planned facilities in India.[29] In 1925, one observer estimated the Indian population in the city to be as high as two hundred, although it was also described as being highly transient due to the irregularity of automobile industry work at that time.[30] With few exceptions, Bangladeshi workers and other South Asian students were unable to sponsor the migration of spouses or to travel back and forth between the United States and India.[31]

For this predominantly male population of Muslim immigrants, the most important social institution to develop in Highland Park and Detroit in the first decades of the twentieth century was not the mosque or the mutual aid society but the coffeehouse. In many ways, the coffeehouse served as a surrogate for both. It also acted as a form of family life. Organized loosely along linguistic and cultural lines, with Indians and Afghans meeting in one or two space, Turks and Kurds in others, coffeehouses provided men with a place to relax and socialize outside of work.[32] The coffee shops were similar to one another in that they provided *narjilah*s (waterpipes), cards, *tawilah* (backgammon), and other ways to pass the time. All served "Turkish" coffee. Many had adjoining restaurants. Alex Ecie, in his interview with historian Alixa Naff, mentioned that the single Syrian men he knew in his early years in Detroit purchased meal tickets from an Armenian restaurant in Highland Park and took their meals there.[33] Coffeehouses also provided meals for their bachelor clientele. Dada Khan, an Indian worker in Detroit in the 1920s, described several Indian restaurants and coffeehouses where he and other workers took their meals, shared news of India, and swapped information about available jobs and housing.[34] Muslim coffee shops were distinctive in their décor. Notably, they tended to feature Arabic calligraphy from the Qur'an, usually the shahada or *fatiha* (the opening verse of the Qur'an), often easily visible from outside the shop. Several shops made prayer rugs available to patrons and set aside a corner or back room for collective prayer on special occasions. Coffeehouses provided immigrant men, whether Christian or Muslim, Afghan or "Hindoo,"[35] with a place for solidarity and mutual acquaintance, and they routinely served as platforms for the organization of more formal ethnonational associations, religious mutual aid societies, social clubs, and fraternal societies.[36]

In 1914, Turks in Highland Park and Detroit created a housing cooperative.[37] They were joined in 1916 by the Arabian-American Society, whose mission was to educate "persons of Syrian nationality in the English language and in the governmental matters of the United States of America, social enjoyment and promotion of good citizenship and to provide reading and club rooms."[38] The latter group was also affiliated with the United

Moslem Association, an umbrella organization that represented "all the Moslem societies in Detroit" and oversaw "sectional branches throughout Michigan and Ohio" as well.[39] In 1916, the Association organized a large celebration of Muharram (the commemoration of the seventh-century martyrdom of Imam Husayn ibn Ali) that included a parade, picnic, and fundraiser for the Red Crescent Society (*Kizilay*) of Detroit. Cosmopolitan and transnational in its ethos, the United Moslem Association was affiliated with another organization described by the *Detroit Free Press* as "Keiriat Island Moslem," most likely a local chapter of Chicago's Eastern European Muslim organization, Khairat ul-Umma. Together, Detroit's Muslims were said to have raised $50,000 in support of the Turkish Red Crescent Society.[40] With the end of World War I, these groups turned their attention to more immediate needs. In 1920, they worked together to officially incorporate a local branch of the *Kizilay*, which assumed responsibility as a Muslim funeral association and purchased a section of Roseland Park Cemetery large enough to accommodate more than five hundred Muslim burials. It was the first explicitly Muslim cemetery plot in Michigan.[41] Finally, in 1922, men from the Indian subcontinent organized the India Club, an association whose membership was purportedly open to all Muslims in the city.[42] Reflecting back on this period, a prominent member of the Syrian community, Kalil Bazzy, who spoke with historian Alixa Naff in 1962, remembered Highland Park in this way: "Every *balad* (village or homeland) had a *jamea* (association or social club)."[43]

This flurry of organizational activity in Detroit was clearly not an isolated phenomenon. Formulated on a diverse array of principles—from concern over the state of the Caliphate in Constantinople or the plight of Muslim communities affected by the Balkan Wars, to concern over the needs of Muslims migrants in the United States, including the push for citizenship and immigrant incorporation—these institutions drew Muslims together on a local, regional, and international scale. A self-described missionary from Sudan, Satti Majid, the "Sheikh of Islam in America," arrived in the United States around 1908 and spent time in Detroit, New York, Pittsburgh, Buffalo, and presumably other locales.[44] In a 1935 interview he gave to the *al-Balagh* newspaper in Cairo, Egypt, he reports organizing Muslims in the United States in 1911 in response to the Italian occupation of Tripoli. His recollections do not neatly map onto events for which documentation is available, but he was clearly involved in the Red Crescent Society in Detroit and in a local group he recalled as the Islamic Benevolent Society—in Arabic, *al-jam'iyya al-khayriyya al-Islamiyya*—another candidate for the "Keiriat Island Moslem" group mentioned above. Majid claims that the first act of this group was to build a mosque next to Ford's factory in Highland Park, after which they "organized another society in this city by the name Islamic Union, and all of these societies worked together to spread the message of Islam under my leadership."[45]

It is unlikely that any of this took place before 1914. The Islamic Union to which Satti Majid refers was probably the United Moslem Association. In 1916, this group was led by Hamid Meshrif.[46] The Association's address, 110 Cottage Grove, was a mere two blocks from the Ford factory, but no evidence remains to suggest that it was built or used as a mosque, just as no evidence exists to place Majid explicitly in Detroit until 1920, when he was recorded (his name spelled "Sait Mahcit") as the president of the *Kizilay*, which officially incorporated its local chapter with the state of Michigan in that year.[47] Majid was one of several Muslim activists in the city, but he did not stay in Detroit for long, perhaps because the city's local Muslim leaders were already well connected and would soon set about building their own mosque. "When I saw the number of Muslims [in the United States]," Majid wrote, "I realized that religious duty necessitates undertaking what God has obliged us to do by way of the prescribed prayers, the fast of Ramadan, and the pilgrimage to the sacred house of God. I also realized that this noble work will not be completed without attaining consensus among Muslims and uniting them upon one view."[48] Clearly, the Muslims of greater Detroit were far enough along in these endeavors that Majid could safely take his skills to other communities.

While coffeehouses, clubs, mutual aid societies, and Red Crescent chapters were important for the social and political life of the community, these male-centered spaces were not considered suitable for the participation of women. For the growing Syrian population, which included many families by 1920, holiday celebrations, Friday prayers, and other Muslim religious and social events were held increasingly in the homes of leading families. Furniture was pulled against the walls, special carpets were laid down, and household prayer spaces were created that easily accommodated men and women, adults and children. Worshiping in homes enabled women to participate more directly in the affairs of the Muslim associations not simply as cooks and supporters but also as hosts of *mawlids* (birthday services in praise of the Prophet and his family), recitations, and other prayer services.[49]

Like their coffeehouses and clubs, the homes of Muslims were important sites of religious and ethnic identity formation. Nonetheless, these private spaces could not hold large gatherings, nor were they welcoming to large parties of single men. They were also inadequate to the task of representing

Islam to non-Muslim Americans, did little to help Muslims reconcile their many differences, and did even less to announce the presence of Muslims in the urban landscape, as other immigrant communities were doing by establishing visibly ethnic houses of worship. Highland Park's Syrian Muslims were well aware of the new churches built in Detroit by Syrian Christians. St. Maron's Catholic Church was established in 1909 and St. George's Antiochian Orthodox Church was dedicated in 1918.[50] The Syrians were equally aware of Muslim associations being established in other parts of the country. As more and more families began to settle in Highland Park, the Syrian Muslims began to long for a mosque of their own, where they could teach Islam to their children, keep Islamic traditions alive in America, and introduce Islam to other Americans. They wanted something more than a male-dominated mutual aid society or social club. At the close of World War I, a plan was set in motion to build a mosque in Highland Park.

America's First Imams: Sunni and Shi'i Difference

Detroit's early Muslim communities were distinctive not only for their size and diversity but because, by 1914, they could already count on the services of (at least) two local imams. One of the first hurdles immigrant Muslims faced in practicing Islam in the United States was the lack of religious leadership. They needed guides to help them understand their obligations as Muslims living in a non-Muslim society. They needed ritual specialists to wash the bodies of the dead, provide proper burials, and perform other, happier rites of passage. They needed preachers and teachers who could speak on their behalf to other Americans. Kalil Bazzy and Hussien Adeeb Karoub were Detroit's first resident imams. For over fifty years, they facilitated the growth of Islam in the city, not through political activism or missionary ambition but by bringing scriptural authority to Detroit's Muslim enclaves, stitching them together through the observance of collective ritual and congregational worship. Both men were living bridges between America and the Muslim world, and they saw themselves as ambassadors of Islam in the United States.

Kalil Bazzy (1886–1982) was the first to arrive in Detroit. He stepped off the street car onto Labelle Avenue in Highland Park, Michigan, in 1913. Unable to speak or read English, he had been told to turn left and follow the numbers on the houses until he came to 199. This was the address of his brother and sister-in-law, who had arranged Bazzy's passage to the United States from Bint Ijbayl, a village in Ottoman Syria. They would take him in and help him settle into his new life. Like so many new arrivals, Bazzy quickly found work on Henry Ford's rapidly expanding automobile assembly line in the model, modern, and—to Bazzy's eyes—monumental structure that loomed over the growing cityscape of Highland Park, where workers were paid $2.70 for a ten-hour day. Bazzy did not need much English to work in Ford's factory, nor did he need much English to get along in the thriving "Syrian colony" that had already taken shape just outside the factory gates, along Labelle and Victor Avenues.[51]

Historian Alixa Naff interviewed Shaykh Bazzy in Dearborn in 1962. His memories were very clear. He described his Highland Park neighborhood, circa 1913, as "Arab. All Arab. All Shi'a from Bint Ijbayl and Tibneen [neighboring villages in what is today Southern Lebanon]. There were Christians, but our neighborhood was Muslim."[52] Alex Ecie, also interviewed by Naff, arrived in Detroit a few years later, and he confirms Bazzy's description: "You could walk up and down Victor Avenue and not hear one word of 'American.' There were thousands of Arabs there, just like Dix Avenue [in Dearborn] today."[53]

After work, Bazzy passed time in the coffee shop of Hussein Abbas, another Syrian immigrant from Bint Ijbayl. Here, amid cups of tea and coffee, tobacco smoke, and the familiar sounds of Arabic, he could share news from home, keep track of other Syrian settlements in "Amreeka," and relax in the company of other newcomers from Ottoman Syria. A pious young man, Bazzy had prayed and actively observed his faith in Bint Ijbayl, a habit he continued in Highland Park without difficulty. "This is a free country," he told Naff. "No one asks you what your religion is, or your sect, or divides you. A person like me used to pray and fast in my home country. Here I prayed too. No one turned me away or opposed me."[54] Bazzy was singled out by others in the Syrian community for his piety and sincerity, not for his religious education. At the time of his arrival, he had received no formal education, religious or otherwise. Bazzy had worked as a shepherd before emigration. It was not until after he arrived in Detroit that he began to teach himself to read and write. Nonetheless, he was a skilled practitioner of Muslim ritual observances, and for this reason he gradually came to be known as *Shaykh* Bazzy.

Shaykh is an honorific used for both secular and religious leaders. Among the Shi'a, the title *Imam*—the one who leads in prayer—is reserved for the first twelve imams of the Muslim age, who were descendants of the Prophet Muhammad and are believed (by the Shi'a) to have been divinely guided and infallible. Disputes over the legitimacy of these imams caused a schism in the early Muslim community. Those who came to be known as

Shi'a believed leadership should remain within the family of the Prophet; they sided with the line of imams that began with 'Ali. Those who did not accept this line of leaders argued that righteous men who were not descendants of the Prophet could also lead the community. They came to be known as Sunni Muslims. The majority of the world's Muslims are Sunni. Most of the religious practices and beliefs of the Sunni and Shi'a are the same, but several important rituals—like prayer—differ in small, but meaningful ways. In the role of shaykh, Bazzy was encouraged to master and maintain these fine distinctions on behalf of local Shi'a, leading them in prayer, reciting the stories and poetry associated with Ashura (the annual commemoration of the martyrdom of Imam Husayn), and preparing the bodies of the Muslim dead for burial. In the 1940s, he traveled to Iraq for several months to study with religious scholars in Najaf. He returned to the United States with several certificates empowering him to marry Muslim couples, perform funeral services, and carry out other official functions of Muslim and American clergy.[55] Shaykh Kalil Bazzy served as a religious leader of the Lebanese Shi'a in greater Detroit from 1913 until his unofficial retirement in the late 1970s.

Hussien Adeeb Karoub (1892–1973) arrived in Highland Park a few months after Bazzy. He too was a Syrian immigrant singled out for his piety. Unlike Bazzy, however, Karoub had received an "elementary education" in his native village of Marj al Angar, in the Bekaa Valley of Ottoman Syria, and he had later traveled to Damascus, where he apprenticed himself to Shaykh Bader Deen at the Suleimaniyyah Mosque.[56] Hussien was fifteen years old when his brother, Mohammed, returned from the United States for a visit in 1912. Mohammed had done well during his five-year sojourn in America. He was eager to marry a girl from the village and return to the United States with a bride and his younger brothers to work beside him.[57]

Mohammed was especially pleased with Hussien's religious training. Mohammed had not encountered anyone with such expertise in the United States, and he recognized the value this training would represent to other Muslim American immigrants. Mohammed, Hussien, and a third brother, Osman Karoub, traveled to the United States in 1912. After working briefly as farm laborers in Danbury, Connecticut, they made their way to Highland Park in early 1914.[58] Not only had they heard promising accounts of work in Henry Ford's factory, but they also knew that Detroit was becoming the center of Syrian Muslim life in the United States. If Muslims were making Detroit their home, they were going to need an imam. Hussien Karoub was well equipped to fill this role.[59]

When the Karoubs arrived in Highland Park, they immediately secured jobs at Ford's factory. Like other immigrant workers, the Karoubs were required to take English language and citizenship classes in the evening in order to qualify for the promised five-dollar daily wage. Like Bazzy, they were eager to make a home for themselves among expatriate Syrians, Muslims in particular. The Sunni Arab community of Highland Park was smaller than the Shiʻi population, but it included a larger percentage of families, most of them from the Bekaa Valley. This group of closely related Muslims was the first to accept Karoub as their imam. Karoub was better educated than most Syrian Sunnis in Detroit, and he could recite the Qurʾan from memory. Despite his young age, his education and religious sincerity strongly recommended him for this important, but unpaid position.[60]

Yet Karoub's religious education in Damascus—the very quality his brother had hoped would qualify him for a leadership position—made him a source of trepidation for many local Shiʻa. In Ottoman Syria, the distinction between Shiʻi and Sunni communities was important. The Shiʻa, a small religious minority in Syria, suffered periodic harassment and persecution by Ottoman authorities and provincial elites, who were Sunni. Conditions were worse for Shiʻa in urban centers like Beirut and Damascus.[61] Faced with the arrival of Hussien Karoub, Detroit's Shiʻa redoubled their support for Kalil Bazzy.[62] Thus, within only a few years of their settlement in Highland Park, Syrian Muslims had recommitted to their distinctive sectarian traditions, effectively dividing their community into the followers of Bazzy and the followers of Karoub.

The city's other Muslims—Turks, Kurds, Afghans, Tartars, Indians, Bangladeshis, Albanians, and other Balkan Muslims—were predominantly Sunni. Members of these ethnonational communities were often familiar enough with Turkish (the administrative language of the Ottoman Empire), Arabic (the language of the Qurʾan and of Muslim prayer), or English (the language of the factory and the larger society), and there is ample evidence that they communicated with one another. They also had their own lay religious figures, men who were respected for their piety and led small gatherings in prayer. Acir Udin Maeh, for example, was the informal imam of the Bangladeshi Muslim community for most of his life. He officiated at weddings, funerals, and holiday celebrations in the Asian community, providing services in Hindi, Bengali, and Urdu, often alongside Hussien Karoub, who also spoke in Arabic and (later) English.[63] Karoub, however, was the only Muslim in greater Detroit with any formal religious education, and he was highly respected for his ability to recite the

Qur'an. Karoub made a conscious effort to acquaint himself with the city's different Muslim communities, seeking out those who were interested in Islam or in need of his expertise. Over time, Karoub came to be recognized as imam to the city's Muslims as a whole, gaining the respect of Sunni and Shi'a alike.[64]

Soon after Bazzy and Karoub settled in Highland Park, World War I broke out in Europe, and the Ottoman Empire aligned itself with the Germans. This conflict wreaked havoc in the Ottoman domains, triggering multiple independence movements and producing Muslim political uprisings in British India as well. It also brought discord to Detroit, where Muslim immigrants faced an intensification of anti-Turkish propaganda, even as they struggled to follow news from home and worried about family members who braved the transatlantic journey despite the conflict. Several Turkish, Arab, and German organizations in Detroit collaborated in 1916 to raise funds for relief efforts in Germany and the Ottoman territories.[65] Across the United States, current and former Ottoman subjects from multiple ethnonational and sectarian backgrounds advocated conflicting political outcomes for the Ottoman Empire. Hussien Karoub was one of at least sixteen thousand Syrians who enlisted in the US Army, for example, once the United States declared war in 1917. Many Syrians were eager to fight against the Ottomans in the expectation that the empire's demise would bring Syrian independence.[66] Arabic-speaking Muslims in Detroit were greatly excited by the Arab Revolt and began a long campaign to convince the US government to support Arab independence.[67] At the end of the war, Turks found themselves embroiled in their own national liberation struggle, one with significant religious repercussions.

By 1918, many of Detroit's Muslims had put down roots in the city and planned to stay there. Those who wanted to return home—to Turkey, Lebanon, or the Balkans—received news that conditions in the countryside were abysmal. The Muslim enclave in Highland Park began to grow again. Veterans of the war returned to Detroit, many as American citizens. A few local Muslims had become wealthy during the war years, as Detroit's economy and population continued to expand. Highland Park was home to (at least) two prominent, affluent Muslim leaders: the grocery store and coffeehouse owner, Hussein Abbas, a loyal supporter of Shaykh Bazzy; and Mohammed Karoub, the older brother of Imam Hussien. Together, and with separate coalitions of supporters, these men began to discuss building a mosque in Highland Park—a mosque that would make Islam part of the visible religious landscape of Highland Park.

The Moslem Mosque of Highland Park

Building a mosque in the United States was a novel proposition. The first purpose-built mosque in England, completed in 1889, was established on the grounds of an Oriental Institute in Woking, with funds provided by Sultan Shahjehan Begum of Bhopal, India.[68] The history of this mosque resembles that of the mosque built at the Columbian Exhibition in Chicago in 1893. While constructed for the purpose of facilitating cultural exchanges between England and India and, in part, for the intellectual amusement of British tourists and day-trippers, it was nonetheless adopted by (and eventually purchased by) Britain's Muslim colonial subjects, who began worshiping there in 1913.[69] In Detroit, no foreign patron or government offered to finance the construction of a mosque. Local Muslims would have to pay for the project themselves. What would the mosque look like? How would it be financed and administered? Who would make decisions on behalf of the facility? Would it have members? A congregation? What functions would the mosque serve? These were challenging questions for the city's Muslims.

At the close of World War I, Mohammad Karoub, brother of Hussien, stepped forward and announced that he would build the first mosque in the United States. He did not organize a committee to help him in this task. Nor did he inquire at local churches to see how they had built their facilities. He simply declared that he wanted to build a mosque and then set about doing so. Although ambitious, such an undertaking was not beyond the reach of a man with Mohammad Karoub's entrepreneurial talents. He had become a successful real estate speculator and developer just before the war. After buying a home for his young family and selling it a year later for a significant profit, he left Ford's factory and set out on his own. Detroit's population continued to grow at a rapid pace during the war, and Karoub made a sizeable fortune trading properties and eventually building apartment houses in Highland Park. By 1921 he was reported to be worth half a million dollars.[70] Channeling the impulse that had led him to bring his clerical brother to the United States, Karoub now developed a plan to provide his brother—and all of Detroit's Muslims—a mosque in which to pray. Having bought up several empty lots along Victor Avenue and a large multistory apartment house, he pledged to invest the profits he made from turning over this property, an estimated $50,000, in the construction of a mosque on Victor Avenue that would be located within a block from the gates to Ford's factory.[71] In 1919 he hired an architect, Theodore H. Degenhardt, to begin work on the project.[72]

Karoub's plan for managing and funding the mosque was never made explicit, but it can be pieced together from local news coverage and from what we know of mosque endowments in the Ottoman Empire, where mosques were the property and responsibility of a state-sponsored religious endowment known as a *waqf*. Villages or urban neighborhoods did not set about building mosques on their own; rather, they petitioned the government for a mosque. Alternatively, a wealthy individual would endow a piece of income-generating property as a *waqf*, which would be administered by trustees designated by the donor. The upkeep of these institutions was supported by *waqf* income, and trustees managed their financial affairs.[73] Karoub apparently envisioned the Moslem Mosque of Highland Park (MMHP) operating on a modified version of this model, with the apartment house acting as the *waqf* property and his brother Hussien acting as the *waqf* trustee. He borrowed from an American business model as well, soliciting "subscriptions" from mosque supporters in and outside the Detroit area. These subscriptions were to support the upkeep and improvement of the facility.[74] Having made a quick fortune in real estate, Karoub now sought to become a patron of the Syrian Muslim community by building America's first mosque. His brother, Hussien, would serve as the resident imam.

Toward this end, the two brothers planned a cross-country trek to solicit donations and drum up enthusiasm for the project.[75] Figure 2.1 shows a poster based on Degenhardt's drawing of the mosque, which Karoub prepared for distribution on their journey. The poster depicts the two brothers as well, Imam Hussien on the left in *tarboush* (a fez-like head covering) and *abaya* (robe), with a Qur'an tucked under his right arm and *masbaha* (a string of prayer beads) in his left hand—items signifying Muslim religious authenticity and authority—and Mohammed on the right, dressed in a suit and bowtie, complete with a stick pin on his lapel—items signifying worldly, American success. Note that the building's design also marries 1920s urban American building materials and styles with a touch of the Orient. The building would have sat well in Highland Park, with its small front stoop, large open first floor, and basement. The mosque's otherwise mundane facade is augmented with ogee arches (similar to those used on the Taj Mahal) over the windows and doors, two strictly ornamental "minarets" capped off with crescent and star finials, [76] and a low-lying ornamental dome. With this deft mix of imagery, the two brothers sought to unify the time and space of Middle Eastern Islam with that of urban America. For good measure, Karoub's apartment building investment plan is included in the lower left corner of the poster.

FIGURE 2.1 Poster used to raise funds for the Moslem Mosque of Highland Park. Courtesy of Carl M. Karoub. Karoub family Collection, Bentley Historical Library, University of Michigan.

The mosque had several interesting internal features as well. As Karoub himself described the building, "the first floor is the mosque dedicated for worship, the second is a school for the youth to learn our Arabic language and the laws of our religion. Next to it [prayer space] is a private modern bath and places for *wudu'a,* place for washing the dead and everything that is needed for purification in every mosque with the most beautiful architecture."[77] Muslims face toward Mecca (technically, toward the Ka'aba in Masjid al-Haram) when they pray, lining up toward the *qibla* (direction, orientation) of the holy city. The most significant and essential feature of any mosque or *musalla* (prayer space) is that it have an architectural feature, usually a niche, that both marks and is known as the qibla. As the finials on the dome and minarets pointed toward Mecca to orient the city's

Muslims outside the mosque, inside the main *musalla* (prayer space) featured a *qibla* as well. Because Highland Park's urban grid made it impractical to orient the building itself toward Mecca, the standard practice in much of the Muslim world, the *musalla* of the Highland Park mosque was constructed as a circle with a thirty-foot diameter and a *qibla* and *mihrab* (prayer niche) facing southeast.[78]

On their 1920 journey, the Karoub brothers visited Arabic-speaking Muslim communities across the United States and presented their proposal for a mosque in Detroit. Most of the Muslims they visited were Sunni Arabs from the Bekaa Valley, although in places like Michigan City, Indiana, or Toledo, Ohio, they also met with Shi'a Arabs, and in Connecticut with a small group of Alawis. Often the families they stayed with on this journey had relatives in Detroit and Highland Park, and the Karoubs generated a sense of excitement on their travels. Hussien was kept busy marrying young couples and praying over the graves of the recently departed, while Mohammed solicited donations. They also visited with non-Syrian Muslims, again drawing on their connections in Detroit's diverse Muslim enclaves. A precise itinerary of their journey no longer exists, but they are said to have raised funds in "every large city in the Eastern states."[79] Imam Karoub made similar pilgrimages throughout his life, visiting Muslim settlements wherever he was invited, stopping in Williamson, West Virginia; Newcastle, Pennsylvania; Mancelona and Grand Rapids, Michigan; Cedar Rapids, Iowa; Ross, North Dakota; and Toledo, Ohio.[80]

This journey was a mapping expedition of sorts, with the Karoub brothers tracing the presence of Islam in the United States as they went. Inspired by the enthusiasm they generated for the planned mosque, Mohammed now wanted a mosque that would unify Muslims locally and nationally, that would provide Muslims with a locus of both sentiment and pilgrimage in the United States. A *Detroit News* reporter captured Karoub's ambitions in the following statement: "To Karoub came the vision of Detroit as a holy city; the vision of a united Muslim congregation drawn from the varied nationalities represented here; a sacred place to which the followers of Mohammed would be drawn from all parts of this continent."[81] Karoub's plans were warmly received, perhaps more so outside Detroit than at home. News stories that ran in the Arabic language papers in New York generated interest in the project overseas as well.[82] "From the king of all Egypt came a Persian rug of the finest weave and the gift of a ring from his own hand. The king of Mecca sent 400 pounds of Turkish money."[83] Karoub also raised money for the project among local Muslims in Michigan. Newspaper sources (written after the fact) also named local Shi'i leaders as financial supporters of the mosque, including Hussein Abbas, William Harb, and Moses Samht.[84]

Construction began on the building in 1920, and in January of 1921 the pace of work was accelerated in hopes of completing the edifice by Eid al-Fitr, the feast marking the end of Ramadan, in June of 1921. The mosque's construction and opening ceremonies were well documented by Detroit newspapers. The *Detroit Free Press*, for example, interviewed Hussien Karoub at the worksite during the Ramadan fast, as he and other volunteer laborers were laying bricks.[85] The paper estimated that up to sixteen thousand Muslims lived in the city and that sixteen languages were spoken among them.[86] James Devlin, a *Detroit News* reporter, also visited the construction site and chatted with Mohammed Karoub. These excerpts from the interview again reveal the Karoub brothers' mounting ambitions. No longer a simple prayer space for local Muslims, the small, still-unfinished mosque was now imagined as an international shrine:

> Mr. Karoub said that since he had resided in the United States for the last seven years, he had been convinced of the need in America of a mosque where the followers of Mohammed might worship, and his civic pride prompted him to distinguish Detroit in the eyes of the world by building in this city a mosque that would draw the Musulmans from all parts of America in pilgrimage to worship.
>
> The presentation of the mosque to the Musulmans of Detroit elevates the city in the eyes of the followers of the prophet throughout the world...It will be no longer necessary for the 400,000 Moslems in America to make their "salat" in their hearts but they have the option of making pilgrimage to Detroit to pray in the house of their God and their prophet after the manner proscribed by their faith.[87]

To realize this vision, Karoub enlisted the support of people who saw in Detroit's Syrian community a potential center for the Arab nationalist movement in the United States. Mohammed al-Mahayssin, a political refugee from Damascus and the representative of King Faisal to the United States, was in Detroit at the time of this 1921 interview, and his views were also sought by Devlin. After praising American support for religious freedom, al-Mahayssin described local Muslims as "content to remain permanently as residents of the city and to show their appreciation of the freedom of worship granted them by being useful citizens and devout believers in the faith of their fathers." He then appealed to American fairness on behalf of Syria's "constitutional king," reminding readers that

King Faisal supported the British during the war and was now expecting "the support and friendship" of the United States in returning him to his Syrian throne.[88] In this narrative, Detroit's mosque serves an important symbolic role, providing Muslims with a place of pilgrimage, a home for their faith, and an intermediary space in which the United States and the Arab world could communicate with one another. The mosque was already an embassy of sorts, representing the interests of both Muslim Americans and the larger Muslim umma. Finally, the article mentions that "the Moslem sheiks of the city, who number 5, look forward to a revival 'that will bring the faithful into communion once more, and bring a blessing on Islam in America.'"[89]

In February, as enthusiasm for the project continued to build, the Karoubs read about the arrival in Philadelphia of a Muslim scholar and missionary from India, Mufti Mohammed Sadiq. Sadiq's arrival made the newspapers because he was taken into custody upon arrival while his application for entry—for the purpose of proselytizing for Islam in the country—was reviewed. Immigration officials sought initially to deny his entry on the grounds that he would advocate for polygamy, despite his assurances to the contrary. After spending nearly seven weeks in detention, Sadiq was eventually granted admittance after he clarified his position on polygamy to government officials.[90] He argued that a distinction should be made between behaviors that are *required* of Muslims, such as prayer, and those that are merely *permitted*, such as polygamy. He assured officials that Muslims were obliged to obey the laws of the countries in which they reside unless those laws specifically contradict their religious obligations.[91] Sadiq took his detention in stride, managing to convert twenty of his fellow detainees to Islam, but the leaders of Sadiq's Ahmadiyya Movement in Lahore were stunned by this discriminatory move by US officials against an Indian national. They were, as Richard Turner points out, apparently unaware of American discrimination against Muslim and Asian immigrants, and they threatened to have American missionaries cast out of India in retaliation.[92] Despite this controversy, the Karoubs were greatly impressed by Sadiq's missionary zeal, his education, and his prolific writing. They decided to invite him to Detroit.

Sadiq's arrival in the city generated great fanfare. The welcoming dinner held for him at a Highland Park restaurant was attended by the mayor and the chief of police of Highland Park, the head of the Ford Motor Company's English School, the head of a local bank, the main Arabic language assistant in the Highland Park Schools, journalists from the English and Arabic press, and Syrian community leaders representing both the

Muslim and Christian establishment in the city. Sadiq addressed the gathering in language meant to put this diverse audience at ease.

A democracy in a republic such as we find in the United States today is exactly according to the spirit of Moslem government that was established in the beginning by the Moslem caliphs, which was a government of the people, by the people, and for the people. When my Moslem brethren try to be good citizens in this country, they perform one of the first great religious duties of their faith.

Be honest to the country and people where you are, be loyal to their flag, try to take your best part in the patriotic, social, benevolent, and charitable works. Learn the American language thoroughly—this is my advice.[93]

Opening Day and the Days that Followed

Four months later, on June 8, 1921, it was Mufti Mohammed Sadiq who again gave an English-language address to a crowd of several hundred gathered for the Eid al-Fitr holiday celebrations and the grand opening of the MMHP (see Figure 2.2).

This is the first Moslem mosque built in this land and I am proud to have the first prayer in it, as the first imam therein. This mosque, although built for the followers of Islam, will be open to the believers of all religions for a place of rest, prayer and meditation.

Mohammedans believe in worshiping but the one God. Mohammet, on whom be peace and the blessings of God, is a prophet of God who teaches us how to come into communion with Him. The religion of Islam treads underfoot all racial prejudices. Islam teaches its devotees that when they go to any other country they must peacefully obey the laws of the government of that country. Thus it is the sacred and religious duty of every Mohammedan here to be a good citizen of America and to learn the language of the country, without which we cannot understand each other rightly.[94]

The prayer itself was led by Hussien Karoub, who also addressed the gathered crowd of several hundred in Arabic, as did Kalil Bazzy. After breaking the fast together, the three imams rode in a Ford automobile, leading a parade of "swarthy orientals, headed by a band, and marching under the banners of America, Arabia, Syria, Mexico, and Turkey" across Woodward Avenue to Ford Field, where they paused briefly before returning to the mosque. The parade was followed by members of the

MOSLEMS CELEBRATE FEAST OF ID-UL-FILTR.

Left to right: Kaliel Bizzy, Mufti Mohammed Sadiq and Hussien Karoub. These three Moslem shieks were central figures in the parade celebrating the opening of the new Mohammedan mosque. Dr. Sadiq, because of his higher rank, was entitled to wear green canonicals, while the others wore white. In the inset is the smallest Mohammedan in the parade. He is a Bedouin and was garbed in native costume.

Mohammedanism had its day in Highland Park Tuesday. From early in the morning, when several hundred of the faithful knelt in prayer on rugs spread upon the mud floor of the incompleted mosque at 265 Victor avenue, until the middle of the afternoon, when the parade of Moslems disbanded, the day was one round of festivity.

prayer service, which did not differ materially in form from a Christian church service, except that the members of the congregation removed their shoes before entering the presence of the altar. The building was so far from completion that the cement had not yet been laid on the basement floor, but linoleum and rugs were spread upon the wet dirt, and a temporary altar was erected.

FIGURE 2.2 Opening ceremony of the Moslem Mosque of Highland Park. Featured from left to right are Kalil Bazzy, Mufti Sadiq, and Hussien Karoub. *Detroit Free Press.*

Mohemmedan Young Men's Association. Women were included in the procession in order "to show that they were Americans."[95] The *musalla* was not entirely completed on opening day, so tarps and carpets were placed over the dirt floor in the basement, and prayers were held there instead.[96] It is unlikely that the several hundred who attended the prayers, meal, and parade could have fit in the basement, but it is certain that they would not have fit in the circular *musalla* upstairs.

Mufti Sadiq was in many ways the ideal candidate to address the media and public officials who gathered to commemorate the mosque's opening. He was a well-trained scholar of Islam who had spent several years in England addressing British audiences, who awarded him with several honorary degrees in response to his efforts in their country.[97] He was also fluent in several languages and could communicate readily with most local Muslims in their native tongues. Finally, his English far surpassed that of Detroit's other clerics. In other respects, however, Sadiq was an unlikely spokesman for the mosque. He was not an immigrant to the United States like Detroit's other Muslims, nor had he helped to build or raise money for the project. Instead, Sadiq was a missionary for the Ahmadiyya Movement of Islam, which was based in Qadian, India. His goal was not to sustain and support Islam among immigrants and their children but to colonize America on behalf of a very particular sect of Islam founded at the end of the nineteenth century by Mirza Ghulam Ahmad.[98] Ahmad claimed to be not simply a *mujaddid* (reformer of the age) but the promised messiah of both Islam and Christianity. His Islamic revival movement was explicitly tied to anti-Christian and anticolonial campaigns in India, and the group rapidly gained adherents.

While the Ahmadiyya refer to themselves as Muslims and adhere to most of the beliefs and practices of other Muslims, they diverge from Islamic tradition when they insist that Mirza Ghulam Ahmad was himself the messiah and a prophet of God. An important tenet most Muslims respect holds that Muhammad was the seal—or last—of the prophets in the Abrahamic tradition. Thus the majority of the world's Muslims have rejected the Ahmadiyya, arguing that they lie outside the fold of Islam. The Ahmadiyya nonetheless have remained among the most active Muslim missionary bodies globally, work which began roughly in 1920, just as Mufti Sadiq was sent to the United States.[99] The Karoubs, like most of Detroit's Muslims at the time, appear to have been initially unfamiliar with the Ahmadiyya Movement and untroubled by the degree to which Sadiq's mission ("to initiate Moslems, Christians, Jews and all into knowledge of Ahmad") differed from their own.[100]

The marriage of Sadiq's missionary agenda, education, and English-language skills with Mohammad Karoub's money and ambition began as a very happy union. Sadiq moved into an apartment at "Karoub House" on Victor Avenue and set about the business of establishing his first permanent mission in the United States.[101] In July of 1921 Karoub underwrote and printed the first edition of the *Moslem Sunrise*, the English-language newsletter of the Ahmadiyya Mission to the United States, which Sadiq edited.[102] As the cover of the first issue of the magazine illustrates (see Figure 2.3), Sadiq seems to have shared Karoub's vision of Detroit and Highland Park as the hub of Muslim life and pilgrimage in the United States. He places them near the center of his rising sun.

The *Moslem Sunrise* was not a project jointly controlled by Karoub and Sadiq; rather, it was a vehicle for Sadiq's mission. In the first issue, Sadiq provided details about his time spent in detention, responded to critical letters he had received after lecturing about Islam for American audiences, issued a very sharp note on why polygamy is not permissible for American

FIGURE 2.3 The cover of the *Moslem Sunrise*, July 1921. MuslimSunrise.com.

Muslims, reprinted several newspaper stories about the opening of the Highland Park mosque and the role he played in it, and acknowledged the generous support he had received from the Karoub family and from many other Arabs in Highland Park and elsewhere.[103] A feature of the *Moslem Sunrise* that he copied from the Ahmadiyya community's equivalent paper in England, *The Review of Religions*, was the inclusion of a brief report on his success at bringing American converts to Islam. Each convert's birth name and newly given Arabic name were listed, symbolizing the shedding of an old identity and embrace of a new one. Mr. Robert Bednell, for example, became Abdullah, and Miss Elizabeth Barton became Zeinab. A secondary list included the names of "Moslem gentlemen and ladies in this country" who "joined the blessed ahmadia movement."[104] Several Arab Muslims appeared on Sadiq's July 1921 list. Of special interest to

Karoub would have been the following: Hussain Haage, Muhammad Moshaikh, and "Othman" Karoub. [105] Osman Karoub was the brother of Hussien and Mohammad Karoub. Did this mean Osman had joined the Ahmadiyya Movement? Had he done so, would he have been considered an apostate by his brothers?

Apparently the brothers did not notice this detail of the English language coverage in the paper. They continued working with Sadiq. In October, when the second issue of the *Sunrise* was published, again with a Karoub subvention, Sadiq was more explicit about his mission. The issue included "a page from the writings of 'Ahmad' (The Promised Messiah and Mehdi,)"[106] which would have been difficult enough for the Karoub brothers to accept. The newsletter also presented an illustration of the Highland Park mosque and described the Karoub family in generous language, emphasizing the role the three brothers played in making the mosque happen. In this brief note, the name of the third Karoub brother was given again as "Osman Karroub Ahmadi," indicating as explicitly as Sadiq could that this third Karoub, brother to the founder and to the imam of the only purpose-built mosque in the United States, had become a member of the Ahmadiyya community.[107] At this point the Karoubs were confronted directly with Mufti Sadiq's heterodox beliefs and with his ambitions toward their community, including their own family. They immediately revoked their hospitality and patronage of the missionary. "[Sadiq's] doctrine was not that of the bulk of the followers of Mohammed here, who clung to the old doctrine, and resented the introduction of a reformed Mohammedanism it is said. The Mufti took leave of his group of followers here, and left for Chicago to continue his missionary work."[108] The *Moslem Sunrise* reflects these changes in the October 1922 edition, which was published from Chicago, not Highland Park, and provided 4448 Wabash Avenue as the group's new address. Sadiq purchased a large house there, renovated part of it as a mosque with a qibla and dome, and used the rest of the space as his home base and the offices of the *Moslem Sunrise*.[109]

This troubling encounter between the Karoubs and Sadiq was only one of several woes that beset the Highland Park mosque over the next few years. The Syrian Muslim population was "deeply shaken" by their encounter with Sadiq, and they were eager to challenge the judgment of the Karoub brothers for having embraced Sadiq so injudiciously.[110] An attack on the mosque and on Mohammed Karoub was launched before the mosque's grand opening, and continued for several weeks afterwards in the pages of *Al-Bayan*, the Druze biweekly Arabic newspaper published in New York but carrying frequent reports from Detroit. In a series of escalating letters and counter-letters, the Syrian community in Detroit raised concerns about Mohammed Karoub's leadership and financial plans for the mosque, his close association with Mufti Sadiq, and his aggressive courting of the media. They also complained that the mosque itself was behind schedule. Karoub defended the mosque, citing the same English-language news coverage relied on above, going so far as to offer $3,000 to anyone who could prove that there was not a mosque, as one writer claimed. Sadiq loyalists also wrote in to defend his mission and his association with Karoub.[111] This controversy made it difficult for Mohammed to raise the final bit of money he needed to complete construction on the building. Added to this controversy was the multistaged opening of Ford's new River Rouge Assembly in Dearborn (beginning in 1918), several miles from Highland Park. Many Syrians were moving to Dearborn for new job opportunities and could no longer commute to the Highland Park mosque without difficulty. The congregation celebrated Eid al-Adha in the mosque in August. After the Sadiq incident, however, the number of worshipers began to dwindle significantly from week to week. In 1922, the building fell into disuse.

I am greatly disappointed that the mosque I built and gave to the people of my faith here is not appreciated; and since I have spent a large sum of money on it, and my purse is bearing the burden of its upkeep and taxes and there are none to worship in it, I can see no other logical things to do but tear the mosque down and sell the lots on which it is built," he [Mohammed Karoub] said. "I would rather tear the building down than sell it to be used for unworthy purposes, for the building has been dedicated to the worship of the God the Moslems revere. I have no word of censure for my people. If they differ with me as to the interpretation of the doctrine of Mohammed, that is their affair and their right. I believe fully in the liberty of conscience.[112]

The very public demise of this mosque was painful, politically traumatic, and embarrassing for Detroit's Muslim leaders. It was not a tale that would be easily recounted to later generations. Karoub's statement about his disappointment suggests that a second rift within the Muslim community was as important to the mosque's failure as Sadiq's heterodox teachings. While not mentioned explicitly, the difference of interpretation he mentions between himself and other local Muslims was likely a reference to divergences between Sunni and Shiʿa, rather than (or in addition to) Sunni and Ahmadiyya, understandings. When Kalil Bazzy was asked about the mosque's demise during his interview with Alixa Naff, he refused to comment on tape. Unfortunately, Naff's record of what he said to her off tape does not survive.[113] Alex Ecie, who arrived in Detroit shortly after these events unfolded, described the demise of the Highland Park mosque to Naff in the following way: "The Sunni and Shi'a cannot get along. I don't care if I have to say it. It is true. So, if they had the shaykh first, the Shi'a, and the Sunni don't like that. And if the Sunni had their shaykh first, the Shi'a don't like that. So they had a fight or something like that and one man got killed. One man got killed. And they sold the place. Some of them, two three guys, they had control just like a committee or something, and they sold the place."[114] Newspaper accounts of the mosque's downward spiral, and of the murder trial that followed, suggest that a tale of conflict between Sunni and Shi'i factions is too simple to account for what actually happened in Highland Park. Rumors and speculation filled the pages of the local press. Presented in the order of their first appearance in print, here are a few of the contemporary theories that account for the young mosque's failure. These items read like cautionary notes in the margins of an instruction manual for new mosque development:

1. The group's thirty-five "trustees...feel they need a place of worship, but they insist that the property rights must be in their own hands."[115]
2. Mufti Sadiq "professed an advanced and reformed movement in Islam" that drove away worshipers.[116]
3. Attendance was "lackadaisical. Friday was their Sabbath and they had to work in the factory that day. If they didn't, they lost a day's pay."[117]
4. Sadiq was not able to convert local Christians to Islam.[118]
5. After a full year of waiting, Karoub had received no money from his "subscribers." With two offers on the building and no worshipers, he decided to sell. Descriptions of the mosque's financial woes grew more elaborate and sensational over time, until a 1924 story accused Karoub, with an "insatiable desire for money and power," of embezzling $100,000 in mosque donations.[119]
6. Turks and Syrians were described as political enemies, uninterested in worshiping together. Apparently, other nationalities were "also at war" with the Arabs. "United under one religious banner? Yes! United in any other way? No!"[120]
7. Karoub wanted the building to serve as both a mosque and a community center focused on providing Americanization services, while others felt it should be a "shrine" alone.[121]

Of these claims, only the fourth is implausible. The mosque was not built for converts. It was built for Detroiters who were already Muslim in 1921, the large majority of whom were immigrants.

After interviewing Muslims from several cultural backgrounds in coffeehouses throughout the city, Carl Muller of the *Detroit Free Press* offered his own analysis of why the mosque failed.

"East is East." It is an unhurried land, the home of Mohammedanism. It is a land of deserts and infinite silence, where the mind turns readily to philosophy. It is a land of minarets and mosques, faint perfumes, crooked streets, pomp and power, poverty and need, fatalism and muezzins calling the devout to prayer from the balconies high up on the spires of ancient temples. It is the setting and the background and the stage property of Mohammedanism.

"West is West." Consider that portion of the west in which the Highland Park mosque was built. From four high towers, as unlike the minarets of the East as the Protestant minister is unlike the sultan, great clouds of smoke belch forth. There is no peace and quiet, but uproar and turmoil. There is no desert silence. Instead there is the unending roar of traffic and the shrill sound of the traffic policeman. Instead of the bright stars of the eastern heavens there are garish electric signs advertising soap, chewing tobacco, underwear, tooth paste and Providence knew what else. There is hurry and strife and madness. There is the background, the setting and the stage property, not for a mosque, but for a convention hall for master mechanics. "East is East. West is West. And never the twain shall meet."[122]

Relying on familiar Orientalist motifs of antiquity, fatalism, and desert tranquility, Muller exoticizes Islam and confines it rhetorically to its "proper" Middle Eastern setting. He implies that Islam does not belong in Detroit. The lines of Kipling he quotes reinforce his conclusion: the Highland Park mosque failed because its location in urban America was incongruous, antithetical even to the practice of Islam.

Murder and Sectarian Conflict

Within a year of the mosque's opening, Mohammed Karoub had given up on the project. Because the building was not being used for worship, the city of Highland Park stepped in to tax the property. Karoub then tried to sell the building, washing his hands of the MMHP. Rather than end here, however, the story took a macabre twist. Those who had contributed money to the building's construction were vehemently opposed to Karoub's decision to sell. They objected on two grounds. First, the building had been consecrated as a mosque, and—as Karoub himself stated above—it would be wrong to convert this sacred space for secular uses. Others complained that Karoub alone would profit from the sale of the property, when hundreds of Muslims had contributed financially. Tension between the various parties eventually coalesced into a conflict between Mohammed Karoub and Hussein Abbas, the wealthy coffee shop proprietor who was Shaykh Kalil Bazzy's biggest supporter.[123]

Hussein Abbas, who began leading prayers at the New Baghdad Café (1002 Hastings Street) under the auspices of a group known as the Moslem Welfare Association, also lobbied city officials to block the sale of the MMHP and attempted to have the building turned over to (or sold to, the record is not clear) this new association, which would then be allowed to complete construction of the facility, maintain the building, and, most importantly, resume worshiping in it.[124] Unable to resolve these differences amicably, Abbas filed an injunction with the city to prevent the sale of the mosque in February of 1924. Although both Sunni and Shi'i Muslims supported the mosque initially, and reportedly prayed together in the mosque,[125] it was a Shi'i delegation who, in the end, were eager to see the mosque survive.

On March 13, 1924, a few weeks after Hussein Abbas filed the injunction with the city, he was murdered in his sleep. He was shot while his wife lay bound and gagged on the bathroom floor. On his deathbed, Abbas named Ahmed Mohammad as his assailant and said the young Turkish man was in love with his wife, Muneera.[126] Muneera told the police to question Mohammed Karoub about the murder. It was Karoub who helped them locate Ahmed Mohammad, who was found with the murder weapon still on his person. He immediately confessed to the crime and also accused Muneera of having "concocted the plot" so they could marry and live off of Abbas's wealth, which reportedly amounted to $100,000. The young Turk and Muneera Abbas were apparently lovers. Both were convicted of the murder and received life sentences.[127] Suspicion was also cast upon Mohammed Karoub, however, because of his well-known dispute with Abbas. During her defense, Muneera Abbas argued that Karoub, not she, had contracted with Ahmed to carry out the shooting. Ahmed Mohammad also implicated Karoub, saying Karoub had hired him to murder Abbas and had even been the one to propose his adulterous liaison with Muneera Abbas. For this reason, Mohammed Karoub also stood trial for the murder of Hussein Abbas. He was acquitted of all charges.[128] The fiasco at the mosque, coupled with this personal tragedy, insured that Mohammed Karoub would never again undertake a mosque-building project in Detroit (or play any public role in the religious life of the community).

The matter of the property sale dragged on in court for another year before it was finally resolved in 1926. Karoub sold the building to the city of Highland Park and divided the proceeds among those who had initially contributed to the mosque. The city sold the building again a year later to the Woodmen of the World, a fraternal lodge, for $14,000.[129] "So now the mosque, with its toy minarets and its many crescents, is to be used in Americanization of the very people it sought to Orientalize."[130]

The Consequences of Failure

The Highland Park mosque may have ended tragically, but it was in many ways the beginning of mosque-building efforts across the country. Mohammed Karoub's initial ambition, which he shared with Muslims nationwide, inspired Muslims in other communities to organize and invest in institutions of their own. At some point in the 1920s, Hussien Karoub, imam of the failed MMHP, left Detroit and sought solace elsewhere. He retraced his first cross-country American tour, visiting Muslim enclaves, relating the sad news of the mosque, and providing the religious services Muslims in small communities throughout the Midwest relied on him to perform.[131] He lingered in Cedar Rapids for months (and returned there frequently in subsequent years), helping their active Muslim community hire an imam of their own, develop an Arabic school and Qur'an school that became the envy of the nation, and establish a mosque that is, perhaps, the oldest functioning mosque in the United States.[132] Many of the mosques that were built in the late 1920s and early 1930s by Syrians across the Midwest (in Ross, North Dakota; Cedar Rapids, Iowa; and Dearborn, Michigan) were inspired in part by the Karoubs' campaign to build the MMHP.

On his travels, Imam Karoub discovered that Mufti Sadiq (the Ahmadiyya missionary) had also passed through many of the same communities, bringing word of the Highland Park mosque and speaking enthusiastically of the importance of mosque building. It is worth quoting from Sadiq's "Advice to the Muhammadans in America," which he published in his second edition of the *Moslem Sunrise*. This text provides the best example from the period of a Muslim visitor to the United States exhorting American Muslims.

There are many Muhammadans in this country who come from Syria, Palestine, Albanian, Servia, Bosnia, Turkey, Kurdistan and India. Their exact number is yet unknown, but they are in thousands. This epistle is addressed to all of them. I beg to be excused to say that in the majority of cases you are Moslems in name only—Islam not playing a practical part in your every-day life. Nay, even your names are generally no more Moslem because you have adopted American names. These are the days of trouble for you. The Moslems are being disturbed and dispersed everywhere. The United States is a very good country for you to live in. I wish millions of Moslems to come over here, settle in this land, make it their home and enjoy the privileges of the citizenship in this free, fertile and rich land. But I must advise you—[133]

Sadiq then lays out a ten-point plan to redress the dire plight of American Muslims. He reminds them to pray and teach their children Islam, among other duties, but the eighth item seems to have been inspired by his stay in Detroit. "Build a Mosque in every town to worship one God, however small and simple it be, but there must be one."[134] Written when his future in Detroit and that of the mosque still looked bright, this statement seems to foreshadow the mosque's fate. "If you cannot build a Mosque, then fix up a room in the house of one of you to meet there everyday to say prayers together," he continues. It was not minarets or carpets that were important to Sadiq but the act of communal prayer, and the reading of the Qur'an. Sadiq was impressed by the opportunity American Muslims had to settle and "enjoy the privileges of citizenship," but he also worried that, as a tiny minority population consisting mostly of men who did not come to the United States for religious purposes, the cost of those privileges would be their faith. Rather than gaining a new territory for "millions of Moslems," he was concerned that America would rob these immigrants of their Islam.

Sadiq did not foresee the trend that historians and sociologists of American religion have repeatedly observed: religion becomes more salient—or significant—for migrant populations as they settle into a new environment. Religion is an important, legally protected arena of identity formation in the United States, especially for ethnic and racial minorities whose political voice is otherwise stifled and whose value as citizens is not fully recognized.[135] "Religion is a refuge for cultural particularity" and for political particularity as well.[136] Perhaps Sadiq did understand this latter point. When he condemned American Muslims for not even being Muslims in name, he was speaking in the language of an evangelist. He wanted America's Muslims to make use of their privileges and find their collective voice, a task he deemed urgent given the "disturbed and dispersed" state of the world's Muslims. He understood that the power of this collective voice was at risk.

Kalil Bazzy, leader of Highland Park's Shiʻi Muslims, was well positioned to understand this warning. Coming from a marginalized religious minority in Syria, Bazzy's ethnic identity was already tightly intertwined with his faith. He had been sidelined in the campaign to establish the Highland Park mosque, which was built by one Karoub to be handed over to and led by another. When the Karoub brothers suffered their crisis in leadership—a crisis that was spiritual, financial, and political—it was Bazzy's allies and supporters who stepped in to contest the sale of the mosque and propose an alternate plan. Freed from the necessity of deferring to Sunni hegemony, the Shiʻa had hoped to lead and manage this institution according to their own traditions. It helped that they had grassroots support and, as we will see in Chapter 3, greater social and political acumen as well. The differential between the Karoubs' financial power and Bazzy's popular support and Arab nationalist ambitions may explain why, in 1924, community hostilities were so elevated that Hussein Abbas's murder could be blamed on Mohammed Karoub.

With Abbas's death, Shaykh Bazzy lost a wealthy and loyal patron, but he did not lose his commitment to establishing Islam, Islamic associations, and mosques in Detroit. The need for a mosque, in Bazzy's view, became more urgent with each passing year. Other pressing matters overtook the city's Muslims in the early 1920s, raising the stakes considerably for the future of Islam in the United States. In May of 1921, the Emergency Quota Act was passed, which severely limited the ability of the Muslim population to grow via new immigration. South and East Asian Muslims were excluded from the right to naturalize, and their co-nationals were denied entry to the United States altogether. Syrians and Turks found themselves defending their right to naturalize as "free white persons" in American courtrooms. Locally, although the Highland Park mosque's opening had initially brought positive attention to the city's Muslims, press coverage soured quickly after the mosque's collapse, exacerbating the anxieties and bigotry of local nativists. Despite the large number of Syrians who had enlisted in the US military during World War I specifically to fight against the Ottomans, Muslims found themselves being featured negatively in stories about the Armenian genocide in Turkey. Finally, Syria was now under French control, and the terms of the Balfour Declaration ensured that European interventions in the region would make Arab autonomy and sovereignty an uphill struggle. These were the issues that Shaykh Bazzy found provocative, but each Muslim enclave in Detroit had its own set of political grievances, and most of them intensified during the 1920s.

The inability of Detroit's Muslims to create a viable mosque significantly hindered their ability to represent themselves as a political, ethnic, and religious constituency in the city and—given the grandeur of Karoub's plans—in the nation as a whole. The consequences of remaining mosqueless made it more difficult for Hussien Karoub and Kalil Bazzy to provide religious services and build alliances across the ethnic and racial divides that defined the Muslim immigrant community. Christian churches in Highland Park began poaching on Arab families, inviting their children to Sunday school, luring them in with treats and toys.[137] Finally, a mosque was needed to provide an institutional setting in which the increasing numbers of interested African Americans might learn about Islam, as was beginning to happen at the State Street Mosque in New York City. A viable mosque was needed to provide a secure space in which Muslims could encounter and challenge one another and non-Muslims could be addressed or converted to the faith. The next chapter explores the consequences of the failure of the Highland Park mosque and examines several new campaigns to institutionalize Islam and develop a sustainable transcommunal Muslim politics in the years that followed.

Eventually, Imam Hussien Karoub, shorn of his brother's ambitions, returned to Detroit and recommitted to his role as a cleric of all the city's Muslims. Given the painful turn of events in Highland Park, it is no wonder that Karoub did not speak often of this first mosque-building campaign; nor did he carefully go about preserving records of this ill-fated experiment. The Highland Park Mosque was not only the first mosque established in Detroit and the first built by and for immigrants in the United States, it was also the first mosque to fail and be publicly forgotten.

CHAPTER 3 | They are Orientals and Love the East
*Locating Muslims in the Racial Hierarchies
of Detroit, 1922–1930*

THE MUSLIM AMERICAN IDENTITY that began to take shape in Detroit in the 1920s did so under conditions in which Islam had assumed heightened political and cultural significance. The city's second mosque, the Universal Islamic Society (UIS), was established in 1925 in direct response to the geopolitical upheavals of the period. Unlike the Moslem Mosque of Highland Park, the UIS was not the brainchild of a wealthy, would-be patron. It was the product of a multiracial alliance of pan-African and pan-Muslim activists who sought, for a brief time, to pursue their political and religious agendas together. These agendas reflected a growing subaltern consciousness among Detroit Muslims that was fed by new US immigration and naturalization laws; polemical media representations of Islam; anti-black racism; and mounting resistance to European colonial policies in Asia, the Middle East, and Africa.

As Orientalist and nativist discourses converged in the 1920s in newspapers, courtrooms, and legislative bodies across the country, Muslims saw their ability to immigrate greatly curtailed. South Asians and Afghans, categorized as non-whites, were now denied the right to naturalize and to come and go freely from the United States. This meant they were cut off indefinitely from their families overseas and, with few (or no) women of similar ethnoreligious origins in the United States, cut off from the possibility of endogamous marriages as well. Their ability to develop ethnic enclaves in Detroit, as elsewhere, was foreclosed. They also found themselves discriminated against in employment and housing markets. Even those who were allowed to naturalize (Turks, Syrians, Kurds, and Albanians) faced a discriminatory quota system that fixed immigration from their homelands at one hundred individuals per year.[1]

Muslims who had hoped their adopted home, the United States, a nation committed to "liberty and justice for all," would support independence movements in their former homelands—Syria, India, Albania, Turkey— were gravely disappointed. Pan-Arabism and pan-Islamism were both ascendant among Muslims abroad, and many in Detroit embraced these movements as well. Pan-Africanism, a movement that linked the plight of black Americans to that of colonial Africa and black populations else- where in the Western hemisphere, was also popularized in this period, introducing Islam to African Americans as their "true" or "original" reli- gion. In part to escape the ravages of American racism, black Americans began to convert to Islam, constructing an alternative identity and con- sciousness and thus an alternative route to economic and social mobil- ity. These diverse populations—immigrants on the path to citizenship, migrants excluded from citizenship, and native-born Americans excluded from the rights of full citizenship—together explored the potential and the limitations of a pan-Muslim politics in Detroit. The UIS provided Detroit's Muslims with a space in which to pursue these agendas. It also gave new Muslim converts and those curious about Islam an opportunity to interact with Muslim immigrants and activists and to gauge their own commitment to Islam.

In addition to tracking the rise of the UIS and the political discourses to which it responded, this chapter explores the less public but equally trans- communal support networks Detroit's Muslims created in order to sustain the everyday practice of Islam in the 1920s and 1930s. These networks were much stronger in Detroit than current research would suggest. Far from being an era of religious and political apathy among immigrants, the 1920s were a decade in which Muslims from many backgrounds sought to develop viable religious institutions, and viable means of representing their faith to others, in a rapidly changing urban environment. The vital- ity of Muslim organizational life in the 1920s contradicted the image of Muslims promulgated by Detroit's vocal nativists, who believed Islam should be prevented from taking root in the city. "They are Orientals and love the East," journalist Faye Elizabeth Smith said of the city's Turks, Kurds, and Syrians in 1922.[2] By exoticizing and racializing the city's Muslims—portraying them as Orientals, a term of exotic danger and appeal—Smith neatly encapsulated the intricate patterns of discursive, judicial, and legislative discrimination that combined to block Muslim set- tlement in the city. The same ideological constructs were used to validate the ongoing colonization of Muslim homelands abroad. Though dismis- sive, Smith's claim was accurate on one point: Detroit's Muslims did love the East. Rather than return to it unchanged, or sit by as it was conquered and exploited, Muslims in Detroit struggled to reconfigure the relationship between East and West. Their love for the East was inseparable from their commitment to Islam, a commitment that brought the city's Muslims together and motivated them to reterritorialize Islam and the East as integral parts of the American city in which they lived.

Polygamy Again, and Armenia

In 1922, the society newspaper *Detroit Saturday Night* ran a series of articles on eight of the city's newest and most "foreign" colonies, entitled "Bits of the Old World in Detroit." Armenian and Chinese populations received especially glowing coverage. The Chinese "admire the United States intensely and devote themselves eagerly to absorbing our habits." Not only are they Christian, but the "colony is made up almost entirely of better class Chinese who came to this country as students, merchants, travelers, or teachers."[3] The Armenians "are the pilgrims of the twentieth century," the "Europeans of Asia," who live "according to Western standards and looking to the West for their ideas."[4]

Written not long after passage of the Emergency Quota Act (May 1921), the series set out to evaluate several of Detroit's immigrant populations in terms of their "fitness" for citizenship. The series focused on the conditions in which these newcomers lived, touching specifically on their gender and marriage customs as a gauge of their moral acceptability. The author, Faye Elizabeth Smith, visited immigrants in their homes and workplaces, in their social halls, coffeehouses, and houses of worship. Her impressions of the local "Turkish colony" were not pleasant. Here is the lead to her story:

> The Detroit Turkish colony is made up of 1,500 young bachelors wedded to polygamy. They consist of Ottoman Turks, Kurds, and Syrian Mohammedans, and have built the only mosque in America, on Victor Avenue, in Highland Park, that Islam may gain a foothold in this country. To set the crescent against the sky of the New World is their only ambition in the occident. They remain only to make money that they may return to the homeland and take unto themselves the delightfully multiple state of matrimony which Mohammed decreed.
>
> No American school will ever set them writing "a bird in the hand is worth two in the bush." The oriental can always wait. Minera Abass[5] is

the only Turkish woman known to be in America today. Her soft eyes and veiled charms, in contrast with the joyous experience of the American flapper, suffer no eclipse. When they chance to see her, they are only inspired to work harder that they may speed the day when they may draw one, two, three, even four queens from the pack.[6]

These images were as familiar to the readership of *Detroit Saturday Night* in 1922 as they are to us today. Following on the heels of popular films such as *The Arab* (1915), *The Garden of Allah* (1916), *Salome* (1918), and especially *The Sheik* (1921), and drawing from the deep well of American Orientalism, readers were fully prepared to see Detroit's Muslims as sexually libidinous, existing outside of time, their women oppressed, and their faces "blank with the mask of the orient."[7] "Grounded in a Social Darwinistic belief in the racial inferiority of Arabs, Kurds, and Turks and sustained by an abiding faith in the superiority of the United States," observes Douglas Little, "orientalism American style became a staple of popular culture during the 1920s through such media as B movies, best-selling books, and mass circulation magazines."[8] In the late nineteenth century, this imagery had focused more specifically on the "terrible Turk." Christian missionaries working among Armenians in the eastern provinces of the Ottoman Empire fed stories to American newspapers on the Armenian separatist movement and its struggles against Muslim Turks and Kurds, a conflict that escalated eventually into ethnic cleansing and genocide. American media presented one-sided, sometimes falsified, accounts of this conflict, in which Turks—and Muslims writ large—were portrayed as explicitly and aggressively anti-Christian.[9] In Detroit, representations of immigrant Turks fueled anxiety about polygamy, but they often focused explicitly on the plight of the Armenians, on the "unspeakable tragedies committed in the name of Allah and Mohammed, His Prophet"—as Smith put it.[10]

By the 1920s, in the aftermath of the Arab Revolt, the fall of the Ottoman Empire, and independence movements against British and French colonial governments, the imagery used to malign Turks and Ottomans was being redirected toward Arab Muslims. Whereas stereotypes of a generally passive people prone to emotional and sexual extremes had been dominant before World War I, more aggressive images of Muslim/Arab fanaticism and radical anti-Westernism began taking shape.[11] Melanie McAlister and William Leach have argued that these representations would eventually be used to rationalize American interventions in the Muslim world. In the 1920s, however, they were used to promote a new consumer culture at home (Orientalist exoticism was a common theme in advertising) and, more importantly, to alleviate—and confirm—anxieties about immigration (by associating the Orient with dreadful and desirable things). American Orientalism also provided an important discursive space in which discomfort over shifting gender roles in the post-Victorian era could be transposed onto Muslims, freeing Americans to package their new gender ideologies as "emancipation" and thus proof of the superiority of Western modernity.[12]

Smith's prurient interest in polygamy borrows heavily from Orientalist traditions. For example, her discussion of gender practices among Detroit's different immigrant populations contains a clear disciplinary message intended to steer immigrants toward the evolving American ideal of autonomous heterosexual married couples.[13] She chastises the Armenians, for example, for relying so heavily on the "picture bride" custom of arranging transnational marriages through the mail, while also acknowledging the circumstances that made this practice, however "unnatural," expedient. She has glowing praise for the domestic habits of the populations she approves of. "Having been a rural people," she writes of the Armenians, "their whole interest centers around the home and family. The women take pride in their households and for food values, palatability and variety perhaps no other nationality in the world has a more nutritious diet."[14] This text could easily have been used to describe Syrian family life in Detroit in 1922, had Smith bothered to visit the homes of local Syrians. Instead, Muslims are all lumped together as "Turks" who "have no women with them and will not marry Christian women. Without homes or children who may come under American educational influences, there is no chance for American ideals to replace those of the old world."[15] Her inability (or is it refusal?) to find women among the city's Muslims provides Smith with a powerful argument against the assimilability of the "Turks."

It is in raising the specter of polygyny, however, that Smith is at her most polemical. Recycling an earlier American Orientalist canard, in which Islamic history and culture were conflated with Mormonism in the campaign to define Mormons as un-American and deny statehood to Utah, Smith now attacks Muslims as un-American in hopes of staving off their access to American citizenship.[16] In 1922, polygyny was not a common practice in the rural districts most Turkish, Kurdish, and Syrian immigrants came from, and it was totally absent in the "bachelor population" of Detroit. Yet Smith evokes this powerful motif to convince readers of the extreme Otherness of "the Turks" and the threat it poses not only to Armenian Christians but to the American family as well. Her essay makes visible an expressly anti-Muslim nativism. The same rhetoric had been used in the attempt to deny the Indian missionary, Mufti Mohammad Sadiq, entry to the United States the previous year in Philadelphia. Smith makes an explicit case against citizenship for "Turks" by stressing their bachelor, working-class, and religious commonality, and emphasizing the distance that separates these features from those of more assimilable, middle-class, and Christian immigrant communities. As she warns her readers, "the Turk comes to America to make money and return to the East. If he may take out citizenship papers to further his ambition he will. To him it is only a form. He gives as little and takes as much as he can."[17]

Muslims, Citizenship, and Ambivalent Racial Categories

Muslim life in the United States in the 1920s was shaped by immigration and naturalization policies that determined which Muslim populations were allowed into the country, which were allowed to naturalize as citizens, and which were able to settle in the United States with intact families and begin the process of reproducing Muslim American communities. These policies informed and reflected the social/racial position Muslim migrants occupied in Detroit in the 1910s and 1920s. Ultimately, immigration and naturalization laws influenced how, and by whom, American Islam was practiced in the first half of the twentieth century.

In 1917, 1921, and 1924, laws were passed to end immigration from East and South Asia outright and to severely curtail it from Asia Minor and other Muslim regions. These laws were in place with minimal abridgments until 1952, and they were not effectively superseded until 1965. During this period, legal challenges to the Nationality Act of 1790—which granted the right of naturalization to "free white persons"—were made on behalf of Syrians (who were Christian, Muslim, Jewish, and Druze) and Indians (who were Hindu, Sikh, Christian, and Muslim). Their exclusion along lines of race and national origin was contested by arguing that these groups (or the individuals within them) should be classified as "white." The resulting judicial and legislative decisions, in tandem with Orientalist media representations, consolidated legal and cultural definitions of "whiteness" that included and excluded Muslims simultaneously. Syrians, for example, were categorized as white and thus allowed to become citizens, while South Asian immigrants were judged to be non-white and denied citizenship.

Detailed accounts of these challenges to the exclusion of Syrian and Indian immigrants have been offered by numerous scholars. I will not repeat them here.[18] I do, however, want to point out that the role religious identity played in these cases is sometimes overlooked by historians of Islam in America, who have tended to argue that early immigrants—particularly Arab Muslims—asserted their whiteness and thus rejected a non-white status.[19] A large majority (between 80 and 90 percent) of Syrian immigrants to the United States prior to 1924 were Christian.[20] Sarah Gualtieri argues that the Syrian claim to whiteness—which was made specifically by Christians—was not premised on "a claim to any special phenotype, but on a reclaiming of a Semitic origin and an emphasis on the Syrian connection to the Holy Land and to Christianity."[21] Syrians did not advance their status as whites because they embraced early twentieth-century American conceptions of whiteness. Instead they adhered to Ottoman-influenced understandings of social difference perpetuated by the millet administrative regime. In this system, religious communities were accorded limited autonomy in regulating their own legal, religious, and educational affairs based on sectarian categories rather than, or in addition to, cultural, biological, or genealogical distinctions.[22]

Syrian American Christians, most notably the Maronites, already perceived themselves to be unlike Syrian Muslims in significant ways and had long associated and identified closely with French and American missionaries. As GhaneaBassiri observes, "the conflation of race, religion, and 'progress'" in the United States in the late nineteenth century was instrumental in defining a "singular national identity" based on "industrial development, commercial capitalism, egalitarian Enlightenment ideals, science, rationality, the white race, and Protestant Christianity."[23] These ideals were precisely those promoted by the American missionaries to Lebanon who played such a pivotal role in launching Syrian immigration and promoting early forms of Lebanese modernity and nation building.[24] When making their case for naturalization as whites, Syrian Christians distanced themselves not only from *blackness* (Gualtieri cites several examples from the early Arab American press) and *Asianness* (which Naff presents as the primary status being projected onto and rejected by Syrian immigrants) but from *Islam* and *Muslims* as well.[25]

By playing up American representations of the Ottomans as despotic oppressors of their Christian minorities, both American missionaries in Syria and Christian immigrants to the United States "exaggerated Ottoman corruption and oppression in order to bolster American support for Syrian immigration" and naturalization.[26] Imagining themselves to be in some essential way different from Syrian Muslims, Syrian Christians successfully argued their way into whiteness (and the right to naturalize). They did so by distinguishing themselves from, and in some cases denigrating, African Americans *and* Syrian and other Muslims. Ironically, Syrian Muslims were granted the right to naturalize along with Syrian Christians once the courts had decided in the latter group's favor. Immigration officials collected geographical and national origins data when processing newcomers; religious identification was technically irrelevant. It was not until 1942 that a Muslim Arab appealed when denied the right to naturalize on racial grounds. Ahmed Hassan of Detroit was denied citizenship because he was "indisputably dark brown in color." Yemeni in origin, his Muslim faith and dark skin were used together to discredit his claim to whiteness.[27] If he had been Syrian, neither his complexion nor his creed would have mattered.

As a consequence of their diverse ethnonational, racial, and geographical origins, Muslims in Detroit experienced multiple patterns of integration into the city's immigrant and minority enclaves. The majority—Albanians, Turks, Syrians, and Tatars—moved steadily toward, and were eventually included within, an ethnic and somewhat provisional whiteness. They settled into working-class neighborhoods and found employment in the city's factories alongside other whites. Many Asian Muslims, who were denied access to the benefits of citizenship (and of whiteness more generally) settled in the area of Greektown or moved to the outskirts of black and mixed-race neighborhoods like Black Bottom. Dada Amir Haider Khan, a Punjabi seaman who found his way to Detroit in 1925 and later wrote a detailed memoir of his sojourn in the United States, described a population of roughly two hundred Indians in the city, most of whom worked in the auto industry and many of whom were without proper immigration papers.[28] This population was highly mobile, and many Asians, tiring quickly of the boom and bust cycle of car production, decided to seek opportunities as peddlers.[29] Like the Syrians who dominated this niche, Bengalis and other Indians found that their cultural origins, broadcast by their relatively dark skin and foreign accents, linked them in the minds of many Americans to an exotic, inherently spiritual East.[30] This image, based in prominent strands of American Orientalism, was exploited by Bengalis in Detroit to sell "spiritual" tokens such as holy water, incense candles, or relics from the "Holy Land." Cast as objects of desire and fantasy, many South Asians specialized in peddling women's lingerie, cosmetics, and silks (which they imported from India). Acir Udin Maeh, the spiritual leader of the Bengali Muslims, met his American wife during his turn as a peddler in Black Bottom. She was one of his customers. Most of the Asian Muslim men who married locally, married black women.[31] Some Indian immigrants, especially those who were lighter skinned in appearance than men from the Sylhet region of Bengal, managed to marry white women during this period, but even they found themselves playing into American preconceptions about their "Oriental" origins. Jamil Akhtar, the wealthiest and most politically active member of the Indian Muslim community, used his chemistry background to establish the Tajj Perfume Company, which specialized in exotic Eastern perfumes. His close friend Hassan Khan, who also married a white woman and raised his family in a white social environment, survived as a conjurer and carnival performer.[32]

To what extent did Muslims in Detroit worship, organize politically, study, and raise their children across the racial divide that marked European, Turkish, and Syrian Muslims as white but South Asian and African American Muslims as something else? Collaborations of this kind were very much the norm for those who placed their Muslim identity above or on par with their ethnicity, for those who rejected American racial categories and embraced Islamic identities instead, and for the anticolonial activists who recognized the pivotal role Western racial and religious constructs played in rationalizing the colonial project.[33] The sense of mutual obligation and camaraderie they found in Islam transcended the enormity of daily life in a society that constantly sorted people into the categories of (not) white, (not) citizen, and (not) immigrant. Of course, not all Muslim immigrants explicitly rejected American racial hierarchies, but neither did all Syrians accept these invidious distinctions when lobbying for the right to naturalize as American citizens.

The Universal Islamic Society: Exploring Pan-Islamism in Detroit

On April 25, 1926, a photograph (Figure 3.1) appeared in the *Detroit News* under the headline "'Allah ho Akbar!' is Chant in Detroit when City's Moslems Gather for Service." The two men shown embracing each other in the picture are Duse Mohamed Ali (on the left) and Kalil Bazzy. The accompanying story is grandiose in language: "It was for the first time in the history of the faith that the throne of Allah was beseeched by communal prayer from Detroit."[34] Here, in black and white, was evidence that Detroit's Muslims had moved on after their disappointment in Highland Park. Organized now as the UIS, greater Detroit's second mosque was not one man's dream but a collective endeavor undertaken by a committee of founders who shared political as well as religious ambitions.[35] As the name "Universal Islamic Society" indicates, this was an explicitly pan-Muslim project.[36]

· EMBRACING THE IMMAN.

FIGURE 3.1 Duse Mohamed Ali (left) and Kalil Bazzy embrace after the Eid al-Fitr
prayer at the Universal Islamic Society in Detroit. Courtesy of the Detroit News
Archives.

The UIS incorporated with the state of Michigan on October 12, 1925,
in order to provide "religious and benevolent services." Its board of direc-
tors included Joseph Ferris (president), Shah Zain Ul-Abedin (secretary),
Kallil Zhidy (treasurer), Mohammad Aiddora, and A. M. Ahmed.[37] The
Detroit News article introduced Duse Ali as the president, Kalil Bazzy as
the imam, and Shah Zain Ul-Abedin as the group's vice president.[38] Duse
Ali was a Sunni Muslim of Sudanese/Egyptian origin; Bazzy was Syrian
Shi'i; Ul-Abedin was Indian. As for the other board members, A. M.
Ahmed (a founder of the older Kizalay Society) was probably Turkish,
and Aiddora and Ferris are names commonly found among Syrian Sunnis.
The 1926 prayer was held not in the heart of an ethnic enclave but at New
Oriental Hall, one in a long line of clubs, coffeehouses, and prayer spaces

used primarily by the city's Indians between the 1920s and the 1970s but also frequented by Arab, Turkish, Afghan, and Balkan Muslims.[39] Oriental Hall was located at 1941 Hastings Street in Paradise Valley, the commercial and entertainment district that adjoined Black Bottom, which would become, in the late 1920s and early 1930s, the city's largest black neighborhood. In the mid-1920s, this strip of Hastings Street was still predominantly immigrant and multiracial. Located near the "bachelor" Muslim enclaves that lay between Hastings Street, downtown Detroit, and the riverfront, the UIS was a quick streetcar ride from Highland Park.

The group's central location, its name, and its mixed board of directors drew Muslims from diverse cultural backgrounds to UIS services. A second photograph that appeared in the *Detroit News* coverage of the holiday prayer warranted special mention in the story itself. "A picture of Mohammedans at prayer would have been regarded as an act of sacrilege among the faithful and as a risky adventure by the photographer," the article explains. Many Muslims consider photography to be "a serious digression from Moslem orthodoxy."[40] Roughly two thirds of those on hand did not pose for this picture. The photographer and journalist were special guests at this prayer, however, and despite "grumblings" of disapproval, "many removed the fezzes, turbans, and bath robes and other parts of the religious panoply of objects too sacred to be shown in a photograph" and lined up again as though in prayer (Figure 3.2).[41] This picture is remarkable for the diversity of Muslims it represents. Dada Khan, who visited the UIS during this period, was impressed by the group's eclectic demography.

I was invited to the meeting of Islamic Association by two Indian Muslims, who knew me from New York. Indeed in the small groups, there were individuals from various races and nationalities, including a blackest Negro from some remote part of Africa.... He had been scarred on both cheeks according to some custom of his tribe [...].

Contrasting with all the local white Christian churches in which the Negroes were not permitted even to offer prayer, the small Islamic group of diverse races was a sort of illustration of Islamic unity. I was asked to speak to the group. I did not know what to speak. At the time I was skeptical about all religions. Yet I did not know any rational argument against any of them. Hence, I said to the gathering that various religions taught various ways for the salvation hereafter though no one has returned to inform us about the other world. But in the present world, despite all sorts of beautiful teaching of all the other religions, it is only Islam that practices real fellowship among all the human beings. The proof of this is right here amongst yourselves.[42]

FIGURE 3.2 Holiday prayer at the New Oriental Hall, led by Shaykh Kalil Bazzy. Courtesy of Liela Abbas. Courtesy of the Detroit News Archives.

Khan's emphasis on Muslim inclusiveness echoes earlier statements made by Mufti Mohammed Sadiq, who often reminded Detroiters that Islam is unequivocal in its support for racial harmony.

> In Islam no Church has ever had seats reserved for anybody and if a Negro enters first and takes the front seat even the Sultan if he happens to come after him never thinks of removing him from that seat. "I tread under the feet the Racial prejudice" said the master-Prophet Muhammad...It is a well-proved fact that Islam is the only religion that has ever destroyed color and race prejudices from the minds of the people. Go to the East and you will find the fairest people of Syria and Turkestan eating at the same table with darkest Africans and treating each other as brothers and friends.[43]

The egalitarian threads that run through these quotes suggest that Muslim activists in the 1920s had their own idealized understandings of the opposition between Islam and Christianity, between East and West, and making these understandings known to Americans was increasingly important to them. Mufti Sadiq, for instance, spent much of his time in Detroit and Chicago defending Islam against its Western critics, a task he clearly considered central to his work as a missionary. The pages of the *Moslem Sunrise* are filled with reports of the public lectures he gave in civic, religious, and educational venues, as well as his prolific correspondence with American newspapers.

The leadership of the UIS engaged in a similar campaign to undo what Dada Khan described as the American tendency to paint Muslims "in the blackest colour due to massacres of the Armenians by the former Turkish Government and legal permission of polygamy by Islam."[44] In 1926 the UIS invited a well-known public speaker, Dr. Sayed Hussain, to Detroit to lecture about Islam and Muslim societies and to provide a countervailing critique of the West, especially European colonial ambitions in the Muslim world. Hussain's talk was held at the University of Detroit, the city's oldest Catholic university, where his comments could be challenged—"heckled and exposed," as Khan put it—by "important Catholic professors and other anti-Muslims."[45] Dr. Hussain provided a classic, self-Orientalizing lecture that juxtaposed the "materialism" of the West to the "spiritualism" of the East, which was followed by a "continuous duel of words" in which Hussain, an Indian Muslim, was held to account for the Armenian crisis in Turkey, among other "embarrassing" topics. Hussain stood his ground, asking if Christianity should be blamed "for killing twelve million young people in the last war." The Muslims and South Asians in the audience were, according to Khan, "jubilant" at Hussain's performance.[46]

Like Dr. Sayad Hussain, Duse Mohamed Ali, president of the UIS, had come to Detroit at the specific request of the society, whose members were familiar with his career as a pan-Africanist organizer in London and New York. Although a practicing Muslim, Ali's public speaking and political activism emphasized secular rather than explicitly religious topics. In this sense, his public persona differed from those of Mufti Sadiq and Satti Majid, who described themselves first and foremost as Muslim missionaries. What were UIS leaders thinking when they invited political activists like Ali to Detroit? They were not expected to lead congregational prayers. Were they summoned to the city simply to deliver public lectures and write editorials in local newspapers? What larger agenda did the UIS hope to pursue?

Duse Mohamed Ali, Race Man in Detroit

Vijay Prashad refers to South Asian guru figures who trade on stereotypes of a timeless, spiritual East to promote religious movements, social theories, and consumer products in the United States as *babas*, or "god men."[47] Hazel Carby intends something slightly different when she discusses the charismatic representations and reputations of black American leaders, referring to them as "race men."[48] What the two terms have in common is that both conflate the bodies, speech, and actions of public men with the social groups these men are thought to, and often eagerly consent to, represent. Preaching the social, economic, or spiritual uplift of their race/ nation/religion, race men and god men often manage to reify and promote essentialized understandings of "identity." Duse Mohamed Ali was one such race man, a pan-Africanist and pan-Muslim leader who came to Detroit in 1926 after first having mentored and collaborated with Marcus Garvey in London and New York. Before considering his role in the UIS, it is worth exploring briefly his profile as a pan-Africanist in the early twentieth century. This profile explains why he was invited to Detroit and what he hoped to accomplish there. Duse Ali's acolyte, Marcus Garvey, was also a significant figure to those in movements like the Moorish Science Temple (MST) and the Nation of Islam (NOI), the latter of which was launched in Detroit in the period immediately after Ali left the city.

Of Egyptian and Sudanese heritage, Duse Mohamed Ali was orphaned young and raised in England by a French foster father. As a young medical student, he performed on the London stage to great acclaim, often playing the part of a Moor or Oriental. In his free time, he frequented the Woking Mosque, an Ahmadiyya-run mission that was a center of Muslim anticolonial activism in Europe. It was here that Ali first encountered pan-Islamism and saw how this political project could intersect with a parallel pan-Africanism. After dropping out of medical school, Ali worked as both an actor and a political activist.[49] He published *In the Land of the Pharaohs* in 1911, a critique of British interventions in Egypt and the Sudan.[50] The book was initially well received among London's colonial subjects, and Ali was recognized as a rising star at the First Universal Races Congress, which was held in London that year. Inspired by this international gathering, Ali soon launched the *African Times and Orient Review*, a cultural, political, and financial journal that became, for a brief time, the primary political organ of the disparate pan-African movements in Europe.[51] Ali's mission statement for the journal read as follows:

The recent Universal Races Congress convened in the metropolis of the Anglo-Saxon world clearly demonstrated that here was ample need for an Oriental Pan-African journal at the seat of the British Empire which would lay the aims, desires, and ambitions of the black, brown, and yellow races— within and without the empire—at the throne of Caesar. For whereas, there is extensive Anglo-Saxon press devoted to the interests of the Anglo-Saxon, it is obvious that this vehicle of thought and information may only be used in a limited and restricted sense in its [communication] of African and Oriental aims. Hence the truth about African and Oriental conditions is rarely stated with precision and accuracy in the columns of European Press.... The voices of millions of Britain's enlightened darkened races are never heard; their capacity underrated: discontent is fermented by reason of systematic injustice and misrepresentation.[52]

Ali's "Oriental Pan-African journal," with its sharp critique of the racial underpinnings of English colonialism, soon caught the attention of Marcus Garvey in New York, who traveled to England and interned with Ali in the period just prior to the launching of the Universal Negro Improvement Association (UNIA) in New York in 1914. It was the UNIA that popularized pan-Africanism among American blacks during and after World War I. By 1920 it had over 100,000 members and 800 chapters worldwide.[53] "By linking the entire black world to Africa and its members to one another," Von Eschen writes, "Garvey made the American Negro conscious of his African origins and created for the first time a feeling of international solidarity between Africans and people of African descent. In a brutal era of Jim Crow, lynchings, and political disenfranchisement, Garvey transformed African Americans from a national minority into a global majority."[54] By adopting the slogan, "One God, One Aim, One Destiny," and by including Muslims like Duse Ali in the pages of *Negro World*, Garvey became an early American promoter of Islam as an African religion with the potential to link non-whites in their opposition to Euro-American racism and colonial oppression.

Support for Ali's journal waned after World War I, and he eventually moved to New York in 1922 to work directly with Garvey, covering events in Africa for *Negro World*. In New York, the two men realized they had developed differing approaches to solving the problems of Africa and its diaspora. After 1922, Ali started a business venture, the American African Orient-Trading Company, that he hoped would enable him to bring economic development to Africa using American dollars and entrepreneurialism. The company faltered, and it was apparently with relief that Ali accepted the invitation of several Indian Muslims to come to Detroit to help them organize a mosque like the one he had known in Woking, where faith and politics brought men from vastly different regions of the globe together for conversation, prayer, and resistance to European colonialism.[55]

While in Detroit, Ali pursued these goals within and beyond the UIS. He became involved with a second organization as well, the America-Asia

Society. This group sought to bring about "more amicable relations and a better understanding between America and the Orient in general than had previously been obtained."[56] According to their incorporation papers, this group was led by Mrs. Consuelo Holmes (president), Shair Mohamed Queraishi (vice president and treasurer), and Duse Mohamed Ali (founder and secretary).[57] Ali acted as the group's impresario, directing and performing in two short "costume dramas," lecturing, and running a speaker series as well. The group was successful enough to attract the patronage of "the Persian charge d'affaires, the Egyptian minister in Washington and his wife, and the mayor of Detroit and his wife," but within a year of its founding, the group succumbed to infighting among "different Asian groups" and disbanded.[58]

In keeping with his more public role of race man, Ali also started an "oriental" theater company in Detroit, which performed several of his original works. They were performing "A Daughter of Judah" at Orchestra Hall in late October 1926 when Harry Houdini died of a ruptured appendix at the Garrick Theater nearby. Ali's troupe quickly moved to the Garrick to fill in for Houdini's canceled shows, where they received positive press for works "oriental in substance" and a star (Duse Ali) who was "a large factor in the success of the plays."[59]

Ian Duffield has speculated that "Duse Mohamed Ali helped to induce some consciousness of Islam among black Americans in the city."[60] The NOI was founded just a few years later (in 1931) only blocks from New Oriental Hall, and Ali's sojourn in Detroit is frequently mentioned in histories of that movement, suggesting that he did play such an inspirational role.[61] Dada Khan's memoir provides the most detailed witness to Ali's activities in the city. According to Khan, Ali was devoted to promoting his Oriental trading company and working with local blacks to create "an association for advancement of coloured and oppressed people."[62] Ali lectured widely on the economic aspects of colonial exploitation and argued that "all the subject and oppressed peoples should organize their own trading and other economic relations independently of the white ruling nations...thus the oppressed people would gain their freedom while the advanced nations without support and trade from the backward colonial countries would be bankrupt."[63] Ali's trading company offered subscriptions, or shares, to American blacks, which disturbed Khan because it drew on the resources of middle- and working-class blacks without offering any means of affecting political change. As Khan saw it, Ali was using his own racialized identity to instill trust among African Americans, while remaining mute on racial conditions in the United States out of fear he would be deported. When elaborating his critique of the colonial order, Ali would "privately or individually" suggest "that Islam alone practiced the brotherhood of all races" and thus offered a means of resistance to colonial domination.[64] Khan's testimony supports the longstanding speculation that Duse Ali played an important role in encouraging an awareness of Islam among African Americans in Detroit, not just as an alternative to Christianity but as an antiracist religious tradition linked to anticolonial political solidarities.[65]

Furthermore, Duse Ali, who performed the role of "Oriental African" on stage and wore a fez when he appeared in public, undoubtedly contributed to the embrace of Oriental sartorial displays among black political and religious movements of the period. In his memoir, Ali stated explicitly that he wore the fez, a hat then popular among urban men in the former Ottoman Empire, because it helped him accentuate his identity as an exotic outsider, thus protecting himself from the insult and injury of American anti-black racism.[66] Sylvester Johnson has suggested that these motifs and symbols were attractive to blacks in the 1920s who were eager to overturn the "racial category of 'Negro' by asserting that this identity was a misleading misnomer because it denied their rightful claim to a rich legacy of pre-American origins and ancestry."[67] Ali's race politics were consistent with this desire to construct a "black ethnicity" that transcended the legacies of slavery and colonialism. His close association with Garvey; his reputation as a leading figure in both the pan-Africanist and pan-Muslim movements; the obvious respect he received in Detroit among immigrant Muslims from Syria, Turkey, Albania, and India; and the attention his lectures and performances garnered among influential Detroiters would have legitimized and augmented the appeal of his sartorial identity displays among the local blacks who knew him. "The tendency has been to see the transnational elements of black culture in the United States as focused exclusively on identifications with Africa," writes Melanie McAlister. "However, in complex ways, African American intellectuals, writers, and artists have looked not only to Africa but also to other areas, particularly to the Middle East, as sites and source for explorations of blackness and the recovery and reconstruction of black history."[68]

Duse Ali was only one of many such explorers in Detroit. Father George W. Hurley, a black pastor active in the 1920s, worked closely with Arab immigrants in the city. Seeking to harness the Arabic language as a means of "uplifting the race," Hurley opened an Arabic language school with Syrian immigrant Elias Mohammed Abraham after "seeing the privileges that are extended to him [Abraham] by the American white man."[69] Father

Hurley wanted blacks to be able to use this language "in case we need our Arabian brethren's help."[70] These social relations were built on a foundation of "black orientalism," which—Dorman argues—was "generative of many African American new religious movements and must be recognized as an important part of the black cultural imaginary in the late nineteenth and early twentieth centuries."[71]

Duse Ali understood this appeal and trafficked in it skillfully. All evidence suggests that his persona, if not his politics, was compelling not only to blacks, Asians, and Muslims, but to white Americans who were also attracted to his anticolonial message or his Oriental mystique. Despite his many personal successes, Ali's ongoing effort to recruit support for his African trading company did not fare well in Detroit. In late 1927 he left for New York at the invitation of yet another Asian group. There he launched a new Oriental Association, replicated some of the theatrical successes he had experienced in Detroit, and tried yet again to promote an anticolonial trading company for Africa, whose benefits never managed to reach those shores.[72]

Islam in Blackamerican Detroit

Little is known, but much is assumed, about the interrelations between Detroit's immigrant Muslims and new converts to Islam in the early twentieth century. The status, or number, of converts who attended the UIS and other Muslim institutions in the city is not clear, and we can say little about the lives of the African Americans who began embracing Islam in Detroit perhaps as early as 1914 (the conversion date claimed by the Laham family).[73] Satti Majid claims to have been in Detroit by that time, and he was certainly there by 1920.[74] Mufti Sadiq arrived in 1921 and immediately began proselytizing Americans on behalf of Islam. He found African Americans especially receptive to his mission. The UIS should also be considered an important institution in this narrative, not simply because Duse Ali was active there, or because the mosque embodied a religious practice that seemed to look beyond race, but also because of its location at the intersection of neighborhoods that housed a mix of immigrants from South Asia, Eastern Europe, and Anatolia, as well as a burgeoning population of workers from the American South. These people frequently lived, worked, socialized, and worshiped close to one another, and they had much in common. They were disproportionately male, disproportionately non-white, and overwhelmingly new to urban life and the industrial economy. Their ethnoracial identities were in flux during a period of intense socioeconomic and geopolitical transition. The politically inclined among them found other common interests, most noticeably a shared desire to change their subaltern status and to oppose Western colonization and exploitation in Asia and Africa. For members of the UIS, Islam provided a transcommunal network, an identity, and a common religious practice through which they could organize for change. For many Americans, some of them newly Muslim or not Muslim yet, this was a seductive ideology.

The early black converts to Islam, certainly those who joined the NOI, were predominately migrants from the rural South. They had come north to escape Jim Crow conditions that blocked their social advancement and subjected them to daily degradation and violence. They soon found that industrial cities like Chicago and Detroit were not the Promised Land. Jobs were available, but southern blacks were at the bottom of the social pyramid, well below European and other immigrants in matters of housing, employment, and other necessities white citizens took for granted. Northern black churches, which were largely middle class and acquiescent in matters of race and social justice, did not reach out to poor blacks from the South, nor did the worship experience provided in these churches meet the expectations of newcomers.[75] White churches often had segregated seating and sometimes separate services for black and white parishioners.[76] Southern blacks responded by creating churches of their own, especially Baptist, Holiness, and Pentecostal congregations. They also pieced together new religious traditions that responded to the social chaos, anti-black racism, and marginalization they were experiencing in their newly urban lives.[77] Islam was one alternative in this complex and quickly changing field of religious experimentation.

The first black converts to Islam were also, in many cases, members of the UNIA who had been introduced to pan-Africanism by Marcus Garvey. Some would even have been aware of Duse Ali through his writings in *Negro World*. Mufti Sadiq attended UNIA events, sometimes spoke at them, and had early success at converting UNIA members to Islam.[78] Not only did Sadiq dress the part of an Asian religious guru, he also encouraged his followers to assume "Eastern dress"; adopt Arabic names; and abstain from pork and alcohol, gambling, and extramarital sex. He trained converts in the basic tenets of Islam, provided them with rudimentary Arabic skills, and empowered the adroit among them to proselytize and lead congregations of their own.[79]

In the 1920s, African American Ahmadiyya mosques sprang up in Cleveland, Pittsburgh, Cincinnati, Dayton, and smaller cities. During his brief time in the United States (1920–1922), and thanks to a busy travel schedule and poor health, Mufti Sadiq was unable to instill a deep knowledge of Islam in his followers. Between 1925 and 1934 there was no foreign-born Ahmadiyya missionary in the United States, and during these years many of Sadiq's converts sought religious training from immigrant Muslims, which weakened the tight hold later Ahmadiyya missionaries sought to exert over their North American flock. Wali Akram (born Walter Gregg) was perhaps the most influential of the early African American Ahmadiyya leaders. He organized and led the First Cleveland Mosque, beginning in 1927. His contacts with Arab and Turkish Muslims in the city and his frustration with the financial obligations the Ahmadiyya order imposed on the congregation eventually led him to declare the group's independence in 1936 and join the growing community of Sunni Muslims.

Other African American leaders were quick to exploit the linkages between Islam and pan-Africanism to build powerful movements of their own. The Moorish Science Temple (MST), founded by Noble Drew Ali (born Timothy Drew), featured a bewildering array of teachings, several of which were (mis)appropriated from the symbols, texts, and traditions of "historical Islam."[80] Sections of the Qur'an, for example, were combined with mystical and quasi-religious texts to form the "Holy Koran" of the movement's founder. Drew Ali argued that black Americans were not Negros but Moors (from Morocco), and he encouraged them to think of themselves as "Asiatics," a term that linked their political status not simply to Africa, but to all of the world's non-white cultures.[81] Like the UNIA, the MST promoted both black nationalism and black separatism, but Noble Drew Ali went much further than Garvey by tying both movements explicitly to Islam and by inventing a new, Asiatic identity for blacks. Both Garvey and Drew Ali encouraged their followers to wear fezzes, turbans, and other garments associated with the exotic East. The MST was founded in Chicago, not far from where Sadiq established his Ahmadiyya mission and where Ahmadiyya converts also practiced sartorial Orientalism. Like Sadiq, Drew Ali expected MST members to change their names, in this case from those imposed by their "slave masters" to names that reflected their new identity as "Moors." MST chapters quickly spread to Detroit, New York, Philadelphia, Newark, and elsewhere.[82]

It was in Detroit that the most influential of these Islam-oriented movements, the NOI, emerged in the early 1930s only blocks away from the UIS on Hastings Street. The movement's founders, Fard

Muhammad (also known as David Ford and Wallace D. Fard) and Elijah Muhammad (born Elijah Poole), had participated in UNIA and MST chapters, Fard in Los Angeles, Elijah in Chicago and Detroit.[83] Like the MST, the NOI appealed to newly arrived southern migrants and drew heavily on Islamic imagery and terminology to articulate a new black nationalist identity that was both separatist and religious. NOI teachings went much further along these lines, however, describing Fard Muhammad as God and Elijah Muhammad as his prophet, and constructing a human origins myth in which "white devils" had been engineered by a demonic character intent on destroying the harmony of humankind (blacks) and enslaving them.[84] Like the MST, the NOI offered black Americans an alternative identity to that of the oppressed Negro. In so doing, it produced an effective model for self-help and "racial uplift," which accounts for much of the group's ultimate success.[85] In its early days, however, which overlapped with the harshest years of the Great Depression, the NOI was beset by tremendous turmoil. One of its adherents committed a confused and much publicized act of human sacrifice, which drew the attention of law enforcement and the media.[86] Unorthodox teachings in the group's new school in Detroit, the University of Islam, also led to police intervention, and Fard was eventually expelled from the city and soon thereafter "disappeared" altogether. Despite this turbulence, the message of Fard Muhammad was a powerful one. The NOI was said to have ten thousand dues-paying members by 1933.[87] When Elijah Muhammad's leadership was challenged in Detroit, he too fled the city, moving the group's headquarters to Chicago, just as Mufti Sadiq had done a decade earlier.[88] Like the Ahmadiyya missionary, Elijah Muhammad found it easier to operate in a city where Sunni and Shi'i Muslims were less prominent and had no mosques or imams to offer a countervailing orthodoxy.

From the perspective of immigrant Muslims and the new black Sunni Muslims, the teachings of the MST and NOI were exceedingly disturbing and not recognizably Islamic. Satti Majid was so distressed by Noble Drew Ali's teachings that in 1929 he traveled to Al-Azhar University in Cairo on behalf of American Muslims to discuss the MST with scholars there. They quickly issued a *fatwa* (ruling) on the group's "errors."

> This man of whom you asked [Noble Drew Ali] has established the clearest proof of his falseness, and the most shining demonstration that he is the greatest liar in the world and the man most [guilty of] perverting [the truth] ... Cry out in the loudest voice that whoever gives credence to this liar

in what he claims has repudiated the religion of God which He approved for His servants, and which he asked all folk of the earth to follow until God shall inherit the earth and those upon it, and has gone against what is known indisputably from the Mighty Qur'an, and deserves eternal and everlasting punishment in Hell, together with this lying slanderer.[89]

Like the other Arab Muslims in Detroit before him, Majid was also displeased with the Ahmadiyya mission, which he described to Al-Azhar leaders in Cairo as heretical, emphasizing the movement's reverence for Mirza Ghulam Ahmad as a living prophet of God. Satti Majid sought support for his own return to the United States as an official Islamic missionary representing Al-Azhar University. This support was not granted due to Majid's lack of formal religious training, and he did not manage to return to the United States. Nor did the *fatwa* he procured stem the popularity of heterodox teachings among black Americans.[90]

Members of the MST in Detroit also confronted Noble Drew Ali with their objections to his heterodox Islamic appropriations in this period. In 1929, Mohammed Ezaldeen (born James Lomax), a high-ranking official in Detroit's Temple, broke with Ali and began exploring Sunni Islam. The following year he traveled to Istanbul, Turkey, under the name "Mehmet Ali." There he requested assistance from the Turkish government to create a safe haven in Turkey for African American Muslims.

> The Detroit Negro, Mehmet Ali, a stranded "Moslem Moses," who came here to seek a "promised land" for American Negroes, today presented to President Mustapha Kemal Pasha his petition for permission to found a colony in Turkey.
>
> "In the name of 28,000 Moslem Negroes suffering from racial prejudice in America, I petition you to accord land on the shores of the Bosporus where we may create a flourishing American town and enjoy Turkey's traditional impartiality to Negroes," he said.[91]

It is important to note that Ezaldeen clearly imagines Islam and Muslims as alternatives to American anti-black racism, proposing even the creation of a separatist colony for blacks in Turkey as a means of escaping prejudice and achieving social and religious redemption. His reference to Turkish "impartiality to Negroes" suggests prior and positive contact with Turkish or other immigrant Muslims in Detroit. Yet unlike the case of Satti Majid's petition to the religious scholars at Al-Azhar, in this case there is no evidence to suggest that Ezaldeen buttressed his appeal by claiming that "28,000 Moslem Negroes" in the United States were being taught a "false" version of Islam by Noble Drew Ali. In 1931, an empty-handed "Moslem Moses" moved on from Turkey to Egypt, where he spent five years studying Arabic and Islam.[92]

Ezaldeen returned to the United States in 1936 and succeeded, in a way, where Satti Majid had not. Ezaldeen established an Islamic "mission" in the United States in 1938, the Addeynu Allahe Universal Arabic Association (AAUAA). This group eventually settled on the outskirts of Buffalo, New York, where Ezaldeen created a successful Muslim agricultural community known as Jabul Arabiyya (Arabic Mountain). For a brief period (1938–1941), Islam flourished in this separatist community isolated from the racial contempt other Americans held for black Muslims. Ezaldeen moved to Newark, New Jersey, shortly thereafter. There he continued to preach against MST teachings and advance Sunni Islam among African Americans.[93]

While MST and NOI teachings diverged from those of "historical Islam,"[94] these movements strengthened the links between Islam and the models of African American liberation first popularized by Garvey, Sadiq, Majid, Duse Ali, and others. Both movements continued to gain adherents. From his headquarters in Chicago, Elijah Muhammad developed a national organization with tens of thousands of members, an annual income in the millions, and an aptitude for promoting the economic independence of African Americans and their physical and spiritual health. As the birthplace of the NOI, Detroit's Temple #1 remained a bastion of support for Elijah Muhammad throughout his life. It is interesting to note, however, that in the 1920s and 1930s, when Detroit was an important center of Muslim activism and immigration, two of the heterodox movements described here— the NOI and the Ahmadiyya—were ultimately compelled to move their headquarters elsewhere, while the local MST congregation was rocked by doctrinal conflicts inspired by the example of local immigrant Muslims. If it is reasonable to argue that the UIS was involved in seeding Islamic consciousness and religious practice among African Americans, it is also likely that its members played a crucial role in driving heterodox Islamic movements, and their charismatic leaders, out of Detroit.

Syrian Nationalism: Translocal Islam?

Duse Ali was a celebrity of the pan-Africanist movement, but he was not alone in bringing a subaltern political sensibility to the work of the UIS.

Detroit's Muslims were active in numerous anticolonial projects in 1925, when the UIS was established. World War I had greatly transformed their homelands. For Turks, the war brought an end to the Ottoman Empire and the birth of a modern, constitutionally secular nation-state. For Syrians, it meant the departure of the Turks and the arrival of the British and the French. For Indians, it meant mounting resistance to the British Empire, organized along religious, nationalist, ethnic, and regional lines. Given the diversity of these political interests, what role did the UIS play in cultivating a subaltern, anticolonial consciousness among Muslims in Detroit?

We have already seen the active part UIS members played in opposing British colonialism in India and Egypt. Evidence of their resistance to French imperial policies in Syria is also abundant. Arab nationalism had been on the rise in Detroit since 1919, when the terms of the Sykes-Picot Agreement were finally made public, revealing the extent to which Britain had betrayed its Arab allies, who were originally led to believe that they would receive political independence in exchange for rising up against the Ottomans. Instead, Greater Syria was divided into several territories that were administered as French and British mandates. The Syrian American community was initially unified in opposition to these plans, but they disagreed vehemently on how the region should be governed and what its political borders should look like. Philip Hitti, a prominent Syrian American historian who participated in these postwar debates, sorted the factions into two principal groups: "There are those among them, mainly Muhammadans and Druze...who aspire to virtual union with al-Hijaz and Mesopotamia in a pan-Arab empire. Others, chiefly Christian, stand for an independent Syria, with an independent Lebanon under French Mandate."[95]

Over the next decade, Detroit, with its sizeable Muslim and Druze populations, became the center of American support for plans to make Syria/Lebanon part of a large, independent, pan-Arab nation. The city's Orthodox Christians also tended to endorse pan-Arab unity. New York, with its Christian-dominated Arabic newspapers and its community of Syrian intellectuals and artists who were mostly Maronite Catholics, became the center of support for an independent Syria, which would include a gerrymandered Lebanese territory that would preserve Christian autonomy under French support and protection. These factions, for the most part, overcame their differences in opposition to the British-backed plan to create a "Jewish national home" in Palestine.[96] Advocates for and against these different political outcomes began visiting Syrian communities in the United States, hoping to drum up financial backing and elicit wider American support for their objectives (see Figure 3.3). Abdul

FIGURE 3.3 Syrian nationalist meeting held at Salina School, Dearborn, Michigan, circa 1925. Courtesy of Hajj Chuck Alawan. Charles Kalil Alawan Collection, Bentley Historical Library, University of Michigan.

Rahman Shahbander, for example, a leading figure in the Syrian nationalist movement, visited Detroit in 1924 and encouraged Syrian Americans to support the liberation of Syria and to reject the Zionist campaign in Palestine.[97]

In 1925, several years into the French Mandate, a revolt against the French colonial army in Syria/Lebanon began in Jebel Druze, historic stronghold of the powerful Druze minority, which was led by the Atrash clan. As the rebellion spread to Damascus, Transjordan, and beyond, it became a full-scale uprising whose aim was to shake off European control, just as the Arab Revolt had overthrown the Ottoman Turks. When news of the "Druze Revolt," as it was called in Detroit's newspapers at the time, broke in the city, the Muslim and Druze populations rallied excitedly behind the New Syria Party (NSP), an international body of exiled and expatriate Syrians who supported the revolt and its objectives. Many in Detroit were not content to sit on the sidelines and observe the conflict. Membership in the party grew quickly. This enthusiasm encouraged Abbas Abushakra, the general secretary of the American arm of the party, to move to Highland Park in 1926, bringing the national headquarters of the NSP with him. Kalil Bazzy, spiritual leader of the UIS, was elected to represent Detroit's Syrians at the NSP's first and second conventions, held in Detroit in 1926 and 1927.[98]

Journalist Charles Cameron captured the mood among Syrians in Detroit in a May 22, 1926, essay entitled "Detroit Druses Watch Revolt."

> In such a time the Detroit Syrian colony seems really like a "Little Syria," for here, on a smaller scale, appear the same divisions of partisan thought and factional sympathy which are disclosed in dispatches from Damascus or Aleppo.
>
> Here, as there, all Syrians dream of autonomy or independence. Here, as there, they differ in their views of the advantages or disadvantages of French mandatory control.[99]

He goes on to describe the fault lines, telling readers that the majority of the Syrian Christian community—with the exception of the Orthodox—hold "aloof from the rebellion," while "Syrian Mohammedans, both Shi'ite and Sunnite, who number upwards of 2,000 in the Detroit metropolitan area" are sympathetic to the uprising.[100] The fact that Kalil Bazzy was a preacher in the city's most prominent mosque and an elected officer in its largest anti-French political party all but guaranteed that the uprising would be portrayed positively among Detroit Muslims.

Speaking on behalf of the NSP, Abbas Abushakra told Cameron that the rebellion was not a religious war or "jihad" on the part of the Muslims but a war of liberation, just as it was not a "crusade" on the part of the French but an effort to reinforce their control of a foreign colony. That such assertions would be necessary provides a vivid glimpse into the preconceived notions of Cameron's readership. Apparently, they were not predisposed to sympathize with an Arab uprising led by Muslims and Druze against a European power.[101]

Several months later, on January 18, 1927, a *Detroit Free Press* story announced that "400 Syrians Protest Visit of Emir Here." The emir in question was Shakib Arslan, the lieutenant of Sultan al-Atrash, leader of the Druze rebellion. Arslan was in Detroit to address the second convention of the NSP. The *Free Press* covered a rival gathering that took place at St. Maron's Church. George Asmar, spokesman for the crowd, was upset that Arslan was visiting Detroit "as an official representative of the people of Syria" rather than as the head of what he dismissively referred to as "Shoof county," the Druze district in Syria.[102] Asmar painted Arslan and the others in his party as political fugitives and described the revolt as an explicitly anti-Christian campaign.[103] "This Arslan and his Druse tribe are the people that persecuted and killed Christians...Arslan was the right-hand man of Kemal and Djemal Pasha, the murderers of the Syrians and the

Armenians."[104] Here we see not only a difference of opinion between the Syrian Muslims and Maronites of Detroit but a willingness on the part of the Maronite spokespeople to associate themselves with Armenians as victims of Turkish/Muslim/Druze violence. Asmar was also willing to link Syrian American Muslims to the Armenian genocide. Incidents like this one illustrate how quickly tropes of anti-Christian violence were taken up and deployed against Muslims in Detroit who had no connection to this violence. Syrian Muslims were compelled to defend themselves against criticisms that likened their independence struggles to a jihad against Syrian, French, and, by extension, *all* Christians. This Orientalist trope was one of several the UIS attempted to discredit; in doing so, its members had to explain both anticolonial politics and Islam to ill-informed, potentially hostile audiences, and their leadership was not reluctant to take up this representational challenge.

Kalil Bazzy was proud of the role he played in the NSP. He traveled as an emissary of the party to solicit donations and other forms of support from Syrian enclaves throughout the Midwest, Northeast, and South, but he experienced limited success due to anti-Muslim prejudice, even among Syrians who supported Syrian independence.[105] In his later years, when his efforts on behalf of the NSP were generally forgotten, as was the party itself, historian Alixa Naff asked Shaykh Bazzy if he had followed any of the early Arabic newspapers that circulated in the United States. He named several for her: *Al-Bayan* (a Druze paper published originally in Detroit), *Mirat al-Gharb, Al-Hoda,* and *Al-Samir* (a Muslim paper published in Detroit). He also gave her the names of their publishers, adding, "they all were my friends. They would visit me and I would go and visit them." Naff, who knew nothing of Bazzy's political interests, was clearly surprised by his response. She asked him how he knew these men. "I was the head of the New Syria Party in Detroit," he responded. When Naff did not follow up, he added, "We did not want the foreigners to rule our country. Syria is for the Syrians, not the French. Iraq is for the Iraqis."[106]

Living as Muslims in the Everyday

The UIS was organized largely by men who were in the United States without families and for whom religious and political identities were tightly intertwined. The record of their efforts, like those of the NSP, survives today in newspaper articles, memoirs, and institutional archives, but these sources tend to dwell only on aspects of Muslim American identity formation that were taking place in the public eye: mosque-building efforts, political organizing, missionary efforts, and campaigns against anti-Muslim prejudice. Much of the important work of establishing Muslim communities in Detroit, and of reproducing them socially, was conducted in the realm of the face-to-face, the oral, and the ritually intimate. Here a less political Muslim identity took shape. For some, this intimate realm was experienced in strictly ethnic terms. Syrians from the Bekaa Valley worshiped with other Syrians from the Bekaa Valley; Turks with other Turks. Being Muslim could mean, in these settings, speaking a particular dialect of Arabic, eating or avoiding certain foods, wearing distinctive clothing, and greeting others in familiar ways. None of these diacritics had to be taught; they were part of a taken-for-granted world of daily experience that, in Detroit, was even more valuable because it helped Muslims understand who they were in relation to a larger, non-Muslim society.

For Muslims from smaller ethnonational communities, for new converts to Islam, for those inclined toward pan-Muslim activism, and certainly for the city's Muslim clerics, this realm of everyday Islam, of intimate study and in-group worship, was an exciting new materialization of the Muslim umma. Historians know very little about the networks that held this early American Muslim community together, or how they operated, but the networks clearly required specialists to sustain them. In Detroit, it was Imam Hussein Karoub who did much of the work of guiding and counseling the city's Muslims, both Sunni and Shi'a, when the city's first mosques were being organized in the 1920s and 1930s. The historical record of this pastoral work exists primarily in the memories of the city's oldest Muslim residents. What follows is a brief examination of how pastoral care was administered to Muslims in Detroit, based primarily on the oral testimony of the children of Detroit's active Muslim leaders of the period.

Carl H. Karoub was born in 1930, and his memories of his father, Imam Hussien Karoub, and his work in the city's Muslim enclaves, are scattered widely in time. From his early childhood, Carl remembers the basement Arabic classes Imam Hussien provided for the children of Highland Park.[107] Mohammed (Mike) Karoub, Carl's older brother, was interviewed by Alixa Naff in 1980. He also remembered his father's basement classes. "One of the objectives was to teach Arabic because of the holy Qur'an," Mike explained. "So it would be almost mandatory, if possible I mean, to teach Arabic...so that the person would benefit from the Qur'an in its original language."[108] Along with Mike and his other siblings, Carl studied Arabic in the family's Highland Park basement. In the 1930s, he noticed that adult students began showing up at his house as well, mostly

African American converts who wanted to be able to pray and recite the Qur'an in Arabic and to understand its message.[109] New Muslim converts, or non-Muslims interested in Islam, would stop by the house frequently and request literature on Islam and copies of the Qur'an. They would visit with Imam Karoub, seek his personal and religious guidance, and listen to his stories about Muslim history or his advice on practicing Islam in the United States.[110]

In the absence of mosques, the Karoub living room often doubled as the official meeting space for the city's Muslims. It served as a semipublic space in which new arrivals to the city, visitors, and new converts to Islam could interact with the local Muslim establishment of the period. Karoub himself was a resource who connected Muslims across their many dif- ferences. New immigrants, according to Alice Karoub, Imam Hussien's daughter in-law, would come to the imam's house and sit with him. "If they came to this country, that was one of their first stops. He was very important to them."[111] American Muslims who lived outside Michigan would also visit the Karoub house and introduce themselves, or reconnect with the imam if they already knew him. These visitors were of all ethnic and racial backgrounds, and of all sectarian orientations. Mike Karoub described to Alixa Naff the visits of Ghulam Ahmed, one of the Ahmadiyya missionaries headquartered in Chicago, who frequently stayed with their family in the 1930s whenever he visited Detroit.

MIKE KAROUB: He used to come to my father's house and sleep at our house. His name was Ghulam Ahmad. He's Ahmadiyya—he used to try and convert us to Ahmadiyya.

ALIXA NAFF: Nobody brought him in? He came of his own?

KAROUB: He was a missionary. Whenever he came into Detroit, he'd come to my father's house. He's a good friend. He had a big turban he wore all the time and a big beard. I was a little boy.

NAFF: How did people react when they saw this strange costume in an American street?

KAROUB: Oh, we didn't react at all. We just thought it was [unintel- ligible]. We didn't look at him with any kind of like, uh, askance. We just thought that was the way he dressed from India, and we accepted it.

NAFF: How did he communicate with your father?

KAROUB: In English. Also, he knew the Holy Qur'an. He read the whole Holy Qur'an in Arabic. As I recall, did he know Arabic? I can't really say if he really spoke. You see, so many people around the world read

Arabic in the Qur'an but can't speak it. You know, like the Turks and Pakistanis—they read real good Arabic, but they can't speak it. So if he was one of those, I can't swear. But he spoke English; he spoke, I think it's Urdu or maybe Hindi, and he was of the Ahmadiyya movement.[112]

On one occasion, Emir Faisal of Saudi Arabia (later King Faisal) stayed in the Karoub home for several days while he was visiting Detroit.[113]

Imam Karoub created Muslim space wherever he traveled. He led prayers throughout the city and performed weddings and funerals throughout his life. He is remembered fondly for "helping people through both their happy events and their sad ones."[114] Azira Maeh, whose father was the unofficial shaykh of the Bengali community, remembers Karoub being at all the funerals she attended in her youth. Maeh's father would be called first when a Bengali Muslim died, and he was responsible for washing and preparing the body for burial, but Karoub often joined him in this work. Azira described the funerals of her childhood in the following way:

> Where I would see Islam expressed was at funerals. And there were always funerals, you know, because it was a population of older men. And I would stand behind the men, you know, and I never felt put upon. I felt protected and that that was the way you practiced for people to be buried.
>
> Now my father let me do some things that—some Muslim people were very upset—like, after he prepared the body and wrapped the body, he would let me crack camphorated ice through the coffin. He would let me put perfume on their face, you know, from Tajj Perfume Company. They would do that, and the camphorated ice.
>
> And one guy said, "You are a girl!"
>
> You know, he wasn't supposed to [let me] do that...
>
> And he would let me stand and look at the bodies. Sometimes it was people that I knew personally, and he would say, "Mr. Khan" or "Safa." Everybody was Safa [uncle]. We would call everybody uncle. And, I was like the son he never had, so, some people were opposed to that. And Imam Karoub would be there. And he would, he would let me do it. I was like 4 or 5 years old...
>
> And, look, it was like being here, being so far from their culture, there had to be some flexibility for them to have survived.[115]

When Maeh's father died in 1967, Imam Karoub officiated at the funeral. He mentioned to Azira that he had buried more than fifty men with her father at his side.

Carl Karoub also mentioned that the Turkish community relied on his father for services, as did the Afghans, Bengalis, and Albanians. His father picked up a few words in each of these languages, and he would schedule events by phone in Turkish. "Imam Karoub...was called in to officiate at the funeral services [of Turkish immigrants] and was invited to the memorial dinners held forty days, and then one year, after burial."[116] Each of the Karoub boys was familiar with the coffeehouses and clubs of the various Muslim ethnic groups, where funeral services would be held when people's homes were not large enough for the occasion. Carl remembered attending ceremonies with his father at the All India Brotherhood near Grand River Boulevard in downtown Detroit.[117]

Azira Maeh and Hansen Clarke, both the children of Bengali fathers and African American mothers, described for me a series of Indian, Asian, and Pakistani clubs that they visited as children. This is where they would celebrate Islamic holidays, watch their fathers pray and chant, sample the mix of Indian and American foods, and enjoy the attention lavished on them in an environment where children were rare. Maeh was also a regular in the city's Turkish and Indian coffeehouses. She described an integrated network of active, practicing Muslims among the Turks, Bengalis, Indians, Afghans, and other "bachelor" populations. These men would meet occasionally in one another's coffeehouses or clubs to pray, discuss politics, and read the Qur'an. "No Muslim was different then," Maeh said. "You didn't even know the difference. In fact, my father would make reference to them all as Mohammadans."[118]

About her father's politics, she remembered, "He blamed the British for every problem in the world!"[119] Like the Karoub children, Azira Maeh might have been more aware of these transcommunal activities than most because her father often led services and meetings. Karoub was a frequent presence at these events: "He was like an angel. There was no one that I have heard who could speak the Qur'an like he did."[120] As a member of a community made up of single Bengali and Indian men—and a few dozen married to African American women, many of whom did not embrace Islam—Maeh's experiences differed significantly from those of the Syrian/Lebanese Muslims of her generation. The latter were raised, for the most part, in households with two Arabic-speaking parents who were connected to an ethnic community that passed gradually into whiteness, into full legal (if not cultural) citizenship, and would begin, in the 1930s, to build effective, long-lasting mosques.

The experience of Detroit's Turks resembled that of the Bengalis more than the Syrians, despite the fact that Turks were racialized as whites and allowed to naturalize, while Bengalis were not. Writing of the early immigrant period, Barbara Bilge claims that fewer than 5 percent of the Turkish population in the city married, and only a handful brought wives with them from Turkey or returned there to marry.[121] Thus, the second generation was small, dispersed, unlikely to identify as Muslim, and concentrated in the homes of a few dozen men who married white Americans, an outcome that is highly ironic, given Faye Elizabeth Smith's original portrayal of Turks as a polygamous, fecund, and religiously colonizing population. In contrast, Bilge describes "Detroit's old Turkish community" as "an ethnic fragment...because of its disparate sex ratio."[122] This community joined with the Syrians and other Muslims for Islamic holidays, and relied on Karoub for religious guidance and services.

Hussien Karoub also brought his faith to the assembly line. According to his son Carl, "they were very good to him at Ford. He would pray right there at the factory. He would take his prayer rug with him to work. The unions were not there. Their immediate supervisor was very cooperative, not just with Hussien, but with other Muslims as well."[123] In his interview with Naff, Mike Karoub suggests that this is one way the city's early Muslim immigrants discovered one another. They saw Karoub, or another devout man like him, praying at the factory.[124]

If factory work was what brought most Muslims to Detroit, its sudden absence removed the foundation of steady employment on which both the public and informal life of the Muslim community rested. After the stock market crash of 1929 and the ensuing economic meltdown, the UIS disappeared from view. Concerns over where to meet for prayer or the nature of political changes taking place overseas paled in comparison to the tremendous anxiety and radical social change brought on by the Great Depression. In the early 1930s, it was local hunger (and prayer), not international politics (and prayer) that brought Detroit's Muslims together.

Religious beliefs which forbid the eating of pork or food prepared with lard, keep 400 Mohammedans out of soup lines and dependent on the charity of their racial friends.

Fate of the 400, all single men who formerly worked in Detroit factories, is discussed at length at meetings of their leaders at the coffee house of Joe Hassan...The men from India, Afghanistan, Arabia, Turkey, and Albania are obedient to the restrictions of the Koran...

"These men are of good character and they do not turn to crimes of violence when pinched by want," [Kermou Alli] declared. "The city provides for others. Most of these Mohammedans have been good citizens of Detroit for five to 25 years and cannot understand why they are given no relief."[125]

Eventually, in 1933, a soup kitchen was made available to the city's Muslim indigents who by then numbered eight hundred. The hardships of the Depression grated at the edges of Muslim unity. "Conflict among the nine different racial groups which represent Mohammedans in Detroit has given [Welfare Department representatives] a trying time for six weeks. Each week some new leader comes forward and renounces those who have been negotiating."[126] It was also reported that the city's "Mohammedan clubs," which had in the past joined together for holiday celebrations, held three separate prayers in 1933, with Turks and Albanians meeting on St. Antoine Street, Arabs on Hastings, and Indians and Afghans next door to the Arabs, also on Hastings Street.[127] Many Muslims left the United States altogether during the Depression. Azira Maeh even suggested that Bengalis were repatriated at US government expense.[128] African Americans did not have this option. Nor did many of the city's more destitute immigrants.

Conclusion

In the 1920s, Detroit's Muslims were preoccupied with many things: becoming citizens, supporting the immigration of friends and family, finding and keeping good jobs, getting married and raising children, and finding a decent but affordable place to live. Their opportunities to achieve these goals were influenced not simply by their initiative and skill but by the shade of their skin, the country of origin written on their immigration papers, and the way their faith was viewed and represented in public discourse. The city's Muslims were also focused on establishing a mosque in Detroit. In 1921 and 1925 they succeeded, briefly, in doing so. These mosques did not last long because—in the first instance—there was not yet a consensus about what they should be or how they should be organized, and—in the second instance—because neither the Muslim population itself nor the political alliances on which these institutions were founded were yet stable. Nonetheless, the Muslims of Detroit were actively invested in practicing and reproducing their faith in the 1920s, and they did so in coalitions that were remarkably diverse.

The history of this period is difficult to assemble because the city's Muslim populations were new, fragmented, and not yet present in terms the larger society could easily recognize and record. Because they were cut off from their families and children, dispersed to the ends of the earth by colonial and anticolonial wars, submerged in the working-class enclaves of greater Detroit then scattered again by a global economic collapse, it is remarkable that we still have a handful of textual and oral historical sources that provide context for media images of the city's Muslims that survive from the 1920s and early 1930s. These materials suggest at every turn that, despite their diverse backgrounds, Detroit Muslims knew one another, worshiped together, and organized together to practice Islam and to build mosques.

Narratives popular today, in which early immigrants changed their names to hide their Muslim identity and otherwise avoided calling attention to themselves as Muslims,[129] cannot account for men like Duse Ali, Hussien Karoub, Kalil Bazzy, or Acir Udin Maeh. These men lived as Muslims at home and in the world. Their names were Arabic in origin, if eventually American in pronunciation, but their identities as Muslims were expressed in a new language, a practical idiom that was sensitive to the real conditions in which Detroit Muslims lived. This idiom was local, transcommunal, flexible, and oriented to the survival of Islam under conditions Muslims did not ultimately control. Over time, the number of Muslims in Detroit who understood this new language grew, as did their desire to situate Islam in institutional forms that were more secure, and more recognizably American.

CHAPTER 4 | Dearborn's First Mosques

IN THE MID-1930S, THE small group of Syrian families who had made a home for themselves in Dearborn and survived the worst of the Great Depression decided it was time to try yet again to build a mosque. They wanted a house of worship, not an outpost of Islam in the West. They wanted a place of their own in Dearborn—a club, a church, a place for prayer and education, a mutual aid society, a gathering place for their growing community, a place for young adults to meet and marry other Muslims. It was parents concerned about raising children in the United States without religious exposure or training who would build Detroit's next mosques, not bachelors and political activists. In 1937, the Progressive Arabian Hashmie Society (Hashmie Hall) was opened as a mosque and social hall on Dix Avenue in the heart of the business district of Dearborn's Southend. In 1938, the Islamic Mosque opened a few blocks away. It too was organized as a mosque and social club. Hashmie Hall was a Shiʻi institution, and the Islamic Mosque was Sunni. The Islamic Mosque, renamed the American Moslem Society (AMS) in 1942, is today the oldest mosque in Michigan, and one of its largest. A second Shiʻi mosque grew out of Hashmie Hall in the early 1960s, the Islamic Center of Detroit. Renamed the Islamic Center of America (ICA) in 1969, this institution is among the oldest, largest, and most influential mosques in the United States.

Why did these mosques survive when earlier ones failed? A partial answer was given to me by Ardella Jabara when she described the religious education she received in Dearborn in the early 1930s. At the time, Jabara (née Simon) lived in an anxious household. Her parents had nine American-born daughters. They felt overwhelmed by the demands of everyday life and were unable to provide even the basics of a religious education for their children. When I asked her about this subject, Jabara told me, "I only prayed once."

That is all I remember. It was during Ramadan. We were fasting, you know. And my mother says, "Come on and," but we had nine girls, kiddo. And she would take us one at a time and show us how to *twadhi* [perform ablutions for] ourselves, as she would say it [the prayer], and by the time she got finished she was all worn out, you know. So we prayed that one time and she said, "Forget it. I can't do this for you every day, every day, five times a day," and all that, you know. So I remember once praying. That is all.[1]

The Simons had moved to Dearborn to be near other immigrant families from the Bekaa Valley (in today's Lebanon), but would this be enough to guarantee a Muslim lifestyle in the United States for their children? During the worst years of the Depression, the Simons and other families in the neighborhood pooled their resources and hired one of the better educated men in the area, Mr. Aishi, to teach Arabic and the Qur'an to their children three days a week in his basement. They fasted during Ramadan, celebrated the holidays, and came together on Fridays in one another's homes for *Jumaa* (congregational) prayers when they were able. But Syrian communities in Cedar Rapids, Iowa; Michigan City, Indiana; and Ross, North Dakota, had already opened (or were in the process of opening) mosques. Other immigrant groups in the Southend were opening churches—Romanian Orthodox, Roman Catholic, Romanian Baptist, Seventh-day Adventist—and ethnic clubs—Romanian, Serbian, Croatian, Polish, Maltese, Italian. "This is what Americans did," explained Jabara, "build churches and clubs." Muslim Americans, at least those who hoped to raise their children as Muslims, would have to build mosques/clubs.[2]

Hashmie Hall and the AMS succeeded because they were situated in tightly knit immigrant enclaves where religious and ethnic identities were perceived to be one and the same. These mosques responded to and reflected this reality by being in equal parts ethnic and religious institutions. They fostered a moral community in which Islamic values and traditions were taught in a safe, accepting atmosphere, among people who shared and treasured these values. Each mosque relied on the support of hard-working, loyal families who considered these institutions their second homes. Yet Hashmie Hall and the AMS were not part of larger denominational structures like those created by Norwegian Lutherans, the Reform Jewish movement, or the Syrian Orthodox. As the United States emerged from the Great Depression and entered an era of unprecedented economic growth, these two congregations remained small and autonomous, a condition they would struggle with well into the 1960s, when a new generation of American-born activists and modernist clerics began to stitch isolated congregations into a national body. In their bid to unify Muslims and transform American Islam, these reformers would describe Dearborn's mosques (and others like them across North America) as ethnic clubs that were not mosques at all. To reconnect with Muslim sensibilities that predate these critiques, this chapter explores the history of the first Dearborn mosques not solely from the perspective of their shortcomings, which were many, but by paying attention to their successes, which were enduring and need to be acknowledged and understood.

Making Space for the Moral Community of Islam

In his seminal work on the incorporation of immigrants who arrived in the United States before the 1920s, *Protestant, Catholic, Jew*, Will Herberg emphasized the centrality of religion to the formation of new American ethnic identities:

> Of the immigrant who came to this country, it was expected that sooner or later, either in his own person or through his children, he would give up virtually everything he had brought with him from the "old country"—his language, his nationality, his manner of life—and would adopt the ways of his new home. Within broad limits, however, his becoming an American did not involve his abandoning the old religion in favor of some native American substitute. Quite the contrary. Not only was he expected to retain his old religion, as he was not expected to retain his old language or nationality, but such was the shape of America that it was largely in and through his religion that he, or rather his children and grandchildren, found an identifiable place in American life.[3]

Contemporary scholars of race and ethnicity are likely to equate the "identifiable place" the descendants of Herberg's Protestants, Catholics, and Jews found in American life with the "privilege of whiteness." It is unclear how many of the grandchildren and great-grandchildren of Herberg's immigrants are still true to the religion of their ancestors. Mary Waters claims that for many third- and fourth-generation Americans, ethnicity is largely "symbolic" and involves, perhaps, "celebrating holidays with a special twist, cooking a special ethnic meal...or remembering a special phrase or two in a foreign language."[4] The roots of this "symbolic ethnicity" can be traced to American ideas about individualism and group belonging. If we believe that all ethnicities or races are equal, and that everyone must belong to a group described in these terms, then to know and accept one's origins can only make an individual more complete.[5] Unfortunately, most Americans do not believe that all racial or ethnic categories are equal, and throughout its history, the laws of the republic have codified this inequality by denying full citizenship according to racial, ethnic, and sometimes religious categories.[6] The degree to which different groups have ethnic options and are free to "choose" them depends largely on the categories to which they belong.

Herberg's older formula does, however, capture the essential role religious institutions played in facilitating the sociopolitical incorporation of the pre-1920s immigrants. A generation later, Raymond Williams described the same process in a more contemporary idiom of identity formation:

> Immigrants are religious—by all counts more religious than they were before they left home—because religion is one of the important identity markers that helps them preserve individual self-awareness and cohesion in a group...In the United States, religion is the social category with clearest meaning and acceptance in the host society, so the emphasis on religious affiliation and identity is one of the strategies that allows the immigrant to maintain self-identity while simultaneously acquiring community acceptance.[7]

Again, emphasis is placed not only on continuity with the past, by preserving a distinctive "self-identity," but on the pursuit of mainstream acceptance. Laurence Moore takes this argument a step further, noting that "religious outsiders"—from sectarian, minority, or immigrant traditions—challenge Protestant hegemony in the United States when they claim special rights and accommodations, a process that sharpens their focus on ethnoreligious particularity and buffers them from the religious (and secular) mainstream.[8] This process requires that certain aspects of ethnoreligious identification be performed in public. They must become visible in order for other Americans to recognize, question, contest, and in many cases accept them as American. The corollary to this formula must also be recognized: outsider religious traditions rely on collective, private spaces where rituals and ideas important to minority communities can be enacted without fear of criticism or harassment.

These twinned spaces, public and private, have been of critical importance to Muslim Americans, whose religious traditions were (and often still are) presumed to lie outside the boundaries of Western civilization, the Judeo-Christian heritage, and a generic whiteness. By developing their own religious associations, Muslims have gradually been empowered to articulate communitarian identities and to represent their "durable presence" in the United States.[9] Yet Dearborn's mosques have always been more than institutional signs of settlement, equally visible to Muslim and non-Muslim observers. They were (and often still are) offered as proof that Islam itself can be American: objectively, functionally, practically, and ritually American.

By focusing on the role visibility played in the incorporation of immigrant, diasporic, or outsider religious communities in the twentieth century, scholars like Herberg and Williams overlooked a process that has been equally important: the objectification of religious traditions. Objectification is a direct result of migration, which leads to the decontextualization of religious identities and subsequent efforts to recontextualize (or reterritorialize) them. For Muslims in particular, this process is not entirely new, nor is mobility its only cause. Dale Eickelman describes the "objectification" of the religious imagination of Muslims as a pervasive effect of modern institutions and state governance, which, over the course of the twentieth century, brought about mass literacy and historically unprecedented levels of popular education to Muslim-majority societies. Because Islam was taken into this transformative process, the result was a new way of experiencing religious identity in which "three kinds of questions come to the foreground in the consciousness of large numbers of believers: What is my religion? Why is it important to my life? And, How do my beliefs guide my conduct?"[10] Eickelman's work is set in contemporary Arab nation-states and focuses on the first generation of citizens who studied Islam in school systems organized according to Western educational standards and institutional forms. He argues that longstanding traditions of religious learning and moral authority have been replaced, devalued, or supplemented by new, largely state-sponsored institutional forms. The latter, which have their origins in colonial and postcolonial rule, have transformed the discourse and practice of most Muslims over the last century, regardless of global migrations.

Early twentieth-century Muslim immigrants to Detroit confronted similar forces of objectification, not because of the educational shifts Eickelman describes but because the migration process detached their Muslim identities from the cultural and governmental supports that had enabled them to live as Muslims in Syria, Turkey, or India. The rituals, histories, and social forms that constituted their Muslim identities were largely, if not completely, unknown in Detroit at the time. Familiar structures of moral authority and the local institutions of instruction and power that constituted Islam were absent or radically transformed in diaspora. In many ways, the religious authorities themselves were also absent, despite the best efforts of men like Satti Majid, Hussien Karoub, and Kalil Bazzy.

For many immigrants, it was enough to reconstitute the props and practices of their faith in Detroit and to hold onto as many "authentic" traditions as possible. This strategy motivated the earliest campaigns to institutionalize Islam in the city. The process was complicated, as previous chapters demonstrate, by the presence of Muslims from so many ethnonational backgrounds, each advocating a particular understanding of tradition. It was also complicated by the uneven distribution of religious knowledge among early immigrants. In the modernizing Muslim societies Eickelman describes, literate and unlettered forms of religious knowledge were mutually constituting; familiarity with the Qur'an was sustained through the collaboration of those who were highly trained and those who relied on and supported literate expertise. This practical division of labor was disrupted by emigration.

> Muslims conventionally represent themselves as "people of the book," yet until recently most Muslims—and certainly those in the Middle East—were not sufficiently literate to read or directly comprehend the Qur'an or other religious texts. Nonetheless, the idea of the book and the text has long pervaded many social contexts....Even where texts are not present, people behave as if they are. The idea of the book, by analogy with the divine text of the Qur'an (Pederson 1984), conveys for many Muslims the idea that valued knowledge is fixed and memorizable....Qur'anic memorization served as a paradigm for subsequent learning in the religious sciences as well as in other fields of knowledge; ideally, texts were mnemonically "possessed."[11]

It is widely believed among scholars that most of the early Muslim immigrants to the United States were functionally illiterate in Arabic and English, and it is certainly the case that the overwhelming majority of Detroit's early Muslims had received little formal religious instruction.[12] Imam Karoub had memorized much (perhaps all) of the Qur'an, and Bazzy eventually studied the Qur'an for a time in Najaf. A few other men, like Acir Udin Maeh and the occasional rival to Karoub's or Bazzy's authority, also possessed Qur'anic knowledge, but most of Detroit's Muslims in the early 1930s had access to "the book" only through a literate friend or relative, through Karoub, or through the ritual traditions—prayer, funeral rites, holiday observances, and homilies—they brought with them from overseas. Attempts to teach children Arabic and Qur'anic recitation were piecemeal and rarely produced impressive results.[13]

This distance from the text haunted the immigrants' new awareness of Islam as one faith among others in the United States. Ill equipped to think of their faith as something they could simply interpret for themselves, their energy went to providing a context in which the traditions and practices they did know could be reproduced and given new life. The process of religious objectification did not come easily to them. In the absence of religious authorities who could sanction or direct such a critical conversation, Detroit's Muslims focused on building mosques. The process of inhabiting these institutions became the principal medium in which Muslims asked and answered existential questions about Islam. Their (dis)agreements over how Dearborn's mosques would be structured served as a discursive space in which the moral community of Islam could be imagined, experienced, objectified, and performed.

Art historian Oleg Grabar, in his search for visual symbols and styles that unify the Muslim umma across its vast cultural spaces, concluded that "Islamic culture finds its means of self-representation in hearing and acting rather than in seeing," for "it is not [architectural] forms which identify Islamic culture...but sounds, history, and a mode of life."[14] Through the spoken word, prayer, and the remembrance of sacred events, space is made Muslim, even though other cultural associations may intensify the process. Grabar's references are aesthetic. Buildings do not need to look like the archetypal mosque to function as mosques. They do, however, need to contain spaces in which prayer can be observed, sermons delivered, and scriptures taught and recited. Thus "it is ritual and sanctioned practice that is prior and that creates 'Muslim space,'" rather than "juridically claimed territory or formally consecrated or architecturally specific space."[15]

In their location outside the Muslim world, Detroit's mosques were the focus of activities that were not strictly religious, and the concentration of these "secular" activities in mosque spaces created new possibilities and problems for Muslims who wanted to *see* evidence of their community. Mosques doubled as ethnic clubs, foreign language schools, funeral parlors, and wedding halls. This swirl of activity made them important sites of Americanization. In this (often profane) work of ethnoreligious identity formation, mosques produced new varieties of Muslim space. The "sounds, history, and mode of life" that pervaded Dearborn's Muslim spaces were not exclusively, or even predominantly, religious in content, nor were they part of deeply historical Islamic traditions. The mosques established in Dearborn in the 1930s were conceptually expansive and physically flexible enough to accommodate and ultimately redefine basic conceptions of sacred and profane, thereby putting Islamic (and twentieth-century American) traditions to the task of cultural preservation as well as communal worship. This process resembled what Gregory Starrett calls the "functionalization" of Islamic discourse. "In general," he writes, "functionalization refers to processes of translation in which intellectual objects from one discourse come to serve the strategic or utilitarian ends of another discourse. This translation not only places intellectual objects in new fields of significance, but radically shifts the meaning of their initial context."[16] In the case of Detroit's early Muslims, existing religious discourses were reified, preserved in the novel institution of the American mosque, and put to work for the strategic and utilitarian interests of the immigrant generation, whose special challenge was the socialization of their American children as Muslims.

Settling into the City

The development of greater Detroit's first sustainable mosques coincided with changes in the American political economy that encouraged home ownership among industrial workers. By the 1930s, it was no longer assumed that immigrant populations would be constantly moving. The unionization of the automobile industry facilitated the upward mobility and social stability of Detroit's working class. Likewise, the demography of Detroit shifted dramatically in the 1930s. Passage of the Johnson-Reed Immigration Act of 1924 effectively cut off significant new immigration from Syria (and other Muslim homelands) and denied Muslims already resident in the United States the expectation that their communities might grow to resemble other well-established ethnoreligious populations in size and influence. Whereas Syrians had originally lived alongside other newcomers in Highland Park and downtown Detroit—in neighborhoods that included blacks, non-Arab Muslims, and other immigrants—their move to Dearborn was part of a widening pattern of residential segregation along racial lines in Detroit and its suburbs.

"Beginning in the 1920s—and certainly by the 1940s—class and race became more important than ethnicity as a guide to the city's residential geography. Residents of Detroit's white neighborhoods abandoned their ethnic affiliations and found a new identity in their whiteness."[17] The Syrian/ Lebanese and many Turks settled in the Southend of Dearborn, a neighborhood of class and racial (white) homogeneity. Most of the Southend's low-income, blue-collar households consisted of twentieth-century immigrants from Eastern and Southern Europe. There was also a sizeable contingent of white Southerners. Detroit's newly arriving black population was excluded from this settlement pattern and forced instead into pre-existing and now extremely overcrowded black neighborhoods such as Paradise Valley. In the 1920s, landlords throughout Detroit were reluctant to rent to southern blacks, many of whom were ill equipped for urban life, and later this reluctance grew to include all blacks. White homeowners, similarly, perceived the influx of blacks as a threat; they refused to sell to black buyers and used racial covenants and the threat of violence to guard their neighborhoods from black settlement.[18]

Dearborn, which incorporated as a city in 1927 and merged with the adjoining villages of Fordson and Dearborn Township in 1928 to arrive at the municipality's current boundaries, has a long history of racial exclusion. The city's population expanded dramatically between 1920 and 1930, from 2,470 to more than 50,000 residents, a growth rate of 1,939 percent.[19] This development was engineered largely by Henry Ford, who bought most of the land between the village of Dearborn and the City of Detroit in 1915 and convinced the federal government to underwrite his plans to build a factory for the production of submarine chasers for the US Navy. His soaring, mile-long industrial complex, the River Rouge Assembly, was opened to production in 1918, whereupon workers began settling in the neighborhood that lay just to the east of the factory, the Southend. This community began to stabilize in the late 1920s as Dearborn itself was laid out and developed, again by Ford, and the factory was converted to automobile production.[20]

Ford planned Dearborn for white residents, but the city was internally divided along class and ethnic lines, with West Dearborn serving as a middle class suburb and East Dearborn as a housing reserve for blue-collar workers. Those with greater resources lived north of Michigan Avenue in housing built largely of brick, while more recently arrived immigrants and white Southerners shared the Southend, whose housing stock was a mix of single-family frame bungalows, frame duplexes, and multi-unit apartment houses occupied mostly by bachelor males. Sensitive to the population pressure being placed on Paradise Valley as the migration of black Southerners quickened in the 1920s and 1930s, and eager to keep his black workers from settling in Dearborn, Ford helped develop a black suburb to the west of Dearborn, which he named—apparently without irony—Inkster. Ford and the city's white residents successfully collaborated to keep black residents out of Dearborn, a policy that has held firm over time.

Today, Dearborn, which shares 40 percent of its border with Detroit, is 4 percent black.[21]

Ensconced in a new neighborhood, with the smokestacks and raised elevators of the world's largest factory complex looming to the west, Dearborn's Muslims began the work of transforming Henry Ford's industrial landscape into one that would accommodate Islam and provide Muslim American futures for their children.

Commitment to American Citizenship

In the 1930s, Detroit's Syrians experienced an imaginative shift in self-understanding that strengthened their commitment to living in Michigan, raising families there, and becoming a permanent settlement in the United States. This shift in emphasis, what Jon Swanson calls the move from "sojourner to settler," was a result of several interrelated trends.[22] Syrian Muslims had been in the United States for a full generation by the late 1920s. Their shared experiences as workers and itinerant peddlers had encouraged greater cooperation, mutual aid, and collectivization of resources, endeavors which had equipped them to behave and think of themselves as an American ethnic constituency. Moreover, when some of them returned to Syria/Lebanon in 1930 to escape the Great Depression, they were shocked by conditions in their homeland. The relative deprivations of life in the countryside made repatriation difficult for these families, especially if their children had flourished in the public schools of Detroit and Highland Park. The Syrians who moved to Dearborn in the early 1930s, however, were committed to remaining in the United States. This commitment motivated them to transform southeast Dearborn into an explicitly Muslim space, one in which continuity with their Syrian past could be emphasized alongside their new identification as American citizens who would participate in local civic life as Muslims.

A common path to Syrian American identity included a Depression-era retreat to Lebanon. It is worth dwelling on this trend, since it shows how transregional migration can, in some contexts, lead to a tactical rejection of the immigrant homeland.[23] Several of Highland Park's Muslim families— part of a larger Muslim exodus from the city—moved back to the Bekaa Valley and the Bint Ijbayl district in Syria in the early 1930s.[24] Their encounters with the Syrian countryside under French control and their reception by kin and fellow villagers compelled them to rethink the opportunities available to them in Detroit. The Maury (Farraj) family, for example, moved to

Rafeet in the Bekaa Valley from Highland Park in 1930, when jobs dried up at Ford. Fatima El Haje (née Maury) said her family, which included several American-born teenagers, found adjustment to life in Lebanon difficult during their seven-year sojourn. The options for employment, education, and overall quality of life in Lebanon simply did not meet the standards of even their roughest years as homesteaders in North Dakota or during periods of economic boom and bust in Highland Park. The Lebanese countryside had received little investment from French administrators during the mandate era, and the economy of the region was also suffering a crushing depression. The Maury family had hoped to return to the United States when the job market improved, but this took longer than anticipated. Fatima recollects that the only reason her mother could tolerate such harsh conditions was because "she thought it was going to be better for us because she didn't want to go on welfare. She hated the idea of people subsidizing her."[25] Young Fatima married Hussein El Haje, a man from her village who was not a US citizen, and then followed her parents back to the United States with him in 1937, shortly after her first son was born.[26]

Michael Berry returned to Syria/Lebanon with his family in 1930 when he was ten years old. His impressions of life in Tibneen were not positive. In his 2008 biography, the eighty-eight-year-old Berry relates his boyish encounter with his parent's home village in terms that accentuate his Americaness. "The lack of facilities," he writes, "lack of playground, lack of reading materials, and lack of paper. Everything that I had here, the things you would expect to find even in the poorest areas, they didn't have overseas."[27] The younger Berrys were amazed to find themselves fetching water by donkey from a well several miles from their home, spending hours a day baking bread over open flames, sleeping in a tiny apartment, and attending an improvised one-room school attached to the village mosque. The school was new to the village in 1930—a rare improvement provided by French authorities—but it hardly impressed the Berry children, who were accustomed to Highland Park's sparkling public schools, newly built in the 1920s. Berry's father was unable to make a living in Tibneen, and the family returned to the United States, now truly destitute, less than a year after their arrival in Lebanon. They settled in Dearborn. Years later, Berry became the supervisor of roads for Wayne County, Michigan, an important political position in the 1970s. He does not romanticize the time he spent in Tibneen. "Had I lived there the rest of my life," he speculates, "I would probably have loaded donkeys with sacks of flour and things of that sort. That would have been my future there, because there were no schools of higher learning in Tibneen."[28]

Berry is not alone in drawing a sharp contrast between life in the United States and life in Syria under the French Mandate. Hussein El Haje was denied entry to the United States in 1937 due to glaucoma. A year later he was finally allowed to enter the country. "I got so excited," he said, "I had $25 with me for my fare to Detroit, and I gave it away to the people."[29] Fatima El Haje, explaining her husband's elation, added, "He made it to America. It doesn't matter if he doesn't have money, doesn't have a job, has to go on welfare. He is here in America. As far as they are concerned back in the old country, he could be a millionaire."[30] Most of the families who had settled in Dearborn in the 1930s had similar stories to tell. By then, talk of returning to Lebanon to start a business, live "like a king," or retire among the grape arbors had begun to fade. So too had talk of sending the children home to learn Arabic, acquire the customs of the "old country," and learn to be good Muslims. These lessons would have to be imparted in greater Detroit.

Motives for Organization

As young girls in Highland Park and Toledo in the 1920s, Gladys Ecie, Fatima El Haje, and Ardella Jabara (whose families were instrumental in establishing the AMS in the 1930s) each attended Christian church services of one kind or another. According to Ecie, "When we were young, we lived on Orleans...And down the block from my dad's place, they had a Catholic church, and on Sunday, everybody went to church. Well, we kids used to go. We learned about the Catholic religion. We learned about different things, you know. It was something you looked forward to when you were a kid."[31] This ecumenical viewpoint was not uncommon among the early immigrants; many felt as much kinship with Christianity as they did distance from it. They were pleased that their children were receiving moral and religious instruction, although they would sometimes correct the Sunday school lessons from a Muslim perspective once the children returned home. The children themselves did not mind the attention paid to them by Christians. Gladys Ecie mentioned the treats she was given at church, while Fatima El Haje was a bit more explicit about the tactics of Christian proselytizers, who apparently saw the Muslim children as potential converts. "In Highland Park," she said, "there was a lady there who was teaching the Christian religion, and we'd go there because we got free gifts." Candy and toys were effective lures for children whose families had very little. The only toy El Haje remembers having as a child was a pair of roller skates; her brother had only a basketball. Both were provided by the Christian missionary, who wanted the children to attend her church.[32]

Over time, Syrian parents began to worry about the inroads these missionary efforts were having on their children's beliefs. To counter the appeal of Christianity, the parents organized programs of their own. In Highland Park in the 1920s, Hussien Karoub had held Arabic and Qur'an classes in his basement. These classes focused on rote memorization, on learning to read and write directly from the complex Arabic of the Qur'an.[33] Highland Park was also home to the United Syrian Citizen's Society that served primarily as a locus for Syrian nationalist and Americanization campaigns of the period, but the group also acted as a religious club for young men.[34] Once enough families had settled in Dearborn, Mr. Aishi—whose first name was never used and is no longer remembered—also provided Arabic lessons. But these were no match for the enrichment opportunities available at local churches, where moral instruction came in the form of colorful, illustrated books and was accompanied by music, food, simplified stories and parables, and treats and toys to be taken home.

Ardella Jabara moved to Dearborn in 1932 from Toledo, Ohio, where she was born. She remembered fondly the prayer services held in her family's living room, as did each of my older informants. "Mom had everything took back so they could pray. And they would come in, I guess it was a feast or something like that, and then they would pray." These weren't large groups, ten to twelve men, as she remembers it. Gladys Ecie recalled meeting her husband, Alex Ecie, at a prayer meeting "at my mother's and dad's. His parents come in...He come here in 1922. He was 15 years old when he come from the old country. His father used to be with my parents, you know." At a typical prayer in her childhood home in Highland Park, "they just prayed. They sat down and prayed, and they had something to eat afterwards and they played cards...Men and women prayed all together. You prayed to the side and the men prayed ahead...Where you put your rug, and it's clean, you prayed." Women would wear a small scarf on their heads during the prayer, but not at other times. "We didn't have too many women who come and prayed. Most of them were single, the boys, so there was a few women, a few kids that sat down and prayed. And they had hymns afterwards, you know. It was nice." She also described other types of services that were held in the home. "It was different. Altogether different. Yeah. It used to be if you had a birth, you had a whole bunch of people come to visit. Or if there was a wedding...You couldn't get them in. If there was a funeral, it was just as bad, you know. They were all together."[35]

Jabara also described another occasion when Muslims gathered in each other's homes—the *mawlid* (a gathering at which hymns were sung and homilies were delivered in praise of the Prophet Muhammad). The children of Essie Abraham, whose family helped establish the AMS and a later mosque, the American Muslim Bekaa Center, also recalled *mawlids* in their parents' home. Robert (Sy) Abraham, Marylynn Abraham Hassan, and Sharon Abraham Korhonen described the mawlids of their childhood in the following way:

MARYLYNN HASSAN: They had what they called *mawlids* at the house, you know...

SALLY HOWELL: What is a *mawlid*?

SY ABRAHAM: A prayer service.

SHARON KORHONEN: ... in your home.

ABRAHAM: Somebody, the men, would come to one house and they would have like a...

KORHONEN: ... sit around in a circle.

HASSAN: Isn't it like a blessing?

KORHONEN: ... and they had the *masbahas* [prayer beads]...

ABRAHAM: ... and they would be...

KORHONEN: ... chanting, praying...

ABRAHAM: ... in the house, and if you looked at them, you would say, "This looks like an African dance from the 1940s," in the old movies you would see, when they gathered around.

KORHONEN: Actually, what I remember is they would sit on the floor with their *masbahas*...

ABRAHAM: ... it used to be prayer services.

HOWELL: And when would they do this?

ABRAHAM: Actually, it was when somebody was sick in the old country, or when someone died, they would have it.

HASSAN: ... or, you know how they say Hail Marys with the rosaries?

HOWELL: Yes.

KORHONEN: That is what it was like.

HASSAN: ... That is exactly what it was. Not exactly, but that is pretty much what it was. If my sister was sick and she got well, we would have a *mawlid*...

KORHONEN: [Referencing a later period] You could have it in the mosque, or you could have it in your home.

HASSAN: ... it would be a celebration that she got well. It would be a prayer for your mom that was ill. It would be a prayer for her brother in the old country. It would be a blessing of the house.

KORHONEN: ... for some good fortune.

HASSAN: ... a new baby.

HOWELL: What was done at these events? What was recited?

KORHONEN: They read out of the Qur'an. It wasn't just chanting. It was like in a verse. And what they would say ...

HASSAN: ... and one man would say it, and then the other men would say it in a chorus like.

ABRAHAM: My grandfather taught me one of them, and it was like [he hums a few bars; tones not words.] They never really had a shaykh or anything like that. It was just a group of men who would get together.[36]

There was disagreement among the siblings about what the older generation of Muslims would actually have been chanting during *mawlid*s. Reciting the Qur'an was common, as was other call and response chanting. The ninety-nine names of God were recited, along with religious poetry. The fact that this American-born generation of Abrahams had no clear idea of what was being recited—that they associated the tradition with Hollywood fantasies about African rituals[37] or with Catholic observances—indicates the distance they felt from their parents' faith. This ritual was associated in their minds with old people and the old country, not with themselves or their futures. The *mawlids* were appreciated by the Abrahams, however. "I remember that *mawlids* were good things," Marylynn assured me. "They had sweets and pastries. There were a variety of reasons to have one, and it was a good feeling after it was over." Nonetheless, this appreciation was not enough to sustain the tradition among the immigrants' children. Without fluency in Arabic, religious chanting sounded like gibberish. These rituals, once common, became exotic and fragile, and all but disappeared.[38]

Funerals were also hosted in private homes, a practice that had not presented a problem when the population was small. As the population continued to grow, however, it became more difficult to host these events in homes. Jabara, Ecie, and El Haje all spoke of the difficulties their mothers and other women in the community faced when receiving guests after someone died. In an amalgamation of Lebanese and American customs, the body of the deceased would be bathed and enshrouded by a family member, often with the participation of Imam Karoub or Imam Bazzy. It would then be laid out in the family's living room. Friends and relatives would gather to pay their respects and to grieve. Mourning rituals often included loud, ritualized chanting and wailing by those closest to the deceased. Others recited the *fatiha* (the opening surah of the Qur'an), offered up supplications on behalf of the deceased and mankind in general, and recited verses from the Qur'an to comfort the family. The bereaved were expected to provide a meal for their guests, a ritual intended to keep them busy and ease their suffering. As the community grew, holding these services in individual homes became burdensome. Yet funeral parlors were expensive and immigrants did not feel free to express themselves openly in such spaces.[39]

Sociologists of religion and American religious historians are quick to point out that immigrants are most likely to establish religious institutions when their American-born children come of age.[40] A keen sense of responsibility for the moral education of their young prompted the Syrians to build Dearborn's mosques, but so did their desire to find their children Arab and Muslim spouses. Confronted by their extreme minority status in the United States, maintaining group endogamy was critically important to Detroit's Syrians and a much overlooked motive for the development of mosques and other religious associations. In most Islamic traditions, men are permitted to marry Christians or Jews because the husband's religious identity is presumed to represent that of the household.[41] The children of Muslim fathers are assumed to be Muslims. By a corresponding logic, the marriage of a Muslim woman to a non-Muslim is not religiously or socially sanctioned. It would result in offspring who are not Muslim.[42] It was hoped that participation in mosque-based social events would encourage young Muslims to know—and therefore marry—one another. This motivation justified making sacred space available for social interactions as well.

Together, the need for a proper Arabic/Qur'anic school, a funeral parlor, a congregational prayer space, and a social space for other community events encouraged the Muslims of Dearborn to try again, roughly fifteen years after the Highland Park debacle and a decade after the Universal Islamic Society, to establish a local mosque. The religious consciousness of the immigrants was invested in forms, words, and traditions that were social in nature, not intellectual in a literary or textual sense, and it was this vernacular, social Islam that they wanted to (and were well qualified to) impart to their children in Detroit. After decades in the United States, however, it had become apparent that traditions like *mawlids*, fasting during Ramadan, celebrating holidays, and attending communal prayers would no longer suffice. In the 1930s, most Syrian immigrants had not yet formalized their religious practice as a set of abstract rules or universal precepts. Yet their children, who were raised in an ethnically and religiously diverse environment, educated in American schools, and painfully aware of their parents' and their own foreignness, did objectify their faith. They needed more than a vernacular Islam to encourage their identification as Muslims. The American-born generation felt alienated from rituals conducted in a language they did not fully understand for reasons they did not fully comprehend. Local Christians seemed to understand what they believed and could explain their doctrines to others, in English. To meet these challenges, Detroit Muslims would eventually need an intelligible, objectifiable, historical Islam that made sense to themselves and other Americans. They would need to understand the Qur'an and know how to assess its many interpretive traditions. As a first step toward these goals, they and their parents would build mosques.

Two Mosques are Better than One

Pnina Werbner, writing about South Asian Muslims in Manchester, England, argues that religious solidarity "is often a feature of early immigrant sociality. Permanent settlement, however, brings fragmentation as numbers increase and associations multiply and often compete internally for moral supremacy."[43] This zone of contest "enables the urban community to reproduce itself in all its cultural and ideological diversity, leading to a process of increasing communal incorporation and institutional completeness, an elaboration of the moral community in all its complexity."[44] Yet it is sometimes difficult for Muslims in diaspora, who are struggling to adjust to their new status as religious minorities or outsiders, to articulate the complexity of their moral community and the meaning of this complexity in a manner that does not also highlight an internal divisiveness (*asabiyah*) they find socially and morally repugnant. Peter Mandaville has also recognized the ideological challenge this complexity poses to Muslim leaders, who "hoped that the circumstances of diaspora would lead Muslims from different parts of the world and cultural backgrounds to focus on that which is common to them all, as prescribed by scriptural norms," and to provide an "opportunity for greater Muslim unity. Too often . . . it seems as if the call for greater unity has been viewed . . . as a call for uniformity—a political maneuver by one school or tendency trying to force its own particular brand of Islam on the entire Muslim community."[45] This tension between the *ideal* of a unified Muslim umma and the *reality* of a highly diverse Muslim community has made it difficult for Detroit's Arab Muslims to discuss, and even to understand, their division into Sunni and Shi'i congregations. Their silence on this topic has contributed to the larger silence that surrounds the early history of Islam in Detroit, obscuring the extent to which Shiʿa and Sunni worked together in the past, just as it obscures the official and everyday settings in which one group sought to impose uniformity on the other, or the two groups bitterly contested one another's efforts on behalf of the whole. Looking at how Muslims imagined and inhabited the institutional spaces they created for themselves in Dearborn, we can recover a history in which conflict and collaboration are essential to the construction of the moral community.

Rather than build one mosque in Dearborn, which all Muslims would then vie to control, the Syrians established two. Rather than build a club and a mosque, they established separate Sunni and Shiʿi associations that performed both functions simultaneously. In the end, it was difference in relation to "ritual and sanctioned practice" that compelled this division into Sunni and Shiʿi congregations.[46] The rituals of prayer vary slightly across the two traditions, but these differences are historically and doctrinally important. Equally significant are differences over moral and religious authority, especially apparent with regard to determining the most appropriate person to serve as imam (prayer leader) for collective prayer. Among Sunnis, any male from the congregation can lead a prayer, with the honor/obligation usually falling on the person with the greatest religious knowledge.[47] Among the Shiʿa, the moral purity and piety of the imam are of great significance. Some Shiʿa believe that following an illegitimate imam in prayer can invalidate the prayer altogether, and many immigrant Shiʿa assumed (in the 1930s) a general prohibition against praying behind a Sunni imam.[48] Given the Shiʿi majority among Dearborn's Syrians and the Sunni majority in Detroit as a whole, these differences compelled a binary development of American Muslim space, with Sunni and Shiʿi mosques evolving side by side rather than converging across differences.[49]

When I began recording narratives about early Muslim communities in Highland Park, Detroit, and Dearborn, I initially found the same reluctance to discuss the separation of Shiʿi and Sunni communities that Linda Walbridge encountered during her research in the early 1990s.

> The early Shiʿa in this area like to stress that there was a lack of Shiʿi/Sunni division in the community, and there is actually strong resistance to discussing this topic. But, obviously, there was a distinction being made between the two sects even in the earliest days…The development of mosques and communities in the Detroit area is complicated, but always there has existed some distinction between the Shiʿa and other Islamic sects.[50]

Most of the older Syrians I spoke with remembered a childhood in which Sunni-Shiʻi divisions did not matter, an adolescence in which the words *Shiʻa* and *Sunni* were not spoken, and a general ignorance of the historical circumstances that led to the division of the Muslim community in the seventh century.[51] My experience was unlike Walbridge's, however, in that I heard many theories about the local rift between the two sectarian groups and how it began. Almost universally, it was blamed on the arrival of newcomers to Detroit, either a new Muslim cleric, a new immigrant cohort, or a combination of the two. The Sunni-Shiʻi division is described as something brought to the United States by outsiders, not as something created or perpetuated in Detroit. According to Gladys Ecie, "We never had it before...The [terms] Sunni and the Shiʻa. 'They are Shiʻa.' I never knew one from another. We kids grew up as sisters and brothers. We never knew Sunni/Shiʻa. 'Til this last bunch come from the old country and they parted us. Imam Chirri [a Shiʻi imam who arrived in 1949] was at the Joy Road [mosque]. We used to go there. Anything they had, we went. Anything we had, they came."[52]

Hussein El Haje blamed a different culprit for this division: "The Shiʻa and the Sunni [were] together. We didn't have divided until what's his name...Chirri, show up. We have a guy, we opened a school at that mosque. We opened a school. We have all the kids, the Shiʻa and the Sunni, all come together to learn from a guy name Ali Shaltout from Egypt ... And he got those kids together and they love him very much. 'Til Chirri show [up]. He split everybody [to] go his way."[53]

Ardella Jabara also shared her thoughts on the subject, articulating the sentiment of the first American-born generation toward this division within their own community.

JABARA: Kalil Bazzy, that's who it was? He was a wonderful person. He didn't differentiate between the Shiʻa and the Sunni. He was just straight like this. A Muslim, that's all, you know. A lot of the Sunni, they kinda liked him because of this attitude and everything, you know.

I'll tell you something, my husband was in South Dakota. He went to church[54] one time. He took the Qurʼan with him...[Someone asked him about] the difference between the Shiʻa and the Sunni.

And my husband said, he told him, "I never heard of it." He never heard of it in the old country neither. He used to live in the old country. And he said, "What do you mean Shiʻa and Sunni?"

[The other man] said, "There is a difference."

So my husband said to him, "Bring me the Qur'an. I want to see the difference between yours and mine." So they open the other Qur'an and he says, "It is the same as mine. There is no difference at all."

What is the difference? He couldn't find it.

There is a difference between Shiʿa and Sunni. I think some people...it is just in their head. I don't know how they do that. This has something to do with way back when Nabi Mohammed was killed,[55] or something like that...

SALLY HOWELL: It was over the leadership after. [I explain the martyrdom of Imam Husayn, who rebelled against the unjust Caliph Muawiyah and whose death solidified the division between Sunni and Shiʿi communities.]

So you said Kalil Bazzy didn't pay attention to this difference. How about Imam Karoub, did he mention it?

JABARA: No. He never mentioned it. He never did.

HOWELL: So when you were growing up, why were there two...

JABARA: Two *jamea*s? Because the Shiʿa wanted to be alone, I guess. That's all.

HOWELL: So they had their church and you had yours and you didn't think about it.

JABARA: No. We cooked the same *mujaddarah*, the same lentils, at our *jamea* that they cooked at theirs!

Jabara's narrative articulates both a commonplace acceptance of this division and frustration over its perpetuation in Detroit.[56] Most people were eager to point out that neither Bazzy nor Karoub exacerbated the division or discriminated among believers when providing ministerial services, yet these narratives do not help us fathom why Dearborn had two distinct congregations or how this division occurred long before the arrival of Imam Chirri.

Kalil Alawan (Hajj Chuck), who was born in 1930 into a Shiʿi family in Detroit, confirmed the overall pattern when he claimed, "The first time I knew anything about Sunni/Shiʿa was when I went to the old country [in 1945].[57] My father never talked about it. Joe's father [Mr. Caurdy, a friend of his father's from the Sunni community] never talked about it. That wasn't a big issue for the kids." He repeated the trope about sectarian divisions arriving from overseas, but he also acknowledged, in a way most people did not, that this division was important for his parents' generation of immigrants, just as it is for today's. "It was a big issue for the adults when they split in the late 30s," he said.[58] Alawan then gave the fullest account available of how the two Dearborn congregations traced their genesis to a decision made in 1935 to maintain, observe, and accommodate this longstanding distinction between the Arab Muslims. In this narrative, Hajj Chuck covers several important points. First, he mentions a meeting he attended as a boy at which a large group of Syrian men discussed purchasing the foreclosed Union State Bank building on Dix Avenue, the main business district of the Southend, for conversion into a mosque. At this meeting, a vote was taken over what to name this new society, and the majority in attendance agreed to name it the "Progressive Arabian Hashmie Society."

HAJJ CHUCK ALAWAN: If that mosque [the Highland Park mosque] was a predecessor of the development, it was also probably a root of the problem, in that [the Sunni said] "Hey. We are Lebanese. We are orthodox Muslims"...[but]...the group was majority Shi'a now. Because when they held the vote, the vote was, we want it to be the "Hashmie Society." And the other group says, "Go ahead. We are not with you."

SALLY HOWELL: And so they [the Sunni] started the American Moslem Society.

ALAWAN: "We are taking our balls and we are going to play over there." "We are right down the road from you." Now, they [the Shi'a majority] bought the bank. That is what they wanted to do. And when they decided to buy the bank, they wanted to name it the Hashmie Hall, Hashemite Society. And "Hashemite" today is benign. I mean it doesn't mean anything. It doesn't mean Shi'a. As I told you, the Kingdom of Jordan is the "Hashemite Kingdom of Jordan." But in those days it meant something to those people. Now when you say the Prophet's family, what clicks in?

HOWELL: *Ahl al-Bayt* [the household of the Prophet Muhammad and his descendants; the Shi'a refer to themselves today as followers of *Ahl al-Bayt*].

ALAWAN: *Ahl al-Bayt.* Yes. Which is the Hashmie [the Prophet was a part of the Bani Hashim clan of the Quraysh tribe and their descendants today are called Hashemites], against the Quraysh or the Bani Umayyad [those who blocked the Bani Hashim leaders from becoming caliphs in the seventh century].[59]

So in their minds it meant something. And they [the Sunni] could see that the Muslim majority [in Dearborn] was on this side. As a matter of fact, the Muslim majority grew to be a very large majority of the Shi'a. Of course today it is predominant, so what the hell are you going to do? But at that time, as a young kid, I won't say it didn't mean anything. I will say that my natural progression went into the Hashmie Society, but my father still associated with...When we came to the community, socially, my dad tried to thwart [the division]...He tried to reconcile the issue.[60]

The Hashmie Society incorporated with the State of Michigan in June 1936 and purchased the Union State Bank building for their new home in the same month (see Figure 4.1).[61] It was the Shi'i majority who voted for this name, which—as Alawan asserts—was explicitly partisan. Alawan did not know the history of the Highland Park mosque or the UIS before our meeting, but he quickly seized on these events to augment his theory about the Sunni's refusal to acquiesce to their minority status. For them, this would have entailed turning their backs on centuries of Islamic history in an effort to accommodate a local majority who followed practices the Sunnis considered unsanctioned innovations.

Alawan saw a parallel between the experiences of the Sunnis in Dearborn and what the Karoub brothers faced in their encounter with

FIGURE 4.1 The Progressive Arabian Hashmie Society on Dix Avenue in Dearborn, circa 1965. Mohammad Jawad Chirri Collection, Bentley Historical Library, University of Michigan.

the Ahmadiyya missionary, Mufti Sadiq, in Highland Park. What he did not realize, or articulate here, was how decidedly different the name "Progressive Arabian Hashmie Society" was from those that had preceded it. The Moslem Mosque of Highland Park (MMHP) and the UIS were names (and groups) that did not distinguish among Muslim sects, ethnicities, or political orientations. The Progressive (not conservative) Arabian (not universal) Hashmie (not Sunni) Society conveyed in its name a legacy of Arab Shi'i marginalization (both local and international) and a refusal to submit again to Sunni hegemony. This name is, in fact, strong evidence that a Sunni-Shi'i rift might indeed have played a part in the demise of the UIS, as it had in the demise of the MMHP. Tired of being marginalized, the Shi'a were willing now to assert their majority status, and their independence. The Arabic-speaking Sunnis, who had up to this point worked alongside the Shi'a to develop a new mosque in Dearborn, also decided to remain independent.

Did the Sunni and Shi'a consider their differences irreconcilable? Did they imagine themselves as two moral communities rather than one? Although the groups chose to preserve their autonomy, they were both Muslim, Syrian, and Arabic speaking. They lived in the same neighborhoods and raised their children together. The two populations worshiped separately, each behind a different imam. Their mosques/ethnic associations were led by different sets of men, each with their own rules and priorities. Yet the two congregations supported one another's fundraisers, attended one another's special events, were married in each other's social halls, sent their children to one another's Sunday schools, and married their children to one another. As Ardella Jabara put it, the two mosques cooked the same lentils (*mujaddara*). Rather than describe this structural bifurcation as divisive, it can be interpreted as proof of the moral and historical complexity of the community and evidence of its institutional completeness (as Werbner argued above). The Sunni/Shi'a split was a reality that could not always be openly acknowledged, but it could never be ignored.

What's in a Name?

The effort to establish a mosque, or mosques, in Dearborn did not begin at the meeting Kalil Alawan attended as a small boy in 1935, nor was the division he witnessed between Sunni and Shi'a the only conflict Detroit's Arab Muslims faced. With very little money, competing ambitions, and differing understandings of their relationship to non-Arab Muslims in the city, the Syrians struggled to establish shared terms and common agendas. Even among the Sunnis there were two factions: one that sought to develop an ethnic, local, and intimate institution; and another that pursued a pan-Muslim, polycultural, or universal mosque. Smaller in number than the Shiʻa, the Sunnis struggled to raise enough money to build anything at all. They settled on a practical plan. They would build the first floor of a mosque initially, a simple structure with a large multipurpose room that could be used for prayer and religious education, but also for funerals, weddings, and social events. As circumstances changed, the economy improved, and the community matured, they would perhaps be able to add a second floor with a space dedicated solely for prayer—a proper mosque, complete with *qibla*, dome, and minarets. This final stage of construction would allow the mosque to serve the long-desired function of representing Islam and the city's Muslims to others in Detroit. The year 1938 is commonly given as the incorporation date for the AMS in Dearborn, although no records exist that tie the AMS to this date. In fact, as illustrated below, the AMS did not incorporate until 1942. The 1938 date is drawn from the building's cornerstone, a relic that has been covered, uncovered, buried, and rediscovered repeatedly over the past seventy years, as the building has undergone one expansion after another. Figure 4.2 features this "cornerstone" as the lintel above the entrance to the mosque in a photograph that was taken in 1952. The date "1938" is engraved between the name "Islamic Mosque" in English, and its Arabic translation "*al-masjid al-Islami.*"

When I set about exploring the early history of the AMS, I was startled to find so many forgotten organizational names and inception dates among the archival papers of the group's founders. Rather than one or two groups, I found five legally distinct entities that undertook mosque-building projects in Dearborn in the 1930s. Making sense of this litany of names was ultimately very helpful to me as I tried to understand how the mosque was first organized, what its relationship was to other early mosque-building efforts in Detroit, and how it related to Hashmie Hall. The list hints at a second conflict that emerged among Dearborn's Muslims, this one unfolding within the Sunni community and based on historical and cultural divisions very unlike the sectarian divide between Sunni and Shiʻa. The following timeline of "start dates" for Dearborn's mosques reveals both the hardship the AMS faced in supporting a mosque financially and the difficulty the community's rival factions had in resolving their conflict over which Muslim public the mosque would serve: the families and community of its founders, or the city's Muslim population as a whole.

FIGURE 4.2 American Moslem Women's Society, 1952, in front of the American Moslem Society as it was initially constructed in 1938. Essie Abraham Collection, Bentley Historical Library, University of Michigan.

Timeline of Important "Start Dates"

1934 – Minaret al-Hoda founded "to build a Mohamadan Mosque" in Dearborn.[62]

1935 – El-Bokka League established, also to build a mosque in Dearborn.[63]

1936 – Progressive Arabian Hashmie Society incorporated. Purchased Union State Bank at 10401 Dix Avenue in July 1936, also for the purpose of creating a mosque.[64]

1937 – Progressive Arabian Hashmie Society celebrates its grand opening as a mosque and social hall.[65]

1938 – Ground broken on a mosque at 9945 Ferndale [later West Vernor Highway].[66]

1939 – Deed for building at 9945 Ferndale granted to the Islamic League.[67]

1940 – Deed transferred from the Islamic League to El-Bokaa League: "To undertake completion of the mosque which this corporation has been attempting to handle, and is willing to undertake and agree to pay all unpaid bills, taxes and liens against said building and relieve this corporation of that burden and liability."[68]

1942 – American Moslem Society incorporated: "To buy, rent, or otherwise acquire a spiritual center known as 'masjid' for the furtherance of Islamic teachings and religious services for old and young and to maintain religious classes for the Moslem Children."[69]

If we remove the name Progressive Arabian Hashmie Society from the list, we can see an orderly progression of names that begins with Minaret al-Hoda [Guiding Light], moves to El-Bokka League, then to the Islamic League, back to El-Bokka, and then rests finally with the AMS. The first, middle, and last names on this list are open ended or "generic," as Hajj Chuck described them. They make no reference to ethnicity or sectarian orientation. The Progressive Arabian Hashmie Society and El-Bokaa League, by contrast, are partisan and ethnic appellations, and both enter the record in 1935. The "El-Bokaa League" was the name adopted by local Sunni Syrians who traced their origins to the Bekaa Valley of Syria/Lebanon. Like its Shi'i counterpart, Hashmie Hall, this organizational label implies ethnic and, in this context, sectarian exclusivity. Without more specific dates, however, it is unclear which partisan name came first, but their simultaneous appearance in 1935 suggests that Muslim leaders sought to build local, ethnically organized mosques under the control of two closely affiliated groups. The bylaws of these groups indicate that both wanted to provide social halls and ethnic clubs for their congregations in addition to the conventional prayer space essential to mosque architecture.

These ethnically particular organizations competed not only with one another but also with a third constituency that wanted to establish a permanent mosque in Dearborn. This third group, which called itself the "Islamic League," emphasized unity over particularity and brought forward some of the vision and ambition that characterized earlier mosque-building efforts in Highland Park and Detroit. In 1938 it was members of the El-Bokka League, however, who broke ground on Dearborn's first Sunni mosque. They began digging the hole for the building's basement and foundation at 9945 Ferndale (later West Vernor Highway), and they did this work "by hand," using only picks and shovels.[70] Despite this tedious, back-breaking work (which has become a badge of honor among the descendants of the men who performed it), the building's deed was registered in February 1939 not to El-Bokka League but to the Islamic League. It was the Islamic League that placed the lintel that read "Islamic Mosque" above the front door when the first stage of the building was completed, also in 1939.

The construction of this modest building placed a tremendous financial burden on the dozen or so Syrian families who first undertook the task. Hussein El Haje and Gladys Ecie recall paying five cents per family member per month to fund the construction, a rate that was ratcheted up as the demand for dollars became more urgent. Others described the multiple picnics that were held, flowers sold, doilies crocheted and sold, and dinners hosted—all to pay for Dearborn's Sunni mosque.[71] Help from Muslims outside Dearborn—those associated with the Islamic League—was also critical. In 1940, responsibility for funding (and leading) the institution again returned to the hands of the El-Bokka League, when Musa Halimi loaned the community the settlement money he received after being injured on the job at the Ford Motor Company.[72] This gift enabled the group to extricate itself from a bank loan on which they were paying interest.[73] The Islamic and El-Bokka Leagues continued to trade leadership of the mosque in the 1930s and 1940s, drawing new coalitions of support for their evolving campaigns to finance the construction of the mosque in a period of great economic duress. One agenda was ethnic. The other was universal. This administrative tug of war finally ended in 1942, when the AMS took over management of the institution.

The AMS's vision for a mosque in Dearborn was quite different from the ethnic club model, and it prioritized the sacred functions of the institution over its social functions. The following goals were formalized the society's bylaws:

1. To promote and improve the spiritual and social life of its members.
2. To teach and inculcate American principles of government and institutions among its members.
3. To preserve and teach all Moslems, irrespective of sect, the doctrines of Islam; to maintain and support a regular spiritual advisor known in the Moslem faith as "Imam" for spiritual services of the members and of all Moslems.
4. To promote peace, love, and mutual helpfulness among its members.
5. To buy, rent, or otherwise acquire a spiritual center known as "masjid" for the furtherance of Islamic teachings and religious services for old and young and to maintain religious classes for the Moslem Children.[74]

The masjid this group sought to acquire was the Islamic Mosque in Dearborn, which they successfully took over in 1942. The imam in question was Hussien Karoub, whose transcommunal vision for the new mosque was clearly championed in this statement of goals, which mentions serving "all Moslems" not once but twice, "irrespective of sect" or membership. Yet Karoub was willing to compromise with the Bekaai leadership and incorporate their vision of a local, ethnic, and social institution into the AMS charter. The names of the "charter members" of the mosque reflect the exacting nature of this compromise. Of the fourteen men whose names appear on this list, seven were from the Bekaa Valley, and the remaining seven were a mix of Turks, Afghans, Indians, a South Lebanese Shiʿa and Arabs from outside the Bekaa Valley.[75]

The AMS was located in Dearborn, in a neighborhood closely identified with Syrian Muslim families, and the institution became a home away from home for these families in coming decades. Women would eventually play as central a role in leading and shaping this institution as did men.[76] The education of children and the match-making of young adults shaped the programs for which the mosque would eventually be known (and later, notorious). The Bekaa families provided most of the money and most of the "sweat equity" to support this institution, which today, over seventy years later, is still called the AMS. The polycultural faction led by Karoub assisted financially as well. Their presence on the board helped ensure that the mosque would remain open and welcoming to the Muslim community as a whole. The competing visions of Muslim space that were seemingly resolved in 1942, when the AMS assumed control of a mosque that consisted mostly of Bekaai Sunni families, did not disappear entirely. Universalists and particularists still vied for control of the AMS, and, as later chapters demonstrate, these battles were waged in an increasingly American idiom of religious identity.

A Space of their Own

It may have been "ritual and sanctioned practice" that marked Dearborn as a Muslim space in the 1920s, when the first immigrants settled there and began worshiping together in their homes.[77] It may have been Syrian and Turkish coffeehouses that made Muslim men visible to others in the city. But it was the opening of Hashmie Hall and the AMS that decisively reterritorialized Islam in Dearborn, giving it legally sanctioned, highly visible, and broadly recognizable forms. Borrowing from urban American institutional models ranging from ethnic halls and clubs to mutual aid societies and Protestant churches, then recombining these with the mosque forms they had known in Syria and (since 1921) in Detroit, Dearborn's Arabs produced new spaces in which Islam could be taught and practiced. Non-Muslims could encounter Islam in these spaces as well, reinterpreting this "Oriental" faith as local, American, and intelligible.

The opening day ceremonies at Hashmie Hall, for instance, were choreographed to highlight the familiar, to assure local audiences that, although the city's Muslims had distinctive traditions and practices, they were also fluent in American styles of public performance. Recycling elements of the holiday celebration, parade, and official pronouncement that had figured so prominently at the opening of the MMHP sixteen years earlier, the ceremonies at Hashmie Hall were far more elaborate.

> More than 1,000 men, women and children of Detroit's Syrian colony, and many persons of the same race from other American cities, came to the dedication ceremonies. First there were exercises at the Salina School, then a parade, and the formal entry into the temple.[78]

This article also suggests many differences between the establishment of Hashmie Hall and the failed venture in Highland Park. The two-year effort to raise the money needed to purchase and renovate the bank, for example, was a success "due largely to the energy of the women of the colony who sponsored innumerable dances, picnics, excursions, auction sales and other entertainments to raise money for a building."[79] This observation illustrates the extent to which Detroit's Syrians had embraced local notions of volunteerism, the public role of women, and civic life in general. While both the "Rev." Hussien Karoub and the "Rev." Kalil Bazzy— already assimilated to the titles of Christian clergy—were "in charge of the ceremonies," public officials from Dearborn and Wayne County were also on hand to address the crowd and lend municipal authority to the proceedings. Rather than emphasizing the Muslim holiday being celebrated, the reporter dwelled on the history and accomplishments in greater Detroit of the Syrian colony, Christian and Muslim, working class and entrepreneurial. After a performance by the Salina School band, "bidding was opened for the honor of cutting the ribbon across the door." "Externally," the reporter tells us, "it doesn't look much like the Mohammedan mosques of the Near East that you see in picture books. It is an old bank building. But the inside has been painted and decorated to make it look as much like the real thing as the structural difficulties permitted."[80] Hashmie Hall was an amalgamated, hybrid space, one through which Islam entered the United States and the United States entered Islam.

The incorporation papers for Hashmie Hall offer a glimpse into the political and social imaginary that shaped its activities and physical layout. The "purposes of this corporation" were:

1. To promote an abiding interest in the social life of the community and in good government; to inspire respect for the law and establish a definite understanding of civic duties; to promote patriotism and to work for international accord and friendship.
2. To encourage and assist members to become naturalized citizens of the United States and to constantly urge that all members exercise the full franchise of their citizenship and conscientiously discharge their civic duties.
3. To engage in Welfare work and charitable aid to worthy members of the Society and their families and to any other persons of Arabian extraction who may be in need.
4. To maintain a building to be used as a Moslem Church and for other religious and educational purposes.
5. To conduct classes designed to teach American-born children of members Arabian History and the Arabic language.[81]

The first item on this list is the promotion of the social life of the community, and this activity does seem to have dominated the calendar and agenda of Hashmie Hall in the memory of its members and supporters. Promoting Americanization and good citizenship were also important in the articles of incorporation. Use as a "Moslem church" is fourth on the list, after the group's status as a mutual aid society and before the education of "American born children." Given these priorities, it should come as no surprise that many of the older Arab Americans I interviewed did not necessarily remember Hashmie Hall as a mosque. It is referred to most commonly by the Arabic term *nadi* (club). Sunni Muslims (and other neighborhood residents) attended parties there on a regular basis. It was a place for weddings, graduation celebrations, fashion shows, and dances. Also held there were political lectures and rallies, events that addressed local American concerns and the group's escalating concern over Zionist ambitions in Palestine. Candidates for public office addressed Syrian and other neighborhood voters. Dignitaries from overseas were hosted and toasted. Scouting troops held regular meetings and award ceremonies there. The United Auto Workers Local 600 rented Hashmie Hall for a year

FIGURE 4.3 A memorial service at Hashmie Hall, late 1950s. Shaykh Kalil Bazzy, bearded, stands in the back row, closest to the picture of the deceased. Shaykh Mohammad Jawad Chirri, in a white turban, stands to the left of the portrait. Courtesy of Hajj Kamel Bazzi.

while their own hall was under construction across the street. The hall was also used to host the funerals of the Lebanese Shiʻa until the early 1960s (see Figure 4.3).

While Sunnis remember Hashmie Hall for the social events that took place on the ground floor, very few Shiʻa describe having attended prayers or other religious observances there. Instead, they speak of the Sunday school programs that were held at Hashmie Hall intermittently over the years, programs attended by both Sunni and Shiʻi children. The question of whether the nadi was also a *jamea* (mosque) is answered, almost universally, in a political fashion. The starkest example of this perspective is provided by Hajj Chuck, who describes both the AMS and Hashmie Hall.

HAJJ CHUCK ALAWAN: We would look down the street, and here was this strange damned building, half out of the ground, with a roof on it, and the stairs going down into it [this is the AMS]. we, I had never been into it at that time…I do remember the Hashmie Hall.

We used to call that the "coal mine." The reason we used to call it the coal mine, first of all, let us understand something. To the American-born, these buildings were far below our standards. It was very hard for us as young kids, or even as teenagers, to buy into them as being religious places, because they were far, far below any standard that we ever observed.

SALLY HOWELL: So for the mosque, you are talking about the fact that it was a basement, and its construction. But for Hashmie Hall you are talking about the way it was decorated, the furniture was run down?

ALAWAN: First of all, it [the AMS] wasn't a mosque. It was a social hall. No matter how you cut it, you can call it any damn thing you want, but to say there was regular Friday prayer there and it was dedicated to that purpose...It was a social hall. And so was the Hashmie Society. There wasn't a place for them to pray in the Hashmie Society until they decided to remodel the upstairs which was in the early 40s or late 30s.[82] They finally cleaned the upstairs, which was all offices of the bank, got rid of the partitions and put a carpet in...We called it the coal mine. The windows were so bad that the soot from the factory used to get in there and you would go in there and you would smell it, inhale it, everything you touched, no matter if you cleaned it now, the next day...We used to call it the coal mine...[83]

When you lived in Detroit, when you looked at churches...you would see these grand edifices, and you'd say, "I am a Moslem." Now this is not something we dwelled on, but I did. [...] I used to go to that mosque and it was terribly below my dignity. Even as a teenager.

HOWELL: Do you mean the mosque [AMS] or Hashmie Hall?

ALAWAN: I'll call it the mosque now. It is Hashmie Hall, ok. Cause when I would go there we would have the kids downstairs and we would have what we called "Sunday school."

Hajj Chuck goes on to mention that his parent's generation, which built Hashmie Hall, was one of peasants. Their expectations were not high. They were not educated. They thought that a "fundraiser in which several hundred dollars were thrown onto a carpet and collected together was a major accomplishment."[84] His narrative suggests not that Hashmie Hall and the AMS were not mosques, but that they were inadequate institutions in the minds of American-born Muslims who wanted their mosques to stand shoulder to shoulder with Detroit's impressive array of churches. They should be clean. They should hold regular Friday prayers. They should be structured around these regular prayers. Finally, although Hajj Chuck does not mention it here, they should have educated and well-trained imams.

Other American-born Muslims who grew up in these institutions had no problem identifying the AMS as a mosque and valued its unique blend of social and religious activities. Sy Abraham, for example, described it as "a meeting place. It had religious as well as social [functions]...in the same space. I don't recall Friday prayer services." According to Marylynn Abraham Hassan, "It kept everybody together." Sharon Abraham Korhonen added, "It was a necessity." While not offering regular Friday prayers until the second floor was added in the 1950s, the AMS did host holiday services, Sunday services, and Sunday school. The Abrahams remembered the kitchen of the mosque with particular fondness, but they also described a space in which dances were held in the afternoon. The furniture could be pushed against the walls, a carpet rolled out in the evening, and the space could then be used for prayer, for a *mawlid*, or for some other religious purpose. Flexibility made the space important in the life of the community, and the Abrahams emphasized again and again that its purpose was both religious and social.

The following announcement for a dance at the mosque provides a clear illustration of how untroubled such combinations were in the 1940s.

General Invitation to My Muslim Brothers in Detroit and Windsor, Canada

I hope that my Muslim brothers will come to the Islamic Mosque in Dearborn this Friday evening, the 8th of October, 1949, for a party featuring Arabic music and American dances in the mosque. This gathering will take place every Friday night at the Islamic Mosque for all of the Muslim youth. Bring and send your children so they can meet us and we can get to know each other and be united. Please help me, children of Islam, so that our group will grow and we can be proud of ourselves in front of others. Separation from each other will do nothing but degrade the status and name of Arabs and Muslims. For this reason, I beg my brothers to make your children attend every Friday night at the Islamic Mosque in Dearborn. I am ready to provide any service my religion requires and this is the duty of every single Muslim.

From the Committee of Muslim Youth   Your servant,
Detroit, Michigan   Mohammed Hassan[85]

Many local Muslims eventually came to suspect that mosque dances might themselves "degrade the status and name of Arabs and Muslims," and they pointed to these mixed-gender events when questioning whether the AMS was ever a mosque at all. Nonetheless, this seamless alignment of sacred and profane services was once common in Dearborn, and it was thought to be vital to the collective life of the Muslim community.

Like most Muslims who grew up in the Southend in the 1940s and 1950s, the Abraham children attended Sunday school at the AMS and Hashmie Hall. Sy Abraham remembers studying with Shaykh Hassan Balooly (a Sunni Muslim leader) at Hashmie Hall in the late 1940s, adding that Hashmie Hall was "strictly a social place." As Sunnis, it is unlikely that the Abrahams would have worshiped in the prayer space at Hashmie Hall, just as Hajj Chuck did not worship at the AMS. The Abrahams did describe the many parties they attended at the "Nadi" and, when Shaykh Chirri was mentioned, Sy explained that, "When he got started there [at Hashmie Hall], it was strictly social and he brought the religion."[86]

Ardella Jabara, who joined the American Moslem Women's Society when it was officially incorporated in 1947 (and was the group's treasurer for over thirty years), also remembers the wide array of programs sponsored by the AMS. For her, religious events such as *mawlids*, holiday celebrations, and Sunday school took center stage, but most of her energy went into organizing the many picnics, bakesales, and *haflis* (parties) at which money was raised to "keep the place up and to make improvements."[87] While women had engaged in fundraising for the mosque from the beginning, they formally organized in 1947 and took over much of the responsibility of organizing the group's fundraising events. Women did not serve on the board of the AMS. The men's group was responsible for making decisions about the religious activities of the mosque, overseeing the building's physical maintenance, and handling membership dues and fees. According to several of my interviewees, the women were more effective and more active than the AMS board.[88] Ardella Jabara recalls with pride a moment when one of her co-workers at the Dearborn public schools described her as "one of the seven women who held up the church." It did not occur to Jabara that the AMS was anything other than a church/mosque, or that any of the activities that took place there and were intended to "keep the community together" might later be judged as inappropriate. For the older generation, the question of whether Hashmie Hall and the AMS were mosques was irrelevant. When I asked him why the AMS was built, Hussein El Haje responded, "Because we need a place to go pray and on the holidays like

Ramadan and Eid al-Adha, we needed a place to pray too. So we built that mosque."[89]

It is unlikely that the founders of the AMS realized it would take them until 1952 to complete the sanctuary and prayer space that proudly occupied the upper floor of the building. The basement, as it was called, was intended to serve as a social hall and classroom and was not designed to function as a mosque (see Figure 4.4). It bore none of the architectural features associated with a prayer space—no *mihrab* (prayer niche), *minbar* (pulpit), or carpeted area set aside for prayer that was never walked on in shoes. Once World War II ended, however, and prosperity returned to Detroit, the AMS set about completing its original plan. "I present you with good news and it is that we have begun immediately to prepare building the second floor of the Mosque and this is clear proof of the dedication and devotion of our good, hardworking women," announced Ali Eisaa, on the second anniversary of the American Moslem Women's Society.[90] If there were any lingering concerns that the AMS was not a proper mosque, they were temporarily resolved in the new push to build a more recognizable

FIGURE 4.4 A 1952 dinner held in the American Moslem Society (basement) to break ground on their expansion. Orville Hubbard, mayor of Dearborn, is seated second from the right. Essie Abraham Collection, Bentley Historical Library, University of Michigan.

prayer space, one that would be set aside for acts of worship and would offer a more dignified representation of Islam to the city's Muslim and non-Muslim residents alike.

Hashmie Hall evolved differently. With the help of an energetic women's auxiliary, Hashmie Hall was much more successful at financing their facility.[91] A larger group than the AMS to begin with, they purchased their building when it was in foreclosure and relatively affordable. Their social hall, which was rented out to the general public, generated income for the mosque. In November 1939, a scant three years after they purchased the former bank, the Hashmie Society hosted a large celebration at which they ritually burned their mortgage papers. The *Detroit Free Press* covered this event, and their story also weighed in on the question of how Hashmie Hall was used. It "houses the mosque of the colony and is used as a social headquarters. Five nights a week the place is turned into a classroom where Arabic is taught, the traditions of Arabia preserved, and lessons in American citizenship given, for, you see, the 45,000 Arabians of Detroit take their American duties seriously and have a great pride in the background of their race."[92]

Hajj Chuck, a founder of the ICA, the mosque which eclipsed Hashmie Hall in the early 1960s, and a committed supporter of this new and improved mosque's religious leader, Imam Chirri, was persistent in his criticisms of Hashmie Hall, which he considered an inadequate, pseudo-mosque. But for his parent's generation, and especially for Shaykh Bazzy, who had struggled for many years without a mosque and had twice failed to create one, Hashmie Hall was a significant achievement. Its creation, like that of the AMS, brought Islam into the public culture of Dearborn, gave focus to the social and religious life of the city's Syrian colony, and attracted new Muslim families to Dearborn. In his 1962 interview with historian Alixa Naff, Bazzy was deeply offended when Naff suggested that Hashmie Hall was converted into a mosque in 1949 (the year Shaykh Chirri first preached there) and had been nothing more than a social club before that date. Bazzy responded with the following account:

KALIL BAZZY: Take *my* word for it. [Emphatically stated.]

ALIXA NAFF: Excuse me. This is what I have heard. Please, of course, correct me. Set the record straight.

BAZZY: The Sunnis had a mosque on Vernor in Dearborn. They had a mosque. When they didn't have a mosque, the Shiʿa used to…the Shiʿa and the Sunnis used to pray together. When we established the Nadi al-Arabi al-Hashmie (the Hashemite Arab Club), the Shiʿa were praying in a [tape unclear]. Nadi al-Hashmie, see, was composed of two floors: the first floor was for community gatherings, and the second floor, because it was a bank building, it was a bank building, up and down, see. We took down all the rooms and turned it into one big room. So the lower, the first floor, [was a] big hall. We took out all the partitions that were there since it was a bank building. And the second floor was a floor of offices. We demolished all those and we turned it into a *musalla* [prayer space]. Religious prayer was on the top in the Islamic mosque on the second floor and the general gatherings, the social [gatherings], stuff like that, whether they were Christians or not Christians, Muslims or not Muslims, the Americans and [tape unclear], it was a permissive club. And that's how the Nadi al-Arabi al-Hashemi was. Its name was a nadi [club] down [stairs] and a *jamea* [mosque] upstairs.

To Kalil Bazzy, Hashmie Hall was a mosque—a club and a mosque.

Conclusion

In the 1930s, despite the economic hardships of the Great Depression, Detroit's Syrian Muslims entered a period of energetic and effective mosque building. They established two imperfect but engaged and enduring institutions. These mosques were, at times, as likely to host Friday night dances as they were to host Friday noon congregational prayers. They were not like the mosques immigrants had known in Syria and other parts of the Muslim world. They represented a newly functionalized relationship to Islam on the part of American Muslims, who sought to reconstitute the moral community of Islam in Detroit by creating a social context in which Islam could flourish and Muslims could "know each other and be united." The emphasis in these mosques was on reproducing vernacular Islam rather than a doctrinal or intellectual tradition. People were, and still are, unsure about the correctness of this agenda. When old-world models of the mosque were held up as explicit points of comparison, Muslims in Detroit often could not say with confidence whether their Islamic institutions were a sign of progress, of adaptability and resolve, or proof that they had somehow gone astray.

CHAPTER 5 | Doctors of the Soul
    | *Building Detroit's Midcentury Mosques*

IN THE AFTERMATH OF World War II, a new generation of Muslim clerics was called to serve American congregations. Formally trained in Islamic sciences and often possessing secular university degrees, these men were advocates of nationalism, economic development, mass education, and other modernist ideologies. They were eager to revitalize the Muslim umma for both political and spiritual reasons. What the new imams saw when they arrived in the United States disturbed them, and they immediately dedicated themselves to reforming the institutions and identities American Muslims had created. They preached a return to—or a step toward—what they, as learned men (*'ulama*), understood time-honored Islamic belief and practice to be. This paradigm shift effectively removed the religious life of early immigrant Muslims in the United States from the historical tradition of Islam. If the immigrants had a relevant identity, it was as Syrians, Albanians, or Indians living in diaspora, not Muslims upholding Islam in the West. As the latter, they had gone astray. Their history, from this perspective, could not be told as a tale of viable Muslim adaptation to life in a non-Muslim society. Instead, it would have to be retold as a salvage narrative, as an example of spiritual retrieval and nationalist awakening led by the new imams of the latter half of the twentieth century.

This narrative transformation began in Detroit in 1949 with the arrival of Shaykh Mohammad Jawad Chirri and Imam Vehbi Ismail, two highly educated young clerics who set about changing local ideas of who the city's Muslims were, how Islam should be practiced in North America, which forms of Muslim American identity should be supported, and which forms should be actively suppressed. Ironically, these religious leaders would eventually embrace many of the institutional habits developed in the early years of Hashmie Hall, the AMS, and other Muslim associations in Detroit. The new mosques Chirri and Ismail built in the 1960s were architect designed and visually recognizable as mosques, but the physical space they allocated to social activities was much larger than the space they set aside for prayer. Instead of doing away with practices they found objectionable when they first arrived in the city, both imams came to regard vernacular forms of American Islam as functionally expedient and complementary to their own visions of a more historically authentic, text-based, and politically relevant Islam.

In fact, Chirri and Ismail represented an Islamic tradition that was as new as the practical innovations they encountered in American mosques. They were eager to reform outdated practices and to purge the errors of the past in order to bring about an enlightened future. They called for a political awakening among American Muslims; they struggled to organize Muslims as a national religious and political constituency; and they strengthened ties between Muslims in the United States and Muslims overseas. It was in pursuit of these agendas that Chirri and Ismail originally criticized American Islam as inadequate, heterodox, and in need of renovation from the ground up. This caustic assessment was appealing to many new immigrants and American-born Muslims, and Chirri and Ismail used this support to build a power base in Detroit that soon acquired international dimensions. What the imams did not foresee as they confidently began their work at midcentury was a future in which Islam would become a medium of resistance to American power in the Middle East and the Muslim world. They also could not have imagined a future in which new Muslim immigrants would see *them* as representatives of an American Islam that was accomodationist and badly in need of reform.

The Soul Doctor

On May 5, 1949, an essay entitled "The Future of the New Generation" appeared in *Nahdat al-Arab*, an Arabic-language newspaper published in Detroit, without a byline but alongside a photograph of Mohammad Jawad Chirri. The piece, whether written by Chirri or for him, was intended to introduce Detroit Muslims to their newly arrived cleric and his mission to America. It offered both a diagnosis and a cure—in the person of Mohammad Jawad Chirri—of the spiritual malaise that had infected the body of the Muslim community.

The Arab immigrant community of this republic, in our opinion, does not face a more truly dangerous issue than that of the new Arab American generation and how to instill in them adequate knowledge and guidelines that will allow for the preservation of good traditions and customs, [given that] their progenitors let go of [these] over time [and let them drift away] in the new American ocean...

Here, the community needs to resort to doctors of the soul...devoted religious servants versed in spiritual and literary knowledge, able to express their culture and learning in order to save the new generation from the danger of melting into the body of an American nation that does not believe in any lofty religion...[thereby losing]...the blessed gift of a religion that has guided and instructed their parents and grandparents before them over many decades.

If the religious domain of Muslims in this country is barren and stricken by drought, we now have a sign that the fertile waters of life will return. This will be accomplished with an outpouring of abundant knowledge, religious devotion, and honorable piety. Yes, the gathering clouds that spelled a dark future for the next Muslim generation in this region have cleared with the coming of Shaykh Mohammad Jawad Chirri, who will be a watchful servant, guide, and religious organizer for the entire Shi'a Muslim community in Dearborn, Detroit, and in other regions.

We have long heard of the shock many feel at the development of the new generation and their fears that they will grow up ignorant of the religion of their forefathers. But now these fearful people have been shown the way...Shaykh Mohammad Jawad Chirri brings them effective medicine and a reliable cure, if only they let go of their past mistakes and make every effort to take advantage of this favorable opportunity...of ensuring our children's salvation from the ill fate that threatens them.[1]

Detroit's Muslims were not alone in experiencing such religious anxiety. Robert Ellwood has identified several patterns that made religion seem more urgent in the United States in the 1950s.[2] Postwar prosperity and the rise of the suburbs contributed to new church construction across the country, and people wanted these churches to reflect a confident, middle-class, modern, and progressive mood. The baby boom produced a growing number of parents who wanted to give their children the values and stability they associated with their own childhoods, values identified with rural churches, inner-city synagogues, or—as in Chirri's mission statement—immigrant homelands and "religious traditions that have been sacred for ages." The Cold War brought with it the fearmongering of McCarthy-era politics and, among Protestant Christians, an evangelical movement that offered itself as the antidote to Communism and moral decline. Finally, the "chasm between the realities of discrimination and the democratic ideals through which America self-identified after World War II was a powerful example not only of hypocrisy but also of the fact that nearly a century after the Civil War, black Americans still remained outside America's national narrative."[3] The Civil Rights Movement, drawing on an activist Christianity, pushed back against this hypocrisy, while the Nation of Islam (NOI), especially in the person of Malcolm X, encouraged blacks to identify with Islam as a religion of resistance and liberation. Overseas, the Cold War generated its own forms of resistance and encouraged a new era of Afro-Asian alliance building. Among Muslims, a new religious sensibility emerged that presented itself as the antidote to Western imperialism and, more specifically, to Zionism and the shocking defeat, subjugation, and displacement of Palestinians it had accomplished. To manage this complex array of spiritual and political trends, Detroit's Muslims needed expert guidance of exactly the sort Chirri was said to possess.

Mohammad Jawad Chirri was among the better educated of South Lebanon's clerics in the early 1940s, having graduated from the Islamic Institute of Najaf, Iraq. After Lebanese independence, he joined forces with Shaykh Mohammed Jawad Mughniyya, another Najaf-educated Shi'i cleric from the South and a highly influential social and religious reformer, to popularize an Islamic theology that emphasized social justice and human rights.[4] In the 1940s, Chirri published several popular books on religious subjects, including *Al-Riyad in Islamic Jurisprudence, al-Tahara, The Fast, A Book of Prayers, Islamic Wills*, and *The Caliphate in the Islamic Constitution*.[5] He gained a reputation as an innovative thinker and social activist who was not afraid to disturb the entrenched Shi'i establishment in the South.

Chirri's journey to Detroit was set in motion in 1947, when Adil Osseiran, a hero of the Lebanese independence movement, the first speaker of the Lebanese parliament, and a Shi'a from Saida in South Lebanon, visited Detroit during a trip to the United States to address the United Nations.[6] Osseiran petitioned the General Assembly on behalf of Palestinians enraged over the partition of their homeland and on behalf of Shi'i pilgrims who were being harassed on the annual hajj in Saudi Arabia.[7] His tour of the Detroit area was a coup for the Lebanese Shi'a, who welcomed him eagerly. Osseiran was hosted at Hashmie Hall and toured the United Syrian Citizens Society (USCS), a mosque/social club that had organized in Highland Park in the 1920s but did not incorporate as a mosque—the Moslem Mosque of Highland Park—until 1958.[8] His visit to these mosques was a great embarrassment to some of the city's younger Muslims, who felt the community should have had more to show for itself after thirty-five years in the area. Their religious leader, Shaykh Kalil Bazzy, was also found wanting by the new generation of college-educated Muslims.

"They greet him [Osseiran] and have a dinner for him, and show him what they have," said Hajj Hussein Hamood, who attended these events. "They don't have anybody but Imam Bazzy," he added, "who is not enough for them."[9] After Osseiran's visit, the Restum family wrote to him and asked if he could help them find a religious leader more like himself: worldly, qualified to address the United Nations on an important matter like the crisis in Palestine, but also a South Lebanese who could speak to the concerns of the Shi'a and empower them in relation to the city's other Muslims. The Restums asked for a religious scholar who was also a trained jurist, someone who could lead American Muslims into the modern time/space of Islam.[10]

Based on Osseiran's recommendation, the leaders at Hashmie Hall and the USCS called Shaykh Chirri to Detroit in 1948.[11] Chirri's vision of a reformed, progressive Shi'ism that emphasized individual religious commitment rather than tradition-oriented, communal religious practices was championed most eagerly in Detroit not by the existing Muslim establishment but by a cohort of young men who were, like Chirri, dismissive of both Detroit's Muslim associations and the old Shi'i elites in South Lebanon. Most of these men were new to Detroit. Part of a small but influential cohort of immigrants who arrived after World War II, they helped bridge the gap between Muslims born in and outside the United States; between those with and without a secondary education; between those who saw Lebanon as an irredeemably foreign, backward place and those who saw it as home. Most of these new immigrants had grown up as French colonial subjects rather than subjects of the Ottoman Empire, and they came to the United States as citizens of the new Lebanese nation-state, which had gained independence from France in 1943.[12] Many were the children and grandchildren of American citizens, émigrés who had returned to Lebanon with financial resources and expanded cultural horizons. These returnees helped to create in Lebanon a distinct form of modernity defined by changing gender and family roles, a new and expanding middle class, urbanization, educational achievement, literacy, and conspicuous identification with the West.[13] The Shi'a of South Lebanon, however, long oppressed by Sunni elites in both Damascus and Istanbul, and controlled by a local network of powerful landowning families, were shut out of the new nation's economic development. This left many young South Lebanese frustrated and willing to try their own hand at emigration.[14] Those with American citizenship often settled in Detroit, while those barred from the United States (by restrictive immigration legislation) typically moved to West Africa or Latin America.

This generation of immigrants, like their American-born Lebanese peers, were likely to possess at least some high school education, and many had college degrees. They were not eager to settle in Dearborn's heavily polluted Southend, preferring the better-off neighborhoods in Highland Park and Detroit; they were more likely to enter private business or a profession than to work on the assembly line; and they were active participants in local mosques, but they expected these mosques to reflect the ethos of a modern, progressive age. With influence that far outweighed their small numbers, these new immigrants helped make Islam palatable to American-born Muslims, and they made a modernizing, reformist Islam palatable to an older generation of Muslims, many of whom sympathized with Shaykh Chirri's desire to correct flaws but were themselves unable to teach Islam in ways their Americanized children could understand and respect.

Hussein Hamood and Hussein Makled typified this new immigration. They were young adults when they moved from South Lebanon to Highland Park, Michigan, after World War II. Hamood's father was an American veteran of World War I, which explains how Hamood arrived in the United States as an American citizen.[15] Makled married a young Lebanese woman whose family had returned to Lebanon from Detroit during the Depression and who also had citizenship.[16] Both began their lives in Detroit on the assembly line, but moved into the grocery business as soon as they were able. Both were active members of the USCS in Highland Park. The USCS (see Figure 5.1) was similar to Hashmie Hall and served in many ways as its Highland Park annex. Both Hamood and Makled eventually became avid supporters of Imam Chirri.

In a 2006 interview, Makled described his impression of Detroit's mosques at the time of Chirri's arrival.

HAJJ MAKLED: There was two places. They're not mosques—they call them "hall." One of them was on Dix Avenue—you probably passed by. It's demolished, nothing over there. And you wonder how people used to be in that place, making a wedding or having a gathering? And it's only . . . you see that piece of empty land over there?

SALLY HOWELL: Yeah, you're talking about Hashmie Hall.

HAJJ MAKLED: Yeah, Hashmie Hall.

FATMEH MAKLED: So small. [She laughs].

HAJJ MAKLED: Now, we had one in Highland Park. We called it United Citizen's Society. When I came here in 1948, the United Citizen's Society was already established and the people who lived in Highland Park, you know, they belonged to that society, or to that Hall...that was the place where we meet, the place where we have our deceased ones when they die, you know we take him from there. It was a place for the community. Like I say, we called it a hall. We never called it a mosque.[17]

HOWELL: Did you do prayers there, like Friday prayers?

HAJJ MAKLED: No, not at the time, no.

HOWELL: And you didn't have anything like...it wasn't, it wasn't in any way a mosque? There was no prayer space, no *qibla*?

HAJJ MAKLED: No, no. Neither that, neither the one in Hashmie Hall. The Hashmie Hall got to be for the prayer after Imam Chirri arrived here, they made the upstairs, they put a few, uh, I still remember, they put a few rugs over there and they use it for prayer.[18]

FIGURE 5.1 The Moslem Mosque of Highland Park, circa 1958. Walter P. Reuther Library, Archives of Labor and Urban Affairs, Wayne State University.

Hajj Hamood, who arrived in Detroit a year later, in 1950, was equally dismissive of Hashmie Hall and the USCS, claiming not only that they were not mosques, but that the only reason they were described as such was for tax purposes. "Again, they called it—just to save, just to not pay property taxes on it—they call it Hashmie," he said.[19]

> They have union meetings. They have the marriages and the New Year and members of the Hashmie Society would meet and everything, and a mosque.

So Imam Chirri came and he said:

> "Is this good for the Muslims? Where people do this and do that and we'll call this a 'place of worship' or something?"
> We are supposed to have a place that—for a school, a place for the community, a place to pray.[20]

Thus Hajj Makled, Hajj Chuck, and Hajj Hamood—three early supporters of Chirri—each speak of Hashmie Hall and the USCS using the same language; they portray these institutions as small, dirty, too social, not adequately oriented toward religion, and—in the words of Hajj Chuck—"completely inadequate to promote a strong, positive identification with Islam" among American Muslims.[21] This critique was articulated by men who took their faith seriously and were eager to compete, as Muslims, in the marketplace of American religious ideas. They were, with few exceptions, products of modern school systems and members of the middle class, whether Lebanese or American. They were educated to expect social, economic, and political advancement and to assert their rights as citizens. They wanted Detroit's mosques to sit on a par with the city's churches. The leadership of Hashmie Hall and the USCS might have shared this ambition in the abstract, but in practice most of them were comfortable with the status quo.

In his first public act in Dearborn, Imam Chirri set about "founding" both a new mosque at Hashmie Hall and a new history for the Shi'i community there. An "opening celebration" for an "Islamic Mosque" was held on May 29, 1949, according to a series of articles that appeared in *Nahdat al-Arab* on June 6 and 17, which describe Imam Chirri asking "the Muslim community in Dearborn to build a mosque for prayer and educational meetings," a project that would enable him to fulfill his mission of "providing the religious guidance the community had solicited from him."[22] During the ceremony, Chirri unfolded a new carpet on the floor of Hashmie Hall and declared the space "a mosque," then led the congregation in prayer "for the first time."[23] This event is memorialized in the narratives of Makled, Alawan, and Hamood, none of whom had been on hand twelve years earlier, when Hashmie Hall celebrated its previous opening as the "first mosque in Dearborn." Many, if not most, of the people who gathered for the second opening would have remembered the earlier event. What they made of Chirri's arrival and his symbolic usurpation of their historic mosque—an act which simultaneously erased its past and announced its future as a house of worship Chirri would control—did not disrupt the fanfare of the occasion, but it was soon to disrupt Chirri's mission in Detroit.

The (re)opening of the Hashmie Hall mosque was well attended. Supportive speeches were made by Shaykh Kalil Bazzy, Joseph Berry, Hussein Makled, and Mohammad Berry. A delegation from the local Albanian community was also on hand, including representatives of the newly organized Albanian Moslem Society of Detroit (a Sunni congregation) and the Bektashi community (a Sufi order closely associated with Imami Shi'ism through the Turkish Alevis). Several Albanians addressed the crowd, among them Baba Rexheb Ferdi,[24] Zainab Ali (representing Iman Vehbi Ismail, who was unable to attend), and Ahmad Ramo, who presented the congregation with a painted Qur'anic inscription on behalf of the Albanian American Moslem Society (AAMS). Letters extolling Chirri's mission, sent by representatives of the Muslim communities in Chicago, New York, and Michigan City, Indiana, were read at the event. Ali Rustum was master of ceremonies. Chirri spoke as well, emphasizing the significance of religious and social cooperation among Muslims and how both were necessary for maintaining Islamic religious obligations and for the equally important work of keeping an Islamic identity alive in America. He entreated the audience to "return to their religion" and, in so doing, uplift the social status of the whole community.[25] Imam Hussien Karoub and other leaders of the AMS, the Sunni mosque located just down the street, are not mentioned in the newspaper coverage, but it appears that Imam Chirri, who had been in Detroit for only a month at the time of this event, was already developing a transcommunal Islamic network of his own. His non-Arab allies, like his most enthusiastic supporters in the Lebanese community, were mostly new immigrants to Detroit and American-born Muslims who sought to institutionalize Islam in unprecedented ways.

Chirri's welcome party at Hashmie Hall was followed a few weeks later by a second event that celebrated the opening of a new school in the "Islamic Mosque." "In keeping with the goal of fulfilling our duties to our religion and our people and of answering the desires of this generous community,"

Chirri wrote in *Nahdat al-Arab*, "we resolved, God willing, to open an Arabic school in Dearborn for the purpose of teaching the Arabic language and the fundamentals of religion."[26] As head of this school, Chirri also requested a salary. This effort to professionalize the role of imam met with a mix of welcome and hostility among local Shi'a. Shaykh Kalil Bazzy, who had long served as the religious leader of the South Lebanese without receiving a penny in payment, was still very much on the scene. His supporters were quick to distance themselves from Chirri.[27]

The idea of a salaried clergy seemed radical to Detroit Muslims, who paid minimal dues to their three mosques, and made donations in the five to twenty-five-dollar range at fundraising events. Neither income stream could provide for the livelihood of Shaykh Chirri. The Shi'a prided themselves on paying off the debts incurred in the establishment of Hashmie Hall and the USCS in a few short years. They were no longer as actively engaged in fundraising as were the supporters of the AMS who, in 1949, were caught up in a multiyear campaign to add a second-floor prayer space to their facility. Hashmie Hall, which initially included a women's auxiliary, apparently disbanded this group once the association's debts were retired, and the group was not fastidious when it came to the upkeep of their Highland Park and Dearborn buildings.[28]

Very quickly, resistance to Chirri's plans began to build. Driven by Lebanese political factionalism and resentment over Chirri's presumptive reopening of a mosque that was already a mosque and rededication of a school that was already a school, this opposition lined up squarely behind Kalil Bazzy. Bazzy's supporters were drawn largely from the Berry family, who were well represented in Detroit and included several of the Shi'i community's better-educated members. A large and powerful family in the area around Tibneen and Bint Ijbayl, the Berrys included their own line of Shi'i clerics whom Chirri had antagonized during his reform campaign in South Lebanon. The Berrys rallied behind Shaykh Bazzy and sought to drive Chirri out of town.[29] In December, a defense of Bazzy's "more than 30 years of service...with his two hands keeping Islam alive in America...without taking a dollar for his services" was quickly mounted in the pages of the same paper through which Chirri appealed to Detroit's Muslims.[30] Once this old guard stepped in to defend the status quo, Chirri's local host, Faiz Humoud, asked the imam to leave his house.[31]

Chirri moved into a small apartment, unfinished and unfurnished, on the second floor of Hashmie Hall. From these reduced circumstances, he continued to appeal to readers of his regular column in *Nahdat al-Arab*, asking them to back his plans to build a new mosque; trust and support him with their "unity"; place their conflicts and division behind them; and empower him to do more than bury the dead, marry the young, and lead the occasional holiday prayer.[32] Despite the urgency of his appeals, support for Chirri's mission did not materialize. His allies among the new immigrants did not yet have the means, financial or social, to build an effective pro-Chirri coalition. Moreover, Chirri's inability to speak, read, or write English meant that the American-born Muslims he championed in his sermons and essays could not read his column in the newspaper, understand his sermons, or even converse casually with him. If Chirri's goal was to teach Sunday school and other classes, represent Islam to the larger society, and guide the young, he lagged far behind imams Bazzy and Karoub in this one very critical skill.

Chirri had come to Detroit to teach Islam "as the Prophet Mohammed had taught it."[33] Alas, like the Prophet Muhammad, Chirri encountered stiff resistance among the leadership of the very community he hoped to redeem and, like the Prophet, he was forced into exile. Alert to Chirri's precarious tenure in Detroit, members of the Asser El Jadeed Arabian Islamic Society of Michigan City, Indiana, the second largest settlement of Shi'i Lebanese in the United States, invited Chirri to serve there instead.[34] Without the benefit of a local imam like Bazzy or Karoub, the Muslims of Michigan City were eager to hire a cleric of their own. Chirri moved to Michigan City in late 1949, less than a year after his arrival in Detroit.

Albanian Soul Doctor: Vehbi Ismail Comes to Detroit

Vehbi Ismail was the second reformist imam to arrive in Detroit in the late 1940s. He was invited to Detroit in 1948 by the AAMS, which had formally organized in 1945. Detroit's Albanian Muslims had been active since the first decade of the twentieth century, but most of the Albanians in Detroit prior to the 1940s were unmarried men.[35] This pattern changed after 1944, when Albania was liberated from German occupation and a new, Communist-led government set about eradicating organized religion in the country. Placing tremendous pressure on religious institutions, elites, and clergy, the government drove a sizeable contingent of the Albanian religious establishment into exile. Many of these exiles made their way to Detroit, where Christian and Muslim Albanian populations were already settled. An Orthodox parish, St. Thomas Church, was being organized in this period, and the Vatra, a national mutual aid society founded in 1912, had a strong local chapter as well. Frances Trix has argued that the influx of postwar Albanian immigrants was much larger than official statistics acknowledged and that roughly one hundred Albanian Muslim families had settled in Detroit by the 1960s.[36] Like contemporaneous Lebanese immigrants, these new Albanian Americans were much better educated than earlier migrants, more likely to arrive as families, and more focused on settling permanently in the United States. It was this population of immigrants who organized the AAMS in 1947 and invited Imam Vehbi Ismail to Detroit the following year.[37]

Born on November 25, 1919, in Schkodra, Albania, Vehbi Ismail was the son of Ismail Alkovaji, the grand mufti of Islam in Albania. Imam Vehbi was raised in a scholarly, religious, and nationalist household. He studied theology at the Islamic University in Tirana, Albania, and then at Islam's leading seminary, Al-Azhar University, in Cairo, Egypt, where he had the opportunity to meet and befriend the Egyptian King, Farouk, who was of mixed Albanian and Egyptian ancestry. Ismail came from a Sunni Muslim family, but his father was the mufti of Albania's diverse Muslim communities, and Ismail was interested in and comfortable with a wide array of Muslim practices. In particular, he was familiar with the Bektashi Sufi order in Albania and spent time with an aspiring leader of this order, Baba Rexheb, who was also a student at Al-Azhar University. Ismail was still in Egypt in 1945 when the Communists took control of the Albanian government and the suppression of religious observances and institutions began. In exile, Albania's religious communities, both Muslim and Christian, were united in the effort to reassert the role of religion in the public life of the nation. Ismail's father led this campaign inside Albania, but as his public role and personal freedom were increasingly curtailed during the late 1940s, he advised his son to remain outside the country, beyond the reach of the new government. These events left young Vehbi to fend for himself, so when invited to Detroit, he accepted the offer, not because he was eager to build a new Islamic center for Albanian immigrants—a goal he little understood at the time—but because it would position him to advocate against the Albanian Communist regime from the heartland of the world's most powerful capitalist nation.[38]

Ismail's initial experiences in Detroit were bumpier than anticipated, in part because of these mixed ambitions. He was a young man, just out of seminary, who had grown up in a conservative but elite household. In Detroit he found himself among not just educated Albanians but also poorly educated, working-class immigrants, many of whom had no formal training and little personal interest in religious matters. In our 2005 interview, Ismail shared his first impressions of Detroit's working-class Albanian Muslims.

> When I came first, in their halls they used to drink [beer]. Because—they think was nothing. Because they didn't know.
>
> Mostly [they] were workers. They came, eh, left their country at sixteen, seventeen years old. And they didn't know anything about religion. But then they wanted to learn, little by little.
>
> When I came first and saw this, I wanted to turn back. My father was a mufti, the head of the Islamic Waqf in Albania. [When I called him and told him I wanted to leave, he] would say, "Why are you leaving?"
>
> I said, "They are drinking."
>
> He said to me, "You read the Qur'an?"
>
> "Yes."
>
> "You don't know the Qur'an first said, 'la taqrabu salat wa andhum sukarah'"... 'don't go to prayer when you are drunk.' Little by little they get used [to observing Islamic prayer]. Then, say it [drinking] is *haram* [forbidden].

In this exchange Ismail's father reminds him that the Prophet Muhammad was also confronted by drinkers and apathetic Muslims in the first days of the Muslim community in Mecca. He was guided by a Qur'anic revelation that encouraged him to be patient with drinkers, preventing them from praying while drunk but not casting them out of the community. Ismail's father suggested that his son stay and work with these American Muslims, educate them about the religious prohibition against consuming alcohol, and gradually encourage them to avoid drinking and other un-Islamic behaviors they had acquired (or continued) during their years in Detroit. For the most part, these workers had not made a sustained effort to organize a congregation of their own or to involve themselves in the activities of Detroit's other Muslim institutions in the preceding decades. In a conversation with Frances Trix, one of these early immigrants summed up the state of Albanian religious life in the city prior to Imam Vehbi's arrival by observing that "the coffeehouse was our church."[39] But in the 1940s, new immigration, especially by families rather than single men, and a newly exilic consciousness spurred on by the Communist takeover of the homeland, led to a new commitment to revitalize and institutionalize Islam in Detroit.

As had happened a decade earlier in the Syrian community, the work of building religious institutions split the Albanians into two groups. Once the leadership of the Sunni community had invited Ismail to town, local Albanians who identified with the Bektashi Sufi order began to search for a religious leader of their own. Sufi master Baba Rexheb settled permanently in Michigan in 1953, and his followers established the First Albanian Bektashi Monastery (*Tekke*) in the nearby town of Taylor, where the Baba could live and teach. The relationship between the Sunni mosque and the Bektashi Tekke seems to have resembled the relationship between Sunni and Shi'i Muslims in Dearborn in previous decades. The two supported one another on most occasions, but made no attempt to merge. Imam Ismail attended the two holiday events observed at the monastery (Ashura and Nevruz, a New Year's celebration which was used to mark the birth of Imam Ali). Likewise, Baba Rexheb attended the two major holiday celebrations (Eid al-Adha and Eid al-Fitr) that were celebrated at the mosque. The two groups supported one another financially; they respected one another's differences and autonomy.[40] Nevertheless, for Imam Ismail, a young, inexperienced cleric who needed to raise money to build a mosque, secure his own salary, and provide religious instruction and guidance, the tekke represented a potential source of competition.

More frustrating to Imam Vehbi was the resistance he faced from outside the Albanian community. Hussien Karoub, who had long provided pastoral care to Detroit's Albanians, apparently felt threatened by the arrival of a younger and better-educated imam. As I was packing up to leave after my 2005 interview with Ismail, he felt compelled to share a final anecdote with me. He said that when he arrived in Detroit, in 1949, Hussien Karoub tried to have him deported. He claimed that Karoub wrote US immigration authorities and advised them to deny Ismail a work permit or green card on the grounds that the Muslims of Detroit already had a cleric and were not in need of a second. Ismail was in Detroit as a political refugee—whether this was his official status or not. Karoub's actions seemed malicious to Ismail, who did not fully understand why Karoub would lobby the US Government to have a fellow imam deported.[41]

Trix, Elkholy, and Walbridge have argued that relations between Albanian Muslims and other Muslims in Detroit were limited at best.[42] Karoub's actions suggest that the various pan-Muslim networks in the city ran deeper and were more important than has previously been acknowledged. Ismail's impressive academic credentials and professional training enabled him to preach and write not only in Albanian but in Arabic as well. Hussien Karoub, who throughout the 1940s and 1950s referred to himself in print and in person as *imam al-muslimin al-'am fi al-walayat al-mutahadida wa Canada* (roughly, the imam of all Muslims in the United States and Canada), apparently felt—as had Shaykh Bazzy in relation to Imam Chirri—that he was being confronted with a serious rival. Beyond Karoub's occasional work performing weddings and funerals, it is unclear how far his ties in the Albanian community reached. Albanians were well aware of the AMS—they emulated the Syrian group when choosing a name for their own society and in the structure of their bylaws—but they considered the group too oriented toward the Arabic language and Syrian ethnicity, and they did not always feel welcome there.[43] In the late 1940s, when the Albanians first organized, the AMS was once again trying to pull the city's Muslims together in support of their mosque—Detroit's "public mosque," as Karoub came to describe it—which was raising funds to complete construction on their second floor addition. Karoub might have been concerned that the two construction projects would compete with one another.

Imam Ismail was not deported, however. Instead, he began to build a following among local Albanians, and he soon became a popular speaker and spiritual advisor among the younger generation of Arab Muslims as well. He was frequently invited to lecture at their mosques in Highland Park and Dearborn, to perform weddings, and, once Imam Chirri returned to Detroit, to participate in the life of the Islamic Center of America (ICA) as well.[44] Events in the Albanian Muslim community were covered in *Nahdat al Arab*, alongside those of the city's Arabic-speaking Muslims, a further indication that the two populations found common ground despite their cultural and linguistic differences. Ismail's willingness and ability to provide leadership for an increasingly educated and multicultural Muslim network enabled him to ultimately replace the aging Karoub in Detroit and nationally as well, just as Karoub had feared he would.

The AAMS was a small group, roughly one hundred adults in 1949, who were well organized politically. When they hosted a convention in Detroit to introduce their new spiritual leader to their members and supporters, Michigan governor G. Mennen Williams was in attendance, as was Detroit mayor Eugene Von Antwerp and the head of the Detroit City Council—evidence that the Albanian community was already well connected to public officials.[45] For the newcomer, Ismail, these connections were important. As a vocal anti-Communist, Ismail had no problem making friends in Republican circles in Michigan and eventually became a close friend of Governor Williams. Imam Vehbi also used the national

FIGURE 5.2 The Albanian American Moslem Society, circa 1955. Walter
P. Reuther Library, Archives of Labor and Urban Affairs, Wayne State University.

infrastructure of the Vatra to introduce himself to Albanian Muslim settlements across the country and in Canada. In 1949 he embarked on the first
of many cross-country journeys to visit Albanian Muslim communities,
provide religious services and counseling when needed, and solicit contributions for the opening of an Albanian mosque in Detroit. By 1950, under
the new leadership of Imam Vehbi, the AAMS was able to move out of its
rented space at the International Institute, on Grand Boulevard in Detroit,[46]
and into a newly purchased building (a former Armenian church) not far
from Highland Park (see Figure 5.2).[47]

In our interview, Imam Vehbi spoke at length about the difficulties of
raising money in Detroit's small, working-class, often newly arrived population of Albanians. Unlike Karoub and Bazzy, who supported themselves
financially with secular employment, Imam Vehbi drew a salary from the
AAMS that came out of the organization's membership dues. *Waqf* support
for religious institutions was the common practice in Albania and Syria
(see Chapter 2), which is why, Imam Ismail explained to me, "we Muslims
are not used to paying very much for mosques. Because every mosque
that was built in [Albania] had property first." Nonetheless, a full-time
salaried position freed Ismail to pursue his academic work in Detroit. His
initial writings in the United States were addressed to Albanian American
Muslims rather than to other scholars, and focused on the basics of Islamic

history, moral principles, and the practicalities of worship and religious observance. It is clear from the level of this writing and its subject matter that he presumed very little prior knowledge on the part of readers. He began publishing a quarterly Albanian-language journal, *Jeta Muslimane Shqiptare* (*The Albanian Muslim Life*) in October of 1949.[48]

The Communist takeover of Albania produced a collective identity, at least among immigrant and exile Albanians in North America, in which Islam and Albanian nationalism were tightly interwoven. Communist rule had radically transformed the political meaning of Islam, and of religion more generally, in everyday life. Holding on to Muslim identity in the United States was as much an Albanian nationalist project as it was a commitment to personal or communal piety, and this political, identitarian motivation also drove work for the journal. It was intended to keep the dispersed Albanian community in touch with one another, to provide religious instruction, and to give voice to the anti-Communist movement among exiled Albanians. Despite his conflict with Hussien Karoub, and perhaps as a means of reconciliation, Ismail printed *The Albanian Muslim Life*—which later became *The Muslim Life* and was distributed to a pan-Muslim readership—at Karoub Printing in Highland Park, from 1949–1963.[49]

A Clinic for the Soul

The impulse to build new mosques, so strongly expressed in Detroit at mid-century, was felt in Muslim communities across North America. Smaller Muslim settlements were eager to create strong ties to each other, to the large urban Muslim communities, and to the larger Muslim world. In the early 1950s, a network of Muslim organizers established the Federation of Islamic Associations of the United States and Canada (FIA) to help Muslims overcome their sense of isolation. The FIA would advocate for their political concerns, expand the contexts in which Islam could be practiced in North America, and educate North Americans—Muslim and non-Muslim—about the history and teachings of Islam.[50]

Abdullah Igram of Cedar Rapids, Iowa, who is credited with having founded the federation and who served as its first president, mentioned three reasons for the group's creation.[51] Igram was personally motivated by his experience serving in the Philippines during World War II. The dog tags available to soldiers at the time required them to identify as Christians (Protestant or Catholic), Jews, or "no religion," which meant that Muslims who died in combat were not granted burial according to Islamic rites. Igram wrote President Truman to request that Islam be recognized by the US Armed Forces in a manner similar to that of Judaism and Christianity. Upon receiving no accommodation, he decided it was time for American Muslims to organize so that issues of this kind could be addressed by a collective body. In 1951, he called a meeting of Midwestern Muslims, mostly Iowans of Syrian/Lebanese descent, to discuss the situation. Older attendees at this meeting had a very different concern. They were worried about how to identify potential Muslim spouses for their children and grandchildren. Increasingly, young men and women were marrying outside the faith.[52]

A third, explicitly political and transnational impetus for organizing was raised at the meeting: the Palestinian refugee crisis. President Truman's support for the creation of Israel in 1948 was seen by many Americans as "election-year politics" that catered to American Jewish voters.[53] The displacement of Arabs from Jewish-controlled sectors of Mandate Palestine, a process that continued after US recognition of the Israeli state, led Arab Americans to organize nationally as a counterweight to American Jewish support for Zionism. Their goal was to encourage an American foreign policy more sympathetic to Arab nationalist agendas. The Cedar Rapids Muslim community convened a national meeting in 1952 and invited every Muslim organization they could identify. Over four hundred people attended, including Imams Vehbi and Karoub from Detroit and Imam Chirri from Michigan City, and the body agreed to organize as an international voluntary association. The FIA was an immediate success among American Muslims, especially those of Syrian, Lebanese, and Palestinian origin. Its annual convention moved from city to city, attracting ever larger audiences and involving hundreds of new members in the organizational life of the Muslim community.[54]

The FIA played a crucial and frequently overlooked role in reinforcing Muslim American identity in the 1950s and 1960s, organizing the North American community at the local and (bi)national level, and bringing American Muslims into more direct contact with Muslim institutions overseas. It is frequently described as having been a social rather than religious organization, a critique that mirrors the language commonly used today to describe American mosques of the period. Hajj Hussein Hamood, for example, scoffed when I asked if he was involved with the association. "There was no sign of Islam in this," he replied. "They used to dance in the Federation. The 'Federation of Islamic' [they called it], and there was no sign of Islam in it. That is how it was."[55] Elkholy, who provides the best written accounting of the FIA's early history to date, offers an assessment of the group that is essentially negative:

> The Islamic Federation's activities up to now have been minimal and, in fact, do not really involve anything worth mentioning except an annual convention. One Toledo respondent complains that this annual gathering itself seems to be mainly for dancing and singing. Another prominent person in the Detroit community described the 1959 convention as "successful in collecting money, but very weak and disappointing in other respects."[56]

Between the years of Elkholy's original research (1958–1959) and the publication of his work, the FIA matured significantly, and Elkholy alludes to this change in his text.[57] He admits, for example, the group's success in forging links between the Muslim American community and several international Muslim organizations, including Al-Azhar University, the Muslim World League, and the governments of several Muslim-majority nations. Unfortunately, Elkholy's harsh and perhaps premature evaluation of the fledgling FIA is what scholars have tended to cite when recounting the FIA and its history.[58]

Contrary to Elkholy's description, the FIA leadership built educational programs and provided instructional services from the very start. Imams Chirri and Ismail were major advocates of this work. By 1952, both men were familiar to Arabic-speaking Muslims across the country due to Chirri's column in *Nahdat al-Arab* and the ample coverage Ismail received in the paper. While Hussien Karoub had been, and remained, a much beloved imam to Arab Muslims in small communities throughout the northern United States and across Canada, Chirri and Ismail quickly gained respect as scholars, institutional leaders, and political activists. Imam Vehbi in particular, due to his status as a Sunni cleric, was asked to visit far-flung Muslim congregations, as Karoub had done a generation before, advising them on how to establish mosque schools for Arabic and Qur'anic instruction. Ismail's journal, *The Albanian Moslem Life*, was made available increasingly in English as well, so it could reach American-born Albanians and other Muslim Americans through the FIA.[59]

The FIA provided a source of forward momentum for Muslims in the United States and Canada, but in the 1950s, the group was still incipient and poorly funded. The FIA incorporated officially in 1954, with a board dominated by Muslims of Arab descent, yet they moved quickly to include individuals and member organizations of Albanian, Bosnian, Yugoslav, Pakistani, Iranian, African American, and other backgrounds, especially in cities like New York, Pittsburgh, Chicago, and Detroit, which had large, ethnically mixed Muslim populations.[60] This diversity was reflected in the Federation's stated goals:

1. To promote and teach the spirit, ethics, philosophy, and culture of Islam to Muslims and their children in the United States and Canada.
2. To participate in and contribute to the modern renaissance of Islam.
3. To establish contacts and strengthen the relationship with the Muslim world community.
4. To expound the teachings of Islam.
5. To point out the common beliefs which other religions share with Islam.
6. To provide a media for religious, intellectual and social needs of Muslims.[61]

The FIA also helped local communities develop mosques. Because the FIA elected officers only from its institutional members (as opposed to individual members), dozens of Muslim groups across the country were motivated to organize, seek nonprofit status, and join the FIA.[62] For communities that were already organized, like those in Detroit and Toledo, the FIA created a feeling of camaraderie and healthy competition. Many mosques were completed in the months before (or sometimes just after) the annual FIA convention was hosted in their community, including the Syrian American Moslem Society of Toledo (1953); the Bosnian American Cultural Association in Chicago (1955); the Islamic Center of Washington, DC (1957); the Windsor (Ontario) Mosque (1960); and the New England Islamic Center in Quincy, Massachusetts (1964).[63]

Detroit, the FIA, and Midcentury Transnational Islam

By the mid-1950s, Imam Chirri's reputation as an effective teacher and community organizer had been securely established through his work with the FIA, his leadership of the Asser El Jadeed Arabian Islamic Society of Michigan City, and his writings in *Nahdat al-Arab*. His years in Michigan City were not misspent. Realizing that he had been unable to communicate with the constituency of American Muslims he most sought to reach— the American-born generation—Chirri set about mastering the English language. Also aware that young Muslim Americans were already well integrated into American society, he made a point of studying American culture, observing and evaluating how religious institutions in Michigan City functioned.[64]

Chirri also came to realize that his early sermons about cultural loss and the threat posed by the religious mainstream may not have been the most productive way to approach a young, relatively educated generation of Americans who avidly embraced their American identities and were poised to enter the middle class. They were keen to identify with Islam, as long as Islam could be made a viable aspect of their middle class American lives. He worked closely with an American convert to Islam, Wilson Guertin. The two produced a book based on their conversations about matters of faith. This book, which was heavily promoted in FIA publications, became a major sourcebook for Muslim converts and other Muslim Americans in the 1960s.[65] Overall, time spent in Indiana allowed Chirri to temper his earlier criticisms of American values and ways of life. He was now better equipped to understand the choices Muslims were making as they sought to practice Islam in the United States.[66]

In Dearborn and Highland Park, however, frustrations had risen as they watched the Toledo Mosque open in 1953 and the AMS complete construction on its second-floor mosque and weekend Arabic school in 1952. Elsewhere, plans were underway to build a grand mosque in Washington, DC. Things seemed to be on the move for Muslim communities across the country, yet Hashmie Hall grew older, dirtier, and less engaged. Finally, in 1955, a delegation of six young Muslim Americans drove to Michigan City from Highland Park and Dearborn to implore Shaykh Chirri to return with them to Detroit. This group swore allegiance to the shaykh and brought with them pledges from several older community members to support the imam and work with him to fulfill his earlier ambition of building a mosque for the Shi'a of greater Detroit. Chirri acquiesced, returning to Detroit in 1955.[67]

"Here a new phase of the Imam's life began," writes Hussein Makled about Chirri's return.

> God prepared American men and women to help the Imam return to Detroit in 1955. At that time the big *jihad* [effort] began. Prayers were held at Hashmie Hall in keeping with Islamic religious principles. Sunday school was held at the same time. The Sunday school was also copied in Highland Park at the United Syrian Society Club. Imam prepared the community to go ahead. He announced that we must build an Islamic center for the community to help them be proud of their religion like other communities. In 1956 the first council [the Islamic Center Foundation Society] was

established, including eight trustees and the support of many people in the community...At the beginning of 1959, the Imam declared that he would travel to Africa to ask for help to build the Islamic Center, and he got it. Actually, the Imam spent the period from 1956 to 1959 preparing the community to sacrifice, convincing many people that they had the power and strength to build.[68]

Progress on the new Islamic Center went hand in hand with progress at the FIA, an institution that continued to inspire American Muslims and provide them with new opportunities and resources. This progress made the American Muslim community more visible to non-Muslim Americans and to Arab embassies and Muslim nongovernmental organizations; it also attracted the attention and ire of American Zionists, which in turn encouraged the further politicization of many young American Muslims. Detroit's Muslim leaders entered a new period of transnational religious and political engagement, and the FIA became the primary vehicle through which Muslim Americans interacted with Muslim religious and political agencies overseas.

In 1957, the FIA hosted its sixth annual convention in Detroit, the first in Michigan. It was a tremendous success. Over two thousand people attended (see Figures 5.3 and 5.4); the crowd was well heeled and ethnically and racially diverse. The local organizing committee included representatives from the AMS, the American Moslem Women's Society, the AAMS, the Albanian American Moslem Youth Club, the Islamic Center Foundation Society, the Islamic Center Women's Society, the Islamic Youth Organization, the Progressive Arabian Hashmie Society, and the USCS. The organizers were drawn primarily from the new Islamic Youth Organization that Imam Chirri had been active in establishing. The Islamic Youth Organization, while predominantly Arab, was open to both Sunni and Shi'a and included several Albanian and South Asian members. A young Charles Alawan (later Hajj Chuck) was chairman of the convention. Imam Chirri was keynote speaker at the banquet, and Imam Karoub led the Jumaa prayer.[69]

This convention gave the city's Muslims a chance to showcase their size and clout to a national Muslim audience, but it was equally significant because it drew organized political opposition for the first time. Among the highlights of the convention was the refusal of the Detroit City Council president and mayoral candidate Louis Miriani to welcome the conventioneers to the city as planned. He sent a statement to the organizing committee explaining why he backed out of this obligation: "I have no

FIGURE 5.3 Federation of Islamic Associations 1957 banquet in Detroit. Courtesy of Joseph Caurdy. Mary A. Caurdy Collection, Bentley Historical Library, University of Michigan.

FIGURE 5.4 Federation banquet detail. Courtesy of Joseph Caurdy. Mary A. Caurdy Collection, Bentley Historical Library, University of Michigan.

objection to local groups but I understand they are bringing in some questionable people from outside, particularly Washington. These people are anti-Eisenhower, anti-foreign aid and anti-American and therefore I will have nothing to do with the meeting."[70] Local Zionist groups protested the appearance of two speakers who were scheduled to discuss the Palestinian refugee situation, Syrian ambassador Farid Zeineddine, and the director of the Arab Information Center, Fayez Sayegh. The 1957 convention is widely remembered for this controversy and the media storm it generated. "I think it was the first time we, as Muslims, made front page news," Hajj Chuck told me, not without pride. As chairman of the convention, it was Hajj Chuck who addressed the media on behalf of the FIA. "We are stunned," he said, "that the acting head of an American city would refuse to welcome a religious group, especially in a country that is dedicated to religious freedom." He then accused Miriani of "attributing the political beliefs of a few to a world-wide religion."[71] Miriani ultimately did address the conventioneers, not to welcome them to the city but to apologize for snubbing them, although his mea culpa was not granted in public.[72]

Following on the heels of Egyptian president Gamal Abdel Nasser's rise to power, his nationalization of the Suez Canal, and the Suez Crisis, Arab nationalist sentiments were running high in 1957. So Mariani's snub was greeted with humor, rather than offense, by the FIA. "Let me tell you," confided Hajj Chuck, "the Detroit convention was the most profitable, the most active convention they ever had...It was dynamic. It set the pace."[73] Aside from the political wrangling that went on with Mariani and the media, the Detroit convention was like other FIA conventions. "You got religious education. You met other Muslims. You were able to express your opinion in seminars and various things," remembered Hajj Chuck. "You would have a big banquet, but every night you were there you would have dancing and music, socializing. People weren't worried about *halal* in those days, so they would go to the coffeehouses and restaurants around and in the hotel and, hey, it was a fun time. It wasn't overburdened with [pause]...It was more secular."[74]

The public controversy surrounding the Detroit convention is proof of the increasing politicization of the Arab American community after the creation of Israel in 1948, but especially after Nasser came to power and Arabs had a leader to be proud of. The shift in orientation was propelled by forces internal and external to the community. The 1958 FIA convention was held in Washington, DC, and one participant, Joe Caurdy, remembers this event as the first time he was insulted because of his ethnic or religious identity. "I came out of the hotel with another guy I only had met at the meeting, and I had my name tag on, and some guy threatened me and my friend because he saw that we were Muslims. It was probably the first time I was in contact with prejudice against us, and he [pause] he actually chased us down the street."[75] Abdo Elkholy, who was in Detroit in 1959, saw vivid evidence of the changing political mood.

> The Arab defeat in the Palestinian War [1948] aroused the anger of Moslems in America but discouraged them as well. The Egyptian Revolution and the rise of President Nasser to world prominence, however, aroused their sense of nationalism. To Moslems in America as well as in the Middle East, Nasser became the symbol of Arab nationalism. In almost every Moslem home in America there is more than one picture of Nasser. In their social and religious events, the Moslems receive enthusiastically and applaud strongly the songs about Nasser. As a prominent woman in Detroit put it to a Jordanian official accompanying King Hussein during his visit in 1959: "Whenever a party is opened in the name of the Prophet, no one is particularly moved. If it is opened in the name of God, no one cares either. But the name of Gamal Abdel-Nasser electrifies the hall."[76]

During this period, the FIA began to facilitate the tours and public addresses of important Arab activists, diplomats, politicians, and leaders when they visited the United States. Often these scholars and officials stopped in Detroit, courting the support of American Muslims. These networks of patronage and politics worked both ways. In 1959, President

Nasser invited the FIA to hold their convention in Cairo. The American delegation had the opportunity to meet with the president, with the head of Al-Azhar University, and with several religious authorities in the country, and Nasser agreed to send four Al-Azhar-trained imams to the United States to help meet the demand for Muslim preachers in America.[77] He also agreed to offer ten Cairo University scholarships to American students and a scholarship for theological training at Al-Azhar University, all to be arranged and administered by the FIA.[78]

Of arguably even greater significance was a solo trip to Egypt and Jordan taken by Shaykh Chirri on behalf of the FIA, also in 1959. Chirri traveled first to Sierra Leone (where he supported a mission project and hospital), then to Lebanon, and finally to Egypt, hoping to raise money for the Islamic Center. While in Lebanon, he presumably met with his friend and former colleague Mohammed Mughniyyah, who was deeply involved at the time in a high-stakes effort to bring about a rapprochement between the Sunni and Shi'i religious establishments in Egypt, Lebanon, Iraq, Iran, and Syria.[79] This issue weighed heavily on Chirri's mind when he had his audience with President Nasser in July of 1959. He made two appeals to the Arab leader. First, he requested financial support for his mosque, which was granted. Second, he asked Nasser to stand behind the effort to bring about Sunni-Shi'i reconciliation. Mughniyyah had been lobbying Mahmoud Shaltout, the religious leader of Al-Azhar University, hoping Shaltout would use his authority to sway leaders across the Sunni world. After a positive meeting with the Egyptian president, Chirri met with Shaltout (see Figure 5.5) and again discussed the matter of Sunni-Shi'i unity.[80]

The next day, Shaltout issued the following legal decree, or *fatwa*:

> 1. Islam does not oblige any of its adherents to be affiliated with a specific *madhhab* [Islamic school of thought]. Rather, we say: Every Muslim has, first of all, the right to follow any of the legal schools that have been properly handed down and whose rules in their specific (legal) effects are laid down in writing. A person who follows one of these schools is entitled to turn to any other without being subjected to reproach.
>
> 2. In the essence of the religious law of Islam (*shar'an*), it is allowed to perform the divine service (*ta'abbud*) in accordance with the rite of the Jaafariyya, which is known as Shi'a *imamiyya*, in the same way as in accordance with all schools of the Sunni.[81]

This proclamation was likely in the works before Chirri's arrival. It smoothed the way toward a Cold War alliance between the United Arab

FIGURE 5.5 Imam Mohammad Jawad Chirri meets with Shaykh Mahmoud Shaltout at Al-Azhar University in Cairo, Egypt, 1959. Courtesy of Adnan Chirri. Mohammad Jawad Chirri Collection, Bentley Historical Library, University of Michigan.

Republic (the sovereign alliance of Egypt and Syria) and Iran that had little to do with Chirri's visit, but the imam's requests were the occasion on which the announcement was made, and Chirri was thrilled to have played a part in achieving this historic recognition of the Jaʿafari *madhhab*—the Ithnaʿashari (Twelver) Shiʿi tradition of jurisprudence—by the leading cleric of the Sunni Muslim world.[82] This moment of Muslim ecumenical esprit proved to be fleeting, but it was nonetheless a tremendous boost to Chirri's status as a scholar and a political activist among Muslim Americans.

The Islamic Center of Detroit

Home again in Detroit, Chirri was able finally to begin work on his long-awaited Islamic Center, using both the cultural capital and the financial capital he had amassed during his travels. The $44,000 Chirri secured from President Nasser, King Hussein of Jordan, and officials in Sierra Leone for the construction of a new mosque was greeted with wild enthusiasm when he returned to Detroit.[83] This funding, and other financial victories and setbacks, animated much of my conversations with the founders and early supporters of the Islamic Center.

HAJJ CHUCK: You see, when you dedicate and you give your sworn promise to somebody, and you can't buy a pencil. And you take it to $100,000 through hard damn work, and you do it within five years, you know that there is a bond there. You know that there is a commitment. There never has been and there never will be again in this community a group with that kind of fervor. We worked damn hard. There was nothing and we brought it up from zero to the Islamic Center of America. American-born, immigrants, young and old, committed to doing something behind the leadership of one man.[84]

Hajj Makled, describing this process in great detail, reveals the kind of pressure Imam Chirri placed on his supporters.

I still remember one [woman] in Highland Park. She gave $300. And one in Dearborn, bint [daughter of] 'Ali Wajni, she gave $300. And people started to give money, you know, $100 here, 300 there...and we thought about making a little dinner, you know. And the first dinner we made, it was in Highland Park, in that Hall where we were at [USCS], and at the time we collected $8,000. And that was a big news in the community. "Hey, hey, hey...they collected $8,000?" "Oh, those people are really...they mean business. Now it's time to fight 'em."
[Laughter]
So...and I remember the time, I remember the time...uh...Imam Chirri came to me...and he was so close to me and, God bless his soul, he said, "Bismallah [in God's name], $100? You paid the whole $100?"
Well to me, yeah, I paid $100, that's $100. I say, "Yeah, what's wrong with $100?"
He said, "You wanna build a mosque, and you pay $100?"
I said, "How much you want me to pay?"
He said, "Ya 'ayb al shum [Shame on you], at least $300. Let the people see that somebody is payin' some money."
His vision was that it could be done, and it's gonna be done. And then he made the trip to Egypt—that was the breaking point.[85]

Makled's sacrifices went well beyond $300. At one point he took out a second mortgage on both his home and his grocery store to help the Islamic Center Foundation Society secure the loan it needed to purchase a building site for the mosque.[86]

Fundraising was only one dimension of Chirri's project. Chirri also continued to write, publishing essays on Islam for American Muslims, and he steadily (re)introduced Detroit's Shiʿa to their heritage as followers of *Ahl al-Bayt*. When he returned to Detroit, he again took up residence in Hashmie Hall. This time, however, he did not wander the streets at night hoping someone would invite him in for dinner. He did not open the doors for Arabic classes that no students were willing to take. Instead, Chirri worked with Imam Vehbi to develop effective Sunday school curricula and language instruction materials. With the help of volunteers in Dearborn (Hajj Chuck) and Highland Park (Sidney Mashike), Chirri organized serious language and Qurʾanic recitation classes at Hashmie Hall and the USCS (renamed the Moslem Mosque of Highland Park). As Figure 5.6 makes clear, upward of seventy-five children attended these programs at Hashmie Hall, and the mosque became a focus of the religious life of the community in a new way. Both the Highland Park and Dearborn Shiʿi communities now rallied together to back Chirri's vision for a progressive, modernist, and newly visible mosque for Detroit.

On September 20, 1963, eight years after Chirri's return to Dearborn, the gleaming Islamic Center of Detroit was officially dedicated on Joy Road and Greenfield (see Figure 5.7). This modernist white brick structure

FIGURE 5.6 Children at Hashmie Hall perform prayer in 1958. Not solely a musalla, this space could host prayers, lectures, classes, and other events interchangeably. Courtesy of Schrifia Aossey Chahine.

FIGURE 5.7 Opening ceremonies at the Islamic Center of Detroit, 1963. Mohammad Jawad Chirri Collection, Bentley Historical Library.

with a light-filled mussalla seamlessly blended midcentury design with Islamic functionality. The prominent dome above the prayer space was the only overt appropriation of Islamic forms in the design (and not a proprietary form at that). The building included a large social hall, a lecture area (also used for funerals, see Figure 5.8), several classrooms, a large office and library for the imam, a commercial kitchen, and a sizeable prayer space. A minaret was added along with new classrooms in 1966, and the size of the social hall was doubled.

The *Jahaliyya* and the Umma: Before and After Chirri

The establishment of the Islamic Center of Detroit (later "of America," ICA) was a collective effort, but Shaykh Chirri receives the lion's share of credit for leading the building campaign.[87] Moreover, his work is often described using motifs drawn from stories of the Prophet Muhammad's life. Chirri, it is said, came to Dearborn when the community was ignorant, like Mecca was before the Prophet Muhammad received the divine revelation of the Qur'an. As the Prophet was rejected by the people of Mecca and

FIGURE 5.8 Hajj Chuck Alawan speaks in the lecture hall of the new Islamic Center of Detroit, 1963. Mohammad Jawad Chirri Collection, Bentley Historical Library.

exiled to Medina, Chirri was rejected by the people of Detroit and exiled to Michigan City. Just as the umma (the community of Muslim believers) triumphed when the Prophet returned to Mecca and ended its *jahaliyya* (its "age of ignorance"), Chirri's return to Detroit ended the city's *jahaliyya* and ushered in a new era in which Muslims began to live as Muslims who properly understood and practiced their faith. The ICA was the proof and the symbol of this transition.

Hajj Hussein Hamood provided the most careful articulation of this "out of *jahaliyya*" narrative.

> The Islamic faith was not the top important item on their list [in 1949 when Chirri arrived in Detroit]. Even I heard that some Muslims who are really with the Masons or the business, or the Americans or something, they deny to their children that they are Muslims. Some people, you know, because really, they are not praying, they are not fasting, they are not going to the hajj, they are not doing—except if somebody make charity—I don't know. I saw people, and you know it was in the time before. I saw older men during Ramadan they smoke a cigar. Or they go to Camp Dearborn and they make food

outside, you know, on Sunday or something. This is the time before Imam Chirri came.[88]

Images of "the time before" surface repeatedly in Hajj Hamood's narrative. Even Hamood himself was not living as a devout Muslim in "the time before."

There was in the community under ten women who covered their hair and their body completely... I don't have to name anybody, but they were here, and how many men who were here—they are about ten people. Less than a dozen people who are practicing their faith fully while living in Detroit and Highland Park and in Dearborn... in 1949, when I came... I wasn't religious myself. I mean, I had, my wife and I, we produced nine kids, OK. And I was working at Chevrolet here at Axle in the beginning, and I had trouble with the system. I wasn't working right, to tell you the truth. And all I know was running to raise my family, and, thank God, I was able to do that. Four or five of them, five of them, they graduated from college.[89]

After a long digression, Hajj Hamood arrives at the moment when the Islamic Center is fully functioning and Shaykh Chirri has accomplished his goal of producing a Muslim community marked not by ignorance, but by faith (see Figures 5.9 and 5.10).

FIGURE 5.9 Women at prayer, Islamic Center of Detroit, 1963. Mohammad Jawad Chirri Collection, Bentley Historical Library.

FIGURE 5.10 Imam Chirri instructs young Muslims in prayer, Islamic Center of Detroit, 1963. Note Shaykh Kalil Bazzy standing to Chirri's left. Mohammad Jawad Chirri Collection, Bentley Historical Library.

Until Imam Chirri start to practice, and to recognize so many things more than what we do in south Lebanon. You know, we have Eid al Mawlid [the Prophet's birthday], and we have Imam Ali's birthday, and we have the day that the revelation came to the Prophet Muhammad, peace be upon him, and we have Ashura.[90] We were the first ones to—we were about forty people or something like that, less, and I suggested to Imam Chirri to do it for three days [rather than the ten customary days]. Do it on Saturday and Sunday and something like that, because I work afternoons.

He said, "Abu Ali." (I wasn't Hajj.) He said, "Abu Ali, in Iraq and in Iran they make it forty days, and you make it too much for Imam Husayn ten days or something?" And the tenth day is supposed to be in the daytime, you know, and I told him that the people will not come. "You want to make it in the evening?" And he said, "Come on. Are you still with that same thinking?" And the next days, honest to God, Sally, they make it in the middle of the day in the middle of the week, and the people, they filled the entire Islamic Center and the people were standing by the wall. There is nothing that unites the Muslims as much as remembering Imam Husayn.[91]

Hajj Hamood is very clear to point out that this *jahaliyya* included American Muslims, the old timers, the first generation, their children, *and* the newcomers—people like himself and others who arrived after World War II. Many of the practices Imam Chirri introduced, such as these Ashura observances, were unknown to Detroit Shi'a, unknown to their parents' generation, and unknown in most of South Lebanon.[92] Chirri brought these "traditions" with him from Iraq, where he had attended seminary at Najaf, and from the experiences he gained working alongside Shaykh Mughniyyah in Lebanon. These men were not simply preachers of Islam; they were reformers. They had lived in Lebanon during its period of liberation from Ottoman and then French imperial rule. The Shi'a of the South, despite their poverty and disenfranchisement from the Lebanese political process, were now relatively free from persecution and at liberty to explore the possibilities of Shi'i identity in the political context of the modern Lebanese nation-state.

Hajj Hamood, himself a midcentury immigrant, was aware of changes taking place among Shi'a in both Lebanon and North America, a vantage that enabled him to see continuities of class, education, and religious experience between American and Lebanese Muslims. Unlike so many contemporary Muslims, he does not blame the religious ignorance of Detroit's Muslims on their having been isolated from *dar al-Islam* (the abode of Islam, the Muslim-majority world) in the United States. Instead, he attributes the weakness of religious identity and education to a Muslim community that was everywhere unfamiliar with Islam as the Prophet intended it to be practiced. Shaykh Chirri led people away from this ignorance. He brought the Qur'an, hadith, respect for *Ahl al-Bayt*, and credible ways of living as Muslims, bringing *dar al-Islam* to Shi'a not only in Detroit but wherever they might be found.

The Albanian Islamic Center

Imam Vehbi Ismail also saw continuities between the religious ignorance of Detroit's Muslims—in this case the Albanian community—and the spiritual negligence of Muslims still living in *dar al-Islam*. The

Albanian refugees who arrived in Detroit throughout the 1950s were often anti-Communist activists and, like many Albanians already in Detroit, not necessarily interested in Islam as anything more than a political identity. Nonetheless, St. Thomas Orthodox Church and the AAMS were the two anchors of Albanian expatriate life in the city, and Ismail's congregation grew rapidly in the 1950s. By 1957 the congregation had outgrown their small, converted church, which they sold to finance the new mosque they would build from the ground up.

Like Imam Chirri, Imam Vehbi learned a great deal in the 1950s about his new homeland. His English improved rapidly. He traveled frequently, worked with the FIA, raised money for the AMS, and added his voice to protests against the Communist government in Tirana. He came to know and appreciate the older Albanians who had lived in Detroit for decades, and he found thoughtful ways of making Islam relevant to their lives. He focused his intellectual energy during these years on providing basic educational materials to the community. He developed a Sunday school and a youth movement, just as Chirri later did when he returned to Detroit. Ismail used the *Albanian Moslem Life* to circulate his ideas and make them accessible to his congregation. Like Chirri, Ismail was a committed ecumenical Muslim leader. He lectured at the USCS and even led a year of study there for a combined Albanian, Pakistani, and Arab youth group.[93] He collaborated with the Bektashi Tekke as well, participating actively in their holiday celebrations and other festivals, contributing financially to their growth, and writing in the *Albanian Moslem Life* about the traditions and historical figures important to them.[94] When Imam Karoub made the hajj in 1959 and was out of the country for almost a year, Ismail rented the AMS for his congregation and, in effect, led both the Albanian and Arab Sunni congregations during Karoub's absence.[95] He never suffered exile from Detroit, as Chirri had. As a Sunni leader with a strong ecumenical commitment, he was greeted by receptive audiences throughout Detroit's Muslim enclaves.

By the mid-1950s, the *Albanian Moslem Life*, its subscription base limited to Albanian speakers, was losing money. Imam Vehbi found it hard to justify investing further time and money in this project when resources were needed to fund his new mosque. The FIA stepped in and began publishing the magazine in English, redubbing it *The Moslem Life*. Ismail stayed on as editor for eight years, continuing to emphasize the basics of Islamic history, beliefs, and practices, but also publishing lectures and speeches delivered at each year's FIA convention and covering news of the Muslim world from an American Muslim perspective.[96] In 1958, Ismail gave the keynote address at the FIA's annual convention in Washington, DC. His speech addressed several audiences. It was didactic—he began by reminding the audience of the five doctrines Muslims hold in common (belief in the unity of God, in the angels, in the holy scriptures, in the prophets, and in the afterlife) and of their four primary obligations (prayer, alms, hajj, and fasting). It was a political and patriotic speech. Ismail quoted from President Eisenhower's recent address at the opening of the Islamic Center of Washington, DC, and from Jamal Al-Din Afghani, a nineteenth-century pan-Muslim and anticolonial activist. It was also a motivational speech. "Moslems everywhere have begun to wake up," he exhorted. "Everywhere around the world we can be witnessing a kind of renaissance and this awakening also can be witnessed among the Moslems here in the United States and Canada."[97]

While not denying the unique position Muslims faced as a minority community in the United States, Ismail clearly saw their awakening as part of a global pattern. The FIA, he argued, was playing a significant role in moving American Muslims from a state of *jahaliyya* toward one of revitalized Islamic belief and practice.

> During those seven years, the influence of the Federation has entered many Moslem homes and reached many Moslem hearts. It has instilled on many of our youth the spirit and teachings of Islam. Many of us, knowing little about our religion, were not aware of the principles of our faith. Due to this ignorance, some developed a sense of inferiority, a complex which made them feel ashamed of their religious beliefs. This inferiority complex was removed from the minds and hearts of many who learned, thanks to the publications of the Federation, how rational the teachings of Islam are. These enlightened people can now feel proud to be members of the universal faith.[98]

In portraying Islam as rational, enlightened, and universal, Ismail was clearly aligning himself and the FIA with a body of contemporary Muslim writers and activists, many of whom lived in the United States or had studied there (Ismail al-Faruqi, for example) and believed Islam could be a constructive part of the West rather than a tradition that rejected Western societies as inherently anti-Islamic (the view associated with Hassan al-Banna, Said Qutb, and Mawlana Mawdudi). Similarly, Ismail was drawing from contemporary American national sources as well. As the Cold War escalated, American political leaders actively promoted an ideology that embraced religious practice as a means of defeating Communism. In

1952 President-elect Eisenhower made this explicit when he asserted that the advantage Americans had over the Soviets was "a deeply felt religious faith and I don't care what it is. With us of course it is the Judeo-Christian concept, but it must be a religion that all men are created equal (sic)."[99] For Ismail, the ideological implications of faith were especially pronounced. To seal his argument, he drew from the Qur'an, arguing that America's reform-minded Muslims, like Americans in general, understood well that "God does not change the condition of a people until they change their conditions themselves."[100]

Ismail put the FIA's national network to work to support his mission in Detroit. He traveled the country extensively in the late 1950s and early 1960s raising money for his new mosque from Albanian Muslims, FIA member institutions, and Albanian Christians. His efforts enabled him to press ahead with his plans to build the Albanian Islamic Center (see Figure 5.11). Its dedication and grand opening, on November 3, 1963, featured many guest speakers, including Hussien Karoub, Kalil Bazzy, Mohammad Jawad Chirri, Baba Rexheb, Abdullah Igram (FIA founder), Ahmad Mohanna (a visiting imam at the AMS), Abdel Halim Naggar (imam of the Islamic Center in Washington), William Hulber (mayor of Harper Woods, where the mosque was located), Dervish Bagram (from the Bektashi Tekke), and Jack Alli (president of the AAMS).[101] Despite their periodic disagreements and backstage rivalries, Detroit's Muslim

FIGURE 5.11 The Albanian Islamic Center, 2008. Photo by Sally Howell.

leadership found practical ways to support one another in the 1960s, as their population—of imams, of mosques, and of Muslims—grew.

Imam Vehbi's career was a model of transcommunal practice, yet the Albanian Islamic Center was an unmistakably ethnic mosque. The founding board consisted entirely of ethnic Albanians, and Imam Vehbi's sermons were conducted in Albanian and English until the 1980s. The mosque hosted Albanian national clubs and youth associations. It included an active Albanian Women's Association. It was open for weddings, dances, and public meetings.[102] The mosque's facade, which was not completed until 1975, was a distinctly Balkan, Ottomanesque design. The interior, however, was like that of most other Detroit mosques.[103] The prayer space itself was relatively small. No barrier separated men and women. The *qibla* faced southeast. The social hall was much larger than the prayer space, casually appointed, and easily rearranged for multiple uses. The commercial kitchen was appreciated for the Albanian food its cooks (mostly women of the congregation) prepared for guests. The imam's office was the heart of the building. Ismail's office walls were lined with an impressive library of Arabic, English, and Albanian books. Located in the suburb of Harper Woods, the mosque overlooks Interstate Highway 94 and has stood as a symbol of the Muslim presence in Detroit to those entering the city from the north and east since its elegant minaret was added in 1975.[104]

The Albanian Islamic Center, Vehbi Ismail's career, and the relationships that linked both to the history of Detroit's other Muslim institutions have received much less attention from scholars than have the better-known stories of Dearborn's mosques and clerics.[105] This neglect stems largely from Ismail's membership in a small, easily overlooked population of ethnic Muslims. Albanians make up only a tiny fraction of American Muslims today, and in the 1950s their numbers were also small.[106] The Bektashi *Tekke* made a conscientious effort for much of its history to remain separate from Detroit's transcommunal Muslim networks, but the same cannot be said of Imam Vehbi, who not only was an active participant in Detroit's multicultural umma but also worked nationally and internationally on behalf of American and Albanian Muslims. In 1967, for example, he was invited to make the hajj as a special guest of the Muslim Students Association and King Faisal of Saudi Arabia. He was part of a small delegation of American Muslims that included Warith Deen Mohammed, the son of NOI founder Elijah Muhammad.[107] The Saudi government was involved in its own cold war against Egypt and Iran in the 1960s, and they were eager to recruit Americans to their side of this conflict.[108] Ismail, by this time, was on comfortable terms with the Saudis, the more conservative and more decidedly anti-Communist of the two Arab factions. Shortly after he returned to the United States from his 1967 hajj, he was invited to serve as imam of the Islamic Center in Washington, DC.[109] This mosque, built largely by and for the Muslim diplomatic community, had a national profile. Its founders and the leadership of the FIA wanted to make the Islamic Center the leading mosque in the country and to empower its imam to speak as a grand mufti of sorts for all American Muslims. Ismail was surprised and honored to be offered this position, especially given that the FIA was controlled by Arab Americans and the Washington Islamic Center by Arab embassies. Fearful of becoming a pawn in Cold War politics, Imam Vehbi demurred in order to continue his work in Detroit.[110]

Conclusion

When I interviewed Imam Vehbi in 2005, he was eighty-seven years old and in poor health. The moral certainty and optimism that pervaded his 1958 address to the FIA was no longer visible. He did not mention the modern renaissance of Islam, or the movement of American Muslims from ignorance to knowledge and pride. Instead, he emphasized the distance that had opened up between the varieties of Islam his congregation practiced in Harper Woods and the identities embraced by new immigrants from Muslim-majority countries. Located east of Detroit, far from the Arab enclaves of Dearborn, the Albanian Islamic Center began to attract South Asian medical professionals who worked at a nearby hospital in the 1960s. These Muslims were not invited to sit on the mosque's board, which was set aside for Albanian members, but they did contribute actively to the educational and religious activities of the mosque (and to its finances). Many of the newcomers were critical of the religious practices they observed at the Albanian Islamic Center, finding them lax. They questioned whether the Albanians who worshiped there were committed to their faith.[111] "Pakistanis are a little strict," Ismail told me. "Some people take some verses of the Qur'an literally. Some take it meaningly. That is the difference."[112]

These conflicts between already American Muslims and recent immigrants initially focused on how the mosque was used for activities that went beyond the explicitly sacred. When I asked Imam Vehbi if they had hosted weddings and dances at the Albanian Islamic Center in this period, he said, "We had. And we didn't have problems here. Anyone who does not like it can go anywhere else." He explained further: "We, to keep the kids, you know, Sally. We had to have some...entertainment. In place of going to bars and clubs, we see you. And we are more in control here. And know each other, get married together...there are benefits. But we don't let them sing songs that are not morally good." Like Karoub and Bazzy before him, Ismail had come to realize that the social practices of his congregation were vital to the continuity of the Muslim faith in Detroit. "It takes time for [new imams and new immigrants] to understand," he added. "You have to live and rule according to the environment."[113]

Opened within weeks of each other, the ICA and the Albanian Islamic Center had much in common. Their congregations were hungry for the revival of Islam. They were eager to transform the lives of Muslims both in their homelands and in diaspora. They were progressive congregations for the most part and, like the city's older mosques, they were used as social halls as well as prayer spaces. Despite the strong misgivings about assimilation Chirri and Ismail harbored upon arriving in Detroit in 1949, within fifteen years both men had established mosques that resembled Hashmie Hall and the AMS. They had become "American" in ways no one anticipated. Behaviors Chirri and Ismail had once considered moral lapses they now tolerated and even endorsed as vital aspects of American Muslim identity. At the same time, these institutions, with their seminary-educated leaders, provided Islamic instruction based solidly on the Qur'an and Sunna. Their Sunday schools taught age-old doctrines and rituals to American children in ways that were entirely new, yet connected Detroit Muslims to national and international networks of believers and to the historical progress of Islamic civilization.

Like Hashmie Hall and the AMS in the 1930s, the ICA and the Albanian Islamic Center functioned in the 1960s as discursive spaces in which knowledge of Islam could be renegotiated, enacted, debated, objectified, and adapted to changing circumstances. The members of these congregations were convinced, as were thousands of members of the FIA worshiping in scores of American mosques, that they had fashioned a religious identity that was confident, forward-looking, universally recognizable as Islamic, and comfortably American. As "doctors of the soul," Chirri and Ismail had successfully overseen the revitalization of Islam in Detroit, and they did so largely by coming to understand and sanction many of the vernacular practices they had at first condemned.

CHAPTER 6

Homegrown Muslim Leaders

Convergences of Race and Class

THE MUSLIM COMMUNITIES THAT emerged in greater Detroit between 1925 and 1965 were numerically overtaken in the 1970s by new immigrants from the Muslim world. From Palestine and South Lebanon, these immigrants came as refugees and displaced persons. From Pakistan and India, they came as university students, doctors, and engineers. From Yemen, they came as unskilled workers escaping civil war and economic hardship. This growing cohort of foreign-born Muslims was joined by newcomers of a very different sort: African American converts to Islam. Some of these new Muslims had migrated from the Nation of Islam (NOI); they had grown weary of the separatism and military discipline that once drew them to the movement. Other black converts were attracted by Malcolm X's public embrace of Islam and his dramatic turn to internationalism, moves that opened up political and identitarian possibilities that were underdeveloped in the mainstream civil rights movement. Still others came to Islam in prison; through avant-garde arts movements; or through interaction with missionaries, preachers, students, and other welcoming Muslims. In 1975, when Warith Deen Mohammed replaced his father as leader of the NOI, he led tens of thousands of members toward a Muslim faith based more closely on Qur'anic teachings and the example of the Prophet Muhammad.

Large-scale immigration from abroad, new convert communities, and the mass conversion of thousands of NOI followers meant that older Muslim communities in Detroit—some of which dated back to the early decades of the century—would be reduced to minority status. Neither the immigrants nor the converts identified strongly with the historical roots of Islam in the city, and both groups had—or would soon develop—a powerful subaltern consciousness. For them, the United States was a purveyor of economic and military policies that threatened Muslims and people of color around the world. The new immigrants and recent converts often saw themselves, and were often seen by others, as people who had no place in mainstream American political and religious culture. Many of them wanted to maintain this separation. The latter stance was especially hard for the older Muslim community to accept. Not only had they struggled to build the mosques and Muslim organizations the newcomers now vied to control, but they had come to see themselves as Americans in the process. They were deeply offended by the anti-Muslim, anti-black, and anti-Arab prejudice that flourished in American culture, but few of them could believe that Islam and American identity were incompatible. Their own lives had taught them that cultural citizenship was an attainable goal for Muslims, despite the many obstacles in its way.

In previous chapters, I look at the careers of foreign imams who encountered American Muslims and immigrant Muslims who encountered American society. This chapter turns the tables, focusing on two American-born Muslim leaders whose careers were shaped by their transformative encounters with immigrant Muslims and converts to Islam. The first of these figures, Imam Muhammad ("Mike") Adib Hussein Karoub, succeeded his father, Imam Hussien Karoub, as spiritual head of the American Moslem Society (AMS) in Dearborn in 1973, but not without a struggle. The younger Karoub's qualifications for the role of spiritual leader were shaky in comparison to those of Chirri and Ismail. Yet like these madrasa-trained scholars, Mike Karoub championed an Islamic practice that was utterly at home in its American setting. He was inclusive of women's leadership, committed to interfaith education, engaged with the social and political concerns of the day, and resistant to the centrifugal forces that threated to spin Detroit's Muslim communities into ethnic and racial isolation. The second figure, Osman Hassanein (born Oscar Hudson), converted to Islam in 1952 and joined the community of the Hajj Sammsan Abdullah Mosque (later Masjid al-Mu'mineen) in Detroit. This mosque became an "international transit station" for Muslim students studying at Wayne State University and the University of Michigan; for Tablighi Jamaʿat missionaries who began passing through Detroit in 1952; and for others (especially NOI members) who were curious about Sunni Islam, Sufi Islam, and the global community of Muslims. The core congregation of this mosque was African American, and Hassanein was Masjid al-Mu'mineen's longstanding president. Like Mike Karoub, Hassanein steered his institution through the political upheavals of the 1960s and early 1970s with a firm commitment to the transcommunal umma of Islam.

Karoub and Hassanein were friends, partners in faith, and close collaborators in the project of bridging the black-white divide among the city's Muslims. They were also active participants in the national Muslim associations that took shape in this period, the Federation of Islamic Associations (FIA) and the Muslim Students Association (MSA, est. 1963). These institutions, which eventually developed rival missions, connected Detroit's mosques to transnational Muslim organizations that were also active in the Unites States at the time, most notably, the Tablighi Jamaʿat, the Muslim World League, and the Muslim Brotherhood. Like Chirri and Ismail (with whom they also worked), both leaders rejected the new fundamentalisms of the period and their impositions on American Islam. Unlike Chirri and Ismail, however, Karoub and Hassanein lacked academic credentials from the world's leading Islamic universities. Their unaccented English and American-inflected Arabic did not instill confidence in the new immigrants, new missionaries, and new converts who came to their institutions seeking a religious home that was culturally familiar and properly Muslim. Both men faced a crisis of authority.

This chapter shows how the AMS and Masjid al-Muʾmineen were, for a time, exemplars of successful Muslim incorporation. Karoub and Hassanein were prominent actors on a national Muslim stage, and their mosques were sites of transcultural encounter and mutuality in matters of belief and practice. They were also bitterly contested social spaces that absorbed the new politics, Islamist movements, converts, religious teachings, and racial understandings that transformed Detroit in the 1970s. Mike Karoub and Osman Hassanein were already Muslim and already American when this era of radical change began. They and their mosques bore the full brunt of the conflicts that ensued.

Coming of Age: The American Moslem Society and its American-born Imam

In 1952, when the AMS broke ground on its new addition (see Figure 6.1), it was part of a national trend. Plans to add a second floor to the AMS had been underway before Imams Chirri and Ismail came to Detroit in 1949, but the arrival of these young, well-educated imams challenged the AMS to represent itself anew as more than a local social club for Syrian Muslims. This shift in orientation motivated the group to complete their new facility. In 1952, when work on the new prayer space, lecture hall, and office was completed, the AMS was the best equipped and largest

FIGURE 6.1 Imam Hussien Karoub in front of the American Moslem Society, circa 1958, after the expansion project was completed. Essie Abraham Collection, Bentley Historical Library.

purpose-built mosque in the United States. Imam Karoub's longstanding practice of describing the AMS as Detroit's *Masjid al-ʿam* (mosque for all Muslims) finally seemed an accurate description. Despite its location in the Southend—Dearborn's industrial, working-class, and highly polluted ethnic enclave—the mosque drew worshipers from across Detroit and from Windsor, Ontario, especially on Muslim holidays or when foreign leaders visited the community (see Figure 6.2). Yet the AMS lacked a leader who could reflect the progressive, modernist ethos of the period.

Compared to Imams Ismail and Chirri, Imam Hussien Karoub seemed old and out of touch with the larger Islamic world. With their impeccable religious credentials, university degrees, and eagerness to make Islam politically and socially relevant, Chirri and Ismail were popular with Detroit's younger, more educated Muslims, both immigrant and American-born, both Sunni and Shiʿa. Imam Karoub was admired and respected across the country, but in Dearborn he was associated with the status quo, with the older immigrant generation and their vernacular expressions of faith.

FIGURE 6.2 Hussien Karoub leads a holiday prayer at the American Moslem Society, late 1950s with Adil al-Aseer at his side. Walter P. Reuther Library, Archives of Labor and Urban Affairs, Wayne State University.

Karoub was not trained as a jurist, and many of the immigrants on the AMS board did not consider him qualified to render authoritative judgments on Islamic law or to engage in Qurʾanic hermeneutics, skills that Chirri and Ismail both possessed. Imam Karoub did not offer inspirational sermons that drew connections between contemporary life and the example and sayings of the Prophet. Instead, he was associated with the Islam of sock hops, bingo, and basement belly-dance fundraisers—events that had flourished under his watchful eye. These practices had kept young people involved and the lights on, but they had not succeeded, from the perspective of many new immigrants in particular, in creating strong American Muslims who could sustain a minoritized Islam in the United States over time. While Imam Karoub's congregation was willing to be patient out of respect for his years of service, some were nervous about the ambitions of one of his sons, who had long served as his father's apprentice and expected to be named the imam of the mosque upon his father's retirement.[1]

Muhammad A. H. Karoub, "Mike," was born in Highland Park, Michigan, in 1924 to Hussien and Maryam Karoub, the fourth of the

FIGURE 6.3 Mike and Hussien Karoub at work together at Karoub Printing in the 1950s. Courtesy of Carl Karoub. Karoub Family Collection, Bentley Historical Library, University of Michigan.

couple's seven children. Mike grew up working alongside his father at Karoub Printing, typesetting the family newspaper, translating articles from Arabic into English, and eventually writing news stories (see Figure 6.3). He also helped with his father's clerical work, chauffeuring the imam—who never drove—around town and around the country, hosting the constant stream of visitors who made their way to the Karoub home, and facilitating his father's interactions with English-speaking audiences. Mike showed an aptitude for Arabic and Qur'anic studies at a young age, and he pursued a degree in religious studies at Wayne State University on the G. I. Bill after serving in World War II. As his siblings pursued independent careers, Mike was mentored closely by their father, and he gradually took over management of the *Arab American Message* and inherited many of his father's clerical duties. Eventually, Mike Karoub described himself, and was generally recognized by Detroit-area Muslims, as "the first American-born Imam."[2]

This title, although comfortably worn by Mike himself, was a curiosity, and as the Muslim community grew and changed around him, Mike spent a good deal of time defending his credentials to new immigrants who considered the title "American-born imam" an oxymoron. When Alixa Naff interviewed Mike Karoub in 1980, she asked him if he received this "title because of your own education or because of heredity from your father?"

MIKE KAROUB: No. Not heredity. No, no. Nothing is heredity. I got it from my own education. And because...

ALIXA NAFF: Because of your own training as an imam?

KAROUB: Yes, my own training, because I earned it by working, by doing, by being active in it. As I told you, my father and mother used to take me with them. Well, in addition to that my father took me to wash bodies with him at a very young age. I began to do that with him when I was, I bet, nine or ten years old. You know, we have to wash the bodies when...

NAFF: Yes, of course...

KAROUB: So, I was doing that. I was attending the weddings with him. And soon I was performing part of the ceremony with him, because of his English.[3]

Mike's response, which makes no mention of religious studies, would not have satisfied his critics. Even to his supporters, who were mostly American-born Muslims of his own generation and their children, this answer would have sounded incomplete. These Americanized Muslims respected the senior Karoub, and they admired Mike as an exciting public speaker, as a university graduate in a community where such degrees were still uncommon, as a teacher who was truly bilingual in Arabic and English, and as an excellent congregational pastor. He was comfortable with the old, vernacular Islam of his father's generation, but equally conversant with the new, more critical and objectified Islam of the modernists. He was familiar to Muslims of every cultural background in the city, and he brought these different cultural communities together in ways no other imam was capable of. The younger Karoub made the city's Muslims feel connected to each other as members of a specifically American Muslim community. Mike could also explain Islam to non-Muslims, new Muslims, and young American Muslims in a style that was well suited to addressing multiple forms of curiosity, ignorance, and fear.[4]

But to his critics, most of whom were postwar immigrants or college-educated Americans with middle-class ambitions, the modest, service-oriented approach to Muslim leadership that both Mike and his father represented seemed out of place. It came across as outmoded, in the case of the elder Karoub, or insufficiently Islamic, in the case of the son. Furthermore, the "volunteer" status of Detroit's imams was seen as problematic in its own right by new immigrants and foreign students like Abdo Elkholy, who argued that "both sheikhs [H. Karoub and K. Bazzy] in Detroit are said to take advantage of their community by collecting as much money from the members as they can. The community, which trusts neither sheikh, does not pay them [a salary]; thus the leaders charge every individual for the religious services."[5] Speaking of Imam Hussien, Elkholy goes on to say that "the education of the volunteer religious leader can by no means be compared with that of Toledo's [Al-Azhar trained] religious leader [Adil al-Aseer]; his personality too suffers by comparison."[6] As for Mike Karoub, his American birth disqualified him outright in the opinion of many immigrants. His informal manner, English fluency, and American education all placed him at a remove from the textual authority they associated with the 'ulama, the scholarly class of Muslim leaders whose authority lay in their familiarity with *fiqh* (Islamic jurisprudence). One such immigrant, Mike Alcodray, expressed common sentiments when he told me that "Mike Karoub was born here and he did not read or write too much [Arabic]—a very little bit. He couldn't even read the Qur'an in the right [accent]...I used to complain to his father about this."[7] Alcodray's primary grievance against the younger Karoub was that he, like his father, was improperly trained and did not have the authority he needed to guide the congregation.

> I think he was a man-made shakyh, Hussien Karoub, in his village back home. Then when he came here, the son like started learning from his father. He did not go anywhere, Mike didn't, to learn to become a shaykh. This used to bother me a little bit. Right? Everybody want to be a fanatic about things...but really, it was not right for him to participate as a shaykh.[8]

Alcodray assumes here that religious authority is located in the Muslim world, not the United States. If Hussien Karoub was himself a self-made shaykh, this was a matter for past generations of Muslims to reconcile, but by the 1950s and 1960s, when the isolation of the community was still real but no longer an obstacle to finding qualified leadership, "it was not right" for the younger, equally self-made shaykh to replace his father as head of the congregation.

Alcodray, like others I spoke with, made specific comparisons between the city's different shakyhs. Imams Chirri and Ismail were in one category, while Mike Karoub, Hussien Karoub, and Kalil Bazzy were in another. Compared to the scholars, self-made imams like Bazzy and the Karoubs were "relaxed in their teachings." Imam Chirri, whom Elkholy described as "not very popular"—perhaps because he was "without religious flexibility"[9]—was a specialist in *fiqh* whose guidance Alcodray and other recently arrived immigrants found helpful. Equally important was his willingness to shake things up. "Chirri came and started going up and down the street to the coffeehouses and tried to pull these people from playing cards," Alcodray remembered, "and drinking and all that, and every week he used to come on Fridays and try to get them out of there."[10] Chirri challenged the status quo,[11] whereas Mike, like his father, was more accepting and easy going. He was part of the American Muslim community Chirri sought to transform.[12]

The conflict between the Karoub model and that represented by Chirri and Ismail was between two different discursive traditions within Islam— one based on practice and experience, on adjustment to local custom; the other based on correct practice and textual authority, on fluency in an ostensibly more global and standardized Islam. The recognition and working out of this distinction was a classic manifestation of what Talal Asad calls "the domain of orthodoxy," in which one party asserts its right to "regulate, uphold, require, or adjust correct practices and to condemn, exclude, undermine, or replace *incorrect* ones."[13] As we saw in previous chapters, and will see again, this formula played itself out repeatedly in the city's Muslim congregations.

Leading the Charge

When the FIA's annual convention was held in Detroit in 1957, it inspired the AMS congregation to ask themselves serious questions about the future. They had added a dome and minarets to the facade of the mosque in time for the convention. Now they began to consider new kinds of programming. Imam Chirri's return to town, his newly launched Sunday school program, and the talk he generated about building a new mosque added to their sense of urgency. Imam Vehbi was equally active among the Albanians, planning to build a grand mosque of his own. As the representative of the Sunni Arab community, the AMS needed an appropriate response. One plan of action, pursued largely by the American Moslem Women's Society (AMWS), was to concentrate on developing education programs for the young and to ultimately open a parochial school next to the mosque. The other, pursued largely by the all-male board of directors, was to evaluate and improve the congregation's leadership.

Mike Karoub and his wife, Aida Karoub, began working with the AMWS to provide a new and more rigorous Sunday school program in the late 1950s. Aida had arrived in Detroit in 1950 as a Lebanese exchange student at Wayne State University. Aida was brought up in a wealthy Greek Orthodox household in Beirut. She met Mike through his brothers, who were students at the time, and married him in 1951. Aida was still a Christian when she began working closely with her husband at the AMS.[14] The couple had become interested in providing religious instruction for their children. Together with a few leaders in the AMWS, they developed an innovative curriculum that divided the students into three classes, each of which was taught using bilingual curricular materials imported from England.[15] This program, with its illustrated texts filled with age-appropriate stories for children, was markedly different from the mosque's earlier educational efforts. These, according to Sy Abraham, had been "hit and miss" and usually involved one teacher, armed with a ruler, in a room with students of all ages and skill levels engaged in rote memorization of Arabic scriptures.[16] Successful as the program was, Aida confessed that "it was hard for them to have me because, I mean, it was not easy to have a Christian teaching Muslim girls, or the Muslim children at the mosque, Sunday school." She also made clear that few people in the congregation at the time had the skills necessary to conduct such classes "because, first of all, I don't think there were many people who were reading at the time or who know how to read [Arabic]."[17]

Meanwhile, the board of directors began to talk openly about finding a scholar, preacher, and institution builder who was also an Arabic-speaking Sunni, preferably from Syria or Lebanon, to replace Imam Karoub upon his retirement, thereby avoiding the likelihood of Mike Karoub inheriting the role from his father. The AMWS, who generally supported Hussien Karoub's leadership and that of his son, resisted this plan. According to Nabeel Abraham, conflict followed:

The men demanded the "preservation" of (in actuality, a return to) "authentic" Islamic traditions, while the Women's Society insisted on maintaining the status quo. The men betrayed their true feelings when they complained that some of the women were "too aggressive," faulting Imam Karoub for failing to preserve "traditional Islamic doctrine," which they believed resulted in the women's assertiveness in congregational matters. As the head of the congregation, the men reasoned, Karoub could have used his influence and knowledge of "the traditions" (sacred texts) to curtail the demands and independence of the leaders of the women's auxiliary. This had not happened, according to the mosque's male leaders, because the imam lacked sufficient "authority" (i.e., his command of theological and legal matters was wanting).[18]

In fact, Karoub shared the women's commitment to the creative, active use of the mosque as both a social and a religious space. The dome, minarets, and musalla did not prevent this usage; rather, they made it easier to keep secular and religious spaces within the institution separate, while reminding those who hosted social events (like weddings) in the mosque that the facility was also a house of worship and they were participating in the life of the Muslim community by holding their functions there.[19]

The AMWS contributed to the success of the AMS through fundraising events, sponsoring youth activities, paying for construction projects large and small. Ardela Jabara, known as "one of the seven women who held up the church," told me that the AMWS was composed of people "who did all the cooking, all the work, and everything else."[20] Many of these women were pious Muslims who prayed daily, fasted during Ramadan, and educated their children about Islam. They attended the Sunday morning lectures at the mosque with much more frequency than did the men (who were equally more likely to attend Friday prayers).[21] Most of them, however, did not pray regularly but expressed their faith and commitment to the Muslim community through their work for the AMWS. Their identification with Islam was socio-religious in nature, and they met their religious obligations by fostering a healthy social life for local Muslims. They fasted during Ramadan, for example, and broke the fast "with a guest at the table."[22] They cooked for mosque banquets. They organized, hosted, and sold tickets for a popular ethnic festival each summer featuring music, dancing, sack races, and generous amounts of food. They left the "business of running the mosque" to the men, but it is hard to determine which association—the men's or women's—actually raised more money for the upkeep of the institution. Nevertheless, it was the AMWS that began planning to build an Islamic parochial school in the lot next to the AMS, an ambitious and costly proposition (that was never realized).[23]

The financial strength of the AMWS helped empower them in relation to the all-male board of directors. So too did the amount of time and energy the "seven sisters" and many others, like Aida Karoub, invested in the institution. In some ways, these women embodied the mosque and dominated its social agenda, a state of affairs simply unheard of in Lebanon and Syria in the 1950s, where mosques were the preserve of men and even the most devout women tended to pray at home.[24] While the extent of the women's involvement eventually became problematic for the men of the AMS, it was difficult for them to vote against the interests of the AMWS lest they alienate the women, lose access to their fundraising skills, and weaken the institution as a whole. Certainly Imam Karoub, whose most avid supporters were women, made no attempt to restrict their increasingly public role, which he seemed instead to endorse.[25]

This pattern of increased influence for women in immigrant congregations (Christian, Muslim, and Jewish) was common in the United States at midcentury, often because these institutions were responsible for the social reproduction of entire ethnic communities and not just their religious beliefs.[26] Immigrant men, even if they opposed the involvement of women, were seldom able to thwart it. They needed the logistical and financial support women could provide. Empowering women became a survival strategy for immigrant religious institutions.[27] The situation at the AMS was symptomatic of these trends. It also reflected a division between those who had been in the United States a long time (who recognized the vulnerability of the Muslim American community and tended to be tolerant of greater female influence) and those who were more recently arrived (who thought women should not be prominent in mosque affairs, regardless of the role they played). At the heart of this tension were conflicting ideas about how mosque spaces should be inhabited. Would the AMS continue to function as both a religious institution (over which men were thought to preside) and a social club (over which women were thought to preside), or would changing Arab world "norms" reassert themselves in the mosque, now that new immigrants were arriving in Dearborn from diverse points of origin and becoming active in the mosque?

Despite the success of the new Sunday school, and perhaps out of concern over Mike Karoub's growing involvement in the institution, the board of the mosque took decisive action against the Karoubs in 1959. While Imam Hussien Karoub was making his pilgrimage to Mecca, a trip that involved a full year's absence from the AMS, the board voted to lease the mosque to the Albanian Islamic Center, whose new facility was under construction. Imam Ismail would lead prayer services at the mosque instead of the younger Karoub, and most other AMS activities were placed on hold to accommodate the needs of the Albanian congregation.[28] Also in 1959, the FIA annual convention was held in Egypt at the invitation of President Nasser. It was during this convention that Egyptian officials agreed to support the FIA by sending four Al-Azhar-trained Muslim clerics to serve in American mosques. The board of the AMS immediately petitioned the FIA and Al-Azhar to receive one of these scholars/imams. A few months later, Dr. Ahmad Mehanna arrived in Dearborn to assume religious leadership of the AMS. He led Friday prayers, offered special religious classes to augment the Sunday school curriculum, and provided other services in the community as requested. According to Aida Karoub Hamed, this development did not sit well with the Karoub family.

> Certain people at the mosque, certain names, wanted someone from Egypt. His name was Dr. Mehanna. Al-Azhar sent him to teach or to be the imam, and they didn't tell my father-in-law or they didn't tell my husband either, because they thought they were kind of stabbed in the back. I mean especially Imam Hussien, my father-in-law…
> So, I said, "Listen. This is not right what is happening." [29]

Aida did what she could to thwart Mehanna's tenure at the mosque.

> AIDA KAROUB HAMED: I almost quit, but I did not. I just stopped. I wasn't selling tickets. I wasn't doing fundraisers. And there were very few people, and there was no money coming.
> I wasn't trying to hurt him directly. I just stopped working. And when somebody who does all the work stops working…
> SALLY HOWELL: … people notice.
> HAMED: […] My father-in-law went back to the mosque. My husband said, "Since he didn't know English well, I will be in English. He will be in Arabic." We had no complaints. And that is how it stayed… for quite a while. [30]

While Aida takes full credit for having sent Dr. Mehanna packing, she does not mention that he remained in Detroit for the full five years of his contract, leaving town only after it had expired. Nabeel Abraham documents a factional dispute in the AMWS between an Aida Karoub-led slate (which was more likely to be US-born and employed) and a Mehanna slate (which was more likely to be foreign-born and unemployed), a dispute the Karoub faction won. But Abraham makes no mention of the repercussions of this dispute for mosque governance or for Mehanna's tenure there. [31] Despite these tensions, Mehanna got along well with people at the mosque, including Mike and Aida

Karoub, but he was especially popular among newer immigrants, who were impressed by his credentials and authoritative manner, and pleased that the mosque now had a progressive imam similar to the city's other Muslim clerics.[32]

Although Mehanna was in every way the antidote to the self-made Karoubs, he did nothing to curtail the participation of the AMWS in the life of the congregation. It is unclear whether he sought this outcome. He is not painted as a "fanatical" figure or one wanting "religious flexibility." It appears that, unlike Chirri and Ismail, he did little to alter the course of Islamic practice in Detroit. He did not intervene in the management of the mosque or in fundraising efforts, although near the end of his five-year contract, he requested and was denied a position on the AMS board of directors. Apparently, board members feared he would "take over" the mosque.[33] Disappointed in this outcome, which may have affected the status of his work visa and which the Karoubs might have had a hand in guaranteeing, Mehanna went back to Egypt in 1964.[34] Hussien Karoub returned to his position as presiding imam at the AMS, and remained there until his death in 1973.

I asked Aida Karoub Hamed to explain to me how and when Mike Karoub assumed the title of imam.

> His father died and they needed an imam because there was nobody at the mosque. So the board met, whatever board they had at the time. It was a good board, all Bekaai, all people who built the mosque really, and they all said—no women of course—and they decided that, they voted on, they wanted Muhammad Karoub to be imam at the mosque. And then he started the sermons. An imam in Islam doesn't…nobody has to appoint him, nobody has to give him a diploma. He is on his own. It is not like you have to be ordained, nothing like that. Since then, which would have been '73 or '74, he worked a lot. He spoke at every church that invited him. He went and I went too. We went together.[35]

Dearborn's American mosque finally had an American-born imam. Mike Karoub had already transformed the position of imam into one that mirrored the profile of the Protestant clergy, especially clergy from nondenominational, locally autonomous churches, where efficacy as a preacher, teacher, pastor, and fundraiser took precedence over seminary training, ordination, and conformity to a denominational hierarchy. Karoub was famous for performing interfaith marriage ceremonies, even of Muslim women to non-Muslim men, a practice he defended because it brought new families into the faith and wove Muslims more securely into the fabric of an ecumenically receptive America.[36]

In addition to his pastoral responsibilities, Imam Muhammad Karoub was a strong advocate for Muslims in American public life and for Arab political causes. Since 1959, he had been the editor of *The Muslim Star*, the FIA's quarterly newsletter. In its early issues, the *Star*'s pages were filled with news of mosque openings, fundraising campaigns, holiday celebrations at mosques, upcoming conventions, international travel plans of FIA leaders and imams, and marriages and funerals of Muslims nationwide. The marriage announcements, in particular, paint a picture of a community in transition, as fewer and fewer endogamous Muslim unions were recorded over time. In the 1970s, these announcements continued, but were augmented by political commentary and prepackaged news from Pakistan, Palestine, Iran, and Egypt—all of it collated, edited, and published by Mike Karoub.[37]

A Muslim Transit Point in Detroit

"Masjid al-ʿam" may have been located in Dearborn at the AMS, but the center of transcommunal Islam in Detroit in the 1960s and 1970s was 1554 Virginia Park Avenue in a small, centrally located Detroit neighborhood that was home to the Muʿmineen Mosque, the city's first congregation of black Sunni Muslims to officially incorporate. This mosque was founded by an American-born imam who, like Mike Karoub, faced regular challenges to his authority as a Muslim leader. Imam Ismail Sammsan (1894–1970) came to Detroit in the late 1940s (see Figure 6.4), roughly when Imams Chirri and Ismail arrived. No existing congregation of Muslims had invited him to town, but he was inspired by the energy and potential of Detroit's black community and the interest it had shown in the NOI, the Moorish Science Temple, and the Ahmadiyya traditions. He wanted to establish a Sunni mosque on their behalf. In a religious tract he disseminated when he first arrived in the city, Sammsan described himself as "Haj Ismail Sammsan, American citizen, ancestral or lineage, 'Arab,' from the 'Tribe of Shabazz,' birthed in the State of Arkansas, May the 1st, 1894."[38] This reference to the "Tribe of Shabazz" suggests that Sammsan might have belonged to the NOI at some point in his past, but he staked his claim to leadership in Detroit on having made the hajj, having spent time in Egypt, and on his faith in the "universal" brotherhood of Islam.[39]

FIGURE 6.4 Hajj Ismael Sammsan Abdullah, circa 1940s, wearing an *agal* and *hattah* from the Arab Gulf and holding a Qur'an. Courtesy of Akil Fahd.

While on his 1947 pilgrimage to Mecca, Imam Sammsan committed himself to establishing the Universal Muslim Brotherhood of Al-Islam of America. In 1952, he and a small gathering of Muslims who worshiped and studied together raised enough money to purchase a spacious duplex in the once prosperous district of Virginia Park.[40] The house on Virginia Park Avenue doubled as Imam Sammsan's residence and site of the Hajj Sammsan Abdullah Mosque (Islamic Mission), an organization whose name changed several times in subsequent years and was eventually known as Masjid al-Mu'mineen (the believers' mosque).[41] Masjid al-Mu'mineen consisted of a steady stream of new believers, which made religious education crucial to the life of the mosque. Indeed, Islamic teaching was pursued at Masjid al-Mu'mineen with a diligence unparalleled in Detroit's other mosques. The members of al-Mu'mineen had mostly come north during the period of the Great Migration and were thus first-generation Detroiters. Their embrace of Islam represented yet another type of migration, one that placed them at a social remove not only from their home communities in the rural South but from other black migrants to Detroit, who were overwhelmingly Christian.[42] Masjid al-Mu'mineen resembled the city's Arab and Albanian mosques in its strong emphasis on social events and mutual aid. It was a center of political activism for the black and other Muslims who worshiped there, and it had a strong women's auxiliary that held fundraisers, cooked holiday meals, and provided youth recreational programs.[43]

For the people of Masjid al-Mu'mineen, the 1950s and 1960s were years very unlike those experienced by the city's Arab and Albanian Muslims. The economic prosperity of the period led to new opportunities for the white working class, yet, as Sugrue contends, "African American workers bore the brunt of economic change...[with] options limited by discrimination and their jobs threatened by deindustrialization."[44] Given their experience of racism, lack of education, and disintegrating labor conditions, the small congregation at al-Mu'mineen was sympathetic to the nationalist and separatist orientation of the NOI. Their conversion experiences, however, were different in important ways from those common in the NOI. In their decision to embrace a universal religious tradition, Robert Dannin argues, groups like al-Mu'mineen sought to "resolve the historical tensions of African-American society by concluding that liberation from racial domination and spiritual redemption are one and the same. The end goals require an indefatigable dedication to transform oneself and one's fellows."[45] The congregation looked inward to transform the self, and outward as well, linking themselves to a global community of believers.

It was in its openness to the city's other Muslims that Masjid al-Mu'mineen distinguished itself most obviously from the NOI, but the nuances of this difference were lost on the Detroit police and the FBI, whose officers contributed to the group's sense of isolation and persecution. Law enforcement agencies had been interested in the NOI since its earliest days, and they were seldom interested in separating black Sunni Muslims from their surveillance programs.[46] The handful of (now very elderly) black Sunnis who were active in Detroit prior to al-Mu'mineen report that their community was slow to organize not because of its small size or lack of funds but because of the persistent intervention of law enforcement agents, who tried to break up their meetings. In an interview with Akil Fahd, Brother Alahab, whose family was among the first to convert to Islam in Detroit, recalled the elaborate evasive maneuvers the group took in the 1940s whenever they gathered for prayer. They would announce the location at the last minute, shuttling frequently between homes, coffeehouses, and other sites to avoid government informants and other interfering individuals (sometimes associated with the NOI).[47]

This misrecognition by government agents haunted the al-Mu'mineen congregation throughout its history. When the association changed their name in 1964, after an apparent lawsuit and factional split, Imam Sammsan included the following statement of purpose in the organization's articles of incorporation:

> To promote the Religion of Al-Islam in its entirety, as expounded in the Holy Qur'an, and illustrated by the Holy Prophet Muhamad over 1300 years ago. Be it resolved, that the incorporated and members of this corporation are not connected with the Black Muslims, nor any other Cult, at home, or abroad, directly, or indirectly, nor any secret society, societies, or the Communist Party. Be it further resolved, that this Religion of Islam, is not prejudiced towards races, colors, language, or national origin. This great religion Islam, abolishes all invidious and class distinctions, thus lays down the basis of a vast brotherhood, in which all men, women, have equal rights, so much so, that no one can trample upon the rights of another, and all praise is due to Allah! The ruler and sustainer of all the Worlds. [48]

Written after the NOI was targeted by the FBI's Counter Intelligence Program (COINTELPRO)—a covert operation intended to subvert groups ranging from the Black Panthers to the Southern Christian Leadership Conference—this statement is phrased as an antidote to multiple mis-identifications. Imam Sammsan was eager to assert that the Mu'mineen Mosque was not connected to the NOI ("the Black Muslims," an appella-tion given them in 1959 by television journalist Mike Wallace), nor to any other cult of interest to the government, including foreign religious asso-ciations like the Tablighi Jama'at (which is discussed later in this chapter), nor to the Communist Party. To members of the NOI—and perhaps to the city's other Muslims—Imam Sammsan was equally eager to affirm that Islam does not condone racism or other variants of discrimination and prejudice. Sammsan sought to correct those in the black community, law enforcement, and the Muslim community at large who were unwilling to see Masjid al-Mu'mineen for what it was: an American mosque for all Muslims. Such grand disclaimers notwithstanding, the community con-tinued to attract the attention of the FBI until its demise in the late 1970s.

Tahira Hassanein Khalid, the daughter of Osman Hassanein, the mosque's longtime president, was aware that the group's mail was tampered with and that some of the Tablighi visitors and new converts who stayed in the mosque for brief periods were government informants. Quoting her father's reaction to this situation, she said, "Bottom line, the only thing they're gonna see us doing, and I'm gonna be clear about that, is that they're gonna see us praying. They're gonna see us serving dinner. They're gonna see me killin' a goat [slaughtering on the holiday for distribution to the hungry]."[49]

Furthermore, by asserting that "this great religion Islam, abolishes all invidious and class distinctions, thus lays down the basis of a vast brotherhood, in which all men, women, have equal rights," Sammsan was appropriating the dominant ideals of American civil religion (both multiethnic and multireligious), which were promoted endlessly during the postwar era. This ideology produced a narrative of American citizenship that "upheld equality, freedom, and the pursuit of happiness as divinely endowed human rights," even as African Americans were excluded from the rights other citizens enjoyed.[50] GhaneaBassiri has argued that black Muslim leaders like Sammsan and Daoud Ahmed Faisal, a Caribbean immigrant who established the State Street Mosque in Brooklyn in 1947 (and perhaps earlier) and produced similarly worded mission statements, were overlooking the historical realities of racial and social inequality in both the United States and the Muslim world in order to develop a more idealized and egalitarian understanding of Islam for the American context.[51]

While the congregants who identified most closely with the mosque were African American, al-Mu'mineen was also home to foreign students who studied at Wayne State University, to an initially small community of Asian immigrants who settled in Detroit in the early 1960s, and to members of the Tablighi Jama'at, a South Asian revivalist missionary movement whose members began visiting Detroit on lengthy *dawa* (Islamic propagation) missions from Pakistan in 1952.[52] The person most remembered today for lending the mosque its air of openness and welcome was not Imam Sammsan, but Osman Hassanein, who joined the mosque in the early 1950s shortly after his conversion to Islam. Hassanein befriended Mike Karoub during this period, and the two worked together over the next twenty years to fortify the transcommunal Muslim community that Mike's father, Hussien Karoub, had served and sustained since the 1920s.[53] Masjid al-Mu'mineen was an anchor for this diverse, international network of believers, especially those who did not have personal ties to Detroit's largest immigrant and ethnic communities, and for Muslims who wanted to establish ties across these communities.

Al-Mu'mineen's policy of openness came at a price. While its educational programs were overseen by Imam Sammsan himself in the 1950s, and by other converts or Mike Karoub in the 1960s, these classes became increasingly hierachical and culturally biased as foreign-born Muslims (international students, missionaries, and newly arrived imams) asserted their authority over the convert population. This trend had actually been appreciated (and sometimes deemed pedagogically necessary) in the congregation's early years, but for American Muslims who wanted to develop their own understanding of the Qur'an and its relevance to everyday life in Detroit, the domineering style of devout immigrants could be frustrating. Among those who felt most alienated by this was Imam Sammsan himself, who left the mosque in 1964 and founded an alternative congregation.[54] In several obvious ways, Masjid al-Mu'mineen's history parallels that of the AMS. The two institutions, and their two American-born leaders, created an important bridge between Arab American and black (Sunni) Muslim communities in the 1960s and 1970s; in effect, this was a bridge between the histories of these populations as well. I explore this link further, but first it is necessary to consider the intertwined careers of Hajj Osman Hassanein and Masjid al-Mu'mineen.

Journey to the Heart of Islam

Osman Hassanein (born Oscar Hudson) converted to Islam in 1953 at a moment of personal crisis. His conversion was part of a larger twentieth-century pattern in which American blacks were attracted to Islam even though (and indeed because) their conversion made them a double minority. Many scholars of Islam and the black American experience have sought to explain why individuals would decide to compound their stigma in this way.[55] Jackson's list, summarized below, is among the most recent and thorough, borrowing as it does from earlier studies.

1. Islam was both "African" and "Eastern," and came with a non-European language as well.
2. It was not practiced by "whites" (or at least not by Northern European, "American" whites).
3. It was associated with resistance movements that maintained a sharp division between insiders and outsiders.

4. It was tied to a historically significant, non-European world civilization.
5. It was deeply fraternal.
6. Its basic teachings were easy to grasp relative to Christianity.
7. It conformed well to a conservative ethos common in the black community.
8. It included Biblical tropes and language familiar to Christians, and thus was easily incorporated into ideas of redemption and divine retribution already common among blacks.
9. As an object of Western fear and contempt, Islam was attractive to those suffering from displacement and moving toward a separatist political stance.
10. Islam, as practiced by the majority of the world's Muslims, was a non-hierarchical tradition, without a unified body to police or represent its claims and teachings.[56]

Each of these features made Islam attractive to Oscar Hudson, if not when he first embraced the faith, then gradually, over the course of his life as a Muslim. I recount Hudson's conversion narrative because it facilitates a deeper understanding of the role he played in shaping Masjid al-Mu'mineen and the larger public culture of Islam in Detroit.

Oscar Hudson was born in Bishop, Georgia, in 1922 or 1923, during a flu epidemic that left him an orphan at eight months old. He was shipped off to an aunt in Dayton, Ohio, who was neglectful and abusive. His daughter, Tahira Hassanein Khalid, remembers him reflecting on his childhood and asking, "Didn't anybody see me? Couldn't anybody see how hungry, how ragged I was?" "Part of his effort in Islam," she continued, was to compensate for these childhood experiences, "to feed people. That's what he did at the masjid; that's how he got people to come in, allowed them to come in and feel a part of a group." Hudson's extended family eventually took pity on him and sent him to live with a sister in Detroit. There his negative experiences were shaped not by domestic abuse but by the harsh realities of Detroit's Black Bottom. He enlisted in the US Army and fought in the Philippines during World War II in a segregated unit. He was trying to escape conditions in Detroit, but the racial exclusion and discrimination he witnessed in the military humiliated him and led him to doubt his prospects in life.[57]

Hudson returned to Detroit after the war, married, and found work in the foundry at Ford's River Rouge plant. Foundry jobs were the most physically demanding in the factory. They were usually reserved for black workers, and later for non-English-speaking immigrants.[58] Hudson was nonetheless grateful to be paid the same as white workers; he was able to provide a comfortable living to his wife and children. Rather than settle in crowded, "second hand" housing in the city, "houses used up by white people," Hudson purchased a postwar bungalow in a new subdivision of Ecorse, a working-class suburb southwest of Detroit. Plagued by the demons of his childhood and struggling to cope with physically challenging work and a rapidly growing family, Hudson became a chronic binge drinker, which placed a significant strain on his marriage. After tolerating his worsening situation for several years, Hudson's wife gave him an ultimatum in 1952: sober up or leave. The thought of abandoning his three young daughters—as he had been abandoned—brought Hudson to the breaking point, but he was unable to give up alcohol on his own.

One evening, as he came out of the factory gates, he was approached by a Muslim co-worker.[59]

TAHIRA KHALID:...who asked, "What's the matter? You look so unhappy." And Dad, not being himself, [said] "I'm just jeopardizing my family, I gotta stop this drinking. I can't do this anymore." And the brother said, "Well, I've got a group of brothers who are studying another religion," and "we gotta understand our identity. We're not who these people say we are, clowns and animals and all of the things...alcoholics, just lowlifes. Come study with me."

I was five [years old when this happened]. And it was Hajj Sammsan's Mosque at 1554 Virginia Park, and he held classes over there...and they had readings, and they would teach us about Islam, the principles of Islam, that all human beings are created equal, that Allah loves us.

There are tests in life, you know. This was our test. It sort of started to make sense to Dad that you couldn't, in order to be a good Muslim, drink, eat pork. They started laying the laws down, and Dad really tried to struggle with that. They started teaching us Arabic.

In his early years at the Mu'mineen Mosque, Hudson changed his name to Hassanein. "They'd all gotten rid of their names," Khalid said, "because the Sheikh said, 'You have the name of your slave master.' Our last name was Hudson. There were no Hudsons in Africa; that's a Dutch name. So my Dad loved that." He became Osman Hassanein.[60]

Khalid also remembers missionaries from the Tablighi Jama'at leading educational programs during her early years at the mosque. The family lived socially in a Muslim-only environment, one shaped not by race or ethnicity but by religious community. The Tablighis, a transnational Islamic revival movement founded in Delhi in the 1920s, sent their members on *dawa* [missionary] trips, eventually around the world. Tablighis focused their energy on educating other Muslims and reviving the traditions of the faith rather than on converting nonbelievers to Islam. Detroit, with its large and well-known community of Muslims, was a primary target of their American campaigns. By the mid-1960s, Tablighi missionaries were also Arab, African American, African, and Indonesian.[61] A steady stream of Tablighis moved through the Mu'mineen Mosque from 1952 on, staying in vacant rooms in the basement, teaching Islam, nurturing the faith among new believers, and providing a community of support for converts and their families. Graduate students at the University of Michigan and Wayne State University, especially foreign students and their families, were also welcomed at the mosque and in the Hassanein home. They gave the mosque a cosmopolitan flair, linking its members to a network of dedicated, sometimes elite Muslims and the revivalist movements in which they were active.[62]

This period was an intense one for the Hassanein family.

> KHALID: A lot times we would go [to the Masjid] every Friday night; we would go Wednesday nights. Our life revolved around it at that point. On Wednesday nights we'd study Arabic, Friday nights *tafseer* [Qur'anic interpretation] as we understood it, and Sunday you'd have some kind of little meeting. And you had the food. It was emulating [creating a new version of] the families that you had broken away from, not only biologically, but socially too.

This latter point is important. Masjid al-Mu'mineen made a concerted effort to construct a new social as well as religious life for its congregation of (mostly) black converts. Like many immigrants, they sought meaning and a sense of community through mutual obligation, regular social activities, a deep spiritual focus, and the sharing of food.[63]

Despite the warm embrace and intense demands of the mosque, Hassanein was still drinking after several years as a Muslim. "He was, to be very honest, still very tortured about things, the pain in his heart from being an orphan, the racism. So the brothers said, 'You know what you need to do? You need to make Hajj. That will solve a lot of your problems.'" Hassanein made the hajj in 1957, but his travels did not end there. He also made a dawa trip to Pakistan with a group of Tablighis. This trip was one of utter deprivation. The missionaries ate little more than what was given to them as charity, slept on the floor in rural mosques, traveled frequently by foot over difficult terrain, and were not adequately dressed for the cold of a Pakistani winter or the heat of a Saudi Arabian spring. Significantly, Hassanein also had no access to alcohol. The experience was transformative for him. He "shed his skin" on the journey, his daughter told me, and became a new man.

TAHIRA KHALID: Something died there. It was unbelievable. Everybody could see that.

And Dad even said about the racism, he said, "You know? I've come to the conclusion: racism's bad…but as long as you've got a bathroom and some soap, [Laughter] you can deal with it. [He is referring to the hardships he faced in Pakistan.] I'm not really that mad about it. I can deal with this, you know. We have to get out here and vote and get ourselves together."

And around that time, the South was exploding and Martin Luther [King] was coming up, and Dad was all into that.

He said, "I can deal with some racist," excuse me, "white boys. I cannot deal with drinking water out of a tin cup, being in the back— I can't, I just can't do it. We still have more going for us here than they have anywhere in the world. I can work with that."

And he, and then…

SALLY HOWELL: That's an amazing conclusion to come to.

KHALID: But that's the same thing Malcolm [X] came to—that that is part of *this* reality. It is not the reality of the universe. And from what I understand, and Dad would always say, "when you are truly ready for reform, Allah *ta'ali* [on high] will send you something to help you make that reform."

Dad couldn't walk. His feet swelled up trying to go around the Ka'aba [while on the hajj in Mecca], trying to make the different [stages]…especially that one between Marwa and Safa [two stages of the pilgrim's journey]. A white man held him up.

And Dad would say, "Allah sent me something to get out of my madness. He sent a European, the very thing I resented the most, is what kept me on my feet, drug me around."

And they stayed in contact for years until that man died or whatever. I think that man was from Grosse Pointe.

Hassanein's experience of the hajj and living as a missionary in Pakistan changed him into a man who embraced Islam fully, a leader of Masjid al-Mu'mineen, and a cultural ambassador for the foreign Muslim population circulating in Detroit during the late 1950s and 1960s. What he saw overseas helped him place his own understanding of anti-black racism in a new framework. Hajj Hassanein was now ready to explore the "reality of the universe," and he did so by opening his heart, his family, and his mosque to the Muslim community of Detroit.

Brothers from the East: Take 1

Those who were active at Masjid al-Mu'mineen in its heyday describe a facility organized somewhat differently from the mosques in Dearborn and Harper Woods. Instead of collecting dues from members, a few elderly members of the congregation, including Imam Sammsan, rented rooms in the Virginia Park house. Members were also expected to pay their annual *zakat* (tithe or alms) to the mosque.[64] The facility also let out rooms in its basement to Tablighi Jama'at missionaries. With so many residents, al-Mu'mineen was able to approximate the functioning of mosques in many Muslim-majority countries; it could be open for each of the five daily prayers, for religious education classes, and for Friday services. Imam Sammsan was "the big cheese" at the mosque, Haitama Sharieff told me, "but the prayers [in the mosque's later years] were called and led by the brothers from the East." The mosque had an ever changing array of teachers (see Figure 6.5). These included graduate students who frequented the mosque, visiting Tablighis; leaders from the city's other mosques, like Imam Karoub; and the mosque's own imams, who were uniformly African American.[65] These instructors would call the prayers, organize *tafseer* (Qur'anic exegesis) classes, provide Arabic instruction, conduct classes on the history of Islam and the Muslim community, and lead the prayers themselves on a daily basis. The heavy emphasis placed on classes and learning, most of which was oriented to adults rather than children, also set al-Mu'mineen apart from the city's other mosques. Most of the teachers were foreigners or new immigrants, but Hajj Sammsan and other leaders from the local black community also held classes. As a center of Muslim intellectual exchange and transcommunal interaction, there was simply nothing like Masjid al-Mu'mineen in Detroit.[66]

Yet the congregation resembled the city's other mosques in vital ways. Islamic holidays were celebrated on the weekends rather than on their actual

FIGURE 6.5 Hajj Hassanein is seated at the lower right, posing with other members of the Masjid al-Mu'mineen congregation and with foreign students and visitors in 1962. Courtesy of Tahira Khalid.

day, due to the work and school schedules of the congregation. Sunday services and Friday evening services took precedence over the *Jumaa* congregational prayer. The women's auxiliary played a significant role in raising money for the mosque, and it did so through hosting bake sales, picnics, and banquets (see Figure 6.6). The American women of the congregation would bring collard greens and fried fish or chicken, while the Indian and Pakistani women would bring biryani, lamb, and other "eastern foods."[67] The mosque hosted funerals and, less frequently, weddings. The facility was occasionally rented out for social functions (see Figure 6.7). There were not enough children for the congregation to have regular Sunday school classes. Instead, families like the Hassaneins attended programs at the AMS, and others were taught in the homes of mosque volunteers.[68] Families with children and teens frequented al-Mu'mineen partly to provide an alternative to the social problems of the era, as was common at the city's other mosques. The congregation was small, with roughly thirty families who were active in a sustained way from the 1950s through the 1970s. Many of the mosque's most active members were male converts who were single or whose families were not Muslim. Scores, perhaps hundreds, of

FIGURE 6.6 Advertisement for a 1973 fundraising dinner at Masjid al-Mu'mineen. Note the bi-cultural options available. Mohammad Jawad Chirri Collection, Bentley Historical Library.

foreign university students, travelers, and new immigrant families also attended the mosque during these years.[69]

After his return from the hajj, Osman Hassanein became a leader of Masjid al-Mu'mineen, serving as its president from 1958 until his death in 1977. In this capacity he engaged actively in the extra-mosque activities of the Muslim community in Detroit. "What happened was people started coming through Mu'mineen Mosque—guess the word got out, and Dad started traveling and meeting more people . . . and what brought us together, um . . . we lived in Ecorse, so we studied a lot in Dearborn," Tahira Khalid remembered. She described studying with Mike Karoub and with Dr. Mehanna. Hassanein spent more and more of his time with the Karoubs, with Imam Chirri, and with the growing population of Indian Muslims who came to Detroit as students. According to Saleem Khalid, Hassanein's son-in-law, these interactions were part of a larger effort to support Muslim social life in Detroit; they were intensely personal, but they had a practical purpose.

I think if you talk to many of the immigrant doctors in the suburbs around here, as graduate students, my father-in-law would go and

FIGURE 6.7 Members of the Women's Auxiliary posing before a birthday celebration at Masjid al-Mu'mineen, 1967. Courtesy of Tahira Hassanein Khalid.

buy meat, halal meat before there was East Dearborn and [halal] markets in the Eastern Market, and he would butcher the meat—he was a butcher—and he would cut the meat and distribute it to gradu-ate students here. So some of these individuals, if you mention his name, their face just lights up, because they remember him not only as a person who was involved in the mosque, but even on a more personal level as a person who came to their homes, brought them meat, and saw to it that as students they were taken care of when they were just making their adjustment, coming from wherever they were coming from to Detroit. He was that kind of person.[70]

Hassanein was also pulled into FIA activities. The pages of *The Muslim Star*, the FIA newsletter Mike Karoub edited and published from 1966–1980, regularly featured announcements from Masjid al-Mu'mineen: news of weddings and funerals, holiday celebrations, fundraising events, and lectures or special services provided by visitors from overseas and from mosques and Muslim associations across North America. However, because of their close association with students at Wayne State University and with the Tablighi Jama'at movement, Masjid al-Mu'mineen also devel-oped a close relationship with the MSA.

The MSA was organized in 1963 by foreign students on the campus of the University of Illinois-Urbana. The group originally sought to counter the secular, socialist-leaning Organization of Arab Students, which had organized a few years earlier to advocate on behalf of pan-Arab nationalism. The MSA was a much more conservative organization. It focused on providing religious support and a religious forum for Muslim students at a time when there were very few mosques in the United States and campuses provided little accommodation to religious minorities of any stripe. As expatriates, the organization's leaders were explicitly political and identified with the Muslim Brotherhood in Egypt (a group that opposed Nasser's leadership and was violently suppressed by Nasser's regime) and the Jama'at-i Islami (a similar revivalist movement that was periodically suppressed in Pakistan). They were adamantly opposed to Nasser, Socialism, Communism, and (much of) American foreign policy. Like the FIA, the MSA included Muslims from diverse cultural backgrounds (which added to its political difficulties), but it was majority Arab.[71]

In 1966, the group held its annual convention at the University of Michigan (a center of secular Arab student activism during this period).[72] Detroit's strongly FIA-identified mosques welcomed the students to town, and the convention banquet was hosted by Masjid al-Mu'mineen (see Figure 6.8). Hajj Hassanein was among the key Detroit organizers of the convention. He arranged for visiting students to stay with local Muslim families, a move he saw as both a cost saver and, more importantly, an opportunity for cross-cultural exchange.[73]

For the first several years of the MSA's existence, the group was on cordial terms with the FIA. Each organization sent representatives to the other's annual meetings, advertised their publications in one another's journals, and cooperated on fundraising. Yet as Nasser's power grew in the 1960s (and his suppression of the Muslim Brotherhood escalated in turn), the FIA's leadership openly celebrated and courted the Egyptian regime's attentions, accepting money, scholarships, and clergy from Al-Azhar; sending regular delegations to Egypt; and holding multiple conventions there—actions that offended MSA leaders.[74]

This political wedge opened up deep ideological differences between the two organizations. The MSA leadership identified not only with the founder of the Muslim Brotherhood, Hassan al-Banna, but with the movement's then active intellectual star, Said Qutb. Qutb had studied in the United States in the late 1940s, an experience that contributed greatly to his political philosophy. He was extremely critical of American materialism, social injustice, violence, mistreatment of Arab immigrants, support

FIGURE 6.8 Mr. and Mrs. Osman Hassanein (third and fourth from the right) at the Muslim Students Association banquet in Detroit, 1966. Haitama Sharieff and her husband Haleem Sharieff are fourth and fifth from the left. Note that the three men on the left, wearing fezzes, are the only ones in attendance who signify their faith by covering their heads. Mohammad Jawad Chirri Collection, Bentley Historical Library.

for Israel, immorality, and hollow religiosity.[75] His critique of the United States resonated with many foreign Muslim students, most of whom had no local mosque like al-Mu'mineen to help them deal with culture shock and homesickness. Qutb also advocated for the overthrow of much of the political establishment of the Muslim world and the creation of new societies managed according to the precepts of the Qur'an and Sunna. He described the Muslim world as languishing in a state of *jahiliyya* (ignorance, see Chapter 5) under the domination of the secular and anti-Muslim West.[76] He spent most of the 1960s in jail and was executed in 1966 for allegedly attempting to overthrow Nasser's regime. For Muslim intellectuals who supported Qutb's vision of an Islamic "renaissance," like many of the MSA's more active members, events overseas intensified their sense of isolation in the United States. They considered themselves the vanguard of a new Muslim political movement, and they began to lose patience with the FIA and its longstanding institutional dynamics.[77] The FIA leadership took a very different position, as did the leaders of Detroit's mosques. These American Muslims were less critical of American values overall and tended not to see Islam and America as irreconcilable. While they were vocally opposed to American support for Israel, to the Vietnam War, and to anti-black racism, the FIA was less critical of Arab national governments and did not advocate for Shari'a law over the institutions of secular and civil society.

As the leaders of the FIA and MSA came to know and understand each other, their relationship quickly soured. MSA leaders were critical of the formal dances and youth mixers that were a part of FIA annual conventions. They also resented the attention given on the convention program (and in FIA publications) to representatives of the Supreme Council of Islamic Affairs (the Egyptian Ministry of Al-Waqf) and the newly established Muslim World League, a nongovernmental organization established by the Saudis in 1962 to promote Islam throughout the world, but also to further the policy concerns of the Saudi regime (which was closely aligned with US political and corporate interests in the region).[78] The MSA was equally critical of Muslim American institutions like those found in Detroit, where attendance at daily prayers was low, Jumaa prayers were de-emphasized, women's auxiliaries exerted genuine leadership, weddings and dances were held in mosques (MSA and other newly arrived immigrant critics did not distinguish between the social halls of mosques and their prayer spaces), and women came and went from mosque facilities (again, not the prayer spaces) wearing the latest fashions and with their heads uncovered.[79] In the 1970s, as many of these students received professional degrees, settled permanently in the United States, and were joined by a new migration of Muslim immigrants, the FIA-identified American Muslims were quickly outnumbered. Their mosques became sites of contention between conflicting views of Islam, of America, and of the relationship between the United States and the Muslim world.

The FIA responded to its MSA critics by expanding the array of services, especially religious services, it provided. In 1976, for example, the group instituted an annual "Islamic Mid-Year Seminar" that was held in January and was "devoted entirely to religion" rather than to social and political concerns. In addition to presenting lectures by clerics like Adil al-Aseer (imam of the mosque in Toledo, Ohio), Mohammad Chirri, Vehbi Ismail, Mike Karoub, and several others, these meetings continued to feature representatives of the Muslim World League[80] and the Egyptian Supreme Council of Islamic Affairs. The FIA also opened an office in New York City in 1977. Led by Dawud Assad, a Palestinian American activist, and linked closely to the Muslim World League in New York, this office handled complaints about discrimination and media misrepresentation of

Islam and Muslims, coordinated FIA communications and membership affairs, served as a nonvoting member of the United Nations, and advocated for the Palestinian national movement.[81]

In the 1960s and 1970s, Egypt and Saudi Arabia competed actively for the support of American Muslims. They did so by sending Muslim clerics and scholars to the United States, supporting new mosque construction (especially after the Arab Oil Embargo of 1973, when the price of oil sky-rocketed and the Saudis became cash rich), sponsoring Arab American delegations to the Middle East, hosting African American delegations on the hajj and *umra* (off-season, lesser hajj), and providing scholarships to Muslim American students for study at religious institutions in Egypt or Saudi Arabia. The Jama'at-i Islami, the Tablighi Jama'at, and the Muslim Brotherhood, although not as wealthy as the Egyptian and Saudi governments and their competing nongovernmental organizations, also actively recruited American Muslim support for utopian religious and cultural projects. Each of these groups was especially interested in wooing African American Muslims, both within and outside the NOI, whom they saw as open to ideological and spiritual influence in ways Arab and other Muslim immigrant communities were not. The groups also sought to influence American politics and culture via these relationships.[82] Some of this financial investment in American Muslim communities and institutions was channeled through the FIA and the MSA, which encouraged a further split between the two as they jockeyed for control over financial resources and devalued each other as "fanatics" and "extreme conservatives," or "too liberal," "too ethnic," and "un-Islamic."

Given Masjid al-Mu'mineen's close ties to the Tablighi Jama'at, local Muslim students, and the city's older Muslim populations, tensions between the MSA and the FIA became increasingly consequential for the mosque. For Tahira Khalid, the rift first expressed itself during her interactions with the MSA at Wayne State during her college years. "A lot of that was still culturally driven by the Arab students who came here and needed something to belong to," she said. "So, you know, it was pretty much male driven. There weren't a lot of women... and they instituted the same policies that came up [elsewhere]," polices that excluded women from leadership positions, enforced the *hijab* [Muslim headscarf and modest clothing] at MSA meetings, and made it difficult for women like Tahira to participate freely.[83] Azira Maeh also tried to join the MSA when she was a student at Wayne State University and felt equally unwelcome, both as a mixed-race person whose Asian origins were questioned and as an American Muslim whose religiosity and identity were challenged.[84] Tahira was invited often by MSAs in the area to speak, but never to join or participate in local chapters.

The ideological tensions between the FIA and MSA also surfaced in al-Mu'mineen's educational programs. Tahira and Saleem Khalid spoke of Mike Karoub and Adil al-Aseer (see Figure 6.2) as men central to their religious education who had encouraged their participation in a large, politically active, and universal community of Muslims.[85] Like Mike Karoub, al-Aseer taught at al-Mu'mineen in the early 1970s. "He came up and he would conduct classes on the weekend," said Khalid, "and I can remember sitting in a number of his classes. He was a trained Islamic scholar, and when I say that, I believe he was actually an Islamic judge back in Palestine. He was an extraordinary Islamic scholar." To Tahira Khalid, these credentials were meaningful, but given her longer familiarity with the politics of the Muslim community, she was equally impressed by al-Aseer's ability to work with people rather than against them.

TAHIRA KHALID: I loved Imam Adil al-Aseer. That was a sweet, that was an incredible, human being. He was Palestinian, and he truly knew the law as well as the Book. Some people know one or the other, but he was diplomatic with his interpretation and he understood our illnesses, too.

[He] was the epitome of scholarship, *hafiz* Qur'an [had memorized the entire Qur'an], who came and taught us, who wanted to smooth the edges out of our understanding. A lot of the things we learned from the Pakistanis were cultural. They really, some of it wasn't Islam. Like, [they claimed that] we didn't have to cover our heads because we were in America. And that wasn't Islam, you know. But that's what maybe they believed, and I'm not sure that everybody who came to us was a scholar. They might have jumped on the Jama'at bandwagon and just came and started teaching folks. That's what Sherman Jackson says in his book. Have you read the *Third Resurrection*?[86]

SALLY HOWELL: Yes.

KHALID: That's a very powerful analysis . . . of what happened. Sherman got it down. That's what happened. We assumed because they were Arabs, [or Pakistanis] they weren't black, they weren't white, they knew what they were talking about. That wasn't always true. And what they did was they talked us out of a lot of our identity. "You shouldn't be doing this; you shouldn't be doing that. That's not Islam." Well, you're doing it, you know. I mean, we can't dance but y'all doing the *dubkeh* [Levantine folk dance]? That's as much shaking, you know.[87]

Despite the fact that Adil al-Aseer and Mike Karoub, teachers Tahira Khalid greatly admired, were Arabs, she (like others in the black Muslim community) began to question the relationship between a universal Muslim faith and particular human cultures. Sherman Jackson, whom Tahira Khalid mentions glowingly, argues that, as immigrant Muslims came to outnumber black Muslims in the 1970s, they assumed a "virtual monopoly over the definition of a properly constituted 'Islamic' life in America."[88] Jackson's claim is made in reference to African American Muslims, but this "monopoly" was felt by non-black Muslims as well. Hajj Hassanein was uniquely positioned to resist this monopoly because he understood that immigrant Muslims were by no means homogenous and that the Islam they preached was not uniform. Islam in Detroit had come to resemble other American religious traditions in that it now operated in a climate of outright competition.[89] Masjid al-Mu'mineen was a marketplace in which competing ideas were aired and evaluated.

This religious marketplace, though rich in doctrines, was poor in dollars. In addition to the diplomatic challenges Hajj Hassanein faced in navigating the factions that vied to dominate Islam in Detroit (see Chapter 7), his congregation entered dire economic straits in the early 1970s. The neighborhood around al-Mu'mineen declined quickly after the Detroit Riots of 1967. One of the incidents that triggered the riots occurred at the corner of Virginia Park and Woodward Avenue (at the Ambassador Hotel), and the white flight that was exacerbated by the 1967 uprisings devastated the formerly middle-class Virginia Park neighborhood, as it did much of the city. The black middle class suffered another blow after the 1973 oil embargo, when Detroit's auto industry—and Michigan's economy as a whole—experienced a major recession and further de-industrialization.

Anti-Arab and anti-Muslim sentiments were expressed openly in the wake of these events.[90] Masjid al-Mu'mineen was not immune to this prejudice. The Virginia Park neighborhood block club turned on the mosque in this period. The house was zoned as a duplex, not as a house of worship or boarding house. Tahira Khalid explained the neighbor's newfound "curiosity" in the following way: "You would see, you know, people with all these different garbs run in, run out. Who knew? Islam wasn't that big of a factor until recently." The city stepped in and sought to evict the residents of the mosque, citing several building-code violations as well as zoning issues.[91] Suddenly, the group was in need of a new facility at a time when their middle-class members were largely retired, the younger generation was largely unemployed, and their non-black affiliates from the MSA had begun to build mosques of their own in the suburbs. It was Hassanein's friends in the FIA who advocated on the mosque's behalf with leaders of the Muslim World League and the government of Saudi Arabia. In 1977, the Muslim World League donated $10,000 to the mosque, which granted it a small reprieve in its Virginia Park home, and in 1978, it received $60,000 for the purchase of a new building.[92] Unfortunately, the check came too late for Hassanein. He died of a heart attack shortly before the mosque's economic crisis was resolved.

After Hassanein's death, the congregation tried to reorganize under the leadership of his son-in-law, Saleem Khalid. They sold the old house and purchased a storefront facility on Detroit's west side, but it was soon clear that many of Detroit's younger black Muslims would not be joining al-Mu'mineen in its new location. They were already praying in several alternate congregations, each with its own mix of domestic and foreign-inspired doctrinal controversies. Saleem Khalid, in his new role as imam, was not as deft at balancing the demands of local and visiting Muslims as his father-in-law had been. Chapter 7 shows how the clash of cultures, the clash of orthodoxies, and the clash of social and political agendas eventually tore Masjid al-Mu'mineen apart.

Brothers from the East: Take 2

The transitional conflicts that beset Masjid al-Mu'mineen in the 1970s also played out at the AMS in Dearborn, a well-established mosque that was already familiar with contests between new and old immigrants, between competing orthodoxies, and between worshipers with very different understandings of the mosque as an American religious institution. The Syrian-Lebanese families who built the mosque and had sustained it since the 1930s were now confronted by a faction of "brothers from the East" not unlike those who first supported al-Mu'mineen and later contributed to its demise.

Abdo Alasry was one such brother. He came to Dearborn from Yemen in 1967, when he was twenty-two years old. His impression of the Southend, the AMS, and the Muslims who populated the neighborhood and the mosque was not positive. "The institution was very bad. If you looked at it from a [Muslim perspective], lot of people they do not practice Islam. They do not pray. It doesn't matter. You could not make a difference between them and other people, you know. Lot of them. You might see a few people practicing Islam, but the majority, no. You see gambling places. You see bars. They have alcohol, a lot of places. Also they had some Arab people being killed in this area, too."[93] Saleem Khalid, from a very different perspective, argues a similar point: "The Dix mosque [AMS] didn't have life. It was totally different from what you see today. It was a place that was opened and closed. Al-Mu'mineen was a different way. People came to Detroit and they asked for the Mu'mimeen Mosque; they didn't ask for the Dearborn mosque."[94]

By the mid-1970s, the population of Dearborn's Southend neighborhood was tipping again toward the foreign born. An urban renewal campaign waged by the Ford Motor Company, the City of Dearborn, and Levy Asphalt had sought (unsuccessfully) to destroy the neighborhood and business district where the AMS and Hashmie Hall were located and to rezone the area for industry.[95] Many of the longtime residents of the neighborhood were bought out by the city and moved to more attractive parts of town. They were replaced by a new, post-1965 immigrant cohort made up of Lebanese, Yemeni, and Palestinian autoworkers, many of them recently displaced by the Israeli Occupation, related political instability in Lebanon, or the independence movements and civil wars that beset North and South Yemen in the 1960s and 1970s. Echoing patterns from the early twentieth century, the newcomers who settled in Dearborn were often bachelors or married men whose families remained in the homeland. Their religious needs and expectations were different from those of the already established congregation at the AMS, which was now predominately American-born. The mosque's board and Mike Karoub, who took over as official imam in 1973, were nervous about the new demographic reality. Karoub wanted a position on the mosque's board, a permanent status that would give him job security, especially as newcomers expressed increasing exasperation with his English-language sermons. He also wanted to wield more power in the institution in opposition to his (and his father's) longstanding rivals.[96]

Nihad Hamed, an Egyptian engineer who was voted in as mosque president at about this time, also sought to have the bylaws changed, so the president of the board could serve a four- rather than one-year term. The idea behind both efforts was to provide continuity for the mosque's existing leadership in a period of obvious demographic flux. Finally, Aida Karoub also suggested that the bylaws be changed so that voting membership in the organization would no longer be open to anyone who was willing to pay the small membership fee. As many of the older Syrian and Lebanese families from the Bekaa Valley left the

Southend, those who stayed were becoming a minority among the new-comers, whose criticisms of the mosque grew louder with each passing day. Aida's plan was to exclude recent immigrants from mosque governance. The board, however, opposed any changes to the bylaws. They feared the influence of Hamed and the Karoubs, who frequently sided with the AMWS against the all-male board in the numerous internal conflicts that beset the mosque. Some on the board clearly appreciated the conservative, old-world values expressed by their newest members and sought to harness the immigrant critique of the Karoubs and the AMWS for their own ends.[97]

While the AMS board debated its bylaw controversy, Tablighi Jama'at missionaries based at Masjid al-Mu'mineen began visiting the Southend neighborhood with greater frequency.

> ABDO ALASRY: The people start coming from there [Masjid al-Mu'mineen] and they start going to the places, to the coffee shops, the stores where the people go. Sometimes they go even to the bar to talk to the people. They do this until 1976, and then some of them start talking to some of the people who are in charge of this mosque, the Lebanese people.
>
> Some people told him [Nihad Hamed], "OK, can we have the key for the mosque? Can we have the key so we can open the mosque and go inside and pray?"
>
> He said, "Yes, we can issue you a key, but you have to pay the bill." Because at that time the society was very poor.[98]

The board agreed to let the new worshipers use the mosque, but only if they would pay rent to cover the costs of power, cleanup, and building maintenance. It struck the newcomers as odd that they should have to pay a fee to pray in the mosque or hold religious classes there, but they agreed to do so. This arrangement was similar to how the social hall of the mosque was rented out for weddings and other parties. Those observing memorial services at the mosque often took up a collection for use of the facility as well.[99] "Back then," Alasry explained, "they used to open up on Friday, and every weekend to teach the kids because they have schools."[100] Otherwise, the mosque remained closed. For men like Alasry, who came from countries in which mosques were never closed and never charged fees, this behavior was inexplicable.

While the newcomers did not complain about the fees, they did complain about the lack of a formal Jumaa congregational prayer at the mosque and the overall laxity of religious observances there. As their complaints escalated into demands, Hamed devised a radical strategy to fend them off. He organized a meeting of the city's Muslim clerics and scholars and asked them to issue a formal edict—to "make *shura*," as Alasry put it— declaring Sunday a legitimate substitute for Friday as the day of congregational prayer for the city's mosques. This consensus of the scholars was then to be accepted as binding by the community as a whole. "Of course, the imams and the scholars are not going to ask for this," Alasry assured me, "to move the prayer from Friday to Sunday. I think it was the members, because the majority does not have knowledge. They want to have it on their day off. To them, they said, 'OK. Everybody can come on Sunday, we'll have the meeting on Sunday.' "[101] The Shura Council rejected this suggestion outright,[102] and the mosque began (or returned to) hosting formal congregational prayers on Friday in addition to their Sunday lectures. Even this positive outcome was problematic for the newcomers, however, because Mike Karoub offered these services in the English language. The prayer itself was led in Arabic, and the Qur'an was read in both languages, but the sermons were in English. Furthermore, Karoub's sermon topics were often offensive to the newcomers; one memorable sermon was given in defense of abortion rights.[103]

If this clash can be viewed as a conflict between competing visions of Islam, one that was confidently American and well adapted to its local environment and another that was not yet American and still uncomfortable in its new setting, then it is clear that the compromises the AMS made to accommodate the Shura Council's ruling would not suffice. The issue of rescheduling religious observances for the weekend resurfaced later that year on Eid al-Adha, which fell on a Wednesday. The English-language faction planned to celebrate the eid on the weekend, as they always had. The Arabic-language faction expected to celebrate the eid on Wednesday. When they showed up at the mosque and demanded to be let in, they were turned away by Hamed and others on the board. "Today is the eid," Alasry remembers the *musalee'een* [those who would pray] crying. "We have to pray today. Today is eid." Eventually, the *musalee'een* broke the lock on the door and went inside to pray.[104]

Shortly after this conflict, another took place that ultimately doomed the Lebanese congregation at the AMS. On this occasion, a Friday evening, the Yemeni faction was hosting a class upstairs in the mosque, and the Lebanese faction was hosting a dance downstairs in the social hall. The building was not soundproofed, and the loud, raucous music was disruptive to the group gathered upstairs. They continued with their class, but when the *adhan* was called for the evening prayer, they expected the music to pause for the prayer itself. When it did not, the upstairs crowd became angry and asked the others to stop the music so the prayer could be conducted in peace. Their request was denied. The Lebanese felt their right to hold a party in the social hall of the mosque was being violated. The Yemenis felt their right to hold a prayer in the mosque was being violated.[105] After this incident, the *musalee'een* decided to take over the mosque's board. In 1977 they elected (Hajj) Fawzi Mura'i president of the AMS board. Hajj Fawzi was a Palestinian from Beit Hanina, a West Bank village on the outskirts of Jerusalem that had been taken over by Israel for the construction of one of its earliest and largest settlements. He was a very conservative Muslim, sympathetic to the Muslim Brotherhood and a staunch supporter of Palestinian rights. His election—by a Yemeni-dominated but culturally diverse block of voters—marked the end of nearly forty years of Lebanese control over the mosque. The two groups attempted to use the mosque jointly, but the new board quickly solicited a new imam from the Muslim World League and established a new set of rules for the mosque.[106]

Imam al-Barakani, a young Yemeni who was trained in Saudi Arabia and spoke little English, was eager to impose a strict regime on the AMS. Mike Karoub again found himself marginalized within the institution, but he continued to provide his Sunday lectures at the mosque. Al-Barakani provided the *khutba* (sermon) for the Friday prayers in Arabic. The Abraham family described to me how the other changes unfolded:

MIRIAM HASSEN: We [had] taught Sunday school for about ten years and then they wanted us to stop.

SHARON KORHONEN: They wanted us to stop the social functions.

SALLY HOWELL: Including the Sunday school?

HASSEN: The Sunday school wasn't "proper."

SY ABRAHAM: When they became a majority of the men's club, they voted everybody out and put their own people in. Then they decided that they wanted to be strictly a mosque. No more dances, no more weddings.

HOWELL: And the Sunday school was somehow inappropriate?

ABRAHAM: Well, they wanted it conducted in a certain way.

HASSEN: It had to be in Arabic. It had to be taught by the right persons.

ABRAHAM: They did not like the ways of the Lebanese Muslims.

HASSEN: No functions. No kids.

HOWELL: Scarves on the women?

ABRAHAM: Yes, they started that. Basically, they started a conservative mosque.

HASSEN: The whole reason they built the upstairs was for prayer and the downstairs was supposed to be social. And they said this was not right...and then they wouldn't let women go upstairs at all.

KORHONEN: I used to get on that rug and pray.

ABRAHAM: Not anymore.[107]

The new rules included gender segregation in all the mosque's activities, including Sunday school classes and congregational prayers. Women had to wear the hijab at all times, everywhere in the building. This hijab could no longer be a simple scarf to cover the hair; it had to cover all parts of the body except the hands, face, and feet. All social functions hosted by the AMWS were banned from the premises. When the women's group protested these moves, the young imam told them, "I am here to teach you the right way; you have gone astray."[108] When the women protested further, they were banned from the mosque outright. The two groups went to court over these new restrictive policies. Abdo Alasry, who was president of the mosque board at the time, explained the court case as follows:

ABDO ALASRY: The reason is, I will tell you, because they [the Lebanese Americans] had their own way. And the people who are coming [the *musalee'een*], they have their own way also. Like before, they have the sisters, they want to come to the masjid like outside. And this is unacceptable, because this is not a club.

SALLY HOWELL: So what do you mean "like outside"? They didn't cover their hair?

ALASRY: Yes. That is the main thing. And we went to the court too, because [they] told the court, "They won't let us go inside." And the women said this.

I was then the president of the society, and we, one brother from Egypt also, asked the judge, "When someone comes to the court, he is supposed to have certain dress?"

He [the judge] said, "Yes."

"Ok," [he explains] "sister, even the judge said you have to have [appropriate] attire...when you go to the mosque."[109]

The other side argued that the mosque itself was one room in the larger facility and appropriate religious attire was observed historically in that room alone. But the judge, siding with the new board, asked the Lebanese faction to turn over their keys to the building. "In the beginning," Alasry explained, "we were ok with them. We said, 'You have the key, you can go in anytime. No you cannot make dances, and [wear short dresses].' They may make a wedding with no problem, but not like with dancing as it used to be in a club. Not in a mosque... belly dancing, that is what I mean. That's why we don't want it here. We couldn't. We said, 'That is not right.' "[110]

A club, a community center, a place for education, and a place for prayer and worship: for the mosque's founders these functions could coexist with minimal conflict and had done so for decades. For the *musalee'een*, however, some of these activities polluted the mosque, degraded its status, and interrupted (perhaps even rendering moot) the religious functions that took place there. Alasry understood the pain this transition imposed on the mosque's founders. "You know, back then they didn't want to [follow the new rules]. It was very hard for them. They had hard feelings. If you tell them put a scarf on your head, it is like you shot them with a gun. They don't want to do it."[111]

I responded, "They did feel that the mosque was their home."

"It was in the beginning, and nobody could deny it," replied Alasry. "But this is not just a home for them or for me or for you or for anybody. This is the house of Allah. And we have to respect that, too."[112]

Conclusion

It is no longer politically correct to speak of human migrations in the language of nature, to describe immigrant waves, or floods, or swells. Yet in the 1970s, this is precisely how immigration from Lebanon, Yemen, and Palestine; from Pakistan, India, and Bangladesh; and from Jordan, Iraq, and Syria was perceived by the older African American, Arab, Albanian, and Asian populations in Detroit. The new immigrants brought demographic power and significance; they brought new teachers and believers to the area's mosques; they brought new resources, new marriage partners, and a renaissance of Arab, South Asian, and Muslim identity. They also overwhelmed the existing Muslim American community numerically. Detroit's "American mosques," built by *already American* Muslims, drew new immigrants to the city and initially welcomed these newcomers with open arms. Yet new immigrants often reacted to Detroit's mosques just as Imams Chirri and Ismail had done a generation before: with disapproval. Many saw the gender dynamics; the reluctance to celebrate holidays and

Jumaa prayers at the appointed times; and the use of mosque spaces for dances, movie nights, and other social functions as American, illegitimate, un-Islamic, scandalous, even *haram* (forbidden by Islamic law). Often the immigrants saw the Americans worshiping and working in these mosques as Muslims in name only. They had hoped the city's mosques would offer them a safe retreat from American values, which they found poisonous and threatening; they wanted their mosques to be spaces of reflection, prayer, and religious study.

Many of the *musalee'een* who took over the AMS in the 1970s were young, single men, or men whose wives and families were still in Yemen or Palestine. They did not consider the education of children at the mosque a priority. They did not have American wives who might want to pray at the mosque, or socialize and participate in religious classes there. These newcomers, when they finally wrested control of the mosque from its founders, established a set of rules that struck the already American Lebanese congregation as foreign and culturally Other, as extreme and unnecessarily conservative, as un-American, un-Islamic, misogynistic, and fanatical. These two factions judged one another not just in religious terms but in political and cultural terms as well. By waging their campaign in a language of moral and religious absolutes, the *musalee'een* foreclosed on negotiation. The mosque remained, as it had always been, a space in which Muslim American identity was debated, enacted, and embodied. But under its new immigrant board, Detroit's Masjid al-ʿam was committed to the systematic rejection of the Muslims who had lived in the city for almost a century and had created the infrastructure of communal life that was now so hotly contested. The takeover of the AMS was a paradigm shift that established a new regime, one not of incorporation or accommodation but of confident orthodoxy and (initially at least) principled separation from the larger society.

Detroit's homegrown Muslim leaders, Imam Mike Karoub and Hajj Osman Hassanein, were pushed aside by these new forms of Islamic practice and belief. Hassanein passed away just as this transition from old to new Islams was unfolding in the city's congregations, but Karoub, and the comfortable approach to Islamic education and practice he had developed over a lifetime of service to Detroit's diverse Muslim communities, did not disappear. Karoub remained a popular figure among many blacks, second- and third-generation Arabs, and the older Turkish and Bengali immigrants and their descendants. He continued to preach throughout his life, eventually moving his printing business and ministry to a small storefront on the outskirts of Highland Park. There he continued to publish the newspaper that he and his father had established in Detroit. He traveled across Michigan and the Midwest performing weddings, funerals, and *mawlids*; leading holiday celebrations; guiding new believers toward the core tenets of the faith; speaking out to non-Muslim audiences in churches, schools, and government offices; and advocating on behalf of Palestine, racial justice, and human rights.[113]

Cast out of the institutional homes of the AMS and Masjid al-Mu'mineen, the old Islam practiced by the Karoub and Hassanein families was not extinguished, but it did become less visible. The voices of homegrown Muslim leaders were less frequently heard. The AMWS, still in possession of their savings account, was able to open a new, smaller mosque in 1982. Tucked inside a former warehouse on a quiet side street (Chase Road) in the Ford Woods section of Dearborn, the group was no longer eager to be thought of as Masjid al-ʿam, as a place of welcome to the area's larger transcommunal Muslim population. They named their new mosque the American Muslim Bekaa Center, in an explicit reversion to their initial launch in the 1930s. The mosque's interior—its social hall, lecture hall, and prayer space all sharing the same multipurpose room—also represented a return to a previous way of inhabiting mosque space. English-language sermons, Sunday lectures and congregational prayers, high school graduation parties, and wedding showers were all equally at home there.[114] This new mosque was founded by a non-Arab woman, a convert to Islam, Essie Abraham. Women at the Bekaa Center did not enter the building through the back door, segregate themselves from the men in any of the mosque's functions except prayer, or allow others to dictate when and how they should cover their hair and bodies. The group's tight-knit Lebanese American board also resolved to maintain control over who could become a voting member or serve on the center's board. When they reconstituted themselves, they did so without their American-born imam, Mike Karoub, his former wife, Aida, or the board president many of them blamed for the loss of the AMS, Nihad Hamed.[115]

The cultural, political, and religious revolutions that overwhelmed and revitalized the Muslim American community in Detroit and across the country in the 1970s brought about changes that seemed radical at the time. Many Muslims retreated to congregations that protected them from the religious and cultural mainstream. Others, like the congregation of the American Muslim Bekaa Center, retreated instead from the apparent dogmatism of the new Muslim population. The cohort of leaders who had worked so diligently to stitch the American Muslim community together in the postwar period—Imams Chirri and Ismail, the Karoubs and

Hassaneins, and the FIA—were pushed aside by a younger, more energetic set of actors whose beliefs and practices would soon come to define mainstream Islam in Detroit. Like their predecessors, this new vanguard intended to live as Muslims in the United States, reterritorializing Islamic discourse and practice in the process. This work of normalization would require new moral commitments and shared political effort across many of the same boundaries the old Islam had struggled to transcend.

CHAPTER 7 | Raising the Bar
Movements of Revival and Change

BY THE EARLY 1980s, the Muslim American establishment was dominated by post-1965 immigrants, a population consisting largely of "students and professionals whose cumulative resources far outstripped those
of their Blackamerican [and other American] coreligionists."[1] The Muslim Students Association (MSA) launched the North American Islamic
Trust in 1973 to help finance new mosque construction. In 1981, the MSA
established the Islamic Society of North America (ISNA), an organization whose mission was to build mosque communities, help parents raise
American children, and manage the flow of resources between Muslims in
North America and those living abroad. The Federation of Islamic Associations of the United States and Canada (FIA), of which MSA activists
had been extremely critical, was quickly marginalized by ISNA and its
rival association, the Islamic Circle of North America (est. 1971). This
proliferation of new Muslim representative bodies at the national level
corresponded to a resurgence of institution building at the local level. In
cities where two or three mosques had once sufficed, suddenly there were
six. Congregations that, over a span of decades, had come to be dominated
by American-born Muslims were filled once again with immigrants, and
African Americans were converting to Sunni Islam in larger numbers than
ever before.

Hajj Eide Alawan, whose family arrived in the United States in the early
twentieth century and helped establish both Hashmie Hall and the Islamic
Center of America (ICA), described these transformations as radical.

Shaykh Chirri had been trying to get us to practice Islam at this level.
[He holds his left hand a foot above the table between us.]

And we were getting there.

[He raises his right hand about three quarters of the way.]

We weren't there yet, where he wanted us to be, but we had a clear goal
in front of us and we were making progress.

Then, Shaykh Berry [another Shiʿi cleric who arrived in 1980] came,
and he raised the bar.

[Hajj Eide's raises his left hand another foot above the table.]

He raised the bar. And a lot of people, they simply couldn't do it. They
simply walked away. A lot of us didn't want to do it. We didn't think
it was right.[2]

Hajj Eide's lament is common among older Detroiters who grew up in the
ICA, the Albanian Islamic Center (AIC), Masjid al-Muʾmineen, or the AMS.
Despite nostalgia for the mosques of their youth and sometimes bitter grievances with the institutions they attend today—over women's roles, dress
codes, the hosting of social functions, and the proper observance of Islamic
rituals in mosques—this older generation of Detroit Muslims realizes that
the dynamic, highly diverse Islamic city they now live in would not have be
possible without the large-scale conversion of African Americans and the
arrival of tens of thousands of new Muslim immigrants. They also realize
that these historical shifts have, in effect, marginalized their own religious
sensibilities and reformed (often for the better) their practice of Islam.

The clash between new immigrants, new convert populations, and
already American Muslim congregations that swept the country in the
1970s and 1980s is an ongoing process for a religious community in which
immigrants and converts continue to outnumber American-born Muslims
who are not converts.[3] For this reason, it is very important to stress that the
radical changes in religious thought and practice I explore in this chapter
were not uniformly the work of converts, nor were newly arrived immigrants always the driving force behind Detroit's Islamic revival movements.
The grandest, most significant revolution of the period took place within the
Nation of Islam. When the NOI's leader, Elijah Muhammad, died in 1975,
his son Wallace Deen Muhammad (who changed his name to Warith Deen
Muhammad in 1980) promptly set about modifying his father's teachings.
He rejected the divinity of W. D. Fard Muhammad (founder of the movement) and abandoned the NOI creation myth, in which white people are portrayed as the devilish creation of an evil scientist named Yaqub. By disposing
of these doctrines, Warith Deen Muhammad led the NOI closer to a Muslim
faith based on the Qurʾan and Sunna, and he did so with the explicit support
of transnational Muslim organizations like the Muslim World League and

the Muslim Brotherhood. At Muhammad's Temple #1, this bold transition was entrusted to a Syrian immigrant named Mazen Alwan. In the prayer space of this historic mosque, renamed Masjid Wali Muhammad in 1976, an American-born imam and a "Brother from the East" collaborated to bring about a new Muslim American practice and consciousness.

For other African American Muslims in Detroit, both those at al-Mu'mineen and those outside it, the bar of piety was raised as well, not by new immigrants or the authoritative voice of a powerful leader but by the clash of religious ideals. The Dar ul-Islam Movement, the Tablighi Jama'at, and various Sufi orders came together to both counterbalance the weight of Muhammad's Temple #1 and offset the self-declared authority of the city's Arab and Albanian mosques, in which white middle-class comforts took precedence (or so it seemed) over living in accordance to the Qur'an and Sunna. The competition for Muslim adherents in the 1970s was fierce, and the opening up of niche markets produced more selective, more nuanced, and more extreme forms of religious expression and consumerism.

At the ICA, the upheavals that mattered most in the 1970s were those taking place overseas. The Islamic Revolution in Iran, the Lebanese Civil War, and the Israeli occupation of South Lebanon brought thousands of immigrants to Dearborn, increasing its visibility as a Muslim stronghold and dramatically altering the practices and beliefs of Shiʿa and other Muslims in greater Detroit. These changes were embraced and resisted by Imam Chirri and his ever-contentious congregation. Rather than acquiesce entirely to the doctrinal and political demands of Lebanese Shiʿi revivalists, the ICA spun off several rival mosques. These institutions were places of spiritual refuge for immigrant Muslims who were impatient with the slow pace at which Imam Chirri imposed gender segregation, new dress codes, and other corrective regimes.

Non-Muslim Americans were also busy constructing new religious and political identities in response to the post-1965 immigration, the youth counterculture that had grown out of opposition to the Vietnam War, the civil rights movement, Roe v. Wade, and second-wave feminism, to name only the most prominent social issues. New forms of orthodoxy and novel conflations of religious identity, ethnicity, and politics congealed in the 1970s, especially among white ethnic Catholics and white evangelical Christians. And, as American interventions in the Middle East increased throughout the 1970s and 1980s, images of Muslims replaced those of Vietnamese guerillas on the evening news. Frequently, Muslims were represented as angry and violent (in the street demonstrations of the Iranian Revolution), as manipulative and greedy (during the Arab Oil Embargo), or as homicidal and anti-Semitic (during Palestinian guerilla attacks at the Munich Olympics). The political objectives of Arabs and Muslims—most Americans could not distinguish between the two—were consistently represented as at odds with the stated foreign policy goals of the United States.[4] The revolutions of the period, at home and abroad, compelled American Muslims to once again see themselves as religious outsiders and to assume that they would now have to work together to resist both political marginalization and, in cities like Detroit, the forms of assimilation that had defined much of their collective past.

Finally, Detroit and its suburbs were also in transition. In 1974, Coleman Young was elected the city's first African American mayor. Young was well respected when he first took office, but his administration could not slow the white flight that became a stampede after the 1967 riots. Deindustrialization and decentralization had both contributed to Detroit's rapid population loss. In 1950, the city's population peaked at nearly two million. In 1960 it stood at 1,670,000. In 1970 the number had dropped to 1,514,000, and in 1980 Detroit's population was 1,203,000. In just thirty years, the city had lost 750,000 people.[5] High unemployment, failing schools, declining property values, and a steady decline in the number and quality of public services hit the city's remaining population hard. Meanwhile, the suburbs continued to expand, and the steady flight of capital, jobs, and other resources to sites outside the city confirmed the widespread belief that Detroit, as a place and an idea, was broken—perhaps beyond repair.

Americans turned to new religious absolutisms in the wake of these crises. The era of multiculturalism and "the culture wars" was about to begin. For Detroit's Muslims, the 1970s and early 1980s were years in which earlier forms of transcommunal cooperation and institution building came rapidly to a close. The city's mosques moved in new directions—cultural, religious, and political—and not all of Detroit's old Islamic institutions, or the American Muslims who worshiped in them, were willing to travel down these unfamiliar paths.

From Nation to Universe

With the passage of civil rights legislation in the 1960s, the NOI gained a modicum of mainstream acceptance. Its commitment to "separation and self-reliance, which was deemed deviant and subversive in the 1940s, 1950s, and early 1960s was tempered as a message of ethnic pride, black community-building, and self-help" in the 1970s.[6] Muslim Americans were also more willing to engage with the NOI. The highly publicized, largely successful effort to bring Malcolm X into the fold of Sunni Islam was undertaken by lay Muslims, religious scholars, and activists in New York City, many of whom were aligned with the Muslim World League. Similar efforts, directed at members of the NOI and other hetero-dox African American groups, played out in temples and mosques across the United States.[7] Leaders at Muhammad's Temple #1, the founding con-gregation of the NOI and home to some of its most dedicated members, resisted dialogue between their congregation and Sunni and Shi'i Muslims with threats of violence and exile.

Hajj Benjamin Hogue, who joined the NOI shortly after graduating from high school in 1949, moved cautiously between Detroit's African American Muslim groups in the 1960s and 1970s. He remembers this time as one of little shared ground between the NOI and its local rivals. Like many members of Muhammad's Temple #1, Hogue had moved to Detroit from the Deep South. The institutionalized anti-black racism he encoun-tered in the North angered him, and he was frustrated by his inability to "find answers" in Christianity. "We had a rather militant organization then," he told me. "The members of the Fruit of Islam [the NOI's unarmed, but well-trained security officers] had a strict code of behavior and...so that attracted a lot of attention and that attracted me. I felt that we needed more discipline in our community at the time. Too many things were going on that were not beneficial to the community, so it was attractive. It was an effort to clean the community up. That is what was attractive at the time, I think, to most people."[8] Anthropologist Zain Abdullah argues that "while the NOI...offered 'a gospel of black redemption,' it was the job of the Fruit to embody that message for the masses," a point Hajj Hogue clearly confirms.[9]

Like other recruits in the 1950s, Hogue had explored Communism and other forms of ideological dissent, but the NOI brought him into a tightly knit organization that offered an alternative to the contempt and hopelessness he saw on the streets of Detroit. As Edward Curtis has argued, the strong emphasis on ritual in the NOI created a powerful moral community committed to a distinctive, intensely ethical way of life.[10] Following the lead of Elijah Muhammad, Hogue refused to reg-ister for the draft in the early 1950s and was sentenced to six years in prison as a result. It was in local prisons that Hogue studied the teachings of the NOI; to a lesser extent, he also acquainted himself with the Qur'an and the history of Sunni Islam. Hajj Hogue's Muslim identity empowered him tremendously in prison, and he became a minister to NOI members who served time during the 1950s or joined the movement from their prison cells. He worked closely with interfaith activists and prison officials to gain recognition for the NOI as a faith community, enabling the group to meet together; order relevant literature; receive visits from NOI ministers; and—after at least one riot—monitor prison kitchens to ensure that the food served did not include pork, lard, or other forbidden ingredients.[11]

While Hogue was a dedicated member of the NOI, he began to question the isolationism of the movement after his release from prison. He was especially concerned about the boundaries its leaders drew between the Nation and other Muslims in Detroit:

> Me and several of the other brothers in the movement began to read the Qur'an and other Muslims started coming around us. They would come and say "*salam alaykum*." They wanted to know what we were coming from, but after they came around us, we began to find that there was a difference, a rather significant difference in how we interpreted what was going on. And I guess that is the period when Warith Deen came along, when he had already been pretty much rejected from the Nation because of his views that certain things that were being taught were not Qur'anic teachings. And so he spent a period of time, and I guess some of the rest of us did, who began to realize that some of the things that they were practicing in the Nation were not actually Islam. We went and visited other Muslims. I used to visit the mosques in Dearborn. There used to be one on Joy Road and Evergreen over there. That was the Shi'i movement [the ICA], but I didn't know the difference at the time. We used to go over there and listen to them talk.[12]

Hogue also spent time with the congregation of al-Mu'mineen in the years before Warith Deen assumed leadership of the NOI.

> Some of us just wanted to learn more. We went on our own and visited these places. There were some groups that felt that we should have been denounced, the one group I think it was called the Dar [Dar ul-Islam]. They wanted to have us excommunicated. They told us we weren't Muslims; created friction. Actually we had more of a problem with the other African American communities than we did with the immigrant communities.[13]

Muslims outside the Nation felt this hostility in reverse. "They would never let us into the place on Linwood when Elijah Muhammad was alive: never, never, ever," recalled Selim Yusuf, now an imam in the local Tijani community. "Elijah Muhammad would say, don't listen to us [Sunni Muslims] because what we were doing was like magic to drive them [NOI members] crazy...because literally some of them came to the mosque and prayed with us."[14] Imam Yusuf went on to describe the fate of an NOI follower who studied Arabic and Islam in Lebanon, and was otherwise well educated, but was destitute when Yusuf met him in the early 1970s. The man had been exiled from the NOI, "because they said he knew too much about the language, and he wasn't using it the way the Messenger, Elijah Muhammad, wanted him to."[15]

Benjamin Hogue also ran afoul of the leadership of Muhammad's Temple #1 when he began to explore alternate versions of Islam, reading the Qur'an on his own, studying Arabic at Masjid al-Mu'mineen, and attending Jumaa prayers there.

BENJAMIN HOGUE: She used to go down there [to Temple #1] a lot, my wife, and they would ask her what was I doing. I think they liked me; they just wanted me to conform, and I wouldn't conform. I'm not very good at bending once I take a position.

Well, I wasn't accepted among them [the NOI]. They had a tradition then. They called it putting you in a certain class where you weren't allowed... like an exile, per se.

SALLY HOWELL: This is the same thing that happened to Malcolm X.

BENJAMIN HOGUE: Yeah right. Exactly. A system where you are not allowed to associate or socialize with the people.

HOWELL: [I direct a question to the Hajj's wife, Halimah.] Were you also shunned?

HALIMAH HOGUE: Well, not exactly, but I didn't go [to Temple #1]...

BENJAMIN HOGUE: Because they were questioning her all the time about what was I doing, and she just got tired of it. More or less, they just wanted to see her to keep track of me for some reason.

HOWELL: And did you go to all the other mosques with him, the immigrant mosques or al-Mu'mineen?

HALIMAH HOGUE: I went wherever he went.

HOWELL: And what was your experience in those places?

HALIMAH HOGUE: I enjoyed it. I mean, I like the religion. And they taught us a lot. I didn't mind dressing and going to hear [their imams]. I was [also] alright at Temple #1 until that last time, when I went back and they started questioning me about him.[16]

Detroit's NOI temples were a bulwark of financial support for the movement. They produced avid recruits for the Nation's elite corps of ministers and for the Fruit of Islam. Members of Temple #1 were proud of their status as the birthplace of the NOI and site of the Sister Clara Muhammad University. They fondly celebrated the "pioneers" in their ranks, the early and now elderly members of the Nation who still attended in large numbers. And, in keeping with their stalwart reputation, temple leaders made it their policy to chase off "brothers from the East" and their African American "imitators" (mostly Sunni Muslim converts), who sought to proselytize among their members.

The exile of Hajj Hogue was difficult for his family. They sent several of their children to the Sister Clara Muhammad School and relied on NOI networks for employment opportunities. Hogue himself had sacrificed much to the movement, serving several years in prison because of his adherence to NOI principles. Like others who had spent decades in the Nation, the Hogues valued the security and sense of purpose they found at Temple #1. The Nation fed them when they were young, poor, and rejected by their families. It gave them work, and the Fruit of Islam and Muslim Girls Training prepared their bodies and minds for a new, more disciplined way of life. Hajj Hogue was respected as a teacher and leader of the movement in Detroit. His place near the center of this tightly knit group made his exile especially painful. The warm hospitality Hogue received from Osman Hassanein and others at Masjid al-Mu'mineen seemed, for all these reasons, even more important to him and his family. Unlike the Dar ul-Islam mosque in Detroit, where divisions between the Nation and other Muslims proved insurmountable, Hajj Hassanein "was interested in us really learning Islam."[17]

Hogue's desire to explore Islam outside the sanctioned spaces of the NOI was motivated by several not uncommon critiques of the movement. In the early 1970s, Elijah Muhammad was gaining credibility as an alternative to the more radical voices of the Black Power Movement. His "do for self" economic programs were creating wealth and upward mobility for the movement's leadership and for its core community in Chicago. In Detroit, however, these socioeconomic gains were less noticeable. Derrick Ali, now an imam at the Muslim Center of Detroit, explained the situation succinctly: "Elijah Muhammad's economic development plans depended on the centralization of the organization in Chicago. The periphery sent money to Chicago."[18] Inevitably, this unequal tributary flow led to resentment. The Messenger traveled in a private jet, but his followers in Detroit were struggling financially and their garages were filled with unsold copies of *Muhammad Speaks*, the NOI newspaper they were forced to hawk on the city's streets, often in direct competition with other members of the movement.[19] For Hajj Hogue, the centralization of NOI resources in Chicago was not simply a matter of financial disparity.

> I left the movement when it got to the point that, to me, the Nation wasn't accomplishing what we wanted it to do. Because it was too... They formed a clique, a group that appeared primarily to be interested in maintaining their own power structure. They surrounded Elijah with that group, and you couldn't have access to him. They made all the decisions, and in some cases we felt that those decisions were not in the best interest of the community. They were in the best interest of maintaining their power structure.[20]

When Elijah Muhammad died on February 25, 1975, his son Warith Deen Muhammad assumed control of the NOI and began to reconcile its teachings with those of other Muslims.

The shock of this sudden break with tradition was especially painful to NOI pioneers and lifelong followers of Elijah Muhammad in Detroit. Yet many disgruntled NOI members were ready to see Warith Deen lead the community in a new direction. Those who had already left the movement to interact with other Muslims in the city were now positioned to help reform a community they considered heterodox and from which they felt increasingly estranged. Integrating these separate worlds would prove to be a momentous challenge. When it came, the transition was striking. In Figures 7.1–7.4, a visual record of this change is captured through the lens of Brother Shedrick El-Amin, who joined the NOI in the 1960s and has served as the community's unofficial photographer in Detroit since the 1970s. Among the most obvious changes in these before and after photographs is the shift from sitting in chairs facing a podium with men and women in sections alongside one another, to the more traditional mosque-like pattern in which men listen to sermons while sitting on the ground facing the *qibla* and women are located behind the men. Whereas uniformed NOI officers (African American males) address the gatherings in the earlier photographs, in the later images a Syrian immigrant without a uniform (Hajj Mazen Alwan) instructs the congregation. This reconfigured space, no longer a temple modeled on Protestant sanctuaries and UNIA lecture halls, was renamed Masjid Wali Muhammad. Alwan served as the masjid's imam during its initial reorganization (1976–1977), then as its principal religious teacher until 1986.

FIGURES 7.1 AND 7.2 A 1974 meeting at Muhammad's Temple #1. Note the use of chairs, the head coverings of the women, and the uniforms worn by speakers. Photos by Shedrick El-Amin.

FIGURES 7.3 AND 7.4 Two 1977 gatherings at Masjid Wali Muhammad (the new name of the former Temple #1). In both pictures, Mazen Alwan, a Syrian immigrant, is instructing the congregation. Photos by Shedrick El-Amin.

Alwan was responsible for implementing Warith Deen Muhammad's directives to the Bilalian community, the new label Imam Warith Deen applied to his followers after officially changing the name of the NOI to "World Community of al-Islam in the West" in 1976. In former temples across the United States, Bilalian Muslims oriented their prayer spaces toward Mecca, instituted the Ramadan fast (held now during the lunar month of Ramadan rather than in December, when the NOI had observed a similar fast), performed the five daily prayers in Arabic, and declared that the hajj required travel to Mecca rather than Chicago.[21] These innovations brought Masjid Wali Muhammad closer to the doctrinal and performative traditions of other Muslim communities in Detroit. Like Elijah Muhammad before them, Imam Warith Deen and Hajj Mazen recognized the centrality of ritual in creating a strong Muslim community, but for these champions of the "second resurrection"—the term Imam Warith Deen used to describe this period of radical transition—new rituals would situate Masjid Wali Muhammad firmly within the larger Muslim landscape of Detroit, effectively bringing to an end the NOI's longstanding commitment to separatism, both racial and doctrinal.

Becoming Muslim Again

As important as these transformations were, they gestured toward deeper, even more wrenching changes.[22] Mazen Alwan, an immigrant Muslim, was brought in to facilitate the conversion process at Temple #1, but he did not instigate or direct it. That role belonged to Imam Warith Deen, who operated at the very center of the NOI establishment in Chicago. The members of Masjid Wali Muhammad realized that new teachings were being imposed on them from above, just as earlier decisions made by Elijah Muhammad and his lieutenants had been. For some, it was difficult to reconcile the new teachings of the movement with those promoted by Elijah Muhammad. "We thought the Muhammad mentioned in the Qur'an was the Honorable Elijah Muhammad, you have to understand," said Saleem Rahmann, a longstanding member of the Nation and later a lay leader at Masjid Wali Muhammad, "and that Master Farad Muhammad was God."[22] It was only by reimagining Elijah Muhammad's theology as a vital stepping stone to the final revelation of Islam, as a period of trial and tutelage, that Brother Saleem and other believers were able to make sense of the radical transition Imam Warith Deen imposed on their community.

We needed to see God and the prophets from our own eyes, our own souls, our own view...Because of slavery, we lost our identity, our self-reliance. To even consider that we had our own souls, our own point of view or anything was so strong that any time anybody came along with something, the only thing that we could do was try to imitate. And you see that among some African Americans who accept Islam and have not gone through this experience that we went through. They, in essence, are imitators. They imitate what they see immigrant Muslims do, the way immigrant Muslims practice Islam. They imitate them and become imitators. Allah has blessed us with something unique, an independent view where we can look at God through our own eyes. That is the real view that Muslims should have. And Warith Deen Muhammad is bringing to the world the true image of Islam and the true image of the prophet Muhammad, what he really was about.[23]

The two-staged structure on which this conversion narrative depends was promoted by Imam Warith Deen, who was careful to avoid representing the teachings of his father as heretical or antithetical to his own understanding of Islam. As he famously put it:

We have been taught many things in the Teachings of the Great Master W. F. [Fard] Muhammad and the Honorable Master Elijah Muhammad that have prepared us for this time—the time of the Second Resurrection. The Teachings have brought us along the road to a certain point towards our destination in scriptural interpretations. When we take it from that point and carry it on into the Second Resurrection, we will understand that the movement is a continuing movement and not a new movement.[24]

Benjamin Hogue finds evidence for the intentionality of this evolutionary conversion in the symbolism of a famous photograph depicting Elijah Muhammad sitting in front of a picture of Fard Muhammad, with the young Warith Deen Muhammad standing at this side (see Figure 7.5). Both Fard and Warith Deen are holding a book in their hands, presumably the Qur'an.

The man [Fard Muhammad] was teaching by his picture. He's holding the Qur'an—a white man holding a Qur'an who is God— why would God need to read a book?

Why would God have to read the Qur'an when he is the one who dictated it?

FIGURE 7.5 Elijah Muhammad, seated, with his son Warith Deen Muhammad, posing
before a picture of Fard Muhammad, Chicago, circa 1960.

He is sending messages that we never saw. That people never thought.
He knew sooner or later somebody was going to see what's going on
here. Warith Deen is the one who figured all this out. But the ones at
the time, when he was trying to explain this to them, they were not
willing to make this adjustment. All the time he was teaching us, this
is a stage that you are going through and when you finally figure out
what is going on, go get yourself a book and study because that is
what God is. He is a body of knowledge.[25]

The picture is read here as a prophesy in its own right, one that fore-
tells that Imam Warith Deen will be the rightful inheritor of his father's
movement, and that the intention of Fard from the beginning was to
bring African Americans to the Islam of the Qur'an and Sunna. Warith
Deen promoted this idea as well, teaching that Fard had worked with
Elijah to invent NOI teachings "as a strategy, a temporary strategy, a
temporary language environment to hold uneducated Blacks...long
enough to come into an independent mind...and then later study the
Qur'an."[26] In a similar prophetic narrative, the unorthodox theology of
the NOI is smoothed over metaphorically by comparing the decades

spent under the tutelage of Elijah Muhammad to the early Meccan years of the Prophet Muhammad, when the fledgling Muslim community was not yet capable of yielding fully to the demands of their new faith. The transition to Imam Warith Deen's leadership is likened to the Muslim community's arrival in Medina, where they were relatively free from persecution and thus expected to express total fealty to the revelations of the Qur'an.[27]

In the 1970s, however, these artful analogies did not satisfy everyone. A religious movement with tens of thousands of active followers could not turn its teachings on a dime, transforming its ministers and members into instant Muslims when they had long been forbidden to explore mainstream Islamic teachings and to associate with other Muslims.[28] The second resurrection brought major upheavals to Masjid Wali Muhammad, as it did to former NOI temples across America. Even the followers of Imam Warith Deen who did not break away from the movement (as Louis Farrakhan did in 1978) frequently resisted his new teachings. According to Eric Sabree, a Muslim who hovered on the boundary between NOI teachings and Sunni Islam in the 1970s, this resistance was inevitable:

> Mainly because they didn't understand. Some because they just wanted nationalism. The black nationalism. Because he [Imam Warith Deen] said white people can come to the temple and then some people didn't like that. So he is changing everything and he's ruining everything. And they really believed what Elijah Muhammad said. They believed so strongly...And you know it kind of hurt him [Imam Warith Deen] too... because they had put so much into the man [Elijah Muhammad]. He [Iman Warith Deen] tried to break that up. You know we have to break this up because he could have continued the whole thing. He could have kept it going. He could have kept it going and people would have been—who knows what we would be doing now. But he broke it up and started taking people towards real Islam.[29]

Sabree's curiosity about what might have become of the NOI had it continued under Elijah Muhammad's teachings is not uncommon. For even the most loyal followers of Imam Warith Deen, the success of Elijah Muhammad's business empire—which had included restaurants, a fish-packing and distribution network, farms, clothing stores, and many other businesses—is an object of nostalgia. Imam Warith Deen sold off most of these assets soon after he assumed leadership of the movement, largely because he found them a distraction from his more overtly religious obligations and because they were a source of corruption and conflict. This income stream was partially replaced by support from overseas in 1978, when Saudi Arabia and other Arab Gulf states made Imam Warith Deen the sole agent for the distribution of their financial aid to American Muslim organizations. Nonetheless, the decision to divest from the NOI's commercial holdings is regretted today by former members of the NOI, who lament the lack of entrepreneurial success and business opportunity among urban blacks.[30]

> BENJAMIN HOGUE: Well, they had a beautiful business model, and I still don't understand why we let all that go...That was a good solid economic opportunity that I feel is missing in the so called orthodox community—something that I feel is missing, why we don't have so much influence in the orthodox community.[31]

This decision had long-term consequences in Detroit. Although most NOI members did not benefit personally from Elijah Muhammad's business endeavors, they are aware that the city's economy has been in free fall since the mid-1970s, precisely the period when Imam Warith Deen became their leader. Many of his strongest supporters question his decision to dismantle the NOI's internal economy. They compare the downward mobility of African Americans in Detroit to the success immigrant Muslims have achieved during this same period and wish that the capital and logistical expertise of Elijah Muhammad's enterprises had somehow been made accessible to their community.[32]

Financial hardships notwithstanding, the followers of Imam Warith Deen encountered far greater challenges on the theological, moral, and ideological fronts defined by the second resurrection. Those who had joined the NOI to participate in its radical critique of unjust racial hierarchies in the United States were often reluctant to embrace a new version of Islam that, in their opinion, demoted the centrality of race struggles. "I would not have joined Islam back in the 1960s," Shedrick El-Amin explained. "I was not interested in the idea of praying and leading a good life and then going to heaven when I died. That is just like the Christianity our people had been fed on for generations. Why would I have changed my life around just for that? Yeah, I was angry when he [Warith Deen] started changing everything around."[33] Suddenly, non-blacks were being brought into the movement, and they were frequently placed in positions of authority over the community in matters of doctrine and practice. Among NOI stalwarts, there was widespread concern that these "white Muslim" teachers would turn their black protégés into a community of cultural and religious "imitators." Sherman Jackson argues that a transformation of this sort is indeed what happened. "Cumulatively," he writes, "this would all evolve into a corporate will to re-create American Islam in the image of an idealized form of 'back-home' Islam...Immigrant Muslims quickly introduced theological, juridical, and revivalist discourses that effectively banished native Blackamerican instincts and understandings to the periphery."[34]

For men like Benjamin Hogue, however, who had worshiped at several non-NOI mosques and had studied Islam with Adil al-Aseer, Mike Karoub, and other non-black teachers at Masjid al-Mu'mineen, this shift in the racial boundaries of the community did not present an insurmountable problem. Indeed, it seemed like a constructive, perhaps even necessary, step forward. Hogue's views, however, were not typical among the NOI rank and file. When Hajj Mazen Alwan was sent to Muhammad's Temple #1 in December 1976 to become the new preacher—now called an imam—his presence was disconcerting, and many members of the congregation publicly and privately resisted the reforms he introduced.

Another Brother from the East

Mazen Alwan moved to Chicago from Damascus, Syria, in 1976 to complete his medical training. While searching for a residency in Chicago, he worshiped at an informal mosque on the South Side that included Syrian doctors, others Arabs, and several African American Muslims. There he befriended a doctor who worked with Imam Warith Deen on the newspaper formerly known as *Muhammad Speaks*, now renamed *The Bilalian News*. Alwan had studied Islam at Jameat Zaid Ibn Thabit al-Ansari in Damascus, and he identified with the Salafi movements then gaining popularity in Syria. He was also affiliated with the Muslim Brotherhood. Alwan's religious knowledge was impressive, and he found himself answering questions brought to him by his new friend. Before long, he was ghostwriting his friend's column in *The Bilalian News*.[35]

Alwan was curious about the NOI and the transition to orthodoxy it was undergoing. He began attending Imam Warith Deen's lectures regularly, and he was soon introduced to the imam. Alwan greatly respected Warith Deen Muhammad, a feeling that was clearly mutual. Alwan was intrigued by the careful methodology the new leader employed to coax his followers away from the teachings of Elijah Muhammad toward those of a more universal Islam.

MAZEN ALWAN: [Quoting Imam Warith Deen] "My father used to tell you that he is the messenger because he wanted you to believe something that is in front of you. And he used to tell you that al-Fard Muhammed is God, and why did he used to tell you this? Because you were Christian and in Christianity they taught you that Jesus is white, has blue eyes. And because he is white and has blue eyes, that you are always admiring the white, the blue eyes, and this is why he told you this is your god, but it is not true that Fard Mohammed is your god. But we give him the credit that he introduced Islam to us, okay? And we give also..." Always he [Imam Warith Deen] used to respect his dad, and he did not show any kind of, you can say, radical criticism with his dad.

Observing this gradualist, respectful approach to change, Hajj Mazen learned how to nudge Imam Warith Deen toward more traditional understandings of Islam without directly contradicting him. He began attending the imam's talks and was fascinated by the different points the imam would emphasize in his lectures, some of which were over six hours long. Speaking with the imam afterward, Mazen would bring out resonances between the Sunna of the Prophet and observations Imam Warith Deen had made in his lecture. In this way, he was able to provide the imam with a more conventional Islamic way of making the same point without directly contradicting or challenging what he said. Others took note and approved of this close relationship as it developed. Representatives of the Muslim World League, who were carefully monitoring the NOI transition in New York and Chicago, granted the young Alwan a salary to enable him to work full time with the imam.[36]

A few months into this collaboration, Hajj Mazen was shocked to hear Imam Warith Deen not only mention him in a sermon but announce that he had been assigned as the imam of "Mosque #1" in Detroit.[37] This news was unwelcome to Alwan, who wanted to stay in Chicago, but it illustrates the heavy pressure Imam Warith Deen was under during this period. His every move was a matter of speculation among his closest followers, among his allies and critics in a global network of Muslim organizations, and among the public at large. Warith Deen was determined to produce Muslim believers, but it was difficult to find well-trained black scholars who both respected his authority and did not belittle Elijah Muhammad's legacy.[38] Given these onerous conditions, the value of teachers like Mazen Alwan was immeasurable.

As Imam Warith Deen systematically overturned the teachings of his father's ministry, he also broke up the authoritarian, hierarchical structure of the NOI, encouraging Muslim congregations to operate as independent mosques. This move was also a matter of great controversy and frustration for his followers.

> BENJAMIN HOGUE: It took an adjustment, because we still had the minister system when he took over, W. D. that is, and the minister had a lot of power and a lot of authority that was based on his political influence, and not necessarily his knowledge of the book. And so, when you go to a knowledge-based credential...the imams and stuff were concerned about what was going to happen. Because they wanted to—they were given a salary. They didn't work. So they thought somebody was going to take their job...At that time they were concerned about what was going to happen to them, and he [Imam Warith Deen] was trying to give them time to make the adjustment, to learn. I think more of it was W. D.'s attempt to get them to learn and become imams, not necessarily to get rid of them, but to give you the opportunity to become what you should be in the first place.[39]

According to Hajj Hogue, Mazen Alwan was sent to Detroit specifically to fill in while the ministers themselves retooled. But the existing ministers had risen through the ranks, knew their congregations well, and were respected political actors within the NOI community; Alwan had no such background. He was precisely the type of "white Muslim" the followers of Elijah Muhammad had long been encouraged to disregard. What is more, when Alwan was appointed head imam of Muhammad's Temple #1, he also became the lead minister for all of the Bilalian congregations in Michigan. This was a highly unusual situation for Alwan and the congregation he came to serve.

At Masjid Wali Muhammad, Alwan was initially well received. His focus on education and correct ritual practice was in keeping with the congregation's past focus and with directives they received from Chicago. As Alwan taught Arabic and the Qur'an and Sunna, he was in turn introduced to African American culture, NOI history, and the nationalist objectives of Elijah Muhammad and his movement. Together, he and his new students built a minbar (pulpit) for the mosque, observed all five of the daily prayers, reached out to other Muslims in the city, and attended to the spiritual and social needs of the community. Alwan was less comfortable managing the masjid's finances, making daily operational decisions for congregations across the state, and maintaining bureaucratic ties to Chicago. Neither did he consider himself a politically appropriate leader for the congregation.[40]

When Alwan's leadership was eventually challenged, however, it was not on financial or political grounds but on his ability to interpret the Qur'an authoritatively and in full agreement with the teachings of Imam Warith Deen.

MAZEN ALWAN: One time I want to make kind of radical change here [to resolve a theological issue] in my speech [which was televised]. I tried to end it. I was talking about Jesus or that this is Issa, Prophet Issa, and then I mentioned that he is Issa, the son of the Virgin Mary, so this is one of the great prophets who we admire and things like that. When I came down from the minbar...before I start to say the prayer, I found many of the men and women raising their hands.
Excuse me, Brother Imam, excuse me.
What is the problem?
This is not the teachings of Imam Warith Deen, this is not the teachings of our Imam.
I said, "Excuse me, what do you mean by this?"
They said, "Brother Imam, Issa was born from Mariam..." [Alwan explains that the NOI did not teach the Virgin Birth of Jesus.] "No he has a father. It was a human birth."
I tell to them, "Didn't your imam tell you that you are like babies, and now you are converted to Islam? And why he assigned me to here? I was not born here. I learned Islam in the East, so I am now coming here to teach you al-Islam, teaching you the principles of al-Islam."
So this is the right thing. I found that many of them opposed this, you know...Imam Warith Deen taught this idea [that Jesus was not born of a virgin], which is in conflict, you can say, of Islam. He was denying what we call a miracle. Whether these miracles were of Prophet Muhammad, praise be upon him, whether these miracles were the other prophets or the great miracles of Jesus, praise be upon him, so it was denied. So bringing this very important issue to those people, those people right away some of them fly to Chicago and told him [Imam Warith Deen] about it, and he became very angry, very furious, you know, that he assigned me to be the leader, and things like that, and to be the imam...
SALLY HOWELL: And you went against his teachings.
ALWAN: That's right. I taught something that is very important against his teaching.

Shortly after hearing reports of Alwan's sermon, Imam Warith Deen himself came to Detroit and preached a large program at the Masonic Temple.

> ALWAN: He mentioned in his speech the point that those Arab Muslims, that they, "when they found out now that we are becoming a strong community, a very great community, they want to come and control us. They want to have authority over us." You know? "It was enough for us that we were slaves to those white people...But now we are free people, and we will not submit to anything." Then he mentioned something important, that "those I [Imam Warith Deen] know, those Muslim scholars, they criticize me the way I interpret the Qur'an, and you can say that I am going to continue saying it because this is the revelation from God to me...And, for this reason, I remove Mazen Alwan from his position."

In this narrative the imam who hired Mazen Alwan and routinely described Detroit's Muslims as "babies" in relation to Muslims from the East is replaced by a more confident leader who refers to the Bilalian community as "strong" and unwilling to "submit" to the authority of Arab Muslims. Likewise, Imam Warith Deen claims a direct "revelation from God" that substantiates his own authority over and above that of Alwan and the cohort of foreign Muslims Alwan represented.[41] Despite this fiery confrontation, after which he was demoted from imam to "teacher" at Masjid Wali Muhammad, Mazen Alwan nonetheless continued in his role as spiritual guide and Islamic instructor to the congregation. Now his lessons would be provided more quietly, in small group sessions of exegesis and interpretation. Another young man, a longstanding NOI member, was named resident imam and took over the weekly broadcasts and public functions of leadership. Mazen Alwan's troubles stemmed both from who he was as a person—a Syrian, a "Caucasian Muslim" from the perspective of the Bilalians, a self-described "brother from the East"—and from the distance that was still to be traveled between the teachings of the Bilalian community and those of Sunni Muslims. The spiritual authority of Imam Warith Deen was at stake. Alwan remained in his position as teacher at the mosque for another five years. He resigned only after the congregation's questions for him surpassed his religious knowledge. He later completed his medical residency in Michigan and joined the medical profession there.[42]

In the 1970s, Alwan was a newcomer to America, and to Detroit. When he compared the untrained but sincere Muslims of Masjid Wali Muhammad to the "born Muslims" who filled the city's older mosques, he often favored the practices and attitudes of his African American congregation. Masjid Wali Muhammad, for example, was the first Detroit mosque to adopt the practice of broadcasting the call to prayer from its rooftop (in 1979).[43] A gathering of brothers stood shoulder to shoulder there each day for the dawn prayer, and the four prayers that followed, while the mosques of immigrants and their children were nearly empty and frequently locked on weekdays. Alwan was alert to these differences. He was a gentle, generous, and thoughtful teacher, but he was also a conservative Salafi and had no patience for the "Americanized" religious leaders he encountered in Detroit: men like Mike Karoub, whom he saw as an accomodationist, or Imam Chirri, who (scholarship aside) Alwan considered an assimilationist whose parochial attachment to his own mosque kept him from giving Detroit's new Muslims the support they needed and deserved.[44] An anecdote Alwan is fond of telling conveys perfectly his admiration for his Detroit congregation and his less-than-favorable impression of local Lebanese American Muslims.

> Imam Chirri and his board were having a conflict and they wanted to sell their mosque. And the Afro-American people, they told me, "Brother Imam, let us go and purchase it." And we went over there, and we had a meeting with them—all of their board meeting, and Imam Chirri was there, and we wanted to discuss about the price of it. But the funniest thing was when he started to introduce the members of the board, "This is brother Mike Johnson, this is brother Joe Smith," in fact, without saying "brother." And then when I introduced the board of directors or the members who were with me, it was, "Oh, this is Abdullah Hussein, this is Saleem Rahman,"—all of their names were Muslim names and they are converted. They are not as Christian, you can say, as those that are supposed to be Muslims. And their names, none of them are Arabic, even though they are Lebanese!

By the late 1970s, Detroit's mosques contained a diverse agglomeration of Muslims: new and old, local and foreign, pious and secular, black and white. Muslims sought each other out in these sacred spaces, evaluated the types of Islam on display, and shared their impressions as they moved through the city. Masjid Wali Muhammad had finally joined this commonwealth of believers. It was unequivocally a mosque, a Muslim house of prayer. It was no longer a site of syncretic Muslim practices and black nationalist rhetoric; nor was it a local franchise in an African American business empire. Imam Warith Deen Muhammad inspired and oversaw this transformation, but it was Hajj Mazen Alwan who introduced Masjid Wali Muhammad to Sunni Islam and to the transcommunal umma of Detroit, teaching old and young Muslims to pray in Arabic, to recite the Qur'an, and to practice their faith in ways that connected them to a world of Islamic thought and collective responsibility much larger than any they had previously known.

Countercultural Islam

Since the 1920s, African Americans have joined and created social movements that use Islamic symbols as tools for building alternative identities and fighting anti-black racism. For some, this activity fostered pan-Africanism. For others, "Moorish" or "Asiatic" identities drew more circumspectly on African associations, filtering them through the civilizational prestige of the Islamic empires of India, North Africa, and the Middle East. By the 1970s, the civil rights and Black Power movements had infused these other-oriented traditions with a new racial awareness that celebrated black beauty, strength, and pride. American notions of blackness were changing rapidly, but African materials remained central to the construction of alternative black identities in Detroit, as did local knowledge of Muslims and Islam.

Malcolm X's powerful ministry for the NOI popularized the linkage between Islam and a new African American identity that was upright, confident, and (most importantly) could stand apart from white America. The Nation continued to attract new adherents until the death of Elijah Muhammad in 1975, but the influence of Malcolm X ran deep even among black Muslims who were not affiliated with the NOI. These communities grew steadily throughout the 1960s and 1970s. Eventually, a generation gap opened between two cohorts in Detroit: (1) those who had become Muslims in the 1950s or earlier, mostly married couples with grown children, who anchored and supported Masjid al-Mu'mineen financially, and (2) those who became Muslim in the 1960s and 1970s. The younger Muslims had not been personally influenced by the black nationalism of Marcus Garvey, Noble Drew Ali, or Elijah Muhammad, nor had they been supportive of the mainstream civil rights movement as many of the older Muslims were. Instead, they admixed ideologies from the Black Power Movement, Malcolm X, the anti-war movement, the counterculture, avant-garde jazz, and conservative Islamic movements to create their own method of turning on, tuning in, and dropping out.[45] Increasingly, these young Muslims were not willing to study at the feet of foreign students or immigrant imams. They identified ideologically with several national or transnational Muslim movements, such as the Dar ul-Islam Movement, which began in the 1960s but was popularized in the 1970s, when Imam Jamil al-Amin (formerly H. Rap Brown) began writing and preaching; or various Sufi brotherhoods like the Tijani movement of Senegal led by Shakyh Hassan Cisse; or the Tablighi Jama'at.[46]

Inspired by countercultural impulses, these African American Muslims indulged in a period of intense religious experimentation and self-examination in groups that ranged from the laid back, to the militant, to the mystical. This broadening spectrum of Muslim options did not bring about the fulfillment of Hajj Hassanein's and Imam Mike Karoub's shared desire for a color-blind, culture-blind Islam in Detroit; instead, it produced identities that were even *more* sensitive to race and culture. Few of these countercultural Muslims sought guidance from the leaders of Masjid al-Mu'mineen. They were radical in ways Hajj Mazen Alwan, the Salafi reformer, would not have deemed legitimate, but they shared his critique of the existing Muslim establishment in Detroit.

Imam Selim Yusuf, who is today the leader of Detroit's Tijani Zawiyyah (a Sufi house of worship), became a Muslim in the early 1970s after his military service in Vietnam. He joined an unaffiliated group of young Muslim artists and activists known as the Beys. He was attracted to their politics, their Arabic fluency, the seriousness with which they studied the Qur'an, and their principled refusals—foremost among them, the refusal to engage with Christians or to participate in the mainstream economy. "It was America in the Sixties, so it's not like they needed to enhance the social order," he told me. "Basically, we created our own social network and we made different things. I mean, we made them literally. We did carpentry on all sorts of levels. Some people were silversmiths. Some people were artisans. Some people were actually in school for social work so they could better interact with the community."[47] The Beys dressed in an exotic mix of African and Arab clothing. They carried big walking sticks and handmade leather bags, wore large turbans, African head scarves, and long dresses made of African cloth. In Imam Yusuf's words, "the only thing we didn't have was the camel!"[48]

The Beys also took part in the drug culture of the era, practiced polygamy, shunned regular employment, and refused to pay taxes. Led by Muhammad Bey Abdul Jalil and his *wazir* (advisor), Furuq Z. Bey, who also led the avant-garde jazz ensemble Griot Galaxy, the "Bey community" was bound together by its commitment to art, knowledge, and faith in Islam. As Robert Dannin observes, "the rise of Orthodox Islam in the postwar era paralleled the development of modern jazz."[49] Many of Griot Galaxy's original members had spent time on the East Coast, where they learned Arabic at the State Street Mosque in Brooklyn and studied music with jazz masters like Dizze Gillespie, who flirted with Islam, and Yusuf Lateef, who embraced it. Like many of the black artist converts of the period, the Beys were committed to the revival and recombination of African and black American social practices, symbols, and aesthetic traditions.

The Beys were nomadic when Selim Yusuf first joined the group, but they eventually settled in Highland Park, where rents were cheap. The group leased a row of storefronts and apartment buildings that they used for collective housing, worship, daycare, and artisan workshops. The Beys threw a street party/concert to raise the funds needed to renovate the block in 1971. Griot Galaxy headlined the concert, which included a mix of jazz, Motown, reggae, and other sounds. Festival fundraisers of this kind were a long-established tradition at the AMS and other Detroit mosques. Dating back to the 1930s, these events served the triple purpose of advertising the Muslim community's presence, celebrating its distinctive ethnic and aesthetic traditions, and generating financial support for the activities and building projects of local mosques.

The Beys took the name Masjid as-Salaam and incorporated with the state in 1971. Masjid as-Salaam resembled the city's older mosques not only in its fundraising methods but also in its gender dynamics. The women of Masjid as-Salaam were visible, active members of the congregation who supported it financially, led educational programs, were involved in politics at the city level, and engaged energetically in dawa. The mosque was initially well received. "People came from all over the city to make Jumaa with us," Imam Selim recalls, "because we were so centrally located in Highland Park, so it was very easy to hit and leave, while the parking at al-Mu'mineen was kind of tight."[50] Their Jumaa prayers quickly grew to 100–150 people, which was more than al-Mu'mineen could accommodate. It was difficult, however, to turn the relaxed, countercultural atmosphere at the mosque and the loose, peripatetic lifestyle of the Beys into a recipe for institutional stability. Detroit's younger, more recently converted, and better educated Muslims came together under one roof at Masjid as-Salaam

but they soon discovered that they were not immune to doctrinal and ideological differences.

The Beys were an open group, and they eagerly explored new ways to
build the local umma. They visited Hajj Sammsan on Detroit's east side,
where he had landed after his split with al-Mu'mineen in 1964. They visited
al-Mu'mineen in Virginia Park. Eventually they scouted out the Dearborn
Muslim scene as well. Imam Yusuf recounts how he first became aware of
Mike Karoub and his work in Dearborn. This episode, which took place
in an Arab restaurant in Highland Park, illustrates the attention-grabbing
habits of the Beys.

> We went in there one day. I remember that clearly. It was time for
> *Maghrib* [the sunset prayer]. I remember that also. And we had to
> get a *wudhu* [a ritual cleansing before prayer]. We went to the res-
> taurant, and we sat down, and this is how it usually went when we
> went someplace. We would go in; we would ask for a cup of a tea.
> We would get a cup of tea, and everybody would literally use the
> same tea bag, and we would literally just use the bathroom to get
> our *wudhu* and everything, and then we would ask, in the restaurant,
> did they had a spot where we could sit and pray, a real quick prayer
> before we sit and drink this tea? And a lot of times the people would
> say, "Yes, right over there!" And we would go over there and make
> *salat* [prayer]. And so, like we were in this place and we said we
> wanted to make a prayer and everything, and the guy kept looking
> at us. And it was African with a mixture of Arab sort of dress [we
> were wearing that day], big turbans...He asked, "Are you going to
> go pray?" I would say, "Yes," and we would make *maghrib*, and he
> heard us reciting the *fatiha* and things like that, and he started telling
> us about what Mike Karoub was doing, his family, how they came
> here, and this, and that, and the other.[51]

Imam Yusuf is now amused by the reactions he and the Beys triggered as they moved through the city. They presented a sharp contrast to
the middle-class conformity and private religiosity of the Muslims who
prayed at al-Mu'mineen, the AMS, the ICA, and elsewhere in greater
Detroit. It is not hard to imagine how the city's more established Muslims
responded to their appeals. "They considered us to be extreme...They
looked at us as...they said we had shahada [had converted to Islam in a
literal sense], we witnessed a lot, but we didn't really have Islam in our
hearts."

SELIM YUSUF: We were always reaching out to everyone. That's what we were doing in al-Mu'mineen, because we were like, "What can we do together?" But, it was just like, "Nothing! Ya'll don't look right; you don't know this, that, and the other. I bet you don't even know your Social Security!" And I would say, "Yeah, you're right. I don't!"

SALLY HOWELL: It's funny because you and Tahira [Khalid] are saying the exact same thing. She said, "My dad was like, 'Get a job! Don't be on welfare and expect people to respect you!' "

KILANI CECE (a member of Imam Selim's current congregation): And they [the Beys] were the opposite! They were hustlers, selling incense, making their own jewelry.[52]

Akil Fahd, a lay historian who spent many years in Imam Selim's Tijani congregation, describes this dichotomy as analogous to the split between the mainstream civil rights establishment and the less enfranchised Black Power Movement. Hassanein clearly fit into the former category. The al-Mu'mineen congregation represented the "do-for-self" mentality so popular among early twentieth-century black nationalists, including the NOI, who saw economic stability as the foundation of community building. At al-Mu'mineen, Islamic values were treated as a means of securing a morally respectable place in American society. Hajj Hassanein clearly felt that the Beys were not on this "straight path."

TAHIRA KHALID: Dad had a real problem with some of them. They didn't work. The women were suffering and Dad would go clashing with some of them. They misinterpreted a lot of the stuff. Some of the groups became very militaristic. They were doing things that weren't quite up to par with Dad. And Dad, like he said, "I'm not afraid of any man," would get into it with them.

"You need to take care of your kids. See, I work every day. You're on the welfare thinking somebody's gonna respect you? You know, you need to get up off your behind and get a job."

And their whole thing, "We need to make our five daily *salat*."

"You need to be feeding your kids and making *salat* after you get home."

That was a running battle. A lot of the brothers talk about it. Dad wasn't scared of anybody. You know, he'd tell them, "Take that mess off your head and go in there and feed your kids. Allah's not gonna be pleased with you. Your kids eating up off food stamps, and you're young, you know."[53]

The Beys were guided by an interpretation of *fiqh* that emphasized difference from the larger society, and from other Muslims. Being free to make all five daily prayers at their appointed times was more important to the Beys than working at "respectable" jobs that would pay well but would not accommodate proper Islamic practice. They treated the Qur'an as an instruction manual for daily life, to be followed as closely as possible, not as an abstract source of moral authority that could be ignored whenever its teachings were unconventional or inconvenient. Responding to the internal dynamics of the black Left and to Detroit's countercultural scene, the Beys were drawn to the spiritual nuances of Islam, which they expressed performatively in their dress, body rituals, food culture, domestic living arrangements, manner of speaking, and artistic production.

This urban cool piety differed in emphasis from that promoted by Mazen Alwan at Masjid Wali Muhammad, but it drew from the same modernizing, reinterpretive sensibility that inspired the Muslim Brotherhood and Muslim World League. In Detroit, reform-oriented, text-based Islamic praxis was expressed in myriad political and cultural idioms, each inflected by the national, ethnic, and racial origins of the communities that embraced it, their position in local subaltern hierarchies, and—just as significantly—the length of time they had spent living as Muslims in America. These revivalist movements were highly critical of the city's existing Muslim institutions, which seemed condescending toward the Beys and Masjid as-Salaam. The Beys in turn dismissed most immigrant and ethnic Muslims, especially the American-born, as assimilationists eager to apologize for Islam.[54] As far as the Beys were concerned, there were no lessons to be learned from Detroit's existing mosques, only mistakes to be avoided. The distance the worshipers at Masjid as-Salaam staked out between themselves and the city's Muslim establishment provided ample room for experimentation. Ultimately, however, this lack of constraint (and the Beys' limited financial resources) led Masjid as-Salaam to self-destruct. By 1982 the mosque was no longer active.

Imam Selim attributes the short life of Masjid as-Salaam to the ideological barriers that grew up rapidly among Muslims in the 1970s and to the destabilizing influence the dissolution of the NOI had on the independent black Muslim scene in Detroit. Before 1975, when the NOI was separatist and heterodox, Imam Selim felt he knew every Sunni and Sufi African American Muslim in the city by name. With the mainstreaming of the Nation, however, hundreds of new Muslims entered the community, intensifying controversies over proper belief and practice. Suddenly, American and foreign Muslim missionary groups were vying for the attentions of the new Muslims. Local models of spiritual authority, already decentralized and endlessly contested, were undermined by obscure doctrinal disputes. According to Imam Selim, African American Muslims were ideologically at sea after 1975. Individuals charted their own course toward Islam, reconciling complex social, moral, and political claims in idiosyncratic ways, with many false starts, and usually without any consistent set of interpretive principles.

> The group I was with, I was personally devastated because our group was torn apart, bit by bit by bit by bit. It wasn't like a death, like someone just stabbed us and we died or something. It was more like you had taken a sheet of paper and were tearing off little pieces. People would come in with new ideologies and new this and new that. "And don't you know this hadith?" "And don't you know what that *ayat al-Qu'ran* was saying?" And stuff like that. It was just like every week there was something new. So they took people, and more people, from the *jami'a* [Masjid as-Salaam] until there was literally almost nothing left.[55]

The dynamism and popularity of the Beys made them irresistible targets not only for proselytizers from overseas, but for well-organized black American Muslims whose activist agendas were at odds with the countercultural ethos of Masjid as-Salaam. Shaykh Mubarrak Mutakalim, for example, worked with the Dar ul-Islam Movement on Detroit's east side when they arrived in the late 1960s from Cleveland, Philadelphia, and New York.[56] Compared to the Beys, this group was more nationalist and militant in orientation and included Black Panthers among its members. The Dar recruited heavily in area prisons as well. Shaykh Mubarrak taught a rigorous Hanafi style of worship and, like the Beys, placed a heavy emphasis on *fiqh*.[57] Detroit's Dar community was much more disciplined, however, and less improvisational in matters of wardrobe and public piety. Mubarrak helped found Masjid as-Salaam in the early 1970s, but he very quickly left again for Detroit's east side.[58] The Dar Movement demanded total loyalty from its members, and it was averse to intra-Muslim ecumenicalism.[59] They were especially hostile to the Tablighi Juma'at, whose members were also gravitating toward Masjid as-Salaam.

"The Tablighi Juma'at was the driving negative force that really split up everything," Imam Selim remembers. "People would leave and go to the Tablighi Juma'at. That was a crazy group of people called the Bayt al-Qureish."

> I mean, there's a thing about righteousness and acting righteous... The Tablighi people... have to wear a uniform. They have to give that,

shake your hand a certain way, and "Don't do this," and "Muhammad did this and didn't do this," and "Muhammad said this and didn't say that." And it's all very subjective because it's looked at through the eyes of a certain school of thought, the Hanafis, the Pakistani Indian culture, and they [the Pakistanis and Indians] will never tell you that, yes, their culture is incorporated into [their] Islam.[60]

Here Imam Selim echoes Tahira Khalid's comments about the Tablighis, noting that they borrowed the social as well as religious traditions of their Pakistani guides and were largely unaware of the extent to which South Asian cultural norms were used to judge the beliefs and practices of other Muslims. In this view, American followers of the Tablighi movement lacked the ability to interpret the Qur'an for themselves and instead superimposed the habits of Pakistani Hanifis on the larger black Muslim community. Detroit's Tablighis did share certain tendencies with the Beys; for instance, they valued the active religious participation of women, they cultivated an antihierarchical ethos, and they rejected the black nationalist militancy of groups like the Dar ul-Islam. The Tablighis were distinctive, however, for the extent to which they insisted on the social isolation of men from women; they were committed to keeping women from public view as well. The Beys considered these behaviors foreign and excessive, a stance taken by members of Masjid al-Mu'mineen as well. The Tablighis in turn criticized the Beys for cultural practices that were "too American" and therefore antithetical to Islam.[61]

"So yeah," Imam Yusuf continues, "we got really, we were decimated. Because, as I said before, we played music. Number one, that was bad. 'Oh yeah! These guys are haram!' We played music. That's how we got the masjid. We put on a concert and raised money, and got the masjid."[62] Soon, the Tablighis split off from Masjid as-Salaam as well. "Some people actually went over to al-Mu'mineen. They left and went over there because they liked the structured type of thing."[63]

Yet even at Masjid al-Mu'mineen, where the "structured type of thing" had long held sway, the new, *fiqh*-inspired movements generated serious conflict. After the mosque's leader, Hajj Osman Hassanein, died in 1977, the problems the congregation faced in the house on Virginia Park continued to escalate. Zoning disputes with neighbors over parking, conflicts among members over how to convert their space into a more architecturally conventional mosque, and the high cost of preserving an old and poorly maintained structure eventually led the group to sell the property. In 1980, al-Mu'mineen opened a new facility on McNichols Avenue, on

Detroit's west side, under the leadership of Saleem Khalid. The move to a renovated storefront inspired their members to dream big. They wanted to reproduce the ethnic enclave model that was then attracting thousands of Arab Muslim immigrants to Dearborn. They envisioned a mosque at the heart of a Muslim neighborhood, where people lived within walking distance of their communal prayer space and were always close to other Muslims. In this new era of spiritual awakening, Saleem Khalid planned to shake things up. His goal was to attract worshipers to al-Mu'mineen from the city's new and still unstable mosques. And, like so many religious entrepreneurs before and after him, Imam Saleem planned to raise the bar of piety.[64]

Tahira Hassanein Khalid spoke to me of the heady and toxic turmoil the black Muslim community experienced in the 1970s when it became clear that the political and economic gains of the civil rights movement were not going to trickle down to street level in Detroit. Parents were worried about their children, who entered a landscape of urban poverty and disadvantage as soon as they walked out the doors of the mosque. Even inside their congregations, they faced the ugly side effects of polygamy, drug use, and parents who shunned regular employment (or were shunned by employers who did not want to hire workers who wore robes, veils, and turbans). All of this brought as much heartache and instability to black Muslim families as it did solidarity and spiritual resolve.[65] Hajj Benjamin Hogue describes the climate of legalism and misdirection that settled over Masjid al-Mu'mineen in its final years:

> BENJAMIN HOGUE: There was an attempt to establish an orthodox mosque among the African American people. We messed it up because of this conflict that we cannot resolve. We want to practice Islam the way they did it in Mecca, down to wearing the prophet's shoes in January with snow up to your wazoo.
>
> HOWELL: And using *miswak* [a wooden twig] to brush your teeth.
>
> HOGUE: And rocks as toilet paper and stuff, you know. The concept of Sunna reached a point to where it has become ridiculous. But they considered that to be such an important part of the religion. That they were unable, we are still unable...
>
> [He recalls a sermon which argued that the Prophet Muhammad wore pants above his ankles in order to avoid being wasteful (damaging valuable cloth as it drags the ground) and prideful (flaunting his wealth in this way).]

HOGUE: They took that as a sin if one does [wear ankle-length pants]. Why, it's like cleaning the teeth—that was the best that they had at the time to clean the teeth, not because there is something magical about the *miswak*, you know. They didn't have toothbrushes. They didn't have toilet paper. They didn't have all this other stuff. He [the Prophet] made decisions based on what was available, but what we did as African Americans is we took that literally...

What I got out of his sermon was our beards are too short and our pants are too long! Now what the heck has that got to do with the problems of some brother sitting out here spaced out on some dope with children to feed? How is that going to help him? You are not even addressing the same world that he is living in.[66]

Brother Hogue and the other Muslims activists I spoke with about the 1970s describe a clash of orthodoxies that animated and destabilized the black Muslim community. Whether they began in the NOI or came to mainstream Islam by more direct paths, African American Muslims in Detroit now shudder when they recall how easily new orthodoxies tore apart both progressive, countercultural groups like the Beys, and more conventional, conservative groups like Masjid al-Mu'mineen. This time of turmoil and transition enabled many Muslims to move toward greater awareness, to become what they would now describe as "true Muslims," but it was also a period in which entire histories, belief systems, and institutions were erased. Those who witnessed these radical changes are often deeply ambivalent about them. They constantly revise their estimates of what the community lost during the 1970s and what they, as individual Muslims, gained.

Hijabi Dialogues

The clash of orthodoxies that beset Masjid as-Salaam and Masjid al-Mu'mineen brought about a pervasive regendering of Muslim space and ritual practice. Haitama Sharieff, speaking of how these changes took hold at al-Mu'mineen, described the old mosque on Virginia Park as a place where men and women had mixed and moved about freely (see Figure 7.6). The congregation's women went uncovered in the streets and wore hats or light scarves inside the mosque. The attic of the building, which had been finished as a large open space, was used for dinners and social events.

FIGURE 7.6 A formal dinner at Masjid al-Mu'mineen in the late 1960s. Notice the variety of hats and scarves the women are wearing, and that both genders dine together. Courtesy of Tahira Khalid.

When it was time for prayer, the furniture was moved aside, a clean rug placed on the floor, and the space transformed into a mosque. The men lined up in front, and the women, who donned appropriate hijab for this purpose, lined up behind the men. The congregation prayed together in one room. Ironically, it was several older men who made a point of consistently covering their heads to mark themselves as Muslim, always wearing Kufi caps or modified fezzes. The young people, male and female, covered only for prayer.[67]

By 1980, however, when al-Mu'mineen relocated to its new home on McNichols Road, Imam Khalid moved to bring it in line with changes occurring in mosques across the city. At Masjid Wali Muhammad, where a strict but permeable gender divide had long been in place and women covered their hair with kerchiefs while in the temple (see Figures 7.1 and 7.2), it was Hajj Mazen Alwan who introduced the concept of the hijab. This issue was controversial at the time and contributed, along with the doctrinal disputes examined earlier, to Hajj Mazen's demotion from imam to teacher.

MAZEN ALWAN: In al-hijab they have, the meaning of al-hijab, especially according to Elijah Muhammad's teaching, it is enough to cover your hair. It is like the nuns in Christianity. Okay, but when I start to say, "No, the hijab is to cover everything from the body of the women except the face and the hands." So the teaching and bringing the verses of the Holy Qur'an and explaining to them and things like that, they [the women] right away accepted and they start to follow it. Many of their men, they were angry at me but not in a nice way. [They said], "You made our women like those women wrapped in a carpet. Why are you insisting on these teachings?" I was explaining that this is very important in Islam to appear as a Muslim, you know?

The men of Masjid Wali Muhammad clearly associated the hijab with foreign Muslims who supposedly oppressed women by "insisting" that they be covered to the extreme. They saw their own practices of gender differentiation as sufficiently modest, while also appropriately respectful of women and culturally familiar.[68] The Afrocentric clothing favored in some Detroit mosques had been strictly off limits to members of the NOI prior to 1975. Elijah Muhammad considered such styles demeaning to African Americans.[69] Mazen Alwan's sudden suggestion that women dress according to his understanding of hijab—not only at the masjid but whenever they went out in public—was a sharp break with precedent. Many Muslims found this new style of dress unattractive and unnecessarily foreign. By making Muslim women highly visible, the hijab also made them vulnerable to harassment. Yet as attention to *fiqh* and the Sunna of the Prophet gradually permeated the Muslim community in Detroit, hijabs began to appear on more and more women.

It is telling that, in Hajj Mazen's narrative, the women of Masjid Wali Muhammad embraced this new practice with little complaint. By adopting hijab, they moved closer to the look popular among their sisters in Detroit's other black mosques, and they showed solidarity with women in the Muslim revivalist movements gaining strength overseas. Among Tablighis in Detroit, full burqas were donned for the first time in this period. At Masjid al-Nur, the Tablighi mosque established in Highland Park in 1978, women were discouraged from attending communal prayers altogether.[70] Mazen Alwan did not advocate for a similar masculinization of mosque space, but the changes he did propose were widely understood as an attempt to reconfigure gender relations within the community, and many Muslims were concerned about where these innovations would lead.

At Masjid al-Mu'mineen, short sleeves, three-quarter sleeves, skirts worn just below the knee, and hair swept up in fashionable hats had for years been the unremarkable norm. Suddenly, these styles of dress were no longer acceptable; in fact, they were denounced as sinful. Curtains appeared in some mosque spaces to divide male and female worshipers, and at others women were moved into separate rooms altogether. As at Masjid Wali Muhammad, this new conservatism struck many of the longstanding Muslims as pointless and retrogressive. Tahira Khalid carefully explained to me that these changes in dress did not follow the introduction of the hijab in Dearborn, which became visible as a trend among local Arabs well after the Iranian Revolution in 1979. Instead, she insisted, this shift in wardrobe was something black Muslims produced by and for themselves, first as an expression of African-identified black consciousness and later as a sign of Islamic literacy, identification, and piety.[71]

Tahira was personally convinced to put on the hijab, after many years of resisting it, by her close spiritual advisor at the time, Imam Adil al-Aseer. Covering, he taught her, is appropriate not only because it encourages modesty, but because it is important that the world see sincere, believing Muslims as Muslims. How else, he asked her, could Americans be made to understand the beauty, values, and commitment of the believers?[72] For Sister Tahira, this decision was difficult. Having been raised a Muslim in a community where most women did not cover, and having participated in mosques throughout the city and country where women covered only for prayer and only in prayer spaces, this distinctive way of comporting the body involved a dramatic step across the threshold of old and new styles of Muslim practice.

Imam al-Aseer's understanding of the hijab as something that makes Muslim women appropriately visible stemmed from a complicated set of principles. In the first place, it recognized that Muslims in the United States are a minority who are easily overlooked, or seen improperly. Only proper visibility would allow American Muslims to gain recognition as a viable religious community. In this sense, the hijab and other forms of distinctive Muslim dress perform a vital function as dawa. Yet in the wake of the 1973 Arab-Israeli war and during an ongoing civil war in Lebanon and the Islamic Revolution in Iran, this sartorial outreach was a highly politicized undertaking. Islam itself was increasingly portrayed in popular US media as un-American and actively anti-American. Women who put on hijab in the 1970s made themselves vulnerable to mistreatment, or at least endless stares and questioning from non-Muslims (and from immigrant Muslims who thought it strange, comical even, for Americans to willingly dress this way). While African head wraps could be interpreted as a fashion statement, as an empowered act of Afrocentric identification, the hijab carried other connotations. It meant that Muslim women, like the Beys, were performing Muslim identity in ways that were meant to be seen as new, alternative, and alien. The hijab carried the aesthetics and body politics of revivalist Islam into the home, the mosque, and the city as a whole.

Carolyn Rouse, who has asked why black women would willingly embrace Islam, a choice that minoritizes them three times over (in terms of race, gender, and religion), has argued that the hijab protects women from stereotypes of African American female promiscuity and provides a space for the acquisition of ritual and religious knowledge, a space in which women can amass their own spiritual power beyond and beneath the gaze of the American public.[73] By the early 1980s, when Sister Tahira first put on the hijab, she was hardly alone. Women at Masjid Wali Muhammad, Masjid al-Nur, Masjid al-Asr, and other black-majority mosques had already accepted these norms. Many of the older members of Masjid al-Mu'mineen, like Sister Hataima Sharieff, did not find this new direction comforting or appropriate. They thought it gave the wrong impression of Islam and of Muslims. Like the men at Masjid Wali Muhammad, who protested Hajj Mazen Alwan's teachings about dress and modesty, they thought the hijab made the Muslim community look backward, unfriendly to women, and out of step with the times.[74]

The arrival of the hijab signaled other, equally significant changes in the status of Muslim women. The most notable and controversial of these changes was the acceptance of polygamy, a custom that is illegal in the United States and has long been defined as "un-American," oppressive of women, and a threat to the Muslim community's ability to practice their faith without legal persecution in this country.[75] Certainly this was how many members of Masjid al-Mu'mineen viewed plural marriage, especially those who had worshiped at the mosque when it was led by Osman Hassanein in the 1960s and 1970s. Not only did polygamy undermine the middle-class aspirations of the community, it also threatened the mosque's status as a beacon of respectability and a safe point of contact between Muslims and non-Muslims and between American Muslims and foreign ones. Nonetheless, the leadership of the reorganized Masjid al-Mu'mineen tolerated polygamy within its new congregation, initially in hopes of attracting members from the city's countercultural black Muslim groups, many of whom engaged freely in plural marriage.[76]

Scholars disagree over the role polygamy played in the chaotic history of the black Muslim community in the 1970s and 1980s. "There were plenty of converts, but also new problems engendered either by confusion or abuse of Islamic ideals," argues Robert Dannin. "One stunning example was the mismanagement of polygamous marriage laws. Another was the failure to stabilize housing and labor according to an Islamic work ethic."[77] Sherman Jackson is less critical of polygamy, suggesting that if Americans were more tolerant of alternative lifestyles, the practice could be seen as a help to many blacks, among whom—he points out—67 percent of children are born to unmarried parents. In this context, he concludes, polygamy might well "strike a balance between interest and principle."[78] Yet at Masjid al-Mu'mineen, when polygamous unions moved from the fringe of the congregation and were adopted by the mosque's leaders in the early 1980s, this decision was met with loud objections, tears, and fisticuffs. Many members stepped away from the mosque, and some left Islam altogether. Immigrant Muslims who had supported the mosque financially were prominent among the deserters. Whatever their reservations about living as Muslims in the United States, they had not come to Detroit to flaunt American laws, challenge its most cherished social norms, and thereby bring negative attention to the Muslim community.[79]

Haitama Sharieff captures the mood of the period vividly in her description of the last event she attended at al-Mu'mineen, where a foreign Muslim's disapproval of gendered comingling was allowed to determine the congregation's behavior.

It was in the 80s. It was on Fenkel, in a new place they were renting.

I don't know where this brother come from, a brother from the East, but we were having this eid and, you know, the ladies would usually go in and cook the dinner and everything. And this brother couldn't stand to see a sister passing.

So the brothers said, "Well, just hand us the food and we'll fix it."

I don't know what was wrong with him, but he put all the sisters in the back, and he put a sheet up in front of them.

So the brother was having a fit. So they said, "We are going to feed this brother in a hurry and get him out."

I don't know where he come from. He was a foreigner and a fanatic and he was having fits. [She mimics someone shouting in a foreign language.] The sisters said, "No! No!" So the sisters were behind the curtain. Some of them were talking loud enough for this guy to hear. "What is wrong with that crazy guy?"[80]

In Sister Sharieff's narrative, this misfit of orthodoxies and cultural expectations is reduced to craziness, to unintelligibility and appeasement.

The most conservative voice—and the loudest—is able to dictate the norms of the group.

When I spoke with Saleem Khalid about these issues, he directed our conversation away from marital politics and gender dynamics, suggesting that the demise of Masjid al-Mu'mineen was more immediately the result of larger shifts in the politics of race, space, and place in greater Detroit in the 1960s and 1970s. The city underwent significant demographic changes, he stressed, as well as rapid deindustrialization, white and middle-class flight, and new immigration. These trends reconfigured the Muslim population in Detroit, marginalizing the black Muslim community and amplifying some of this community's more countercultural practices (polygamy being an obvious example). In this period, low-income Yemeni immigrants moved into the city, replacing the (frequently elite) Indian and Pakistani immigrants and foreign students who had once attended Masjid al-Mu'mineen and supported it financially. These South Asian students, who gradually assumed professional status as doctors, lawyers, engineers, and pharmacists, began opening mosques of their own in the distant suburbs, where they were settling with their families. In 1977 the Muslim Center of the Western Suburbs was opened in Canton, and in 1978 the Islamic Association of Greater Detroit was established in the far northeastern suburb of Rochester Hills. Both congregations were overwhelmingly South Asian. Immigrants could now attend mosques where Urdu, Hindi, and Punjabi were spoken. They could insist on gender norms, educational standards, social practices, and religious observances that were familiar to them.[81] Yemeni workers also opened mosques in this period, most notably the Islamic Mosque of Yemen of Detroit in 1976.[82] Arab students could, by 1981, choose among three Yemeni and four Lebanese mosques. African Americans would soon be able to choose among eight black-majority mosques. Masjid al-Asr opened in 1978, and Masjid al-Nur and Masjid al-Haqq followed in 1981. Three former NOI temples in the city were converted into mosques during this period as well. Instead of becoming more relevant as Detroit's black Muslim population grew from a few hundred to a few thousand, Masjid al-Mu'mineen suddenly faced tremendous competition.

Saleem Khalid agreed that the sources of doctrinal and ideological discontent I have explored in this chapter were critical to the dissolution of Masjid al-Mu'mineen, but he insists that the growth of the suburbs, fueled by anti-black racism, also pulled the Muslim community apart.

SALEEM KHALID: It propelled Islamic sprawl outside the city. Where do you find the Muslims? They are not setting up shop on Cass Ave., on the East Side, and people will give you a thousand different reasons, and at the end of the day, at the bottom of that recipe, is racism. Now it doesn't have to be overt. It can just be, "We are a lot more comfortable in Canton." "We are a lot more comfortable in Rochester [middle-class suburbs]." I understand that.

SALLY HOWELL: The schools are better...

KHALID: The insurance rates are lower. The incidence of break-ins and car thefts is lower.

HOWELL: The houses are newer...

KHALID: I understand. So, you see, racism played a role. It played a role back then, but you don't dwell on it. You keep moving; that is what you have to do and that is what people did back then. They understood that people weren't going to come and set up shop in the middle of Detroit. If they were going to give dawa, they were going to give dawa from a distance. If they were going to raise money for an Islamic center in Detroit, it was going to be a little less than they were going to raise for somewhere else.

That was part of our reality.

Khalid's assessment is true. Despite the steady discrimination and prejudice Arab and Asian Muslims have faced in the United States since 1967, they have been better positioned to secure for themselves the benefits of suburban life than have black American Muslims. This obvious racial disparity played a central role in the weakening and demise of Masjid al-Mu'mineen. The group's long battle for transcommunal relevance and its desire to make Islam welcoming and attractive to non-Muslims were no longer realizable goals. After several years of in-fighting and recriminations, Masjid al-Mu'mineen closed its doors in 1985. By the time I began my research in 2004, the mosque was seldom discussed, its members had been absorbed into newer congregations throughout the city and suburbs, and most Detroit Muslims did not know that a mosque like Masjid al-Mu'mineen had ever existed.

The immigrants who worshiped at the mosque as students or young professionals in the 1960s and 1970s sometimes refuse to acknowledge that Masjid al-Mu'mineen was a mosque at all. Compared to the well-financed, architecturally significant mosques found across Detroit's suburbs today, Masjid al-Mu'mineen's location in a renovated house in a marginal urban neighborhood, without a permanent musalla, without a dome or minarets, and without a foreign-born imam might explain its ex-post-facto demotion from "mosque" to something else in the minds of the post-1965 revivalist activists who once prayed there. The introduction of more conservative gender norms and the move to a new space in 1980 did not dispel this dissatisfaction. The Detroit Muslims who today deny that al-Mu'mineen was ever a "mosque" often make similar claims about the AMS under the leadership of the Karoubs. In this respect, they resemble an earlier generation of Lebanese Muslims who claimed that Hashmie Hall was not a mosque. More than a statement of cultural or religious bias, this refusal to grant the status of mosque to Detroit's early Muslim congregations is a stance meant to deflect attention from the Islamic beliefs and practices that held sway in the past and the intense contests for control over sacred space that erupted in the city's mosques whenever old and new Islams came into contact with each other. The Islam practiced at al-Mu'mineen in its prime cannot be described today without dredging up painful memories of the ideological disputes, abrupt gender transitions, and race-based abandonment that brought about the mosque's failure.

Perhaps this is why former members of Masjid al-Mu'mineen prefer to remember the individual survivors, not the institutional losses. When I asked Tahira Khalid what she made of this momentous period of transition in the history of Detroit's black Muslim community, she responded with a mix of confidence, defiance, and pride:

> Many persons continue to be impressed by the fact that this generation of men and women like Hajj Sammsam, Dad [Osman Hassanein], Brother Sharrief, Sister Sharrief, my mother, Rokiyah and Jamil Ibrahim, had the vision and fortitude to build something of such significance as an international mosque and were not so brainwashed in their imposed marginality that they could not conceive of a vision beyond the indoctrination which was meant to dictate and diminish their life journeys. The success of this movement maybe cannot be found in concrete buildings, but many of the children of these individuals are Islamic scholars, lawyers, teachers, and hold on to their Islamic identities with pride.[83]

If the purpose of Masjid al-Mu'mineen was to equip a new generation of Muslims to recreate the moral community of Islam in the wilderness of America, and to do so against forces of racism, exclusion, and debilitating ignorance, then it is possible to remember it—among the few who are privileged to remember it—as a success.

Islamic Revolutions

At the ICA and the AIC, similar attempts to (re)define orthodox belief and practice took place in the 1970s and early 1980s, and similar conflicts ensued. Once again, established Muslim American institutions were confronted by the expectations of new immigrants and newly converted Muslims. Led by progressive imams with scholarly credentials, housed in buildings that reflected midcentury trends in architectural design, and filled with worshipers who had lived in the United States for a generation or more—the ICA and the AIC faced off against the new immigrants, new ideologies, and new transnational Muslim organizations that arrived in Detroit in the 1970s. One of these congregations reformed much of its historical practice as it struggled to accommodate new forces. The other remained resolute.

By the late 1970s, thousands of Muslim immigrants were arriving in greater Detroit each year as a consequence of liberalized immigration laws and political unrest in the Middle East and Asia. These newcomers felt very differently about their faith, the countries they left behind, and their future place in the United States than had earlier migrants. They arrived in a city with old and active mosques, with ethnic newspapers, coffeehouses, restaurants, halal butchers, grocers, bookstores, Arabic-language television and radio programs, social service agencies, political advocacy groups, and village and national clubs. These institutions explain why so many Muslims were drawn to Detroit in the first place, but they cannot explain why the newest Muslim immigrants frequently felt marginal and stigmatized, or why members of the larger society would view them with suspicion and actively discriminate against them.

The negative image of the new immigrants was mirrored in the specter of the Muslim militant/terrorist, a stock character in Western media culture. "In the United States," Melanie McAlister writes, "the 1980s began with the nightly spectacle of Americans held hostage by Iranian militants in Tehran. During the 444 days of their captivity, which began on November 4, 1979, and ended on January 21, 1981, the day Ronald Reagan was inaugurated as president, the hostages in Iran became a national symbol."[84] Documenting the dramatic increase in anti-Arab discrimination and violence that took place in the United States in the 1980s, Nabeel Abraham argues that this violence was focused more directly on Muslim subjects and Islamic institutions as the decade progressed.[85] In this tense atmosphere, Islam was simultaneously vilified in the United States and valorized in much of the Middle East. To make matters worse, the United States was embroiled in culture wars of its own making over issues like the equal rights amendment and a white backlash against the accomplishments of the civil rights movement. If America seemed like a hostile, ideologically unsettled place to many of its native-born citizens, could newly arrived Muslim immigrants (themselves accused of harboring anti-American sentiments) find safe haven in the mosques and other Muslim spaces that proliferated in Detroit? For many, the answer was yes, but only if the social and religious norms that prevailed in Detroit's mosques, and in the daily lives of local Muslims, could be transformed into something more familiar. And gender dynamics, once again, were a central idiom in which this familiarity would be perceived, recreated, and imposed.

"Racialized immigrants," according to Yen Le Espiritu, "claim through gender the power denied them through racism," but this project, so essential to critical race theory and postcolonial immigration politics, does not sufficiently explain why new Muslim immigrants to Detroit (like the black converts of the same period) became singularly obsessed with the social interaction, physical appearance, and spatial placement of men and women in Detroit's mosques.[86] Nabeel Abraham, in his analysis of the Yemeni takeover of the AMS in 1978, argues that newly arrived Arab immigrants, especially the more devout among them, brought to America very different cultural models of mosques as gendered spaces.[87] In the Arab world of the 1970s, women rarely visited mosques at all, and they played almost no role in their daily operation. As we saw in Chapter 6, immigrants from the Yemeni and Palestinian countryside were scandalized to see women, hair uncovered, presiding over Sunday school classes and social functions in American mosques. They insisted that propriety, as they understood it, be restored. These new immigrants often considered themselves authorities on Islam because, unlike so many of the already American Muslims in Detroit, this group spoke fluent Arabic, had grown up in Muslim-majority countries, had received standardized Islamic instruction in the public schools, and had witnessed firsthand the growth of Islamic revival movements overseas.

These problems became especially complex at the ICA, where Imam Chirri, who had worked so diligently as an Americanizer of Islam, an interfaith pioneer, and a committed Cold Warrior, found himself greatly inspired (and politically marginalized) by the Islamic Revolution in Iran, a Shi'i people's movement led by men of religion like himself, men he revered and most Americans despised. The Shi'i population in Dearborn exploded in the 1970s, as Lebanese immigrants and refugees poured into the area to escape the ravages of civil war and Israeli occupation. Chirri's political and spiritual embrace of the Islamic Revolution was in keeping with the political sensibilities that prevailed among new immigrants. With few exceptions, they saw this revolution's emphasis on religious nationalism, social justice, widespread political participation, independence from imperial overlords, and a return to authentic regional traditions as the antidote to their own military and cultural occupation. Chirri credited Ayatollah Ruhollah Khomeini—the spiritual and political leader of the new Islamic Republic of Iran—with being a great *mujaddid* (reviver) of Islam. To the dismay of many of his longtime supporters, Chirri embraced Khomeini as his personal *marja'* (spiritual guide).[88]

The Ayatollah's popularity among the newly arrived South Lebanese in Dearborn in the early 1980s cannot be overstated. Yet to many of the city's older Muslim Americans, this was an unmitigated disaster. Julia Haragely, who was born in Michigan City, Indiana, in 1920 reminded me that it was Khomeini who referred to the United States as the "great Satan" and whose regime was responsible for a horrific purge of suspected dissenters.[89] "[The Islamic Center] started to change when all this mishmash happened with the rise of Khomeini," she told me. Quoting the newcomers, she continued, " 'Oh, Khomeini could be Muhammad Ibn al-Hassan.' You know who that is? The Mahdi! Come on, I don't buy all that."[90] And to Haragely's consternation, Imam Chirri seemed to embrace similar ideas. In an undated press release that must have been published in 1979 or 1980, Chirri suggested that Khomeini was the fulfillment of several prophecies made by the sixth and seventh imams of the "House of the Prophet Mohammed," who said, "A man from the people of Qum will invite mankind to accept the true religious ideology. He will be followed by people who are as solid as pieces of steel." This leader would bring about the return of the Mahdi, who would join with the risen Christ to "religiously unite all mankind."[91] Chirri's appeal to seventh- and eighth- century religious leaders in his campaign to convince interfaith activists and American journalists of Khomeini's legitimacy reveals just how abrupt and unqualified his own spiritual transformation was.

In the newly intense political atmosphere ushered in by the Iranian Revolution, the relaxed gender regime of the ICA became a source of extreme anxiety for recent immigrants, and increasingly for Chirri as well. Suddenly, he was expected to defend mores that allowed women to move about the mosque with hair uncovered, men and women to greet one another with handshakes and a kiss on each cheek, and adolescent boys and girls to dance with each other at weddings and mosque fundraisers.

HUSSEIN HAMOOD: [Imam Chirri] used to shave [his beard]. He used to shake hands [with women], and he used to...accept the women uncovered. Ok.

Just when they started to have [political] parties in Lebanon, Hizbullah and Amal and that sort of thing, there is a young man over here and he stand by the door [of the mosque] and he tell you if you are not covered you cannot get in or nothing.

And he [Imam Chirri] said, "Oh no. Those women, those daughters, those girls, they came from Troy and Sterling Heights, from Warren [distant suburbs]. They passed by so many [non-Islamic] things that they can go and have fun and different things, and they [instead] want to hear the word of God, and they come over here to Joy Road [where the mosque was located in Detroit]. You tell them—let them come inside. I will speak to them."

And he says in his sermon, "Your ancestor is Umm Hashim (for example) or Umm Ali [women of the Prophet's lineage], and they will be proud of you when you are covered."

That is how he would do it.[92]

In this example, Imam Chirri is represented as a master of gradual persuasion. Like Mazen Alwan, Chirri realized that he could not turn his congregation on a dime. He knew that change would be as difficult at the ICA as it had been at other well-established mosques in Detroit. Nonetheless, turning his congregation in a new, more visibly pious direction did indeed become Imam Chirri's objective, and it is clear from this example of a young immigrant seeking to impose hijab on all who entered the mosque that Chirri was subjected to tremendous pressure himself in this regard. In Julia Haragely's description of the period, it was "fanatics" and "fundamentalists," much more than Chirri himself, who felt local efforts at reform were not unfolding quickly enough.

They came out after the rise of Khomeini. That's when the fundamentalists came out. We would go to the mosque, and we sat in the lecture room, men and women together. No one said anything about it. If you went in the prayer room to pray, you covered your hair.

All of a sudden I understand somebody sent to the Najaf. That's the university, you know [Chirri's alma mater]. Somebody said that he wasn't following the faith. The women wore lipstick and makeup and stuff like that...

Anyways they started to pressure you to cover your hair.

Well, I balked. I tell you, I refused. I refused.

My husband was very active at the mosque. He used to go help, you know, to make Xeroxes. He would go to the bank and stuff like that. He would take the imam to the bank, and after Imam Chirri retired, he would wash the dead. My husband, he did it for ten years until he got real sick...

We would have weddings [see Figures 7.7 and 7.8]. We would have music.

Anyway, they wound up banning music. When she [the bride] is marching down the aisle, now they're saying prayers.

Oh, come on. Give me a break.

Haragely's exasperation over the changes that took place in her community in the 1980s runs very deep, so much so that she began to describe herself as a "secular Muslim" to fend off the constant barrage of questions she heard from newly arrived immigrants who wondered why her hair was uncovered, whether she had made hajj, and if she considered herself to be Sunni or Shi'a.[93] Imam Chirri, who identified strongly with Khomeini's revivalist movement, embraced many of the postrevolutionary etiquettes and orthodoxies introduced by the new Shi'i leadership in Iran, Lebanon, and Detroit. He urged his followers to do likewise. As a result, many conservative men no longer shook hands with women. Beards became ubiquitous. Women washed the makeup off their faces, and the hijab became commonplace. The piano was removed from the lecture hall at the ICA, and fathers escorted their daughter brides to the accompaniment of Qur'anic recitations rather than the traditional American wedding march (see Figures 7.7 and 7.8). The celebratory wedding banquets that were held at the ICA no longer included dubkeh bands or deejays who played popular American dance tunes. If families wanted the old-style festivities, they hosted them outside the mosque, in the Italian and Polish banquet halls of east Dearborn.[94]

These changes happened because the worshipers at the ICA, like those at Masjid as-Salaam and Masjid al-Mu'mineen, sought increasingly to follow the "example of the Prophet," a behavioral standard that American Muslims had understood differently in the past. Men and women were equally affected by this shift to a more literal expression of piety. Lila Amen, who grew up attending the AMS in the 1960s, and her husband, Mohsen Amen, a South Lebanese immigrant who arrived in the 1970s, offer an interpretation of the Islamic Revolution and the changes it produced among Lebanese Muslims in Detroit that differs markedly from the views of Julia Haragely. Here, the Amens describe the sudden, transformative effect these events, and a new generation of Muslim teachers, had on their lives.

FIGURE 7.7 Imam Chirri presides over the wedding of Miriam and Carl Eastman, Islamic Center of America, 1974. Courtesy of Miriam and Carl Eastman.

FIGURE 7.8 The groom, Carl Eastman, throws the bride's garter belt to the awaiting groomsmen, Islamic Center of America, 1974. Courtesy of Miriam and Carl Eastman.

LILA AMEN: First, it was Skeikh Abdel Latif [Berry]. He...took a room at ACCESS [the Arab Community Center in Dearborn] and used it for Friday prayers. Then it started to grow, rapidly grow. This was in 1980, 1981. Of course the Islamic Revolution in Iran kicked off in 1979. I believe it was in 1981 that Al-Sayyad Mohammed Hussein Fadlallah came to town. Then a whole group of people just woke up. It was very strange. He came to town. He was a very big figure from Lebanon. I'll never forget that they had this event out at a country club in Southfield, the Bonnie Brook. Hundreds of people went there. I think it was more out of curiosity. It was a political time...

[Mohsen interrupts. He had attended this event.]

MOHSEN AMEN: Everybody that I knew was there. And I saw Al-Sayyad Mohammed Hussein Fadlallah. I knew him since I was a little boy, 'cause he used to be a shaykh right in my neighborhood. He knew my father. I asked him if he remembered me. He said, "Yes, I do remember you. You are the son of so-and-so." And he reminded me of things I used to do when he was making sermons. For me, that was like I was sleeping and somebody woke me up from a dream. I came back home. I put the Qur'an in front of me and I started crying. I didn't know what to do. I had forgotten how to pray. I forgot everything. I didn't even know how to recite the *fatihah*. I forgot all about that. Then I start to read, read. And I start to do my *salah*, and I cried. My wife saw me. She said, "What the heck is wrong with this man? He goes to a dinner and he comes back like there is something wrong with him."[95]

These moments of collective transition were intensely political and deeply emotional. Fadlallah's personal touch and his fiery rhetoric captivated a crowd of several hundred men in Southfield, many of whom were reawakened to the faith of Islam, just as millions of Shi'a around the globe had been inspired by Khomeini's revolution. The Bonnie Brook Social Club was not the ICA, and the event described above was organized not by Imam Chirri but by a rival Shi'i cleric who had arrived in Detroit in 1980, Abdel Latif Berry.

At first, the rapid influx of new immigrants to Detroit invigorated the ICA. New immigrants meant potential spouses for the American-born, a growing congregation, a renewal of the Arabic language, and much more. A revitalized Muslim community also meant that many families like the Amens, longstanding community members, were coming to the mosque in greater numbers. The ICA offered a space of familiarity and welcome. It was a mosque with a well-trained, Arabic-speaking, Shiʻi cleric who was close to many of the leading Lebanese clerics of the day. Chirri also shared the new arrivals' outrage over injustices in Lebanon and Palestine and frustration about how the Islamic Revolution was destabilizing the relationship between the United States and Iran. Yet Imam Chirri's mosque looked foreign and unintelligible to these new arrivals. How could it be, they asked, that English was the dominant language of the mosque? Why were uncovered women found around every corner? Why did women seem to run the institution?

As these moments of confusion and concern accumulated, it became clear that the status quo at the ICA could no longer hold. Shaykh Abdel Latif Berry, the new cleric who so deeply influenced the Amens and other young Muslims, was, like Chirri, a scholar trained in Najaf. Berry was from an impressive line of clerics and, more importantly, had deep roots in the same Lebanese villages from which much of the new Dearborn was migrating. The Berry family is large and powerful, both in Lebanon and in greater Detroit. In the 1950s, they had supported Kalil Bazzy and opposed Chirri when the ICA was first being organized. Now, having arrived fresh from the war zone and having worked closely with Al-Sayyad Mohammed Hussein Fadlallah, one of the most influential spiritual guides of the new Islamic awakening in Lebanon and a close affiliate of the factions that coalesced into Harakat al-Amal[96] and Hizbullah,[97] Abdel Latif Berry quickly began to articulate a critique of the failed praxis of the ICA. He also began organizing a rival mosque in 1981, the Islamic Institute of Knowledge, which grew exponentially after Sayyad Fadlallah's emotional lecture at the Bonnie Brook Social Club. This is why men like Hajj Eide Alawan (mentioned at the opening of this chapter) attributed the new religious standards imposed at the ICA to Shaykh Berry's arrival rather than directly to the Revolution in Iran. It was Berry who legitimated the more conservative institutional praxis among the Lebanese Shiʻa in Detroit and, to quote Hajj Eide again, "raised the bar."[98]

It can be argued that the Islamic Institute of Knowledge did more than propagate a vibrant, intensely conservative model of piety in Detroit; it also served as a pressure valve, siphoning the "fundamentalists" and the "fanaticals," as Julia Haragely described them, away from the ICA. For Imam Chirri and the large congregation who remained with him at the ICA, struggles over internal mosque dynamics were only one front in a much larger ideological contest. Chirri was still heavily invested in the crisis and the accomplishments of the Islamic Revolution. Shortly after the Shah was forced into exile in 1979, a large four-by-six-foot portrait of

Ayatollah Khomeini was placed inside the social hall at the ICA with the accompanying caption, "I have come to perfect your religion." This image created tremendous anxiety among Sunni members of the congregation, the remainder of whom dropped off the board. Many stopped attending the mosque's functions altogether.[99] Chirri continued to lecture publically about Islam on his weekly radio program, "Islam in Focus," and to local university groups and interfaith gatherings, but he now attacked the excesses of the former Shah and his successors in addition to his more regular criticism of the Soviet Union.[100]

"We found [the Shah] worse than Hitler in the rating of crimes," he told one gathering of clergy. "Hitler killed people of nationalities with which he was at war. This man killed his own people, and he stole $20 billion, unique in the annals of history."[101] The Iranian students who held the American embassy personnel hostage, Chirri argued, "may be wrong, but they want to show us about oppression...They asked for the Shah when he was alive and he escaped that. But whether we are Christian or Moslem, an apology for wrongdoing is not wrong."[102] The hostage crisis was an event that Imam Chirri took very personally. He was thrilled and awed by the revolution, and he was distressed to see his own country taking such a hard line on the new regime. He traveled to the White House and met with President Jimmy Carter about the hostage situation. He offered his services to the government to negotiate on behalf of the United States for the release of the Americans. He used the occasion of Ashura in 1979 to telegram Iran's foreign minister, imploring him to "free unilaterally the men of the American Embassy in the name of the Imam Al-Husayn the leader of the martyrs as a major sacrifice on your part for his glory and in the interest of world peace."[103] The Carter administration did not take Chirri seriously as a negotiator, so in December of 1979 he traveled to Tehran on his own. His goal was to personally reconcile his spiritual and national homes in this moment of intense international crisis and political miscomprehension.[104]

While in Tehran, Imam Chirri met with Ayatollah Hussein-Ali Montazeri, Khomeini's second-in-command, and joined the imam in attending an outdoor Friday prayer service in which "over a million worshippers participated."[105] Addressing the crowd and praying before them were awe-inspiring experiences for Chirri. Shortly after his return, he issued a press release from the ICA that detailed how free and open the recent Iranian elections for president had been, how the people were much better off under the new government, and how local media in Detroit should report—with less bias—the many ways in which the Iranian Revolution had brought about positive change.

> We ought not to treat the Islamic revolution in Iran as a problem, we should rather consider it a blessing. The religious zeal which was kindled by the Iranian revolution is a shield to the Muslim world and ultimately to the free world. It offered the Iranian nation and other Muslim nations an alternative to Communism or any other ideology. The masses of the people of Afghanistan and Iran do not fight Communism in order to protect their wealth, because they are not wealthy. They do resist Communism only to preserve their religion...
>
> We were not receptive to the Islamic Revolution since its inception. We ought to change our attitude towards this revolution and to turn 180 degrees. Probably our government is not in a position to do this at the present, but you, the people of the highly respected media, can do the job by informing the people of the positive side of the revolution.[106]

Here we see a Cold Warrior speaking through the gauze of religious revival. Islam, Chirri argues, is the answer to the Soviet threat. It is not the problem Americans seem determined to think it is. Chirri's message illustrates his deeply held conviction that Islam, as much as Christianity and Judaism, is an authentically American religious tradition at home and a force of liberation and change abroad. In the early 1980s, he would increasingly direct his anti-Communist and pro-Islam arguments toward the growing population of new immigrants from South Lebanon. In one such address (likely delivered in 1980), the "Soviet Union no Match for Islam," Chirri insisted on the link between Islam and freedom, even as public opinion and American policies insisted on just the opposite. Interestingly, a surviving video of this event illustrates how quickly the ICA congregation was adapting to the new gender regimes of the period. Chirri himself now wears a bushy beard, a larger, "Iranian-style" *laffi* (turban), and a full-length robe and cloak. He is joined at the front of the lecture hall by several clerics, including Abdel Latif Berry. He speaks from a new mihrab (raised pulpit) rather than a lectern. The audience is segregated by gender, with men in front and women at the rear of the hall rather than in mixed family groupings familiar from the past. The women's section stands out because of the white, loosely fitted headscarves that cover the hair and shoulders of most of those on hand. (The hijab itself is still a few years off.)[107]

If these transitions seem sudden and dramatic, they were greeted as such by Chirri's longtime loyalists and opponents alike. For Imam Vehbi Ismail, spiritual leader of Detroit's Albanian community, himself an adamant Cold Warrior and reviver of Islam, the changes that overtook the congregation at the ICA and his old friend and colleague, Imam Chirri, were painful to watch. While he would not have disagreed with Chirri on the value of Islam to America or the fight against Communism overseas, he saw the newly politicized Islam and anti-American rhetoric of Khomeini as disruptive, and he thought the new expressions of religiosity that were sweeping over Dearborn were counterproductive.

In 1979, Ismail's home country, Albania, was still under Communist rule, its mosques shuttered, its Christian and Muslim clergy in prison or exile. Ismail's primary political objective had long been to overthrow the Enver Hoxha regime and establish a democracy that protected the religious freedom of all Albanians. These political ambitions were completely in line with US foreign policy, whereas Chirri's support for the Iranian Revolution was easily (mis)construed as anti-American. More critical still, immigration from Albania was not significantly affected by the Immigration and Naturalization Act of 1965.[108] The new immigrants who visited the AIC in the 1960s and 1970s were mostly from India and Pakistan or from the Middle East, not from Albania. While these newcomers voiced their concerns over the customs they observed at the AIC, Ismail made it clear to them that they would have no say in the management of his institution. Its board was (and remains) open only to Albanian members. The Albanian refugees who had arrived in Detroit between the 1950s and the 1970s often had received no religious education under Communist authorities and were more interested in the AIC as a home for their political and ethnic identities rather than as a platform for a new religious one. Thus in 1978, many of the non-Albanian immigrants Ismail had turned away from leadership positions worked together to establish the Islamic Association of Greater Detroit (described above).

As Imam Chirri and thousands of new immigrants began to impose a new social order in Detroit's mosques, Imam Vehbi Ismail plotted a separate course. In an interview I conducted with him shortly before his death, Ismail describes a visit the AIC received in 1981 from a representative of the Muslim World League, the Saudi-backed organization that paid the salary of Mazen Alwan and supported Salafi reform in mosques across North America.

In 1981 came the head of *Rabita al-'Alam al-Islami* [the Muslim World League] here. He went to Dearborn first, and they called me. They said, "Please tell the women to put [on the hijab]." Because most of our people don't.

And, he came, and I did not tell the women. But I told him that Dearborn had asked me to do it. I told Dearborn, "If they don't listen to me because it is ordered, or is good religiously, why [should they] make it [cover their hair] for Ali al-Harakan?"

His name was Ali al-Harakan.

I said, "I did not tell them."

And I didn't.

The only mosque that [he] gave $10,000 to was our mosque.

He said, "I like your sincerity."

I said, "Why to [ask the women to cover], to cheat you, to tell my wife [to cover]?"

My wife does not put [wear a hijab]. She is born here.

The Qur'an says *la ikrah fi ad-din* [there is no compulsion in religion]. I tell her she has got to have [it, to wear the hijab]. She does not want this.

And then there is a misunderstanding. In the Qur'an, the Qur'an tells to man, "lower your eyes." It tells the same to woman. So why does the woman have to wear those [scarves]?[109]

Imam Vehbi also argued that there is no need to segregate men from women in the mosque—for social events, or in separate prayer rooms—another issue which became significant in the late 1970s. "We don't [segregate] a man and woman," he said. "They sit together, one facing another, all equal. All the Muslims are brothers. The one that comes here thinks that my wife is his sister. We don't look in different ways."[110]

As these observations suggest, the two scholar imams who had revived Islamic practices and institutions in Detroit and nationally in the 1950s and 1960s, and the mosques they had established, went separate ways in the 1970s. Both imams had become "American" to an extent neither would have thought possible in 1949, when they arrived in the United States. Behaviors Chirri and Ismail once considered moral lapses they now tolerated and even endorsed as vital aspects of American Muslim identity. But the external pressures their congregations faced in the early 1980s led one imam toward a newly politicized and revitalized Islam, while the other clung tightly to the (now) old Islamic American practices his community had developed in Detroit.

Conclusion

The bitter disputes that shook the Muslim American community in the 1970s radically altered the atmosphere and the manner of worship in Detroit mosques. These changes, in effect, eradicated the Muslim American praxis that men like Mike Karoub, Vehbi Ismail, Mohammad Jawad Chirri, and Osman Hassanein spent their lives promoting. This outcome was not limited to Detroit.[111] Often made in the name of a purified Islam, the reforms that swept through American mosques were focused, time and again, on public, highly visible expressions of faith; on the role women played in mosques; on how women and men dressed; and on the conventions that would guide cross-gender interactions in mosque space. Religious conversion and transnational migration are themselves gendered processes; likewise, mosques are gendered spaces shaped by conversion and migration. In the 1960s, Detroit's mosques were spaces that encouraged autonomy and active participation for men and women alike. For earlier generations of Muslim women, these spaces were emancipatory and affirming. Basing his claims on research he did in the 1950s, Elkholy argued that without the participation of women, Detroit's mosques would probably not have existed. He found gender to be an insignificant variable when measuring the religiosity of Detroit Muslims and when attempting to "intelligently discuss Islam."[112] Imam Chirri also learned this lesson early in his career, arguing that the most important thing he realized while in exile in Michigan City was that "the power of the church is in the woman's hands."[113]

The tales of transformation and social discord I tell in this chapter are as much about culture and politics as they are about religious beliefs and ritual purity. Nonetheless, the idiom of orthodoxy intentionally simplifies these transitions, moralizing them and obscuring much that was at stake historically. The storm surge of new Muslims and new Islams that swept through Detroit in the 1970s effectively washed away much of Detroit's past as an Islamic city. Even careful scholars, like Linda Walbridge, find themselves reproducing this narrative of erasure.

> In Dearborn, there is a new interpretation of the purpose of the mosque. It is actually part of a process that was started in the early part of this century. The mosque initially was used for all social events, many of which had nothing to do with religion. Then, an earlier group of the new wave of immigrants came. Steeped in tradition, they tried to bring the mosque in line with what was done in Lebanon, so they moved weddings out of the mosque [the ICA]. A slightly later group, strongly influenced by political changes in the

Middle East, arrived, and once again the mosque (particularly the Majma'
[the Islamic Institute of Knowledge]) became a center for all types of occasions. But all of these occasions have been redefined as religious.[114]

Here Walbridge states that at the Majma', the mosque Abdel Latif
Berry founded in 1982, weddings were again permitted to take place. This
occurred only because music and dancing were no longer a part of the
celebrations, couples wore "Islamic attire," and the ritual was observed
according to strict religious guidelines of gender segregation. For her, this
new order "redefined" wedding parties and other social activities as "religious" occasions rather than events that, as she sees it, had "nothing to do
with religion" prior to these reforms.

Imams Chirri and Ismail, lay leaders like Hassanein and his daughter
Tahira Khalid, and virtually every proponent of old Islam in Detroit I spoke
to for this research were well aware that the "social events" that took place
in their mosques were actually critical to the spiritual life of their congregations. They were thus deeply religious activities. If, at the Majma' and
the transformed ICA, hijabs rather than hats or hairdos were worn "for all
types of occasions" and men and women sat in divided spaces rather than at
common tables, this might indeed have granted the weddings, political lectures, health clinics, and memorial services a new and inherently religious
value. But these innovations were certainly not the only way to create or
experience religious value. Detroit's Muslim leaders had long understood
the purpose of the mosque in the United States. The mosque functioned
as a discursive space in which knowledge of Islam could be negotiated,
enacted, debated, objectified, and adapted to changing circumstances. By
1981, the older religious leaders and their followers were fully aware that
each generation of immigrants and converts would have to work out its
own understanding of what a proper mosque should be. What they had not
anticipated, however, was the fact that their own understandings of Islam
would ultimately be rejected as irreligious and merely social.

The transformations of the 1970s and 1980s were seen by many of
Detroit's Muslims as an urgently needed purification. For others, these
were years of marginalization and intolerance. Without choosing sides
in a conflict that has already become historical, and whose meanings are
still changing, it is perhaps best to note the ironic outcome of these struggles. By the 1980s, after decades of arrival, reform, and cultural survival,
Detroit had actually become what two Syrian immigrants, Mohammed
and Hussien Karoub, dreamed it would be when they built the city's first
mosque in 1921: a beacon of Islam in the West.

CHAPTER 8 | Conclusion
| *Everything Old is New Again*

Mosques in Detroit, which have never been many, have
been remodeled rooms of American buildings, and the only
mosque ever built here was built for a somewhat remodeled
Mohammedanism.

CHARLES CAMERON, *Detroit Saturday Night*, JULY 7, 1926

The Shamys had been scandalized by the Mishawaka Muslims.
They had one of the oldest mosques in America up there, founded
by Arab Muslims who had come to America as far back as the
1870s. But slowly, over generations, they had mixed American
things in with real Islam, Wajdy explained, so that now they
needed a refresher course in real Islam from the Dawah Center.
None of the women up there wore hijab and none of the men
had beards—they didn't even look like Muslims. And they did
shocking things in the mosque, like play volleyball with men and
women together, *in shorts*. And they had dances for the Muslim
boys and girls—dances! "Mishawaka Muslims" became a byword
for "lost Muslims" in *The Islamic Forerunner*.

MOHJA KAHF, *The Girl in the Tangerine Scarf*, 2006

Charles Cameron was a careful and sympathetic observer of Detroit's
Muslim immigrants in the 1920s, but like more critical journalists, and
like many of the city's Muslim pioneers, he was not convinced that Islam

belonged in Detroit. Remodeled rooms and a "somewhat remodeled Mohammedism" were precisely what it took to anchor Islamic practices and Muslim communities in the United States in the early twentieth century, and this renovation project is ongoing. It is reconfiguring the life space of Muslim immigrants and their descendants, of Muslim converts and their families, and it is steadily transforming the religious cultures of North America. Cameron sensed that this remodeled Islam was a diminished version of something that properly flourished elsewhere, a sentiment Mohja Kahf's fictional characters, observing the mosque in Mishawaka[1] half a century later, would wholeheartedly endorse. To missionary representatives of a new Islam, the old Islamic habitus on display in Mishawaka does not look or feel like the "real" thing. If Cameron suspected that Islam would eventually fade away in Detroit, Kahf's characters, who visit an active, apparently healthy mosque, are convinced by their encounter with uncovered, clean-shaven, mixed-dancing, volleyball-playing Muslims that Islam in Mishawaka has been utterly "lost." I am prepared to disagree, but I must acknowledge that Cameron's assessment and Kahf's playful description show a strange agreement across decades and cultures. They continue to haunt the narratives of old (and new) Islam in the United States in ways that need to be understood.

Islam is still seen as an outsider religion in the United States by Muslims and non-Muslims alike,[2] and it will remain so for as long as American foreign policy subjects Muslim populations to drone assaults, military invasions and occupations, embargoes, extraordinary renditions, secret detention, and torture; and for as long as our domestic policy singles out Muslims for no-fly lists, targeted surveillance, and entrapment schemes carried out by federal investigators, paid informants, and agent provocateurs.[3] Muslims "here" are connected to Muslims "there" not only in the most literal sense, through kinship or economic relationships, or in a generic religious sense, through shared habits of worship, but also in a moral sense that plays on the imagined loyalties that characterize Muslim, American, and Muslim American identities. There is currently little Muslim Americans can do to reverse the negative charge carried by the identity labels applied to them by the larger society. Although they face suspicion and outright hostility, new converts to Islam and new immigrant Muslims are quick to realize that their status as stigmatized outsiders is only one side of their newfound reality. On the other side, they find legally protected spaces in which they can build their own public sphere, their own Muslim American praxis, and their own moral community in the United States. They quickly set about doing so.

For much of the past century, the newest Muslim Americans have found older Muslim American communities they could collaborate with in this process. I have tried to document the outcomes of this collaborative remodeling effort in Detroit. By focusing on the accomplishments of this project (along with its many failures) and by showing how it has been represented by interested observers—journalists and scholars, new immigrants and new converts, activist reformers and Muslim missionaries—I hope to have restored to the Muslim American past, especially that of the early twentieth century, a sense of balance.

Amina McCloud has pointed out that "most scholars writing about Islam in the African American communities have focused their efforts on the...teachings of the Nation of Islam [leading to] a lacunae in our understanding of the dynamics of Islam in society." She goes on to say that "we have relatively little informed data about the growth of Islam and development of an equally large Islamic population outside the Nation of Islam, that of Sunni African Americans who have been active in the major urban areas of the United States since the first quarter of the 20th century."[4] The same is true of the much larger population of Muslims who migrated to the United States prior to 1965 and actively developed institutions here from the early 1900s forward, but who produced a thin and fragile record of their efforts. Their history too is overshadowed by that of the more flamboyant, syncretic movements that represented themselves in the English language and captured the attention of federal agents, the popular media, and scholars of their day, generating an extensive paper trail for historians and other writers to follow. The Ahmadiyya Movement, the Moorish Science Temple, and the Nation of Islam were embraced by African American populations that were still struggling for emancipation from the racist legacy of slavery and the lived reality of Jim Crow laws in the American South. Displaced by the Great Migration, many northern blacks found in these proto-Muslim movements the means to accelerate their own political, intellectual, and spiritual growth. Islam, especially that shaped by the NOI, was part of African American political culture in the twentieth century, and it played a distinctive role in the Civil Rights and Black Power Movements.[5] By contrast, the effort to establish more conventional Sunni and Shiʻi communities (whether undertaken by American-born blacks or immigrant Muslims) was a quiet and marginal, if equally transformative, enterprise. Perhaps it is for this reason that Kambiz GhaneaBassiri cautions us that "while the communities and institutions formed in the interwar period set roots for Islam in America and thus helped shape consequent developments in the history of Islam in America, they did not circumscribe the future practice of Islam nor the subsequent character of Islamic institutions in this country."[6]

If, however, we give greater attention to what was accomplished by early Muslim Americans outside the NOI and other syncretic movements, the character of future Islamic practice in the United States—especially Muslim *institutional* practices—can indeed be seen. To bring these qualities into focus, we must avoid the often pejorative terms that are so frequently used to describe early immigrant Islam: "ad hoc," "individualistic," "assimilationist," "disorganized," "apologetic," "ignorant," and "lost," to name but a few. Narrative tropes that emphasize weak religiosity, apathy, discord, and inevitable decline are themselves historical, and they favor themes of rupture and loss. They keep us from seeing what is familiar about the past and what is recurrent in the process of making Islam and Muslims part of life in the United States. Moreover, they prevent Muslim Americans from realizing the extent to which their incorporation in American society is not only possible in the present and future but has already been achieved by Muslims of earlier generations.

As I argue throughout this book, the idea that Islam in America was (until very recently) small, insignificant, and corrupted is a claim made by a diverse array of observers, each with a moral stake in how American Muslims were to be seen and judged. This claim, in other words, is itself a historical artifact. In the 1920s, Muslim missionaries (most often foreigners representing heterodox variants of Islam) exhorted Muslim Americans to do a better job of living up to the ideals of their faith. They simultaneously warned new believers that the Muslim communities that already existed in Detroit (and elsewhere in the United States) should not be accepted as proper guides to the faith. Meanwhile, anti-immigrant journalists (and the occasional Christian missionary) reassured their audiences that Islam did not belong in America and could not gain a toehold here because Muslims would not and could not act as free white citizens. By the 1940s, reformist Sunni and Shi'i imams (again, foreign-born) criticized their predecessors and Detroit's existing mosques, hoping to galvanize support for newer, more ambitious Islamic institutions. The Muslim students who arrived in the 1950s and 1960s, most of them immigrant intellectuals from elite backgrounds who had little in common with the working-class Muslim Americans they met and worshiped with, were generally disparaging of the institutional practices they observed in Detroit as well. When they set about deconstructing American religious culture, capitalism, and domestic politics in order to inspire a new Islamic awakening in their homelands, they found the example of established Muslim

American communities useful only as a cautionary tale, as an example of what had gone wrong in the past and might go wrong again in future. As Eric Lincoln and Lawrence Mamiya have argued, "other-wordly religious transcendence can be related dialectically to the motivation, discipline, and courage needed for this-worldly political action."[7] The activism that came to dominate the Muslim American community by the 1980s clearly affirmed the understanding that effective moral change could not be based on the beliefs and practices that had evolved, over several decades of accommodation, in Detroit's mosques.

A discourse of this kind, especially when used to motivate people already disoriented by migration, religious conversion, or both, tends to be critical of the status quo and averse to the historical experiences that produced it. Hayden White, writing about the character of historical narrative, suggests that the trends I have been examining as idiosyncratic features of Muslim American history are by no means unique to it. "The growth and development of a historical consciousness," he contends, "is intimately related to, if not a function of, the impulse to moralize reality, that is, to identify it with the social system that is the source of any morality we can imagine."[8] For many of Detroit's Muslims, the social and moral system that was most worth imagining in the 1980s was the revivalist Islam sweeping through the Muslim-majority world. The old mosques, Islamic organizations, and everyday expressions of Muslim American identity no longer mattered. They had little moral value worth preserving.

The new, self-aware, expressly politicized, and *fiqh*-based Islam favored by a new generation of American Muslim activists came with a built-in critique of the old Islam and the American Muslims who practiced it. Rather than work with the Federation of Islamic Associations or other existing Muslim American institutions, the new activists established the Muslim Students Association and (in Detroit) invested in several new mosques that sprang to life in the 1970s and 1980s. Attuned to the legal and interpretive regimes then struggling to gain authority in prominent Muslim-majority nations, and vexed by the obvious fact that they were living beyond the "canopy" of this tradition—that is, outside *dar al-Islam* (the abode of Islam)—these newcomers (both immigrants and converts) had to reinvent themselves not simply as practitioners of Islam or as Muslim believers but as interpreters of Islam in a decidedly non-Muslim sociopolitical context.[9] They did this gradually, as earlier generations of Muslim Americans had also done. They extended the (legal and cultural) canopy of Islam to provide cover for their lives in the United States. And they did so largely on their own, rejecting, or never seriously considering, the innovations developed by their Muslim American predecessors.

In 1982, when MSA leaders found themselves raising families in America, they created a new national organization, the Islamic Society of North America, to help their members (re)build Islamic infrastructure in America—to establish mosques and Islamic schools, to represent the interests of Muslim Americans on the national stage, and to clarify their understanding of what it meant to be Muslim Americans. The creation of ISNA came at an opportune time. In 1979–1980, the FIA faced an internal leadership battle following an unexpected influx of petrodollars from Gulf Arab funders. The group self-destructed. ISNA picked up exactly where the FIA left off in terms of real services provided, but it did so from a very different ideological perspective. Moving from the isolationism of their early MSA years, ISNA's position was one of gradualist incorporation, or, as Mucahit Bilici describes it, "protectionism through partial involvement" in the "American environment."[10] Weakened and ignored, the FIA and the leadership of the old American mosques it represented were relegated to obscurity, an obscurity that freed a new generation of Muslim activists to construct an alternative Muslim American identity, a new vision of Islam unencumbered by the moral ambivalence that many of the newest immigrants and converts felt toward the identities and institutions of their predecessors. To put it simply, the Muslim American identities that rose to prominence in the 1980s were unencumbered by the history of Islam in America.

At the national level, it was possible for ISNA to ignore and delegitimize the record of the FIA. In Detroit, however, where the older Muslim institutions and activists were familiar to the new, this act of rewriting and overturning the past was personal and, as I illustrate in Chapters 6 and 7, it was very painful. The demise of the FIA in Detroit entailed a drawn-out legal battle between Mike Karoub and Nihad Hamed and their various supporters.[11] The "unity prayers" organized jointly by the MSA and the city's new activist/leaders between 1976–1980, which sought to bring together all area Muslims for one large collective prayer, ignored outright the FIA-identified congregations of the Albanian Islamic Center, the original American Moslem Society congregation, and the Islamic Center of America. When I discuss this period with the Muslim leaders who built the city's new mosques in the 1970s and 1980s, they are uniformly uncomfortable about offering their opinions of the mosques and Muslim leaders they encountered upon arrival in Detroit. Very few are willing, as Abdo Alasry was (see

Chapter 6), to put their critique of these institutions on the record. Perhaps this is because the struggle for control of the AMS, which Alasry led, was decided in a court of law and is already on the record, so to speak. Others tell me that they do not want to engage in backbiting or in judging the piety or motivations of others. Some are hesitant because they are well aware that they now represent American (and Americanizing and Americanized) mosques. They understand that the mosques they built in the 1970s and 1980s are themselves subject to criticism by recently arrived immigrant Muslims today. On the record, several people told me that Masjid al-Mu'mineen and Hashmie Hall were never really mosques at all. They did so because this distinction was essential to their narratives about newer mosques they played a role in building, and because such assertions can be read as technical statements about architecture, the balance between social and religious functions in "real" mosques, or the manner in which women should move through mosque spaces. But off the record, I have been told alarming things about the earlier generation of Muslim leaders that echo the Mohja Kahf epigraph above: Hajj Hassanein was not "really" a Muslim; Khalil Bazzy and Mike Karoub were not "really" imams; members of Imam Warith Deen Muhammad's community were "really" half Muslim and half Christian. And so on.

Claims of this sort are harsh judgments based on deeply held moral, religious, and cultural assumptions, and I do not repeat them here to embrace or debunk them. I repeat them because they belong to a much larger historical pattern. They are judgments not simply of local men, mosques, or communities, but of American Muslims as well. Mohammad Mardini, a Syrian-born imam, was hired by the American Muslim Bekaa Center, the reconstituted congregation of the original AMS, shortly after he arrived in the United States in 1981. Now a champion of the older Muslim American community, he was originally shocked by "how American" they seemed. "They looked and acted just like Americans. It was hard for me to accept. I still thought of Americans as non-Muslims, and of Muslims as living in America but not really being Americans."[12] In his gentle way, Imam Mardini speaks here for many new American Muslims who simply did not (and still do not) recognize the older communities of American Muslims as being authentically Muslim. Their perspective is shaped by their own cultural understanding that *Islam* and *America* are terms that exist, if not in opposition to one another, then at least in a state of mutual tension, or exclusivity. In this worldview, the terms *Muslim* and *American* do not overlap, nor can they dwell comfortably in one another, despite the presence of Muslims in the Americas from the earliest days of European and African arrival.

It is this problem of recognition, this sense that Islam is essentially foreign to America that explains why the history of old Islam in the United States so consistently slips into oblivion. Many scholars today tell us that the Muslim American community has suffered through a period of crisis brought on by the 9/11 attacks that has propelled Muslims into the national spotlight and compelled them, at long last, to claim their place—their sense of (not yet) belonging and their (diminished) rights as citizens—in the United States. This process is traumatic. Like other forms of trauma, it can lead to forgetting or to tactical reconfigurations of the past.[13] While I agree that geopolitical crisis has indeed fueled demand for recognition and rights by Muslim Americans in the face of tremendous pressure, I do not think that ideas of trauma and forgetting can explain widespread ignorance of the Muslim American past, especially when this ignorance is shared by Muslims and non-Muslims alike. Nor do I believe the demographic newness of the Muslim American population can account for the trend—in Detroit, as nationally, the majority of Muslim American adults are immigrants, and the majority of adult African American Muslims are first-generation Muslims—although the perpetual representation of Muslims as new, as without deep roots in the Americas, is a contributing factor. Beyond all these issues, I would argue that it is the sense of alienation newcomers have, both as new Americans and as new believers, toward their own status as Muslims living in the United States that has led them to consistently misrecognize, misunderstand, and marginalize Islamic practices and Muslim communities that appear to be comfortably at home in America.

In this book I have tried to show that the history of Islam in Detroit can be written and has been experienced in ways that do not privilege alienation but instead situate this sensibility within encompassing processes of incorporation and exclusion. This approach has implications for the present. It suggests that the Islamic practices and thriving institutional forms found among American Muslims today are products of a distinctive American context, that they are evidence of continuity between past and present, and that they cannot be accurately understood as the result of a great upheaval in which one religious praxis was overturned by another. I have illustrated how this transformative religious conflict did indeed take place in Detroit, but I have also shown how it began much earlier than most Muslims today realize. The call for a return to proper Islamic practice was heard in the

Highland Park Mosque in 1921, at Hashmie Hall in 1949, at the ICA in 1963, and at Masjid Wali Muhammad in 1976.

The pattern has repeated itself many times, and I am struck by the institutional forms and religious practices that have survived these coups and revivals, managing to reassert themselves as Muslim Americans work out the logistics of life in the United States. Like their predecessors, the newest immigrants and converts are coming to feel more at home in America today[14] not because the United States is a welcoming place—in the post-9/11 era it would be impossible to make this argument—but because they are making America a more Muslim place by raising their families here; building mosques; and participating in the social, economic, and political worlds around them. In doing so, they face cultural and institutional challenges similar to those faced by their predecessors. The responses to these challenges are strikingly similar. Over time, this cycle of challenge and response has yielded new generations of American-born Muslims and Muslim-born Americans who do not share earlier anxieties about a supposed incompatibility between Islam and American life. Comfortable within their own skin as Muslim Americans, and increasingly adept at playing minoritized forms of identity politics, these new generations—whether they came of age in the 1930s or the 1990s—confront existential dilemmas unique to their own position in an unfolding and ever shifting historical process. They must struggle to be recognized as authentic Muslims by Detroit's steady stream of new Muslim arrivals, and they must struggle to be seen as authentic Americans by a larger, non-Muslim society.

This latter, reciprocal process presents challenges of a different sort because many non-Muslim Americans share the feeling that Islam is an alien faith, especially those who have not known (or been aware that they have known) Muslim Americans personally. In places like Detroit, where Muslims are so well established and have been covered in the media for a solid century, their presence is registered for the most part as familiar and relatively uninteresting by locals who have lived among, attended school with, and worked alongside Muslim Americans throughout their lives. No longer seen as aliens, these American Muslims are often startled to hear their neighbors or co-workers express hostility toward Islam, followed by a quick disclaimer that sounds something like, "Of course I don't mean you. We all know you're an American." In communities where Muslims are indeed newcomers, or where they were less visible in the twentieth century, it takes time for familiarity to develop and for non-Muslims to take for granted the presence of Muslims (however real or unreal) in their local landscape. It takes time too for Muslims to find ways to identify publicly as *Muslim* and *American* without triggering alarms. Mosques have long provided the means to announce a community's presence in just this way.

In the middle decades of the twentieth century, Detroit's mosques were sites defined by a complicated mix of social and religious functions. They anchored ethnic identities among Muslim Americans; they announced the presence of Islam in the United States; they made the city's Muslims visible, especially to each other; and they enabled the Muslim community to reproduce itself over time. These mosques were sites of Americanization, globalization, and political and social incorporation. They were translocal spaces, connecting Muslims in Detroit to other parts of the Muslim world, and they were transcommunal spaces, connecting ethnoracial and sectarian congregations to one another in an overarching Muslim public. I have focused my analysis on how Muslims from very different social and cultural locations have intersected in Detroit's mosques and have transformed these spaces, like the Muslim American identities they contain, over time. These dynamics of encounter—when accompanied by recognition and transcommunal attunement—have encouraged (and sometimes compelled) a kind of Islamic self-awareness. Pluralism and intra-Muslim ecumenicalism enabled the city's Muslims to develop a religious praxis and moral community that emphasized the things they had in common as Muslim Americans. At mid-twentieth century, Detroit Muslims realized that not all Muslim traditions and discourses were created equal, and that their desire for Islamic community could extend only so far. Detroit's mosques were intensely political spaces, not simply because they connected the United States to the Muslim world or because they nurtured a uniquely *Muslim American* identity, but because they connected Muslims to one another across multiple boundaries, creating *Muslim* identities that were genuinely new and not always easy to express.

As the Muslim community grew in the 1970s and 1980s, Detroit's mosques were able to shrug off many of the social and ethnic functions they had served for prior generations. Private institutions and a Muslim marketplace developed to satisfy these needs. As the relationship between the United States and much of the Muslim world soured after the 1967 Arab-Israeli War, placing intense pressure on Arab Americans in particular, new secular and explicitly ethnic institutions emerged to speak on behalf of constituencies that defined themselves in ethnic rather than religious terms. The prominent social service agencies, political lobbies, and civil liberties organizations associated with Arabs in Detroit all have their origins in the political activism of the 1970s and 1980s. And as mosques generally became more *fiqh*-based, banquet halls and village clubs opened nearby. There families could celebrate weddings and other happy occasions with music and dancing, if they so desired, or with belly dancers and open bars. Islamic schools opened in conjunction with the city's mosques, and so did charter schools that offered Arabic language instruction and a more conservative social atmosphere (such as gender segregated classrooms and conservative dress codes) than the public schools provided. By the 1990s, Detroit was home to Muslim cemeteries and funeral parlors; Muslim radio programs and newspapers; Muslim university professors and public school principals; halal butchers, obstetricians and gynecologists, dentists, judges and elected officials; Muslim poets, writers, and musicians. The city's Muslim population grew from several thousand in the 1930s to at least 200,000 in 2010. Greater Detroit has over seventy mosques (a number that now changes almost constantly, usually in an upward direction), an uncounted number of clergy, dozens of Islamic schools, and even an Islamic university.

Mosques are no longer the primary engines of ethnic and racial identity formation among Muslim American populations. They are part of a vast and complex market of institutions, public and private, that compete for the attention of Muslim Americans, enriching, facilitating, and sometimes undermining Muslim American identity. This Muslim public sphere, which intersects with Arab, African American, South Asian, Eastern European, and other ethnoracial and immigrant publics, has enabled mosques in Detroit (and elsewhere) to concentrate on the everyday practice of the faith. Today's mosques do not have to work as hard as did the mosques of the 1940s and 1950s to provide a sense of community, to sustain Muslim American identities by providing their primary content, context, and collective inspiration. Today's mosques can specialize. In the language of commerce, they can develop niche markets, focusing their attention on religious and moral education, ritual, and piety.

Yet in some ways, today's mosques have to work much harder. In a community of dramatically increased size and visibility, where multiple institutions make relentless claims on the individual Muslim's time and loyalty and where dozens of approaches to interpreting Islamic tradition are cultivated in close proximity to one another, Detroit's mosques are now full participants in American religious pluralism. They compete not only with Christian churches and secular ethnoracial organizations, but with one another for the attention and support of believers. Perhaps this explains why the larger mosques, with no exceptions, have reverted to the intensely social model rejected by the conservative reformers of the 1970s. Not only do the larger mosques boast prayer spaces that can hold over a thousand worshipers, but a guided tour of these facilities will feature a mix of several of the following: a shining commercial kitchen, a banquet hall, a lecture hall, a gymnasium, a daycare facility, sparkling his-and-her ablution rooms, a weekend or private school, a soup kitchen, a mortuary, a multimedia library, state-of-the-art classrooms, a recording studio and editing suite. Gifts shops, book stores, and coffee shops are also increasingly common. One Detroit mosque, after successfully spinning off an independent free health clinic, is now home to a "Jazz Café." If this inventory of special features is not enough, one can sample the rich array of extracurricular activities Detroit's mosques provide, activities that are oddly reminiscent of the "social events" that repulsed conservative reformers a generation or more ago: yoga classes, chess clubs, spelling-bee practice sessions, athletic leagues, after-school homework programs, interfaith and ecumenical councils, art exhibits, open-mike poetry slams, musical performances and plays, children's concerts, appearances by clowns and magicians and face painters, Red Cross blood drives, Boy and Girl Scout troops, and so on. Finally, some of these institutions require that women wear appropriate hijab when they enter the building. A box of scarves is usually made available by each entrance to accommodate non-Muslims and those who do not wear hijab daily. In some cases, this box and the attire associated with it are found at the door of the musalla, a placement that is reminiscent of the more relaxed practice of earlier decades. In even the most conservative mosques, rules about hijab wearing are often relaxed for non-Muslim visitors such as government officials, health-care workers, journalists, and students.

In this environment, the tension between the ideal of an all-inclusive Muslim umma and the equally strong pull of ethnic solidarity, or particularistic interpretative traditions, remains powerful. The majority of Detroit's mosques today are identified with a discrete ethnic, national, racial, or linguistic group, but increasingly mosques are forming around neighborhood identities, around strong leaders, or around a common vision. Within each of these mosques, there are predictable factional cleavages based on length of time spent in America (or in Islam), income level, and education. All of these institutions compete to draw worshipers, to lock in the time and energy commitments of volunteers, and to gain the trust of donors. The most important idiom in which Detroit's mosques market themselves and compete with one another, however, is that of perceived religious orthodoxy. In this realm, congregational splits are rarely the traumatic upheavals that shook Detroit in the 1970s and 1980s. They are now a common occurrence, and most large mosques spin off smaller ones, which are almost always defined as more conservative (or less so) than the original. It is nowadays much easier to start a new mosque than to take over a well-established one. Conservative mosques have one primary advantage over others: clarity of vision, rules, and practice. Less conservative mosques also have significant advantages: their social and religious flexibility and their more convincing hold on the politics of integration, Americanization, and—very often—socioeconomic success. At stake in these divisions are issues of openness in worship and interpretation, policies toward women, and engagement with the broader landscape of both American and Muslim ecumenicalism. In the post-9/11 era, the old divide between already American Muslims and new American Muslims no longer translates as neatly as it once did into conservative and liberalizing sensibilities in matters of mosque politics.

It would appear, then, that Detroit's mosques—even traditional, conservative ones—have arrived at a comfortable relationship with American pluralism. This arrangement is not exactly new. The history of Detroit's mosques and Muslim communities shows clearly that Islam, against common perception, is a long-standing American faith tradition. In the past and the present, Detroit's Muslims have sought and have been granted accommodations. Those granted today, when Muslims form large voting blocs in the city, are so extensive that the compromises made by the city's early mosques—shifting Muslim sacred calendars into alignment with secular or Christian ones—are unnecessary. In cities like Dearborn and Hamtramck (both over 40 percent Muslim), public schools are closed on Islamic holidays.[15] Nowhere in greater Detroit are Muslim students penalized for staying home, and most employers recognize these holidays as well. Similarly, many Muslim workers can easily extend their lunch breaks on Friday to accommodate *Jumaa* prayers, if they so desire. Muslims in Detroit are not a small or exotic religious minority; in some areas, they are the majority and have been for decades. Their faith is widely recognized and its particulars often understood by non-Muslims in ways that are still hard to imagine outside Detroit.

Has this complex of greater numbers, much greater wealth, and obvious institutional maturity made Detroit's Muslims immune to the familiar critiques launched against them in the past—that they are assimilationists, weak in their faith, and suffer from an irreversible pattern of cultural decline and loss? Not entirely. Do new Muslim Americans, disoriented by the shock of arrival, still doubt that Americans can really live as Muslims?

Yes, they do. Both narratives can be heard from *minbars* across the city on Friday afternoons. Islam is an emergent faith not a static one, and it is the obligation of clerics to exhort their congregations to resist back-sliding and to take their faith seriously. New converts complain, "If I had known Muslims before I knew Islam, I might not have converted." They are frustrated by taken-for-granted, often lax approaches to Islamic faith and practice displayed by co-religionists who have been Muslim all their lives. New immigrants, likewise, complain about the dating habits, dress codes, and social mores of the American-born Muslims they encounter in and outside the city's mosques.

And Detroit is a stronger magnet today than it was in the past for anti-Muslim activists who find mosques and Arab ethnic festivals an attractive setting for Qur'an burnings and protests against Shari'a law and Islamic extremism. To the horror of Muslim and non-Muslims onlookers, these anti-Muslim agitators carry pig heads on spikes, denounce new mosque openings, organize mass prayers to remove Islam from Detroit, and host sensational conferences on "honor killings" and the dangers of Muslim incorporation. Like the FBI operatives who harass Detroit's Muslim community leaders, drive radiation detection devices past the city's mosques, and surveil and infiltrate area mosques, these anti-Muslim activists are not convinced—despite all the evidence that surrounds them—that Islam and American life are already functionally integrated in Detroit and are becoming more so.[16]

The work of seeking accommodations, establishing mosques, and speaking out on behalf of Muslim causes did not begin in the 1980s, or even in the 1950s. It began in the era of World War I. It began when Muslim immigrants from the Ottoman Empire sat in one another's homes and coffeehouses and discussed the things they had in common as Muslims. It began when they prayed together next to a moving assembly line at Henry Ford's Highland Park factory. It began when they gathered to celebrate the opening of the Moslem Mosque of Highland Park. This historical space, like the space of the mosque itself, is one in which the moral community of Islam can be imagined, created, and contested *in the present*. The American mosque is not a building whose architecture, functions, and congregational dynamics can be established once and for all. Its qualities are constantly reconfigured according to the needs of a changing Muslim American public and the aspects of Islamic tradition this public seeks to promote and observe. Rooms and customs that once flourished in this sacred space can fall out of fashion. They are then papered over, expanded, or transformed into something new. The Muslim American past in Detroit is constantly undergoing such reconstruction. The lintel that once stood over the door of the AMS in Dearborn, reading "Islamic Mosque 1938," is now buried behind an obscure door beneath a set stairs. Most visitors, and many regulars, do not know it is there. Likewise, the old Islam practiced in Detroit can seem like an out-of-the-way curiosity rather than a monument to the religiosity and commitment of the city's first Muslim communities. Many people do not know it was there.

This work has captured only small portions of a small history. Much of what the early Muslims of Detroit thought, experienced, and believed is no longer knowable.[17] I am prompted to conclude, nonetheless, that their experiences were not as different from those of today's Muslims as we have been led to believe. Like today's new Muslim Americans, the people who built the Highland Park Mosque, or the AIC, or Masjid al-Mu'mineen were a mixture of the devout and the less so. They were challenged by the differences they observed among the city's other Muslims. They were described as unworthy of citizenship in local and national media and were frequently denied the opportunity to become or enjoy the rights of citizens. They built mosques and dreamed of American futures for their children. As these mosques celebrate their fiftieth and seventieth—and soon enough, their one-hundredth—anniversaries, they will be filled with new members who know little about the histories of these institutions or the people who built them. Still, these American Muslims will be richly equipped to extend, repeat, alter, deny, and recreate those histories in terms appropriate to their own lives. This is the viable future of a forgotten past.

NOTES

Chapter 1

1. The mosque is also referred to as the "Dix Mosque," an appellation that appears frequently in the literature about Muslim communities in Detroit. See especially Nabeel Abraham, "Arab Detroit's 'American' Mosque," in *Arab Detroit: From Margin to Mainstream*, ed. Nabeel Abraham and Andrew Shryock (Detroit: Wayne State University Press, 2000); Janice Terry, "Community and Political Activism Among Arab Americans in Detroit," in *Arabs in America: Building a New Future*, ed. Michael Suleiman (Philadelphia: Temple University Press, 1999).

2. According to the 2003 Detroit Arab American Study, 58 percent of Yemeni Americans in the Detroit area arrived in the United States after 1990 (DAAS Team 2009, 43).

3. For a detailed examination of anti-Muslim sentiments in the post 9/11 period, see Christopher Allen, *Islamophobia* (London: Ashgate, 2011); John Esposito and Ibrahim Kalin, *Islamophobia: The Challenge of Pluralism in the 21st Century* (New York: Oxford University Press, 2011); Stephen Sheehi, *Islamophobia: The Ideological Campaign Against Muslims* (Atlanta: Clarity Press, 2011); Andrew Shryock, *Islamophobia/ Islamophilia: Beyond the Politics of Enemy and Friend* (Bloomington: Indiana University Press, 2010), 1–28.

4. For a comprehensive examination of the longstanding incorporation of Detroit's Arab and Muslim communities, see Nabeel Abraham, Sally Howell, and Andrew Shryock, *Arab Detroit 9/11: Life in the Terror Decade* (Detroit: Wayne State University Press, 2011).

5. Estimating the size of the Muslim American population is difficult because the US Census does not record religious identifications. The figure of 200,000 given here is an extrapolation based on the size of Detroit's Arab American community. According to the 2007 American Community Survey, Arab and Chaldean populations in the metropolitan area had reached 210,000; slightly less than half of this population is Muslim. See Kim Schopmeyer, "Arab Detroit after 9/11: A Demographic Portrait," in *Arab Detroit 9/11: Life in the Terror Decade*, ed. Nabeel Abraham, Sally Howell, and Andrew Shryock (Detroit: Wayne State University Press, 2011), 29–65. Based on the number and size of their mosques, Arabs are the single largest Muslim population in the area,

comprising roughly half of Detroit's Muslims. See Ihsan Bagby, *A Portrait of Detroit Mosques: Muslim Views on Policy, Politics and Religion* (Clinton Township, IL: Institute for Social Policy and Understanding, 2004). See also Pew Forum on Religion in Public Life, *Muslim Americans: No Signs of Growth in Alienation or Support for Extremism* (Washington, DC: Pew Research Center, August 2011).

6. Raad Alawan, *New Beginnings: The Story of the Islamic Center of America* (Dearborn, MI: Islamic Center of America, 2005).

7. Raad Alawan, *Oldest Mosque in Michigan Celebrates 70 Years* (Dearborn, MI: American Moslem Society, 2009).

8. Hussein El Haje passed away in August 2009. He was ninety-seven.

9. Hussein El Haje, interview by Sally Howell, Dearborn, Michigan, 2005. All interviews are indexed in the bibliography. Unless otherwise noted, all translations are mine.

10. Curtis, *Muslims in America: A Short History* (New York: Oxford University Press, 2009), describes a similar transition which took place in the same period at the Islamic Center of New England in Wooster, Massachusetts.

11. Kambiz GhaneaBassiri, *A History of Islam in America* (Cambridge: Cambridge University Press, 2010), 3.

12. GhaneaBassiri, *History*, 3.

13. These figures recombine the foreign-born and U.S.-born findings from the 2007 Pew survey into distinct ancestry categories. Gallup describes the population as 28 percent white, 35 percent African American, 18 percent Asian American, 18 percent Other, and 1 percent Hispanic. Gallup did not ask about ethnic or national origins, making it impossible to differentiate Arab Americans from those with European origins, Pew Forum on Religion and Public Life, "Muslim Americans: Middle Class and Mostly Mainstream" (Washington, DC: Pew Research Center, 2007); Mohammed Younis, *Muslim Americans Exemplify Diversity, Potential: Key Findings from a New Report by the Gallup Center for Muslim Studies*, 2009.

14. The statistics here are from Pew Forum on Religion and Public Life, "Muslim Americans: Middle Class and Mostly Mainstream."

15. For diverse Muslim populations, theories of segmented assimilation are especially relevant. See Alejandro Portes and Ruben Rumbaut, *Immigrant America*, 2nd edn (Berkeley: University of California Press, 1996); Alejandro Portes and Min Zhou, "The New Second Generation: Segmented Assimilation and Its Variants," *Annals of the American Academy of Political and Social Science* 530, no. 1 (1993): 74–96; Mary Waters, *Black Identities: West Indian Immigrant Dreams and American Realities* (New York: Russell Sage Foundation, 1999); Karen I. Leonard, *Making Ethnic Choices: California's Punjabi Mexican Americans* (Philadelphia: Temple University Press, 1992); Vivek Bald, *Bengali Harlem: And the Lost Hisories of South Asian Americans* (Boston: Harvard University Press, 2013).

16. Peter L. Berger, *The Sacred Canopy: Elements of a Sociological Theory of Religion* (New York: Doubleday, 1969); W. Herberg, *Protestant, Catholic, Jew: An Essay in American Religious Sociology* (Garden City, NY: Anchor Books, 1960).

17. Seymour M. Lipset, *American Pluralism and the Jewish Community* (New Brunswick: Transaction Publishers, 1990); R. Stephen Warner, "Work in Progress: Toward a New Paradigm for the Sociological Study of Religion in the United States," *The American Journal of Sociology* 98, no. 5 (1993): 1044–1093.

18. Tracy Fessenden, *Culture and Redemption: Religion, the Secular, and American Literature* (Princeton, NJ: Princeton University Press, 2007), 4.

19. GhaneaBassiri, *History*, 67.

20. R. Laurence Moore, *Religious Outsiders and the Making of Americans* (New York: Oxford University Press, 1986), 46.

21. Fessenden, *Culture and Redemption*.

22. Nadine Naber, "Introduction: Arab Americans and U.S. Racial Formation," in *Race and Arab Americans Before and After 9/11: From Invisible Citizens to Visible Subjects*, ed. Nadine Naber and Amaney Jamal (Syracuse: Syracuse University Press, 2008); Helen Samhan, "Not Quite White: Racial Classification and the Arab-American Experience," in *Arabs in America: Building a New Future*, ed. Michael Suleiman (Philadelphia: Temple University Press, 1999); Therese Saliba, "Resisting Invisibility: Arab Americans in Academia and Activism," in *Arabs in America: Building a New Future*, ed. Michael Suleiman (Philadelphia: Temple University Press, 1999).

23. Sally Howell and Andrew Shryock, "Cracking Down on Diaspora: Arab Detroit and America's 'War on Terror,'" *Anthropological Quarterly* 76 no. 3 (2003): 443; Sally Howell and Amaney Jamal, "Belief and Belonging," in *Citizenship and Crisis: Arab Detroit After 9/11*, ed. DAAS Team (New York: Russell Sage Foundation, 2009).

24. Zahid Bukhari et al., eds., *Muslims' Place in the American Public Square: Hopes, Fears, and Aspirations* (New York: AltaMira Press, 2004); Jocelyn Cesari, *When Islam and Democracy Meet: Muslims in Europe and in the United States* (New York: Palgrave Macmillan, 2006).

25. Peter Mandaville, *Transnational Muslim Politics: Reimagining the Umma* (New York: Routledge, 2001), 50.

26. Mucahit Bilici, "Being Targeted, Being Recognized: The Impact of 9/11 on Arab and Muslim Americans," *Contemporary Sociology: A Journal of Reviews* 40, no. 2 (March 2011): 133–137.

27. Derek Gregory, *The Colonial Present: Afghanistan, Palestine, and Iraq* (Malden, MA: Blackwell Publishing, 2004), 4.

28. Iftikhar Malik, *Islam and Modernity: Muslims in Europe and the United States* (Sterling, VA: Pluto Press, 2004); Edward W. Said, *Orientalism* (New York: Vintage, 1978); Armando Salvatore, *Islam and the Political Discourse of Modernity* (Ithaca, NY: Ithaca Press, 1999).

29. Lila Abu-Lughod, *Remaking Women: Feminism and Modernity in the Middle East* (Berkeley: University of California Press, 1998); Lara Deeb, *An Enchanted Modern: Gender and Public Piety in Shi'i Lebanon* (Princeton, NJ: Princeton University Press, 2006); Dale F. Eickelman, "Islam and the Languages of Modernity," *Daedalus* (Boston) 129, no. 1 (2000): 119–135; Timothy Mitchell, *Questions Of Modernity* (Minneapolis: University of Minnesota Press, 2000).

30. Timothy Marr, *The Cultural Roots of American Islamicism* (Cambridge: Cambridge University Press, 2006), 18.

31. Gregory, *The Colonial Present*; Ussama Makdisi, *Artillery of Heaven: American Missionaries and the Failed Conversion of the Middle East* (Ithaca, NY: Cornell University Press, 2009); Melanie McAlister, *Epic Encounters: Culture, Media, and U.S. Interests in the Middle East Since 1945* (Berkeley: University of California Press, 2001); Vijay Prashad, *Everybody Was Kung Fu Fighting: Afro-Asian Connections and the Myth of Cultural Purity* (Boston: Beacon Press, 2001).

32. Marr, *Cultural Roots*, 297.

33. Terry Alford, *Prince Among Slaves: The True Story of an African Prince Sold Into Slavery in the American South* (New York: Oxford University Press, 1986); GhaneaBassiri, *History*.

34. Faye Elizabeth Smith, "Bits of the Old World in Detroit: The Turks," *Detroit Saturday Night*, April 22, 1922.

35. Douglas Little, *American Orientalism: The United States and the Middle East Since 1945* (Chapel Hill: University of North Carolina Press, 2002); McAlister, *Epic Encounters*.

36. See especially Jacob Dorman, "'A True Moslem Is a True Spiritualist': Black Orientalism and Black Gods of the Metropolis," in *The New Black Gods: Arthur Huff Fauset and the Study of African American Religions*, eds. Edward E. Curtis IV and Danielle Brune Sigler (Bloomington: Indiana University Press, 2009), 116–144.

37. Evelyn Alsultany, "The Changing Profile of Race in the United States: Media Representations and Racialization of Arab- and Muslim-Americans Post-9/11" (Stanford University, 2005); Naber, "Introduction: Arab Americans and U.S. Racial Formation"; Jack Shaheen, *Arab and Muslim Stereotyping in American Popular Culture* (Washington, DC: Center for Muslim-Christian Understanding, History and International Affairs, Edmund A. Walsh School of Foreign Service, Georgetown University, 1997).

38. Anny Bakalian and Medhi Bozorgmehr, *Backlash 9/11: Middle Eastern and Muslim Americans Respond* (Berkeley: University of California Press, 2009); Louise A. Cainkar, *Homeland Insecurity: The Arab American and Muslim American Experience After 9/11* (New York: Russell Sage Foundation Publications, 2011); Baker et al., *Detroit Arab American Study DAAS*, 2003; Abraham, Howell, and Shryock, *Arab Detroit 9/11*.

39. She echoes Max Weber in her use of the term enchanted to signify a modernity colored by a religious sensibility.

40. Deeb, *An Enchanted Modern*, 5.

41. Jocelyne Cesari, ed., *Encyclopedia of Islam in the United States [2 Volumes]*, annotated edition (Westport, CT: Greenwood, 2007); Edward E. Curtis IV, *Encyclopedia of Muslim-American History*, 2-Volume Set, 1st edn (New York: Facts on File, Inc., 2010); Edward E. Curtis IV, ed., *The Columbia Sourcebook of Muslims in the United States* (New York: Columbia University Press, 2009).

42. Atif Wasfi, *An Islamic-Lebanese Community in U.S.A: a Study in Cultural Anthropology* (Beirut: Beirut Arab University, 1971).

43. Yvonne Haddad, *A Century of Islam in America* (Washington, DC: American Institute for Islamic Affairs, 1986), 2. Since Timothy Smith's work in the 1960s, scholars have long accepted that migration intensifies religious commitments, at least in the short term. See also Handlin and Bodnar, and virtually every other scholar of migration and religion since. John Bodnar, *The Transplanted: A History of Immigrants in Urban America* (Bloomington: Indiana University Press, 1985); Oscar Handlin, *The Uprooted*, 2nd edn (Boston: Little, Brown, 1973); Timothy Smith, "New Approaches to the History of Immigration in Twentieth-Century America," *American Historical Review* 71 (July 1966): 1265–1279.

44. Abdo A. Elkholy, *The Arab Moslems in the United States: Religion and Assimilation* (New Haven, CT: College and University Press, 1966); Yvonne Haddad,

"Maintaining the Faith of the Fathers: Dilemmas of Religious Identity in the Christian and Muslim Arab-American Communities," in *The Development of Arab-American Identity*, ed. Ernest McCarus (Ann Arbor: University of Michigan Press, 1994); Linda Walbridge, *Without Forgetting the Imam: Lebanese Shiism in an American Community* (Detroit: Wayne State University Press, 1997); Wasfi, *An Islamic-Lebanese.*

45. The "not really mosques at all" claim is pervasive in my interviews with the leaders of mosques established in the 1970s: Abdo Alasry, 2008; Ghaleb Begg, March 24, 2001; Eide Alawan, 2005; Ather Abdul Quader et al., May 20, 2011; Mahmood Hai, May 24, 2012. For concerns expressed about women in mosque spaces, see Nabeel Abraham, "Arab Detroit's 'American' Mosque"; Walbridge, *Without Forgetting the Imam.*

46. Elkholy, *The Arab Moslems in the United States*; F. Trix, "The Bektashi Tekke and the Sunni Mosque of Albanian Muslims in America," in *Muslim Communities in North America*, ed. Yvonne Haddad and Jane Smith (New York: State University of New York Press, 1994); Barbara Bilge, "Voluntary Associations in the Old Turkish Community of Metropolitan Detroit," in *Muslim Communities in North America* (New York: State University of New York Press, 1994).

47. Richard Brent Turner, *Islam in the African-American Experience* (Bloomington: Indiana University Press, 1997) provides the most direct criticism of Detroit's Muslim leaders for not having intervened with the NOI. The point is also made frequently by African American Muslims in Detroit today.

48. Gladys Ecie, interview by Sally Howell, Dearborn, Michigan, 2005.

49. Elkholy, *The Arab Moslems in the United States*, 19, attributed the presence of two mosques in Dearborn to the "persisting sectarianism, carried over from the old country by the first-generation immigrants." He also noted the "disruptive" and "divisive" role Shaykh Chirri played when he first arrived in Detroit in the late 1940s, when he is said to have "found the sectarian conflict dying in the Detroit community" and "decided to revive it" (76). In the Albanian community, a Sunni mosque and a Bektashi (Sufi) retreat were also established as both competitive and complementary institutions in the 1940s.

50. Elkholy, *The Arab Moslems in the United States*, 46–47.

51. Andrew Shryock, Sally Howell, and Nabeel Abraham, "The New Order and Its Forgotten Histories," in *Arab Detroit 9/11*, 381–393; Michael Suleiman, "A History of Arab-American Political Participation," in *Arab Americans and Political Participation,* ed. Philippa Strum (Washington, DC: Woodrow Wilson International Center, 2006).

52. Gregory Starrett, *Putting Islam to Work: Education, Politics, and Religious Transformation in Egypt* (Berkeley: University of California Press, 1998), 9.

53. Deeb, *An Enchanted Modern*, 20.

54. Dale F. Eickelman and James Piscatori, *Muslim Politics* (Princeton, NJ: Princeton University Press, 2004).

55. Sylviane Diouf, *Servants of Allah: African Muslims Enslaved in the Americas* (New York: New York University Press, 1998); Michael A. Gomez, *Black Crescent: The Experience and Legacy of African Muslims in the Americas* (Cambridge: Cambridge University Press, 2005); Alford, *Prince Among Slaves*; Curtis, *Muslims in America*; GhaneaBassiri, *History.*

56. For the later point, see especially Edward E. Curtis IV, *Islam in Black America* (Albany: State University of New York Press, 2002); Edward E. Curtis IV, *Black Muslim*

Religion in the Nation of Islam, 1960–1975 (Chapel Hill: University of North Carolina Press, 2006); McCloud, *African American Islam*; Gomez, *Black Crescent*; C. Eric Lincoln, *The Black Muslims in America* (Boston: Beacon Press, 1961).

57. Yvonne Haddad, "The Islamic Identity in North America," in *Muslims on the Americanization Path?*, eds. Yvonne Haddad and John Esposito (Atlanta: Scholars Press, 1998), 21–22.

58. Elkholy, *The Arab Moslems in the United States*; Wasfi, *An Islamic-Lebanese*.

59. Walbridge, *Without Forgetting the Imam*, 44–45.

60. For the "churches" reference, see Elkholy, *The Arab Moslems in the United States*; Abraham, "Arab Detroit's 'American' Mosque"; Walbridge, *Without Forgetting the Imam*.

61. Muqtadar Khan, "Living on Borderlines: Islam Beyond the Clash and Dialogue of Civilizations," in *Muslims' Place in the American Public Square*, ed. Zahid H. Bukhari et al. (Walnut Creek, CA: AltaMira Press, 2004), 98.

62. See Mucahit Bilici, "Finding Mecca in America: American Muslims and Cultural Citizenship" (University of Michigan, 2008).

63. Sherman A. Jackson, *Islam and the Blackamerican: Looking Toward the Third Resurrection* (New York: Oxford University Press, 2005), 3.

64. Jackson, *Islam and the Blackamerican*, 4.

65. Jackson, *Islam and the Blackamerican*, 4.

66. Aminah Beverly McCloud, *Transnational Muslims in American Society* (Gainesville, University Press of Florida, 2006), 25.

67. The only noteworthy exception to this pattern remains Robert Dannin, *Black Pilgrimage to Islam* (New York: Oxford University Press, 2002). GhaneaBassiri, to his credit, bemoans the lack of good source materials prior to World War II and blames this not on the weak religiosity of the early Muslims but on the lack of academic research into this subject. See especially chapters 4 and 5, GhaneaBassiri, *History*.

Chapter 2

1. Eric Davis, *Representations of the Middle East at American World Fairs 1876–1904*, 2006; Adele Younis and Philip Kayal, *Coming of the Arabic Speaking People to the United States* (Staten Island: Center For Migration Studies, 1995).

2. *Scribner's Magazine* 14:606, quoted in Younis and Kayal, *Coming of the Arabic Speaking People*, 606.

3. West African slaves, who perhaps numbered in the tens of thousands, "came as Muslims and lived as Muslims" despite the brutal conditions of slavery. Deprived of the opportunity to reproduce Islam through the generations, they nonetheless sustained it in their own lives and, where possible, found personal and political empowerment through Muslim networks. Sylviane Diouf, *Servants of Allah*. See also Alford, *Prince Among Slaves*; Allan D. Austin, *African Muslims in Antebellum America: Transatlantic Stories and Spiritual Struggles* (New York: Garland Publishers, 1997); Michael A. Gomez, *Black Crescent*.

4. Adele Younis, *The Coming of the Arabic-Speaking People to the United States* (Boston: Boston University Graduate School, 1961), 183.

5. Asad Hussain and Harold Vogelaar, "Activities of the Immigrant Muslim Communities in Chicago," in *Muslim Communities in North America*, ed. Yvonne Haddad and Jane Idleman Smith (New York: State University of New York Press, 1994).

6. Marc Ferris, "To 'Achieve the Pleasure of Allah': Immigrant Muslim Communities in New York City, 1893–1991," in *Muslim Communities in North America*, ed. Yvonne Haddad and Jane Idleman Smith (New York: State University of New York Press, 1994), 221.

7. Akel Ismail Kahera, "Urban Enclaves, Muslim Identity and the Urban Mosque in America," *Journal of Muslim Minority Affairs* 22, no. 2 (2002): 369–380; Patrick D. Bowen, "Satti Majid: A Sudanese Founder of American Islam," *Journal of Africana Religion* 1, no. 2 (2013): 194–209.

8. Elizabeth Munger, *Michigan City's First One Hundred Years. Bygone Places Along the "Hoosier Line": The Monon Railroad Line Third Subdivision*, 1969, http://www.monon.monon.org/bygone/thirdsub.html. "A History of the Islamic Mesjid of Michigan City" is included in the Naff Collection, NMAH #78, 1-K-1-b, anonymous, undated.

9. Bill Yahya Aossey, *The Role of the Islamic Center and Its Necessity in the Development of Muslim Communities in North America*, Naff Collection, National Museum of American History, 1978. It can be argued that it is the oldest, but not the first mosque built in the United States.

10. Elizabeth Boosahda, *Arab-American Faces and Voices: The Origins of an Immigrant Community* (Austin: University of Texas Press, 2003).

11. "Arabian Colony," *Detroit Journal*, July 21, 1897.

12. For images of a few of the gravesites, see Building Islam in Detroit, "Featured Mosques," n.d., http://biid.lsa.umich.edu/.

13. Reynolds Farley, Sheldon Danzinger, and Harry Holzer, *Detroit Divided* (New York: Russell Sage Foundation Publications, 2000).

14. Farley, Danzinger, and Holzer, *Detroit Divided*. In 1920, 30 percent of Detroit's population was born overseas and another 36 percent were the children of at least one immigrant parent. Of the city's 40,000 black residents, 87 percent were born outside Michigan.

15. Charles Cameron, "A Street of All Nations," *Detroit Saturday Night*, June 12, 1926.

16. Ford established his corporate headquarters and factory in Highland Park (and later in Dearborn) to avoid paying Detroit taxes and meeting city zoning regulations. Capital flight was thus a part of Michigan's auto industry at the start of mass production. See Joe Darden et al., *Detroit: Race and Uneven Development* (Philadelphia: Temple University Press, 1987); Thomas Sugrue, *The Origins of Urban Crisis: Race and Inequality in Postwar Detroit* (Princeton, NJ: Princeton University Press, 1996).

17. For a breakdown of Syrian arrivals by sex, see Gregory Orfalea, *The Arab Americans: A History* (New York: Olive Branch Press, 2006). For a breakdown of those arriving from Ottoman territories by ethnicity/nationality, see Rifat Bali, "From Anatolia to the New World," in *Turkish Migration to the United States*, ed. A. Deniz Balgamis and Kemal Karpat (Madison: University of Wisconsin Press, 2008).

18. Alixa Naff, *Becoming American: The Early Arab Immigrant Experience* (Carbondale: Southern Illinois University Press, 1985); Bilge, "Voluntary Associations".

19. Bilge, "Voluntary Associations"; "Mohammedans to Celebrate Feast," *Detroit Free Press*, September 28, 1916.

20. P. K. Hitti, *The Syrians in America* (New York: George H. Doran, 1924); Naff, *Becoming American*.

21. Bilge, "Voluntary Associations," 387; "Moslems Here Build Mosque," *Detroit Free Press*, January 21, 1921; "Moslems Celebrate Feast of Id-Ul-Fitr," *Detroit Free Press*, June 9, 1921; "Mohammedans to Celebrate Feast," *Detroit Free Press*.

22. Leonard, *Making Ethnic Choices*; Bilge, "Voluntary Associations"; Kambiz GhaneaBassiri, *History*.

23. Hekmate Nassar was one such Syrian Christian, who married Hassan Restum and came with him to Highland Park in 1920. As a former school teacher, she was respected as the most educated woman in the community. She taught both Arabic and the Qur'an in her basement in Highland Park for decades, with a large cross hanging from the wall. William Restum, interview by Sally Howell, August 17, 2014.

24. Bilge, "Voluntary Associations"; Kemal Karpat, "The Turks in America," *Turcs d'Europełdots et d'Ailleurs, Les Annales de L'Autre Islam* 3 (1995): 232–233.

25. The United States v. Bhagat Singh Thind decision ruled that Asian Indians were non-whites and thus ineligible to naturalize as citizens. Sarah M. A. Gualtieri, *Between Arab and White: Race and Ethnicity in the Early Syrian American Diaspora* (Berkeley: University of California Press, 2009); Karen Isaksen Leonard, *The South Asian Americans* (Westport, CT: Greenwood Press, 1997).

26. Vivek Bald, "Overlapping Diasporas, Multiracial Lives: South Asian Muslims in U.S. Communities of Color, 1880–1950," *Souls* 8, no. 4 (December 2006): 3–18.

27. Azira Maeh, interview by Sally Howell, Detroit, 2005; Halimah Akhtar Gutman, interview by Sally Howell, Long Island, New York, May 26, 2010.

28. Maeh, interview.

29. Dada Amir Haider Khan, *Chains to Lose: Life and Struggles of a Revolutionary Memoirs of Dada Amir Haidar Khan*, vol. 2, ed. Hasan Ghardezi (Karachi, Pakistan: Pakistan Study Center, 2007), 442. See also, Ford R. Bryan, *Henry's Lieutenants* (Detroit: Wayne State University Press, 1993), 238.

30. Khan, *Chains to Lose*, 441.

31. Bald, "Overlapping Diasporas"; Karen McBeth Chopra, "A Forgotten Minority: Historical and Current Discrimination Against Asians from the Indian Subcontinent," *Detroit College of Law Review* (Winter 1995): 1269.

32. Journalist Charles D. Cameron studied the "Syrian" enclave in some detail in 1926 and published his reports in the weekly society newspaper, *Detroit Saturday Night*. His reports on the coffeehouses of the Syrians are carefully observed; see especially July 7 and May 22, 1926.

33. Alex Ecie, interview by Alixa Naff, Detroit, 1962, Series 4/C, NAAC.

34. Khan, *Chains to Lose*.

35. Just as *Turk* was commonly used to refer to anyone from the Ottoman Empire in this period, the term *Hindoo* referred to those from the Indian subcontinent and was not a religious designation per se.

36. Cameron, "A Street of All Nations"; Bilge, "Voluntary Associations"; *Shayk Khalil Bazzy*, interview by Alixa Naff, Detroit, 1962, Series 4/C, NAAC; Ecie, interview.

37. Bilge, "Voluntary Associations"; Trix, "The Bektashi Tekke". In her history of the Albanian Muslim communities of Detroit, Frances Trix argues that the Sunni Arabs congregated with the other Ottoman Muslims, but that the Shiʻa Arabs congregated by themselves.

38. "Articles of Association of the Arabian-American Society," State of Michigan, County of Wayne, March 23, 1916, Collection of Kamel Bazzy.

39. "Mohammedans to Celebrate Feast," *Detroit Free Press.*

40. "Mohammedans to Celebrate Feast," *Detroit Free Press.*

41. Bilge, "Voluntary Associations."

42. Gutman, interview; Maeh, interview.

43. Bazzy, interview.

44. Bowen, "Satti Majid."

45. Satti Majid, "al-Islam fi-Amrika," *al-Balagh*, 1935, 120. An alternative reading of Majid's recollections about Detroit would have him on hand for the opening of the Highland Park Mosque in 1921 (see below) and the Universal Islamic Society in 1926 (see Chapter 3).

46. "Is Head of Detroit Moslem Association," *Detroit Free Press*, September 28, 1916.

47. "Mohammedans to Celebrate Feast," *Detroit Free Press*; Bilge, "Voluntary Associations."

48. Majid, "al-Islam fi-Amrika," 117, quoted in GhaneaBassiri, *History*, 174–175.

49. Gladys Ecie, interview by Sally Howell, Dearborn, Michigan, 2005; Michael Berry, interview by Sally Howell, Dearborn, Michigan, 2007; Najah Bazzi, interview by Sally Howell, Plymouth, 2006.

50. Sally Howell and Amaney Jamal, "Belief and Belonging."

51. Bazzy, interview.

52. Bazzy, interview.

53. Ecie, interview. Dix refers to the intersection of Dix Avenue and Vernor Highway in the Southend of Dearborn, the main business district in the heart of Dearborn's Arab/Muslim enclave from the 1930s–1970s.

54. Bazzy, interview.

55. Bazzy, interview; Hussein Hamood, interview by Sally Howell, Madison Heights, Michigan, 2007.

56. John Devlin, "Mosque: Its Builders," *Detroit News*, January 21, 1921.

57. Alice Karoub, interview by Sally Howell, Northville, MI, 2005; Carl Karoub, interview by Sally Howell, Farmington Hills, MI, 2005.

58. Karoub's sons and grandchildren disagree over the precise date of his arrival in Michigan. His ship crossed the Atlantic in April of 1912 and was at sea and heard the distress calls of the Titanic. Hussien's son Karl thought his father arrived in Michigan in 1914, but his other son, Mike, understood his father to have arrived before the five-dollar workday at Ford. This would have placed him in Michigan in 1913 (C. Karoub, interview by Howell; M. Karoub, interview by Alixa Naff, Detroit, MI, 1980, Series 4/C, NAAC.)

59. Carl H. Karoub, interview; Carl M. Karoub, interview.

60. Ibid.

61. A. R. Norton, *Hezbollah: A Short History* (Princeton, NJ: Princeton University Press, 2009).

62. Bazzy, interview. Bazzy mentioned that he taught himself how to perform weddings, wash the dead, etc., and that the community "were happy when one of their own learned to do those things," implying that he learned these skills only after another man— perhaps Karoub—had already begun providing these services.

63. Maeh, interview. Mr. Maeh led the Bengali community of Detroit until his death in 1967. Imam Karoub officiated at his funeral and mentioned at the time that the two men had performed over fifty funerals together.

64. Bilge, "Voluntary Associations"; Trix, "The Bektashi Tekke"; Maeh, interview.

65. "Mohammedans to Celebrate Feast," *Detroit Free Press*.

66. A few Muslim conscripts were given honorable discharges when they refused to take up arms against the Turks. Hamood, interview; Hitti, *The Syrians in America*; Michael Suleiman, "A History of Arab-American Political Participation," 155. Karoub was not able to serve in the conflict due to an injury he had received at Ford's (Jeff Karoub, personal communication, August 28, 2012).

67. Lawrence Davidson, "Debating Palestine: Arab-American Challenges to Zionism 1917–1932," in *Arabs in America: Building a New Future*, ed. Michael Suleiman (Philadelphia: Temple University Press, 1999).

68. See "Shah Jahan Mosque—Britain's First Purpose-built Mosque Est. 1889," n.d., http://www.shahjahanmosque.org.uk/.

69. Jorgen S. Nielsen, *Towards A European Islam (Migration, Minorities and Citizenship)* (New York: St. Martin's Press, 1999).

70. "Mountain in Mohammed's Path," *Detroit News*, December 9, 1924.

71. "Moslems Here Build Mosque," *Detroit Free Press*.

72. Mufti Mohammed Sadiq, "Arabian Hospitality," *Moslem Sunrise*, July 21, 1921. Degenhardt received no remuneration for this work, but performed the task as "his sacred duty."

73. Timur Kuran, "The Provision of Public Goods Under Islamic Law: Origins, Impact, and Limitations of the Waqf System," *Law Society Review* 35, no. 4 (2001): 841–897; Jon E. Mandaville, "Usurious Piety: The Cash Waqf Controversy in the Ottoman Empire," *International Journal of Middle East Studies* 10, no. 3 (1979): 289–308.

74. "Gold the Root; Death the Bud," *Detroit News*, July 24, 1924.

75. C. M. Karoub, interview.

76. Devlin, "Mosque: Its Builders." Devlin also mentioned that a crate of "turbans" was located inside the main door so men entering the mosque could cover their hair for worship. It is unclear if he had this detail wrong and the scarves were, in fact, intended for women. This would indicate that the mosque was used by both genders.

77. Mohammed Karoub, "al-ihtifal al-kabir bi-ʿid al-fitr al-mubarik," *Al-Bayan*, June 14, 1921, translation by Nader Seif.

78. A 1921 *Detroit Free Press* article, "Moslems Here Build Mosque," is the first to document the direction in which Detroit's Muslims placed their *qibla*. The circle within a square layout of the interior was an impractical solution to the problem of creating an artful *qibla* in the already small building, reducing the size of the main room from forty-five by thirty feet to a thirty-foot circle.

79. "Gold the Root; Death the Bud," *Detroit Free Press*.

80. C. H. Karoub, interview; M. Karoub, interview.

81. "A Dream Fades: Sale of Mosque Finis to Mohammedan Vision," *Detroit Free Press*, July 9, 1924.

82. Mufti Mohammed Sadiq, "One Year's Moslem Missionary Work in America," *Moslem Sunrise* 1, no. 1 (July 1921). Mufti reports that news of the mosque's opening was reported in *Al-Bayan, Al-Hoda*, the *Toledo Blade*, and several other papers.

83. "A Dream Fades," *Detroit Free Press.*

84. Carl Muller, "Faith of Islam Withers in Detroit Atmosphere," *Detroit Free Press,* April 20, 1924; "Gold the Root; Death the Bud," *Detroit Free Press.*

85. "Moslems in Detroit Mark Turk's Victory," *Detroit Free Press,* September 9, 1922.

86. "Moslems Here Build Mosque," *Detroit Free Press.*

87. Devlin, "Mosque: Its Builders."

88. Devlin, "Mosque: Its Builders."

89. "Moslems Here Build Mosque," *Detroit Free Press.*

90. Sadiq, "One Year's Moslem Missionary Work in America," 12–13.

91. Sadiq, "One Year's Moslem Missionary Work in America," 12–13.

92. Turner, *Islam in the African-American Experience* .

93. "Moslems Avow Loyalty to U.S.: Laud Religious Freedom at Oriental Dinner to Highland Park Notables," *Detroit Free Press,* February 12, 1921.

94. Mohammed Karoub, "al-ihtifal al-kabir bi-`id al-fitr al-mubarik," *Al-Bayan,* New York, June 14, 1921. The quote is from "Moslems Celebrate Feast of Id-Ul-Fitr," *Detroit Free Press.*

95. "Moslems Celebrate Feast of Id-Ul-Fitr," *Detroit Free Press.* Chapter 3 provides a lengthier discussion of the symbolic role women played in illustrating the "modernity" of Detroit's Muslims in the local media.

96. Kamel Mansour al-Habhab, "Slow Down You Exagerators (in Arabic)," *Al-Bayan,* June 9, 1921.

97. Dhost Muhammad Shahid, "Mufti Muhammad Sadiq: Founder of Ahmadiyya Muslim Mission in the United States of America," *The Muslim Sunrise,* July 31, 2013.

98. William Richards, "Moslem Mufti Seeks to Make Detroit Islam," *Detroit Free Press,* February 13, 1921.

99. Turner, *Islam in the African-American Experience*; Yvonne Yazbeck Haddad and Jane Idleman Smith, "The Ahmadiyya Community of North America," in *Mission to America: Five Islamic Sectarian Communities in North America* (Gainesville: University Press of Florida, 1993), 49–78.

100. "Mosque, Empty, Will Be Razed: Highland Park Will Lose Picturesque Shrine to Islam's Faith Soon," *Detroit News,* August 9, 1922.

101. Sadiq, "One Year's Moslem Missionary Work in America." Sadiq provides 74 Victor Avenue, Karoub House, as his personal address and that of the newsletter in the first issue of the *Moslem Sunrise.*

102. "Seeds of Islam, Find no Root," *Detroit Free Press,* September 24, 1922.

103. Sadiq, "Arabian Hospitality."

104. Sadiq, "One Year's Moslem Missionary Work in America," 12.

105. Sadiq, "One Year's Moslem Missionary Work in America," 13.

106. Mufti Mohammed Sadiq, "My Advice to the Muhammadans in America," *Moslem Sunrise,* 1921, 28. This violates one of the primary tenets of Islam: that the Prophet Muhammad was the final prophet in the Abrahamic tradition.

107. Mufti Sadiq, "Untitled," *Moslem Sunrise,* October 1921.

108. "Mosque, Empty, Will Be Razed," *Detroit Free Press.*

109. Sadiq does not mention having been driven from Detroit by the Karoubs or other Muslims in the city. Instead he thanked "brother J. B. Khan Ahmadi and other

brethren in Detroit for offering arrangements for my permanent staying in Detroit, but I think Chicago is a better place for our central office in this country than any other city and therefore I have established a central mission here. However, our missionaries will be touring round and visiting Detroit as often as possible." Mufti Sadiq, "Brief Report of the Work in America," *Moslem Sunrise* 2, no. 3 (October 1922): 112.

110. "Gold the Root; Death the Bud," *Detroit Free Press*.

111. See, especially, Mohammed Karoub, "3,000 Riyal will be Paid to Anyone who can Prove that there is no Mosque in Detroit," *Al-Bayan*, June 9, 1921, 3; al-Habhab, "Slow Down You Exagerators (in Arabic)."

112. "Mosque, Empty, Will Be Razed," *Detroit Free Press*.

113. Bazzy, interview; Naff personal correspondence.

114. Ecie, interview, 1962.

115. "Mosque Sheik Quits, Works as Watchman," *Detroit Free Press*, November 11, 1922.

116. "Mosque, Empty, Will Be Razed."

117. "Seeds of Islam, Find no Root."

118. "Seeds of Islam, Find no Root."

119. "Seeds of Islam, Find no Root" and "Gold the Root; Death the Bud," both *Detroit Free Press*.

120. Muller, "Faith of Islam Withers."

121. "Hussein Abbas Murdered in His Sleep," *The Highland Parker*, March 14, 1924. This suggests that Karoub might have had a financial ambition for the mosque that revealed itself only after the building was officially opened. Karoub could have charged rent for Americanization services from Ford.

122. Muller, "Faith of Islam Withers."

123. "Gold the Root; Death the Bud"; "Mountain in Mohammed's Path."

124. "Highland Park Mosque Still Houses 'Faithful,'" *Detroit News*, August 20, 1922; "Moslems in Detroit Mark Turk's Victory." This second story notes that the gathering included 250 worshippers and that a similar prayer took place in Highland Park. Mehmed Shefik Zia also presided over the service, which illustrates again that the Muslim organizations created in Detroit in the period were multi-ethnic.

125. Bazzy, interview; Ecie, interview, 1962.

126. "Hussein Abbas Murdered in His Sleep."

127. "Turk Confesses Murder for Love, Death of Hussein Abbas, Wealthy Syrian Grocer, Attributed to Wife's Plotting," *The Highland Parker*, March 26, 1924.

128. "Mountain in Mohammed's Path"; "Karoub Freed in Killing Case," *Detroit News*, December 24, 1924.

129. "Woodsmen of the World to Get Mohammedan Mosque," *The Highland Parker*, July 7, 1927.

130. "Seeds of Islam, Find no Root."

131. M. Karoub, interview.

132. Abdullah Igram, interview by Alixa Naff, Cedar Rapids, IA, 1980, Series 4/C, NAAC; Aossey, *The Role of the Islamic Center*.

133. Sadiq, "My Advice to the Muhammadans in America."

134. Sadiq, "One Year's Moslem Missionary Work in America."

135. Robert Wuthnow, *Between States and Markets: The Voluntary Sector in Comparative Perspective* (Princeton, NJ: Princeton University Press, 1991), 295.

136. R. Stephen Warner, *A Church of Our Own: Disestablishment and Diversity in American Religion* (New Brunswick, NJ: Rutgers University Press, 2005), 30.

137. Ecie, interview, 2005; Khan, *Chains to Lose*.

Chapter 3

1. This was the official quota for both Turkey and Syria, although the Syrian quota was uniformly exceeded. Gregory Orfalea, *The Arab Americans*.

2. Smith, "The Turks," 8.

3. Faye Elizabeth Smith, "Bits of the Old World in Detroit: China," *Detroit Saturday Night*, March 4, 1922.

4. Faye Elizabeth Smith, "Bits of the Old World in Detroit: Armenia," *Detroit Saturday Night*, March 18, 1922, 8.

5. "Minera Abass" was Muneera Abbas, the woman discussed in Chapter 2 who was found guilty of conspiring to kill her husband, Hussein Abbas.

6. Smith, "The Turks."

7. Smith, "The Turks"; Melanie McAlister, *Epic Encounters*.

8. Douglas Little, *American Orientalism*.

9. Sidney Whitman, *Turkish Memories* (New York: Charles Scribner's Sons, 1914); Roderic Davidson, "The Image of Turkey in the West: In Historical Perspective," *The Turkish Studies Association* no. 5 (1981): 1–6.

10. Smith, "Bits of the Old World in Detroit: Armenia," 4.

11. Little, *American Orientalism*, 20.

12. McAlister, *Epic Encounters*; William R. Leach, *Land of Desire: Merchants, Power, and the Rise of a New American Culture* (New York: Vintage, 1994). See also Susan Nance, "Respectability and Representation: The Moorish Science Temple, Morocco, and Black Public Culture in 1920s Chicago," *American Quarterly* 54, no. 4 (2002): 623–659.

13. In Detroit this project was also supported by the settlement houses of the period and by the "Sociology Department" of Ford Motor. Ford's famous five-dollar workday was provided to those who graduated from the company's Americanization program and submitted their households to inspection by the company's social workers. See Martha May, "The Historical Problem of the Family Wage: The Ford Motor Company and the Five Dollar Day," *Feminist Studies* 8, no. 2 (1982): 399–424; James Barrett, "Americanization from the Bottom Up: Immigration and the Remaking of the Working Class in the United States, 1880–1930," *Journal of American History* 79, no. 3 (1992): 996–1020; John Ehrenreich, *The Altruistic Imagination: A History of Social Work and Social Policy in the United States* (Ithaca, NY: Cornell University Press, 1985).

14. Smith, "Bits of the Old World in Detroit: Armenia."

15. Smith, "The Turks."

16. "Not inaptly or without logical force has Joseph Smith been designated the Mohammed of America. Between the prophet of Arabia and the prophet of Nauvoo (each claiming divine, prophetic powers) there is a strong family resemblance and a more than singular coincidence of experience," T. B. H. Stenhouse, *The Rocky Mountain Saints* (New York: Appleton and Company, 1873), 203. Stenhouse was affronted by

both Mormonism and Islam because they dared to claim "divine, prophetic powers" that extend beyond the teachings of the Christian Bible. Beyond this structural similarity, both also condoned the practice of polygamy, a "strong family resemblance" indeed. See Timothy Marr, *Cultural Roots*, 186.

17. Smith, "The Turks."

18. Nadine Naber, "Ambiguous Insiders: An Investigation of Arab American Invisibility," *Ethnic and Racial Studies* 23, no. 1 (2000): 37–61; Nadine Naber, "Introduction" Sarah Gualtieri, "Becoming 'White': Race, Religion and the Foundations of Syrian/Lebanese Ethnicity in the United States," *Journal of American Ethnic History* 20, no. 4 (2001): 29–58; Ariela Gross, *What Blood Won't Tell: A History of Race on Trial in America* (Cambridge, MA: Harvard University Press, 2008); Alixa Naff, *Becoming American*; Lisa Suhier Majaj, "Arab American Ethnicity: Locations, Coalitions and Cultural Negotiations," in *Arabs in America: Building a New Future*, ed. Suleiman (Philadelphia: Temple University Press, 1999).

19. See, especially, Jackson, *Islam and the Blackamerican*; Lincoln, *The Black Muslims in America*; Turner, *Islam in the African-American Experience*.

20. Arab American historians have traditionally followed the estimates provided in Hitti, *The Syrians in America* and Naff, *Becoming American*, but Kemal Karpat, working from Ottoman rather than American sources, estimates the percentage of Muslims in the Syrian migration to have been higher, between 15 and 20 percent; "The Ottoman Emigration to America, 1860–1914," *International Journal of Middle East Studies* 17, no. 2 (1985): 175–209. GhaneaBassiri, who accepts these larger numbers, suggests that anti-Turkish and anti-Muslim sentiments discouraged many immigrants from identifying as Muslim; *History*, 143.

21. Gualtieri, "Becoming 'White'," 41.

22. Ussama Makdisi, *The Culture of Sectarianism: Community History and Violence in Nineteenth Century Ottoman Lebanon* (Berkeley: University of California Press, 2001), has argued that the sectarianism that developed in Ottoman Syria in the seventeenth and eighteenth centuries was a product of "indigenous and imperial histories" that linked Syrian Christians (especially Maronite Catholics) to French and later American missions. The Ottomans, it was assumed, would protect and punish Muslims and the French would do likewise for the Maronite communities, though both groups were nominal subjects of the Ottoman Sultan (2).

23. GhaneaBassiri, *History*, 98.

24. Akram F. Khater, *Inventing Home: Emigration, Gender, and the Middle Class in Lebanon, 1870–1920* (Berkeley: University of California Press, 2001).

25. Gualtieri, "Becoming 'White' "; Naff, *Becoming American*, 108.

26. GhaneaBassiri, *History*, 142.

27. Gualtieri, *Between Arab and White*. Elderly Arab American interviewees were quick to point out that "Syrians" were declared white in the Dow case of 1909. "We have Dow!," I was told when the racial ambiguity of Arab Americans or anti-Arab racism was discussed (Helen Okdie Atwel, interview by Sally Howell, Dearborn, MI, December 2, 2000; Julia Haragely, interview by Sally Howell, Dearborn, MI, 2007; Aida Karoub Hamed, interview by Sally Howell, Farmington Hills, MI, 2005).

28. Dada Amir Haider Khan, *Chains to Lose*, 446–490.

29. Vivek Bald, *Bengali Harlem*; Khan, *Chains to Lose*. See also Karen I. Leonard, *Making Ethnic Choices*, who observed that many Punjabi and other South Asian immigrants who made their way to California in the 1920s and 1930s spent time in Detroit before moving west.

30. See Naff, *Becoming American*, for the most detailed description of peddling among Arab immigrants in the early twentieth century.

31. Of the several dozen men who married Americans, roughly half of their wives became Muslim. Hansen Clarke, interview by Sally Howell, Lansing, MI, 2006; Maeh, interview.

32. Gutman, interview.

33. Dada Khan's memoir, discussed in greater detail by Vivek Bald, describes a South Asian community in Detroit that was active politically across a wide range of labor and anticolonial issues. See Khan, *Chains to Lose*; Bald, *Bengali Harlem*.

34. "'Allah Ho Akbar!' Is Chant in Detroit When City's Moslems Gather for Service," *Detroit News*, April 25, 1926.

35. Here I use the term mosque to stand for any institution organized for the express purpose of hosting congregational prayers. See Regula Qureshi, "Transcending Space: Recitation and Community Among South Asian Muslims in Canada," in *Making Muslim Space in North American and Europe*, ed. Barbara Metcalf (Berkeley: University of California Press, 1996), 46–64.

36. Ian Duffield translates the name of the group, from Ali's memoir, as the "Central Islamic Society." He assumes Ali was a founder of this group and that they copied the name from the group that managed the Woking Mosque in England, Ian Duffield, "American Influences of Duse Mohamed Ali," in *Pan-African Biography*, ed. Robert A. Hill (Los Angeles: University of California Press, 1987), 41. See Duse Mohamed Ali, "Leaves from an Active Life," *The Comet* (n.d.); "Articles of Association (Ecclesiastical Corporation)" (State of Michigan, Department of Commerce, October 12, 1925). Satti Majid also refers to this mosque in his writings as the "Islamic Union," Satti Majid, "al-Islam fi-Amrika," *al-Balagh* (Khartoum, 1935), 1.

37. "Articles of Association (Ecclesiastical Corporation)."

38. "'Allah Ho Akbar!,'" *Detroit News*.

39. Khan, *Chains to Lose*, 477.

40. "'Allah Ho Akbar!,'" *Detroit News*.

41. "'Allah Ho Akbar!,'" *Detroit News*.

42. Khan, *Chains to Lose*, 478.

43. Mufti Muhammad Sadiq, "Thee Only Solution of Color Prejudice," *Moslem Sunrise* 1, no. 2 (October 1921): 41–42.

44. Khan, *Chains to Lose*, 477.

45. Khan, *Chains to Lose*, 477.

46. Khan, *Chains to Lose*, 480–481.

47. Vijay Prashad, *The Karma of Brown Folk* (Minneapolis: University of Minnesota Press, 2000), 2.

48. Hazel V. Carby, *Race Men (W. E. B. Du Bois Lectures)* (Cambridge, MA: Harvard University Press, 2000), 25–26.

49. Ali, "Leaves from an Active Life"; Duffield, "American Influences of Duse Mohamed Ali."

50. Duse Mohammed Ali, *In the Land of the Pharaohs* (New York: Appleton and Co., 1911).

51. Ali, "Leaves from an Active Life"; Duffield, "American Influences"; Turner, *Islam in the African-American Experience.*

52. Ali, 1912, quoted in Turner, *Islam in the African-American Experience*, 84.

53. Theodore G. Vincent, *Black Power and the Garvey Movement* (Berkeley, CA: Ramparts, 1971).

54. Penny M. Von Eschen, *Race Against Empire: Black Americans and Anticolonialism, 1937–1957* (Ithaca, NY: Cornell University Press, 1997), 10.

55. Ali, "Leaves from an Active Life"; Duffield, "American Influences."

56. Duffield, "American Influences," 41.

57. Michigan Department of Energy, Labor, and Economic Growth, "Articles of Association. America-Asia Society," March 12, 1926. Halimah Gutman, daughter of Jamil Akhtar, remembers Mr. Queraishi as an activist for the Indian Independence Committee that was established in the 1940s. Like Gutman's father, Queraishi married a white American. The education and middle-class standing of several of the Indian immigrants in this period is noteworthy.

58. Duffield, "American Influences," 40; Ali, "Leaves from an Active Life," 7. Dada Khan's memoir suggests that these tensions were due, in part, to religious prejudice between Hindus and Muslims. He also mentions that the celebratory dinner organized in honor of Dr. Hussain (described above) was ruined when one of the organizers invited the British Consul in Detroit. Many "nationalist minded Indians including myself...refused to attend." Khan, *Chains to Lose*, 482.

59. "Theater Notices," *Detroit Free Press*, October 29, 1926.

60. Duffield, "American Influences," 41.

61. See Hisham Aidi, "Let Us Be Moors: Islam, Race and 'Connected Histories,'" *Middle East Report* 7, no. 229 (2003): 42–53; Jackson, *Islam and the Blackamerican*; Turner, *Islam in the African-American Experience.* Scholars have not reached a consensus about when the NOI was established. I use 1931 because this is when Elijah Poole and W. D. Fard first met in Detroit. The Allah Temple of Islam (ATI) was the first ministry launched by Fard in the area, in 1930 or 1931: Erdmann Doane Beynon, "The Voodoo Cult Among Negro Migrants in Detroit," *American Journal of Sociology* 43, no. 6 (May 1938): 894–907; Claude Andrew Clegg, *An Original Man: The Life and Times of Elijah Muhammad* (New York: St. Martin's Griffin, 1998). Fard renamed the group the Nation of Islam in 1933 to circumvent a court order to disband the ATI. Karl Evanzz, *The Messenger: The Rise and Fall of Elijah Muhammad* (New York: Vintage, 1999), 94.

62. Khan, *Chains to Lose*, 477.

63. Khan, *Chains to Lose*, 476–477.

64. Khan, *Chains to Lose*, 478–479.

65. According to Evanzz, *The Messenger*, 5, Elijah Poole (Mohammad) and Duse Ali were in the city at the same time. Poole was an active member of the UNIA and might have been familiar with Ali's writings in *Negro World*. But Poole was also active in the MST; it is unlikely that Ali would have associated with this group.

66. Duffield, "American Influences."

67. Sylvester A. Johnson, "The Rise of Black Ethnics: The Ethnic Turn in African American Religions, 1916–1945," *Religion and American Culture: A Journal of Interpretation* 20, no. 2 (July 1, 2010): 126.

68. McAlister, *Epic Encounters*, 87.

69. Dorman, " 'A True Moslem Is a True Spiritualist,' " 116.

70. Dorman, " 'A True Moslem Is a True Spiritualist,' " 116.

71. Dorman, " 'A True Moslem Is a True Spiritualist,' " 117.

72. Ali, "Leaves from an Active Life"; Duffield, "American Influences."

73. The 1914 date is from Akil Fahd, February 12, 2007.

74. Barbara Bilge, "Voluntary Associations," 394.

75. James Gregory, *The Southern Diaspora*; Angela Denise Dillard, *Faith in the City*; Dorman, " 'A True Moslem Is a True Spiritualist.' "

76. The segregation of Detroit's churches, especially Roman Catholic ones, came up frequently in my interviews with African American Muslim converts. One church on Woodward Avenue, for example, had different hours for black and white services. "That's just not right," said Haitama Shareiff. "White" institutions like the Catholic Church were viewed as racist; independent black churches were often viewed as exploitative, Sharieff, interview; T. Khalid, interview; Hogue, interview.

77. Hardy, "Fauset's (Missing) Pentecostals"; Dorman, " 'A True Moslem Is a True Spiritualist.' "

78. Mufti Mohammed Sadiq, "Brief Report of the Work in America," *Moslem Sunrise* 2, no.1, 1923, 167.

79. Dannin, *Black Pilgrimage to Islam*.

80. See Sherman Jackson for a thoughtful and straightforward discussion of these borrowings, *Islam and the Blackamerican*, 45.

81. Curtis, *Islam in Black America*. For a close reading of the long history of the deployment of the term "Moor" see Anouar Majid, *We Are All Moors: Ending Centuries of Crusades Against Muslims and Other Minorities* (St. Paul: University of Minnesota Press, 2012).

82. Curtis, *Islam in Black America*.

83. Curtis, *Islam in Black America*; Evanzz, *The Messenger*.

84. For details on NOI teachings, see Curtis, *Islam in Black America*; Evanzz, *The Messenger*; Jackson, *Islam and the Blackamerican*; Turner, *Islam in the African-American Experience*. See Michael A. Gomez, *Black Crescent*, 296–301, for a thoughtful examination of the intellectual and historical threads that linked the NOI to the MST and to Garveyism.

85. Curtis, *Islam in Black America*; McCloud, *African American Islam*.

86. For the most detailed account of these events, see Evanzz, *The Messenger*.

87. Beynon, "The Voodoo Cult Among Negro Migrants in Detroit."

88. Evanzz, *The Messenger*; Michael A. Gomez, *Black Crescent*.

89. Ahmed Abu Shouk, J. O. Hunwick, and R. S. O'Fahey, "A Sudanese Missionary to the United States: Satti Majid, 'Shaykh al-Islam in North America,' and His Encounter with Noble Drew Ali, Prophet of the Moorish Science Temple Movement," *Sudanic Africa* 8 (1997): 137–191.

90. Rogia Abusharaf, *Wanderings: Sudanese Migrants and Exiles in North America* (Ithaca, NY: Cornell University Press, 2002). For evidence of the Arab community's reading of Ahmadiyya teachings as heresy, see Chapter 2.

91. "Urges Turk Negro Colony," *New York Times*, June 30, 1930.

92. Dannin, *Black Pilgrimage to Islam*, 47–55.

93. M. Naeem Nash, "Muhammad Ezaldeen (1866–1957) Founder of the Addeynu Allahe Universal Arabic Association," in *Encyclopedia of Muslim American History*, ed. Edward Curtis (New York: Facts on File, 2010), 175–176.

94. Sherman Jackson's term for the Islam practiced initially in the Arabian Peninsula, spread through contact with believers, and based on the Qur'an and Sunna, *Islam and the Blackamerican*.

95. Hitti, *The Syrians in America*, 59–60.

96. Lawrence Davidson, "Debating Palestine," 355; Michael Suleiman, "A History of Arab-American Political Participation," 155.

97. "Syrian Emir Heads to Detroit," *New York Times*, March 28, 1924.

98. Kamal Bazzy and Yehia Shamy, *Shaykh Khalil Bazzy: 75 Years in Religious and Immigration Services* (Beirut, Lebanon: Dar Al-Mahajaj, 2012); Shaykh Khalil Bazzy, interview by Alixa Naff, Detroit, MI, 1962, Series 4/C, NAAC.

99. Charles Cameron, "Detroit Druses Watch Revolt," *Detroit Saturday Night*, May 22, 1926, 10.

100. Cameron, "Detroit Druses Watch Revolt."

101. Cameron, "Detroit Druses Watch Revolt."

102. Cameron, "Detroit Druses Watch Revolt."

103. "400 Syrians Protest Visit of Emir Here," *Detroit Free Press*, January 18, 1927.

104. "400 Syrians Protest."

105. Bazzy and Shamy, *Shaykh Khalil Bazzy*, 69–78.

106. Bazzy, interview.

107. Michael Berry, born a decade earlier in 1920, remembers attending this school before he moved to Lebanon with his family in 1930. Originally, the school seemed to be for boys only. Hekmate Restum also taught Arabic and the Qur'an in her Highland Park basement from the 1920s–1940s. A similar basement school for both boys and girls opened in the 1930s. Michael Berry, interview by Sally Howell, Dearborn, MI, 2007; Ardela and Julia Jabara, interview by Sally Howell, Romulus, MI, 2007; William Restum, interview by Sally Howell, August 17, 2014.

108. M. Karoub, interview by Alixa Naff, Detroit, MI, 1980, Series 4/C, NAAC.

109. Mike Karoub, who apprenticed himself to his father as a teen and became an imam himself in adulthood (see Chapter 6), would continue to teach Arabic to new converts throughout his life. I often meet elderly African Americans who studied with one of the Karoubs.

110. Carl H. Karoub, interview by Sally Howell, Livonia, MI, 2005.

111. Alice Karoub, interview by Sally Howell, Northville, MI, 2005.

112. M. Karoub, interview.

113. "The Big Party," *Al-Daleel* 3, no. 9 (1945); A. Karoub, interview.

114. Michael Karoub, "Golden Jubilee Celebration Marks Fifty Years of Service to Arab-Americans an Islam," *Golden Jubilee Celebration of the Reverend Imam Hussien Adeeb Karoub* (1962): 7–8.

115. Maeh, interview.

116. Bilge, "Voluntary Associations," 393.

117. C. H. Karoub, interview.

118. Maeh, interview; Clarke, interview.

119. Maeh, interview.

120. Maeh, interview.

121. Bilge, "Voluntary Associations."

122. Bilge, "Voluntary Associations," 390.

123. C. H. Karoub, interview.

124. M. Karoub, interview.

125. "Religion Bars 400 from Soup Lines: Mohammadans Can't Eat Relief Food," *Detroit Free Press*, December 12, 1932.

126. "Mohammedans Get Their Own Soup Kitchen," *Detroit Free Press*, January 12, 1933.

127. Philip Adler, "Allah Hears Supplication for Doles From Detroit," *Detroit News*, December 30, 1932.

128. Maeh, interview; Turner, *Islam in the African-American Experience*; Curtis, *Muslims in America*; McCloud, *Transnational Muslims*; GhaneaBassiri, *A History of Islam in America*.

129. Curtis, *Muslims in America*; GhaneaBassiri, *A History of Islam in America*; McCloud, *Transnational Muslims*; Turner, *Islam in the African-American Experience*.

Chapter 4

1. Ardella and Julia Jabara, interview.

2. Ardella and Julia Jabara, interview.

3. Herberg, *Protestant, Catholic, Jew*.

4. Mary Waters, *Ethnic Options: Choosing Identities in America* (Berkeley: University of California Press, 1990).

5. Waters, *Ethnic Options*, 147–168.

6. For three of many possible examples, see Marr, *The Cultural Roots of American Islamicism* on Mormons; Makdisi, *Artillery of Heaven* on Native Americans; and Sherene Razack, *Casting Out: The Eviction of Muslims from Western Law and Politics* (Toronto: University of Toronto Press, 2008) on Muslims.

7. Raymond Williams, *Religions of Immigrants from India and Pakistan: New Threads in the American Tapestry* (Cambridge: Cambridge University Press, 1988).

8. Moore, *Religious Outsiders*.

9. Le Roy Etienne, "Les Musulmans et Le Pouvoir En Afrique Noir," *Journal of Legal Pluralism and Unofficial Law* (1984): 143–145; Robert Leveau, "The Islamic Presence in France," in *The New Islamic Presence in Western Europe*, ed. T. Gerholm and Y. G. Lithman (New York: Mansell, 1988), 107–122.

10. Dale F. Eickelman, "Higher Education and the Religious Imagination in Contemporary Arab Societies," *American Ethnologist* 19, no. 4 (1992): 643.

11. Eickelman, "Mass Higher Education," 644.

12. Bilge, "Voluntary Associations"; F. Trix, "The Bektashi Tekke"; Yvonne Yazbeck Haddad and Jane Idleman Smith, *Muslim Communities in North America* (Albany: State University of New York Press, 1994); Alixa Naff, "The Arabic-Language Press," in *The Ethnic Press in the United States*, ed. Sally Miller (New York: Greenwood Press, 1987), 11.

13. Even the children of Bazzy and Karoub, with one important exception, were not able to read or recite the Qur'an as adults. The communities in Cedar Rapids and Toledo did a better job of educating the second generation, perhaps because they were more middle class. See Kambiz GhaneaBassiri, *History*, 190; Elkholy, *The Arab Moslems in the United States*.

14. Oleg Grabar, "Symbols and Signs in Islamic Architecture," in *Architecture and Community Building in the Islamic World Today* (Millerton, NY: Aperture, 1983).

15. Barbara Metcalf, *Making Muslim Space in North America and Europe* (Berkeley: University of California Press, 1996).

16. Starrett, *Putting Islam to Work*.

17. Sugrue, *The Origins of Urban Crisis*.

18. Kevin Boyle, *Arc of Justice: a Saga of Race, Civil Rights, and Murder in the Jazz Age* (New York: Henry Holt, 2004); Sugrue, *The Origins of Urban Crisis*.

19. Heather Barrow, "'The American Disease of Growth': Henry Ford and the Metropolitanization of Detroit, 1920–1940," in *Manufacturing Suburbs: Building Work and Home on the Manufacturing Fringe*, ed. Robert Lewis (Philadelphia: Temple University Press, 2004).

20. Barrow, "'The American Disease of Growth.'"

21. David L. Good, *Orvie: The Dictator of Dearborn: The Rise and Reign of Orville L. Hubbard* (Detroit: Wayne State University Press, 1989); James W. Loewen, *Sundown Towns: A Hidden Dimension of American Racism* (New York: Touchstone, 2006); 2010 US Census.

22. Jon Swanson, "Sojourners and Settlers in Yemen and America," in *Sojourners and Settlers: The Yemeni Immigrant Experience*, ed. Jonathon Friedlander (Provo: University Press of Utah, 1988), 65.

23. Naff, *Becoming American*; Khater, *Inventing Home*. Both Naff and Khater suggest that this pattern of migrating back to Lebanon and then finding life there unsatisfactory, resulting in a permanent resettlement in the United States, occurred a generation earlier for Syrian Christians.

24. Khater, *Inventing Home*, and Orfalea, *The Arab Americans*, agree that the number of Syrians who left the United States in the 1930s greatly exceeded the number of arrivals. Turkish and Albanian Muslims also returned home in large numbers, reducing their presence in the city by half in the 1930s. See Bilge, "Voluntary Associations," and Trix, "The Bektashi Tekke."

25. Fatima El Haje, interview by Sally Howell, Dearborn, MI, 2005.

26. F. El Haje, interview.

27. Susan Giffin, *Michael Berry* (Bloomington, IN: AuthorHouse, 2007).

28. Giffin, *Michael Berry*, 12.

29. H. El Haje, interview.

30. F. El Haje, interview.

31. G. Ecie, interview.

32. F. El Haje, interview.

33. M. Karoub interview.

34. "United Syrian Citizen's Society Celebrates 'Independence Day,'" *Highland Parker*, July 8, 1926; "Brotherhood of Nations Picnic a Success," *Highland Parker*, September 2, 1926.

35. G. Ecie, interview.

36. Abraham Family, interview.

37. See Judith Weisenfeld, *Hollywood Be Thy Name: African American Religion in American Film, 1929–1949* (Berkeley: University of California Press, 2007).

38. Abraham Family, interview. In the 1980s, the Lebanese Sunni community hired a new imam, Mohammad Mardini, who revived the *mawlid* tradition among the older generation. Today the tradition is alive and well among new immigrants. Mohammad Mardini, interview by Sally Howell, Ann Arbor, MI, 2006.

39. G. Ecie, interview; F. El Haje, interview; Jabara, interview.

40. Raymond Williams, *Religions of Immigrants from India and Pakistan: New Threads in the American Tapestry* (New York: Cambridge University Press, 1988); R. Stephen Warner and J. G. Wittner, *Gatherings in Diaspora: Religious Communities and the New Immigration* (Philadelphia: Temple University Press, 1998).

41. Christians and Jews are referred to as "people of the book" in the Qur'an. Islam is a prophetic tradition that accepts the major prophets of the Torah and New Testament. As such, neither Christians nor Jews are considered *kufar* (unbelievers), and Muslim men can marry women of either faith.

42. Most, but not all, imams in Detroit have refused to marry Muslim women to non-Muslims unless these men first embrace Islam. M. Karoub, interview.

43. Pnina Werbner, *Imagined Diasporas Among Manchester Muslims: The Public Performance of Pakistani Transnational Identity Politics* (Oxford: James Currey, 2002), 63.

44. Werbner, *Imagined Diasporas*.

45. Mandaville, *Transnational Muslim Politics*.

46. Metcalf, *Making Muslim Space*.

47. Linda Walbridge, "The Shi'a Mosques and Their Congregations in Dearborn," in *Muslim Communities in North America*, ed. Yvonne Yazbeck Haddad and Jane Idleman Smith (New York: State University of New York Press, 1994).

48. Michael M. J. Fischer and Mehdi Abedi, *Debating Muslims: Cultural Dialogues in Postmodernity and Tradition (New Directions in Anthropological Writing)* (Madison: University of Wisconsin Press, 1990).

49. Abdo A. Elkholy, *The Arab Moslems in the United States*, describes a similar pattern occurring in Toledo. When the Sunni majority planned to build a mosque there, the Shi'a withdrew from the association and did not, for the most part, join others for prayer. They nonetheless supported this institution financially, and were "content to see their children active in both the social and religious activities of the mosque" (73–75).

50. Linda Walbridge, *Without Forgetting the Imam*.

51. While several of the people I interviewed mentioned not having heard the word *Shi'a* until the1950s or later, all of the Shi'a I spoke with, and most of the Sunnis as well, were familiar with a term now considered derogatory, *mitwali*.

52. Ecie, interview.

53. The first printed appearance of the word Shi'a that I have identified was in an announcement of the arrival of Shaykh Mohammad Jawad Chirri to Detroit in 1949 (see Chapter 5). Elkholy, *The Arab Moslems in the United States*, also attributes the visibility of this division to the arrival of Chirri. "He came to America several years ago where he found the sectarian conflict dying in the Detroit Community. He decided to revive it ... as a means of increasing his own power" (76).

54. Many of the Sunni who attended the AMS in the 1940s and 1950s were accustomed to referring to this mosque, and to mosques in general, as "churches." In this anecdote, her husband was in a mosque, most likely the mosque in Ross, North Dakota.

55. The Prophet Muhammad was not killed. He died of natural causes. The division between Sunni and Shi'a took place decades after the Prophet's death. Jabara's error suggests that her education in this regard was rudimentary, perhaps due to the reluctance of the older generation to discuss religious factionalism.

56. Jabara also narrated several incidents that indicated Shi'a difference from Sunnis. These narratives illustrated the social inferiority of the Shi'a from her perspective.

57. Alawan's family was from Damascus where they suffered ongoing persecution for their minority status. For the Shi'a, the significance of the difference was much more important than it was to the Sunni majority.

58. Charles Khalil Alawan (Hajj Chuck), interview by Sally Howell, Dearborn, MI, 2005.

59. Quraysh is the tribe into which the Prophet Muhammed was born, along with most of those from Mecca at the time of his birth. After the Prophet's death, the leadership of the Muslim community, the caliphate, was initially granted to several of his closest supporters. The fourth caliph, Ali, was a cousin and son-in-law of the Prophet, and a member of the Bani Hashim family within the larger Quraysh tribe. It was an Umayyad caliph who blocked the rival claim of Ali. This dispute over the caliphate led to the division of the early Muslims into Shi'a—those who were the followers of 'Ahl al-Bayt—and the Sunni—those who did not oppose the Umayyad caliphs.

60. C. Alawan, interview.

61. Michigan Corporation and Securities Commission, "Michigan Articles of Incorporation of Progressive Arabian Hashmie Society," July 20, 1936.

62. Letterhead of Minaret al-Hoda, including foundation date and primary objectives, Essie Abraham Collection, Folder, Islamic Organizations, Box 1, Bentley Historical Library, University of Michigan.

63. Incorporation papers of El-Bokka League, Essie Abraham Collection.

64. "Michigan Articles of Incorporation of Progressive Arabian Hashmie Society," July 2, 1938.

65. "Moslems Dedicate Temple to Fulfill a 20-Year Dream: Detroit Syrian Colony Conducts Ceremonies; Building to Be Church and School," *Detroit News*, May 31, 1937.

66. Dearborn Department of Records, Dearborn Historical Society.

67. "Minutes of Special Meeting of Minarat al-Hoda," Essie Abraham Collection, Box 1: Islamic Organizations Folder, Bentley Historical Library, February 20, 1939.

68. "Minutes of Special Meeting of Minarat al-Hoda."

69. "Articles of Incorporation of American Moslem Society," Essie Abraham Collection, Box 1: American Moslem Society Articles of Incorporation Folder, Bentley Historical Library, 1942.

70. H. El Haje, interview.

71. Ecie, interview; Jabara, interview; Abraham, interview; H. El Haje, interview.

72. H. El Haje, interview.

73. Paying and receiving interest is not sanctioned in Islamic jurisprudence. The practice was also expensive and both of these early Dearborn mosques were eager to

remove themselves from their obligations to bank lenders as quickly as possible. Owing money to a member of the congregation was far preferable and more affordable.

74. "Articles of Incorporation of American Moslem Society."

75. Ibid.

76. Nabeel Abraham, "Arab Detroit's 'American' Mosque," 629.

77. Metcalf, *Making Muslim Space.*

78. "Moslems Dedicate Temple to Fulfill a 20-Year Dream." Coverage of this opening also stressed that this was the "first temple in Detroit Metropolitan area." "Moslems to Open Dearborn Temple: Will Dedicate First One in Detroit Area Sunday," *Detroit Free Press,* May 29, 1937.

79. "Moslems Dedicate Temple to Fulfill a 20-Year Dream."

80. Ibid.

81. "Michigan Articles of Incorporation of Progressive Arabian Hashmie Society."

82. As described above, the building was not purchased until 1937 and the prayer space renovation was completed in 1939.

83. The Southend, surrounded as it was by Ford's Rouge facility—a soup manufacturer, a sausage producer, and a cement factory—suffered from terrible air quality in this period. See Barbara Aswad, "The Southeast Dearborn Arab Community Struggles for Survival Against Urban 'Renewal,'" in *Arabic-Speaking Communities in American Cities,* ed. Barbara C. Aswad (New York: Center For Migration Studies, 1974), 79.

84. Eide Alawan, interview by Sally Howell, Dearborn, MI, 2005.

85. Mohammed Hassen, "General Invitation to My Muslim Brothers in Detroit and Windsor, Canada," trans. Ryan Ferris, *Nahdat al-Arab,* October 5, 1948.

86. Abraham, interview.

87. Jabara, interview.

88. Abraham, interview; G. Ecie, interview; Jabara, interview; A. Hamed, interview.

89. H. El Haje, interview.

90. Najla Abu Khalil, "The American Women's Muslim Society Celebrates Its Second Anniversary Since Its Establishment," *Nahdat al-Arab,* February 11, 1949.

91. Once these debts were paid, however, the women's society of Hashmie Hall faded from view, see Abraham, "Arab Detroit's 'American' Mosque."

92. "Arabian Colony Holds Mortgage-Burning Rites," *Detroit News,* November 13, 1939.

Chapter 5

1. Ryan Ferris and Andrew Shryock, trans., "The Future of the New Generation," *Nahdat al-Arab,* May 5, 1949. Note that the word *Shi'a* is used in the text, an important innovation of Chirri's agenda.

2. Robert S. Ellwood, *1950: Crossroads of American Religious Life* (Louisville, KY: Westminster John Knox Press, 2000).

3. GhaneaBassiri, *History,* 228.

4. Rainer Brünner, *Islamic Ecumenism in the 20th Century: The Azhar And Shiism Between Rapprochement And Restraint* (Leiden: Brill, 2004). Mughniyya's work also influenced Musa al-Sadr, the Iraqi theologian and activist who is credited with having given birth to the Amal political party in the early 1970s and challenging the Communist Party in Lebanon for the support of the Shi'i masses.

5. These titles are taken from an English-language book Chirri published in Detroit. See Mohammad Jawad Chirri, *The Shiites Under Attack* (Detroit: Islamic Center of America, 1986).

6. The Lebanese government was set up to create a balance of power between the three majority communities: Christians, Sunni Muslims, and Shi'i Muslims, while in reality guaranteeing Christian—and in many ways Christian/Sunni—dominance.

7. Hussein Hamood, interview by Sally Howell, Madison Heights, MI, 2007. Osseiran, along with both Chirri and Mughniyya, was involved a political campaign to reconcile Sunni and Shi'i Islam that included leading Shi'i clerics (in Lebanon, Iraq, and Iran) and the leadership of Al-Azhar University in Egypt, the center of Sunni scholarship in the Arab world. Brünner, *Islamic Ecumenism*.

8. Michigan Corporation and Securities Commission, "Michigan Articles of Association (Eccliastical Corporation) of Moslem Mosque of Highland Park," April 4, 1958.

9. Hamood, interview.

10. Hussein Makled, "The Founding of the Islamic Center of America," 1990, Hussein Makled Collection, Bentley Historical Library, 3.

11. C. Alawan, interview; Hamood, interview; Makled, "The Founding."

12. Orfalea, *The Arab Americans*. From Arab-sending nations as a whole, the average annual immigration rate was just under one thousand people a year between 1950–1960.

13. Khater, *Inventing Home*.

14. Norton, *Hezbollah*; Emryrs Peters, "Aspects of Rank and Status Among Muslims in a Lebanese Village," in *People and Culture of the Middle East*, ed. L. E. Sweet (Garden City, NY: Natural History Press, 1970).

15. Hamood, interview. Hajj Hamood's father was an American veteran of World War I, but he refused to fight against the Ottoman Empire during the war, arguing, "This is my country. I can't fight against my own country." He was offered an honorable discharge.

16. Hussein, interview by Sally Howell, Dearborn Heights, MI, 2005.

17. When the USCS incorporated with the State of Michigan in 1958 as the Moslem Mosque of Highland Park, its goals included hiring an imam, purchasing a building to convert into a mosque, providing regular religious services, and providing religious education for "old and young persons of the Moslem faith." "Michigan Articles of Association (Ecclesiastical Corporation) of Moslem Mosque of Highland Park."

18. Makled, interview.

19. Hajj Hamood arrived in Detroit well after Hashmie Hall was established. While he admitted that the group did have a place set aside for prayer, a space he referred to as a "mosque" in our interview, he was unaware that Hashmie Hall had originally been founded to serve as a mosque for local Shi'a; Hamood, interview.

20. Hamood, interview.

21. Chirri published a regular series of sermons in the pages of *Nahdat al-Arab* from May 1949 to June 1950. The style of these sermons is somewhat repetitive and didactic (and does not lend itself to artful translation). Chirri addresses personal piety, the need for better education, and the political condition of the Shi'a universally, but is careful to avoid criticizing Detroit's mosques directly.

22. "Opening Ceremony of the Islamic Mosque in Dearborn, Michigan," *Nahdat al-Arab*, June 6, 1949.

23. "Opening Ceremony," *Nahdat al-Arab*.

24. "Opening Ceremony," *Nahdat al-Arab*. Baba Rexheb settled permanently in the Detroit area in 1952 (and once the Bektashi *Tekke*, his monastery, was completed in 1954 he no longer ventured out to other Islamic centers in the area—apart from the Albanian Islamic Center). See Hussein Abiva, "Baba Rexheb: A Sufi Saint for America," in *First Symposium on Bektashi-Alevism at Suleyman Demirel University*, 2005. Kaskelen, Kazakhstan; Frances Trix, *Albanians in Michigan – A Proud People from Southeast Europe* (East Lansing: Michigan State University Press, 2001).

25. "Opening Ceremony," *Nahdat al-Arab*.

26. Mohammad Jawad Chirri, "New School to Open at Islamic Mosque in Dearborn," *Nahdat al-Arab*, June 24, 1949.

27. Bazzy's refusal to accept payment for his services, insisting, "my reward is from God," has taken on legendary qualities in the present. See Walbridge, *Without Forgetting the Imam*; Bazzy and Shamy, *Shaykh Khalil Bazzy*.

28. Walbridge, *Without Forgetting the Imam*; Abraham, "Arab Detroit's 'American' Mosque," 629.

29. This group was also not fond of Osseiran, who won his position as Speaker of the House by defeating the candidate the Berrys supported. Makled, interview; Hamood, interview; E. Alwan, interview. They also sponsored an extended trip by Kalil Bazzy to Najaf in Iraq to beef up his Islamic credentials in the period between Osseiran's visit to Detroit and the arrival of Chirri. In 1948, Bazzy returned to Detroit bearing several certificates authorizing him to perform many of the same rites he had been performing in Detroit since 1914: bury the dead, marry the young, and adjudicate religious controversies (Bazzy and Shamy, *Shaykh Khalil Bazzy*, 154–160).

30. A Muslim, "My Opinion: On the Esteemed Shaykh Khalil Bazzy Who Is the Preferred Religious Leader of the Immigrants," *Nahdat al-Arab*, December 13, 1949.

31. Makled, interview; Hamood, interview.

32. Chirri, "New School to Open at Islamic Mosque in Dearborn."

33. Makled, "The Founding," 2.

34. First organized in 1914 as the Bader Elmoneer Society of Michigan City, Indiana, this group had close ties to Detroit's Arab community. Michigan City began drawing Muslim immigrants to work in the railroad industry for Pullman and Haskell-Barker in the late nineteenth century. Many of Detroit's Shi'i families spent time there before settling in Michigan. See Munger, *Michigan City's First One Hundred Years*.

35. Trix, "The Bektashi Tekke."

36. Trix, "The Bektashi Tekke."

37. Trix, "The Bektashi Tekke"; Trix, *Albanians in Michigan*.

38. Vehbi interview by Sally Howell, Harper Woods, MI, 2005. Ismail was recommended for this position by Mohammad Makke, an Albanian missionary based in Ohio who had corresponded with Ismail when he was still at Al-Azhar University.

39. Trix, "The Bektashi Tekke," 367.

40. Trix, "The Bektashi Tekke"; Ismail, interview.

41. Ismail, interview. I was not able to confirm this claim from other sources. My request (1133346-000) for Ismail's FBI file was denied on the grounds that his files had

been destroyed. Personal communication, Federal Bureau of Investigation, September 15, 2009.

42. Trix, "The Bektashi Tekke"; Elkholy, *The Arab Moslems in the United States*; Walbridge, "The Shi'a Mosques and Their Congregations in Dearborn."

43. Trix 1994. "Bektashi Tekke."

44. Ismail, interview; Alawan, interview.

45. Trix, "The Bektashi Tekke."

46. In 1948, the International Institute also hosted meetings of the Pakistan Association of Detroit and the Young Pakistan Association, including holiday celebrations for Eid al-Adha and Eid al-Fitr, and a memorial service for Mohammad Ali Jinna. "Moslems Here End Month of Fasting," *Detroit News*, August 7, 1948; John Najduch, "Moslem Holy Day Observed: Pakistan Group Here Prays for Peace," *Detroit News*, October 14, 1948. Young Pakistan Association spokesperson, Mohammad Munir, also joined the board of the AMS and served in a leadership role there for at least a decade.

47. Ismail, interview. Imam Vehbi mentioned that Arab Muslims in Dearborn, and both Christian and Muslim Albanians contributed to the purchase of this church. Further evidence of cross-cultural mutuality in the city, Ismail traveled across the United States again several years later and raised money to help complete the second floor of the AMS.

48. Ismail, interview.

49. Ismail, interview; C. Karoub, interview.

50. Igram, interview; Alawan, interview.

51. Igram, interview, 1960.

52. C. Umhau Wolf, "Muslims in the Midwest," *The Muslim World* no. 50 (1960): 39–48.

53. Douglas Little, *American Orientalism*.

54. Igram, interview; Sidney Mashike, "Historical Perspective on the Federation of Islamic Associations in the U.S. and Canada," *Muslim Star*, July 1977; Elkholy, *The Arab Moslems in the United States*.

55. Hamood, interview.

56. Elkholy, *The Arab Moslems in the United States*, 47.

57. Elkholy, *The Arab Moslems in the United States*, 47.

58. Yvonne Yazbeck Haddad, "Arab Muslims and Islamic Institutions in America: Adaptation and Reform," in *Arabs in the New World: Studies on Arab-American Communities*, ed. Sameer Abraham and Nabeel Abraham (Detroit: Wayne State University, Center for Urban Studies, 1983), 209; Larry Poston, *Islamic Da'wah in the West: Muslim Missionary Activity and the Dynamics of Conversion to Islam* (New York: Oxford University Press, 1992); G. M. Ahmed, "Muslim American Organizations," in *The Muslims of America*, ed. Yvonne Haddad (New York: Oxford University Press, 1991).

59. C. Alawan, interview; Ismail, interview; E. Alawan, interview.

60. Wolf, "Muslims in the Midwest," observes that Pakistanis were not officially represented among the group's member organizations, but they nonetheless attended the conventions as individuals. He also points out that the NOI did not join because FIA leaders "do not believe [Elijah Muhammad] could subscribe to the objectives of the Federation," 17.

61. Wolf, "Muslims in the Midwest," 17.

62. Igram, interview; C. Alawan, interview. The group had forty members in 1977; Poston, *Islamic Da'wah in the West*, 198.

63. See Poston for a partial listing of these.

64. C. Alawan, interview; Ronald Amen, Dearborn Heights, MI, August 12, 2010; Makled, interview.

65. Chirri, *Inquiries About Islam*.

66. Makled, interview; C. Alawan, interview.

67. Hamood, interview; C. Alawan, interview; Makled, interview.

68. Makled, The Founding," 3. Makled and Chirri's other supporters do not today mention that he faced one last hurdle upon his return to Detroit. When Chirri applied for US citizenship in 1956, for the second time, he was accused of infidelity to his wife in Michigan City, of polygamy, and of not being a religious cleric. Citizenship and Immigration Services investigated these charges and concluded that Chirri had divorced his wife in Lebanon in 1950 before embarking on an American marriage, and that the allegations that he participated in a *muta'a* (temporary) marriage to a widow from Detroit were false. The charges were dismissed and Chirri was naturalized on July 23, 1957. "U. S. Citizenship and Immigration Services FOIA/PA Request Regarding Mohamad Jawad Chirri," April 5, 2011.

69. C. Alawan, interview.

70. "Snub by Miriani Incenses Moslems: Mayor Candidate Refuses to Greet Delegates at Party," *Detroit Free Press*, August 3, 1957.

71. "Moslems Answer Miriani Rebuff: Convention a Religious Party, Acting Mayor Is Informed," *Detroit News*, August 3, 1957.

72. C. Alawan, interview.

73. Alawan, interview.

74. Alawan, interview.

75. Joseph Caurdy, interview by Sally Howell, Saline, MI, 2005.

76. Elkholy, *The Arab Moslems in the United States*.

77. C. Alawan, interview; Hamood, interview; Aida Karoub Hamed, interview. A problem raised annually at the FIA convention was the lack of trained clerics to lead the growing number of mosques in the United States.

78. Elkholy, *The Arab Moslems in the United States*; Ismail, interview.

79. Brünner, *Islamic Ecumenism*.

80. Adnan Chirri, interview by Sally Howell, Dearborn, MI, 2005; Alawan, interview; Chirri, *Inquiries About Islam*, "About the Author."

81. Quoted in Brünner, *Islamic Ecumenism*, 289–290.

82. Brünner, *Islamic Ecumenism*, 289–290.

83. The Shaykh was given $10,000 by King Hussein of Jordan and $7,000 by officials in Sierra Leone. Because his trip was facilitated by the FIA, these donations were controversial. When Chirri returned to the United States, he was forced to give half of the money to the FIA. The $44,000 commonly attributed to Nasser was actually half of the total dollars Chirri raised on the trip from several sources. Makled, interview.

84. C. Alawan, interview.

85. Makled, interview.

86. Makled, interview; Alawan, interview.

87. Shaykh Chirri appreciated the role women played in the Michigan City mosque so he encouraged women's participation in planning, building, and operating the Islamic Center of Detroit. As Hajj Hamood described this, "the ladies of the Islamic Center

really are the backbone. They raise money and they work and they make the people go for the prayer and the services, and the children go to Sunday school." Hamood, interview.

88. Hamood, interview.

89. Hamood, interview.

90. Ashura literally means "tenth." It refers to the tenth day of the month of Muharram, on which Imam Husayn, his family, and his supporters were massacred on the fields of Karbala by the forces of the Caliph Muawiya. The holidays mentioned here are celebrated more commonly among the Shi'a, with the exception of Laylat al-Qadr (the night of the first revelation).

91. Hamood, interview.

92. Deeb, *An Enchanted Modern*; Norton, *Hezbollah: A Short History*.

93. Ismail, interview. C. Alawan, interview.

94. Trix, "The Bektashi Tekke."

95. Ismail, interview. A. Hamed, interview.

96. Ismail, interview.

97. Vehbi Ismail, "Islam and the Federation," *The Moslem Life* VI, no. 3 (1958): 22–33.

98. Ismail, "Islam and the Federation," 31.

99. Quoted in GhaneaBassiri, *History*, 234.

100. Ismail, "Islam and the Federation," 33.

101. "Albanian Mosque Celebrates Grand Opening," *Muslim Star*, December 1963; Ismail, interview.

102. Ismail, interview.

103. The mosque was designed by Frank Bimm, a German convert to Islam who donated his time and work to the mosque. Prior to the addition of a minaret and semi-dome, the mosque looked like a modern office complex or medical clinic and included no Islamic distinguishing feature other than its name.

104. The minaret and domed entrance, which cost $112,000, were funded by King Khalid of Saudi Arabia. This gift reflects the prominent role Ismail played in transnational Muslim networks of the period. Ismail, interview.

105. For a different perspective on the connections between the Albanian and other Muslim communities in Detroit, see Elkholy, *The Arab Moslems in the United States*; Trix, "The Bektashi Tekki"; Trix, *Albanians in Michigan*; Frances Trix, *Spiritual Discourse: Learning with an Islamic Master* (Philadelphia: University of Pennsylvania Press, 1993).

106. Ismail himself placed the number at one thousand when he arrived in Detroit in 1949, while Trix and other scholars estimate there were five thousand Albanians in the country as a whole by the late 1930s. Immigration and Naturalizaton Service figures for the years between 1941 and 1960 only count 144 Albanians entering the country. Far more than this number arrived in Detroit alone during these year, which suggests these statistics are unreliable. See Trix, "The Bektashi Tekke"; Dennis Nagi, *The Albanian-American Odyssey: A Pilot Study of the Albanian Community of Boston, Massachusetts* (Carbondale: Southern Illinois University Press, 1989).

107. Ismail, interview.

108. Edward E. Curtis IV, "Islamism and Its African American Muslim Critics: Black Muslims in the Era of the Arab Cold War," *American Quarterly* 593 (2007): 683–710.

109. Ismail, interview.

110. Ismail, interview.

111. Ghaleb Begg, interview, March 24, 2001; Ather Abdul Quader et al., interview, May 20, 2011.

112. Ismail, interview.

113. Ismail, interview.

Chapter 6

1. Mike Alcodray, interview by Sally Howell, Dearborn, MI, 2005; Abraham Family, interview; Jabara, interview; Abraham, "Arab Detroit's 'American' Mosque," 629.

2. Karoub was not aware of American-born Muslim leaders like himself within the Arab American community, but his title was overreaching in that it overlooked African American imams in Detroit and elsewhere. M. Karoub, interview; C.M. Karoub, interview; C. Karoub, interview by Sally Howell, Livonia, MI, 2005; A. Hamed, interview.

3. M. Karoub, interview, 1980.

4. Abraham Family, interview; C.M. Karoub, interview; Alice Karoub, interview; Tahira Hassanein Khalid, interview by Sally Howell, Detroit, MI, 2008; Saleem Khalid, interview by Sally Howell, Detroit, MI, 2008.

5. Elkholy, *The Arab Moslems in the United States*, 97.

6. Elkholy, *The Arab Moslems in the United States*, 97.

7. Imam Mike Karoub was fluent in both colloquial and classical Arabic.

8. Alcodray, interview.

9. Elkholy, *The Arab Moslems in the United States*, 137.

10. Alcodray, interview.

11. Alcodray was also highly critical of Imam Chirri for reinforcing divisions between Sunni and Shiʿa.

12. C. Alawan, interview; Fatme Boomrad, interview by Sally Howell, Dearborn, MI, 2005; Caurdy, interview; G. Ecie, interview.

13. Talal Asad, *The Idea of an Anthropology of Islam* (Washington, DC: Center for Contemporary Arab Studies, 1986), 15.

14. Hamed has since converted to Islam.

15. Similar materials were distributed by the FIA. Their use was novel at the time. Abraham Family, interview; Boomrad, interview; A. Hamed, interview.

16. Abraham Family, interview; Jabara, interview.

17. A. Hamed, interview, 2007. Christian women married to Muslim men had, in fact, long served as Arabic and Qurʾanic instructors in the Detroit area beginning in Highland Park in the 1920s. See Chapter 2.

18. Abraham, "Arab Detroit's 'American' Mosque," 287–288.

19. A. Hamed, interview, 2007; Abraham Family, interview.

20. When I asked Jabara to name the seven women, she did not want to leave anyone out. These names she provided (eleven in all) are in their colloquial forms: Umm Omer (Mrs. Okdie), Umm Alia Ecie, Marat Said Ali, Essie Abraham, Miriam Simon, Gladys Ecie, Ardella Jabara, Fatme Bomourad, Mrs. Caurdy, Hind Balooly, and Mrs. Boshammy. Jabara was treasurer of the American Moslem Women's Society for roughly thirty-five years. Jabara, interview.

21. For a description of this participation, see Elkholy, *The Arab Moslems in the United States*, 133.

22. Abraham Family, interview.

23. Boomrad, interview; Caurdy, interview; Jabara, interview. See also Ninian Smart, *Dimensions of the Sacred: An Anatomy of the World's Beliefs*, 1st edn (Berkeley: University of California Press, 1999), for an exploration of how such work contributes to the religious life of communities worldwide and is often undervalued.

24. In some Sunni traditions, it is believed that men receive an extra blessing for joining congregational prayers, but women do not. Participation of women in mosque activities, including prayer, is not common in most of the Muslim majority world, although this pattern is now undergoing rapid change in many Muslim societies.

25. Abraham, "Arab Detroit's 'American' Mosque"; A. Hamed, interview, 2005; Jabara, interview.

26. Warner, "Work in Progress."

27. George Sheba, "Caroling with the Keralites: The Negotiation of Gendered Space in an Indian Immigrant Church," in *Gatherings in Diaspora: Religious Communities and the New Immigration*, ed. R. Stephen Warner and Judith G. Wittner (Philadelphia: Temple University Press, 1998), 265–294; Warner, "Work in Progress"; Cheryl Gilkes, *Saints in Exile* (Oxford: Oxford University Press, 1995).

28. Ismail, interview; Abraham Family, interview.

29. A. Hamed, interview, 2007.

30. Hamed, interview, 2007.

31. Abraham, "Arab Detroit's 'American' Mosque," 288.

32. El Haje, interview; Alcodray, interview.

33. Abraham, "Arab Detroit's 'American' Mosque."

34. Hussein El Haje mentioned that Mike Karoub "turned the guy in to immigration because he took his job away from him." El Haje, interview.

35. A. Hamed, interview, 2007.

36. Karoub, interview, 1980.

37. Several dozen issues of the *Muslim Star* are now available for research in the Mohammad Jawad Chirri Collection at the Bentley Historical Library at the University of Michigan.

38. "The Universal Muslim Brotherhood of al-Islam in America," collection of Ihsan Bagby. The group incorporated with the State of Michigan on November 18, 1952. "Articles of Association, Hajj Sammsan Abdullah Mosque Islamic Mission," Michigan Department of Licensing and Regulatory Affairs.

39. Sammsan perhaps knew Mohammed Ezaldeen (see Chapter 3) from his travels.

40. Much of the money came from Sammsan himself, who suffered a debilitating work injury and received a lump-sum disability payment from his employer. Advised to have his leg amputated, he "prayed on it" instead. When his leg healed, Sammsan used his money to purchase the duplex. Hatima Sharieff, interview by Sally Howell, Clarkston, MI, 2008.

41. It was also known as the Hajj Sammsan Abdullah Mosque, then as the Universal Consolidation of Islam, HOLY MOSQUE, before it settled into its final name in 1966, "Articles of Incorporation, Universal Consolidation of Islam, Holy Mosque" (Michigan Corporation and Securities Commission, October 16, 1964), Michigan Department of Licensing and Regulatory Affairs; "Certificate of Amendment to the Articles of Incorporation, Hajj Sammsan Abdullah Mosque," Michigan Corporation and Securities Commission, August 17, 1966, Michigan Department of Licensing and Regulatory Affairs.

42. Haitama Sharieff mentioned the suspicion and hostility her husband's family expressed toward Islam. When she became a Muslim in 1948, her mother-in-law asked her, "Isn't it true that Muslims like to jump out windows and kill themselves?" Sharieff, interview.

43. Sharieff, interview; T. Khalid, interview.

44. Sugrue, *The Origins of Urban Crisis*, 155.

45. Dannin, *Black Pilgrimage to Islam*, 7.

46. Police interest in the NOI began in 1931 with Fard Muhammad's close association with the Japanese radical Satohata Takahashi, who established the Society for the Development of Our Own in Detroit in 1930. The combination of anti-American (and pro-Japanese) political rhetoric with criminal behavior such as murder and truancy (see Chapter 3) guaranteed government interest in the early NOI; Evanzz, *The Messenger*. Scrutiny of dissonant black religious groups by law enforcement can be traced to World War I, when the Universal Negro Improvement Association attracted similar interest, and even back to the era of slave codes that prohibited blacks from meeting without the explicit approval of whites. See Mark Ellis, *Race, War, and Surveillance: African Americans and the United States* (Bloomington: Indiana University Press, 2001); Johnson, "Religion Proper and Proper Religion: Arthur Fauset and the Study of African American Religions," in *The New Black Gods: Arthur Huff Fauset and the Study of African American Religions*, ed. Edward E. Curtis IV and Danielle Brune Sigler (Bloomington: Indiana University Press, 2009), 145–170.

47. Personal communication, Akil Fahd, August 2006.

48. "Articles of Incorporation, Universal Consolidation of Islam, Holy Mosque."

49. T. Khalid, interview. Hajj Hassanein used one room in the basement of the mosque to slaughter sheep according to Islamic tradition, which is one reason Hassanein was so well known to Detroit's Muslim communities. He provided this service long before the area's first "halal" meat distributor, Saad Brothers, opened in the Eastern Market in 1976. See http://saadmeats.com/about-us/, accessed on July 27, 2012.

50. GhaneaBassiri, *History*, 250.

51. GhaneaBassiri, *History*, 250.

52. For an overview of this organization and their mission work in the United States see Barbara Metcalf, "New Medinas: The Tablighi Jama'at in America and Europe," in *Making Muslim Space in North American and Europe*, ed. Barbara Metcalf (Berkeley: University of California Press, 1996), 110–130; Poston, *Islamic Da'wah in the West*.

53. Hamed, interview, 2005; T. Khalid, interview.

54. Selim Yusuf and Kifani Cece, interview by Sally Howell, July 7, 2011; T. Khalid, interview; Benjamin Hogue, interview by Sally Howell, July 10, 2012; Fahd, personal communication, August 25, 2010.

55. Curtis, *Black Muslim Religion in the Nation of Islam*; Dannin, *Black Pilgrimage to Islam;* Leonard, *Muslims in the United States*; Carolyn Moxley Rouse, *Engaged Surrender: African American Women and Islam*, 1st edn (Berkeley: University of California Press, 2004); Turner, *Islam in the African-American Experience*; C. Eric Lincoln and Lawrence H. Mamiya, *The Black Church in the African American Experience* (Durham, NC: Duke University Press, 1990).

56. Jackson, *Islam and the Blackamerican*, 44.

57. T. Khalid, interview. This section is based on my interview with Tahira Hassanein Khalid. Unless otherwise noted, all quotes and information are from this source.

58. Dan Georgakas, *Detroit, I Do Mind Dying*, 1st edn (Cambridge, MA: South End Press, 1998).

59. It is likely that this co-worker was Mustapha Bey, who was known to solicit new members outside the city's different factories. Bey was an active proselytizer even before Hajj Sammsan came to Detroit in the late 1940s (Sharieff, interview).

60. T. Khalid, interview.

61. Metcalf, "New Medinas."

62. T. Khalid, interview.

63. Sharieff, interview; T. Khalid, interview.

64. Giving *zakat*, customarily defined as alms, is among the primary obligations of all Muslims. Hajj Sammsan's request that his congregation give *zakat* directly to the mosque (and thus to the travelers and its other guests and residents) was an innovative application at the time.

65. The frequent reports the mosque's "Corresponding Secretaries," Hatima Sharieff and Tahira Hassanein placed in the *Muslim Star* in the 1960s and 1970s suggest that the position of imam changed hands frequently.

66. S. Khalid, interview; T. Khalid, interview.

67. Sharieff, interview.

68. Interestingly, the children of Asian families residing in the city did not join in educational programs at the mosque. T. Khalid, interview; Sharieff, interview.

69. T. Khalid, interview; Sharieff interview; Akil Fahd, personal communication, August 20, 2012.

70. S. Khalid, interview. Hassanein was also a familiar presence in the Bengali community in Detroit, where he is remembered as the city's first halal butcher, Maeh interview, 2005.

71. Ahmed, "Muslim Organizations in the United States."

72. Ibrahim Abu-lughod, *The Transformation of Palestine: Essays on the Origin and Development of the Arab-Israeli Conflict* (Evanston, IL: Northwestern University Press, 1971); Nabeel Abraham, "National and Local Politics: A Study of Political Conflict in the Yemeni Immigrant Community of Detroit, Michigan" (Detroit: University of Michigan, 1978); Michael Suleiman, "'I Come to Bury Ceasar, Not to Praise Him': An Assessment of the AAUG as an Example of an Activist Arab-American Organization," *Arab Studies Quarterly* 9, no. 3, 4 (2007): 75–95.

73. T. Khalid, interview; "Al-Mumineen Mosque Welcomes Convention of Muslim Students," *Muslim Star* 6, no. 42 (October 1966): 7.

74. Nasser was a Socialist, but he was also a staunch anti-Communist (although an ally and, after 1967, a client of the Soviet Union). The Iranian Revolution and the Iran-Iraq war that followed also created tensions within the MSA and between it and the FIA, as did conflicts in India, Pakistan, and elsewhere. Ahmed, "Muslim Organizations in the United States"; Steve Johnson, "The Muslims of Indianapolis," in *Muslim Communities in North America*, ed. Yvonne Yazbeck Haddad (New York: State University of New York Press, 1994); Poston, *Islamic Da'wah in the West*.

75. Said Qutb, *Amrika Allati Ra'ayt Fi Mizan Al-insaniyya* (Cairo: Al-Rasala, 1951).

76. S. Qutb, *Ma'alim Fi al-Tariq* (Dar al-Shuruq, 1964).

77. Johnson, "The Muslims of Indianapolis"; Poston, *Islamic Da'wah in the West*.

78. Poston, *Islamic Da'wah in the West*.

79. A. Hamed, interview, 2007; Alawan, interview; Ismail, interview.

80. Rabita al-ʿAlam al-Islami, the Muslim World League, supported mosque construction in the United States, funded the salaries of foreign imams working in the United States, distributed Qur'ans and other religious texts, and eventually opened an office in New York that had nonvoting member status at the United Nations. They also conducted research on Muslims and Islamic institutions in the United States. GhaneaBassiri, *History*, 262–263.

81. "Federation of Islamic Associations Second Annual Islamic Mid-Year Seminar," *Muslim Star* 18, no. 133 (October 1977): 11; "FIA-A Catalyst Organization," *Muslim Star* 18, no. 130 (July 1977): 5.

82. Curtis, "Islamism and Its African American Muslim Critics": 683–710; Evanzz, *The Messenger*; Marsh, *The Lost-Found Nation of Islam in America*; Herbert Berg, *Elijah Muhammad and Islam* (New York: New York University Press, 2009), 105–126.

83. T. Khalid, interview.

84. Maeh, interview. The FIA's Muslim Youth Association, which was also active in Detroit during this period, did not reach out to these women either.

85. Saleem Khalid "took shahada" [made a public confession of faith] under Karoub's watchful gaze at a ceremony at the AMS in Dearborn, and Karoub later performed the wedding of Saleem and Tahira. The couple named their son after Adil al-Aseer.

86. Jackson, *Islam and the Blackamerican*.

87. T. Khalid, interview.

88. Jackson, *Islam and the Blackamerican*, 4.

89. Daniel Stout and Judith Buddenbaum, *Religion and Mass Media: Audiences and Adaptations*, ed. Daniel A. Stout and Judith M. Buddenbaum (Thousand Oaks, CA: Sage Publications, 1996); Peter Berger, "The Global Picture," *Journal of Democracy* 15, no. 2 (2004): 76–80.

90. Abraham, "Anti-Arab Racism; Suad Joseph, "Against the Grain of the Nation," in *Arabs in America: Building a New Future*, ed. Michael Suleiman (Philadelphia: Temple University Press, 1999); McAlister, *Epic Encounters*.

91. "Al-Mumineen Mosque Vs. City of Detroit," *Muslim Star* 15, no. 108 (April 1975): 6.

92. "The Al-Mumineen Mosque, Inc., Will Remain Open," *Muslim Star* 18, no. 128 (May 1977):10. Saleem Khalid was not as enthusiastic about the FIA. He felt that the organization tried to monopolize all contacts between Detroit Muslims and major funders like the Muslim World League. S. Khalid, interview.

93. Abdo Alasry, interview by Sally Howell, Dearborn, MI, 2008.

94. S. Khalid, interview.

95. Terry, "Community and Political Activism"; Aswad, "The Southeast Dearborn Arab Community Struggles," 53–84.

96. A. Hamed, interview, 2005; Abraham Family, interview; Alcodray, interview; Abraham, "Arab Detroit's 'American' Mosque."

97. Alasry, interview; A. Hamed, interview, 2005; Nihad Hamed, interview, Farmington Hills, MI, 2005. See also Nabeel Abraham, "Arab Detroit's 'American' Mosque," for a detailed account of these events.

98. Alasry, interview.

99. Abraham Family, interview; G. Ecie, interview.

100. Alasry, interview.

101. Alasry, interview.

102. Alex Balooly, interview by Sally Howell, Dearborn Heights, MI, 2008. Mike Alcodray also mentioned this decision, which convinced him that Mike Karoub was unqualified to lead the AMS.

103. Abraham Family, interview; Alcodray, interview.

104. Alasry, interview; N. Hamed, interview; Abraham, "Arab Detroit's 'American' Mosque."

105. Ibid. For many conservative Muslims, music is associated with immorality and the sensual and is thus considered *haram* [forbidden]. The *musalee'een* could not pray or recite the Qur'an while loud music was blaring in the mosque. Even Muslims who do not object to secular music would have difficulty praying under these circumstances.

106. Alasry, interview; Abraham Family, interview; Abraham, "Arab Detroit's 'American' Mosque."

107. Abraham Family, interview.

108. Abraham, "Arab Detroit's 'American' Mosque," 292.

109. Alasry, interview.

110. Alasry, interview.

111. Alasry, interview.

112. Alasry, interview.

113. Carl M. Karoub, interview; A. Hamed, interview.

114. In 1980 they hired a young Lebanese imam, Mohammad Mardini, trained in Saudi Arabia, who fit in comfortably with their style of worship and revived among them the *mawlid*s and other services that Hussien Karoub had first encouraged them to practice.

115. Abraham Family, interview; El Haje, interview.

Chapter 7

1. Jackson, *Islam and the Blackamerican*, 71.

2. E. Alawan, interview.

3. Pew Forum, *Muslim Americans*.

4. American support for the Afghan insurgency after the Soviet invasion of Afghanistan in 1979 may have confused this narrative somewhat for Americans and conservative Muslims alike.

5. Darden et al., *Detroit*, 19.

6. GhaneaBassiri, *History*, 283.

7. Curtis, "Islamism and Its African American Muslim"; Poston, *Islamic Da'wah in the West*; Jackson, *Islam and the Blackamerican*; Manning Marable, *Malcolm X: A Life of Reinvention*, Reprint (New York: Penguin Books, 2011).

8. Hogue, interview.

9. Zain Abdullah, "Narrating Muslim Masculinities: The Fruit of Islam and the Quest for Black Redemption," *Spectrum* 1, no. 1 (August 2012): 142.

10. Curtis IV, *Black Muslim Religion in the Nation of Islam*, 136.

11. Hogue, interview. Frequently the NOI and other Muslims collaborated in prisons, sharing religious instructors, studying Arabic together, and exchanging literature. The different Muslim populations in Michigan's prisons also viewed one another

competitively, vying for recruits and privileges within the system. See Ahmed Rahman, "Story by Ahmed Abdul Rahman," *Transformations* (n.d.); Dannin, *Black Pilgrimage to Islam*.

12. Hogue, interview.

13. Hogue, interview.

14. Selim Yusuf and Kifani Cece, interview by Sally Howell, July 7, 2011.

15. Yusuf and Cece, interview.

16. Hogue, interview.

17. Hogue, interview.

18. Derrick Ali, interview by Robert Dannin, August 29, 1989.

19. Ali, interview; Saleem Rahmann and Gary al-Kassab, interview by Sally Howell and Andrew Shryock, Detroit, MI, 2005; Eric Sabree, interview by Robert Dannin, August 30, 1990.

20. Hogue, interview.

21. Hogue, interview; Curtis, *Black Muslim Religion in the Nation of Islam*; McCloud, *African American Islam*.

22. Rahmann and al-Kassab, interview.

23. Rahmann and al-Kassab, interview.

24. Wallace Deen Muhammad, "The Destruction of the Devil," *Muhammad Speaks*, July 11, 1975, quoted in GhaneaBassiri, *History*, 287. See also Berg, *Elijah Muhammad and Islam*, 123–125.

25. Hogue, interview.

26. Quoted in Berg, *Elijah Muhammad and Islam*, 125.

27. Hogue, interview; Rahmann and al-Kassab, interview; Jackson, *Islam and the Blackamerican*.

28. Elijah Muhammad provided several of his sons with an extensive religious education, made sure that they were taught Arabic, and allowed them to study in Saudi Arabia and elsewhere in the Muslim world as young adults. Often Muslim immigrants were hired to work in NOI temples to provide Arabic instruction, but they were advised to stick to the script of NOI teachings and not to discuss variances between this tradition and those based on the Qur'an and Sunna. See Curtis, *Black Muslim Religion in the Nation of Islam*; Turner, *Islam in the African-American Experience*; McCloud, *African American Islam*; Essien U. Essien-Udom, *Black Nationalism: A Search for an Identity in America* (Chicago: University of Chicago, 1962).

29. Sabree, interview.

30. GhaneaBassiri, *History*, 289.

31. Hogue, interview.

32. Almost every former NOI member I spoke with made explicit reference to this regret. Eventually, Imam Warith Deen Muhammad took limited action in response. In 1994 he published a book entitled *Islam's Climate for Business Success* (Sense Maker, 1994) and established a Collective Purchasing Conference to help Muslim small business owners procure and sell Islamic clothing, halal meat, books, cleaning supplies, music, and other products.

33. Shedrick El-Amin, interview, July 10, 2012.

34. Jackson, *Islam and the Blackamerican*, 72.

35. Mazen Alwan, interview by Sally Howell, West Bloomfield, MI, 2007.

36. Alwan, interview.

37. Quoted in Alwan, interview.

38. Alwan was initially convinced that his removal from Chicago to Detroit was insti-
gated by Ahmad Sakr, the US representative of the Muslim World League who feared that
Alwan (a Muslim Brotherhood supporter) was growing too close to Imam Warith Deen.
What looked initially like exile was in fact a significant promotion, and Sakr insisted that
Alwan quit his new job. This falling out resulted in Alwan's disassociation from the Muslim
World League. He received his salary directly from Masjid Wali Muhammad. Alwan, inter-
view. On the objectives of the Muslim World League and Muslim Brotherhood during this
period, see Curtis, "Islamism and Its African American Muslim Critics": 683–710; Poston,
Islamic Da'wah in the West.

39. Hogue, interview.

40. Alwan, interview.

41. Hajj Alwan also had much to say on this subject of divine revelation, accepting finally that Imam Warith Deen meant something more along the lines of "inspired"
than "revealed." The question of ongoing revelation is one that often sparks division
between Muslims, and Alwan would have found it an insurmountable division between
himself and Imam Warith Deen had they not been able to agree, ultimately, on the softer
English-language definition of the word.

42. Alwan, interview.

43. Isaac Weiner, *Religion Out Loud: Religious Sound, Public Space, and American
Pluralism* (New York: New York University Press, 2013).

44. Alwan, interview.

45. Dannin, *Black Pilgrimage to Islam*; McCloud, *African American Islam*; Rouse,
Engaged Surrender describe similar alternative Muslim communities.

46. The Dar ul-Islam Movement developed out of the State Street Mosque in
New York. See Dannin, *Black Pilgrimage to Islam*; Jackson, *Islam and the Blackamerican.*

47. Yusuf and Cece, interview.

48. Yusuf and Cece, interview.

49. Dannin, *Black Pilgrimage to Islam*, 58.

50. Yusuf and Cece, interview.

51. Yusuf and Cece, interview.

52. Yusuf and Cece, interview.

53. Akil Fahd, interview, August 19, 2012.

54. T. Khalid, interview.

55. Yusuf and Cece, interview; Alwan, interview.

56. Yusuf and Cece, interview.

57. Fahd, interview.

58. Fahd, interview.

59. Fahd, interview; Yusuf and Cece, interview.

60. R. M. Curtis, "Urban Muslims: The Formation of the Dar ul-Islam Movement,"
in *Muslim Communities in North America1*, ed. Yvonne Haddad and Jane Idleman Smith
(New York: State University of New York Press, 1994).

61. Yusuf and Cece, interview.

62. Yusuf and Cece, interview; Fahd, interview.

63. Fahd, interview.

64. Yusuf and Cece, interview.

65. T. Khalid, interview.

66. T. Khalid, interview.

67. Hogue, interview.

68. Sharieff, interview.

69. Rahmann and al-Kassab, interview; Catherine Ziyad, interview by Sally Howell, Detroit, MI, 2008. See also Curtis, *Black Muslim Religion in the Nation of Islam*; Rouse, *Engaged Surrender*.

70. Curtis, *Black Muslim Religion in the Nation of Islam*.

71. Fahd, interview; T. Khalid, interview.

72. T. Khalid, interview.

73. T. Khalid, interview; Fahd, interview; Yusuf and Cece, interview.

74. Rouse, *Engaged Surrender*, 18–21; Ziyad, interview.

75. Ziyad, interview; T. Khalid, interview.

76. See Introduction.

77. Anonymous. Several of my conversations about the introduction of polygamy at Masjid al-Mu'mineen were conducted off the record to protect the privacy of those involved.

78. Dannin, *Black Pilgrimage to Islam*.

79. Jackson, *Islam and the Blackamerican*, 166.

80. Anonymous.

81. Sharieff, interview.

82. Saleem Khalid, interview, considers this process to have begun well before Elijah Mohammed's death. It was set in motion when both Warith Deen Mohammed and Malcolm X made the hajj or studied Islam formally in Egypt and Saudi Arabia in the 1960s.

83. Sally Howell, "The Competition for Muslims: New Strategies for Urban Renewal in Detroit," in *Islamophobia/Islamophilia: Beyond the Politics of Enemy and Friend*, ed. Andrew Shryock (Bloomington: Indiana University Press, 2010). Today this mosque is known as Masjid Mu'ath bin Jabal and is one of the city's largest.

84. Tahira Khalid, personal communication, September 13, 2012.

85. McAlister, *Epic Encounters*, 194.

86. Abraham, "Anti-Arab Racism and Violence in the United States," 162.

87. Yen Le Espiritu, "Gender and Labor in Asian Immigrant Families," in *Gender and U.S. Immigration: Contemporary Trends*, ed. Pierrette Sondagneu-Sotelo (New York: Sage Publications, 1999), 279.

88. Abraham and Andrew Shryock, *Arab Detroit: From Margin to Mainstream*, ed. Abraham Nabeel and Andrew Shryock (Detroit: Great Lakes Books, 2000).

89. C. Alawan, interview, 2005; E. Alawan, 2012; Haragely, interview; Hamood, interview.

90. Quoted in Christopher Buck, *Religious Myths and Visions of America: How Minority Faiths Redefined America's World Role* (Santa Barbara, CA: ABC-CLIO, 2009), 136. Haragely, interview.

91. Haragely, interview.

92. Imam Mohammad Jawad Chirri, "A Press Release," Islamic Center of Detroit, n.d., Mohammad Jawad Chirri Collection, Box x, Bentley Historical Library, Ann Arbor, MI.

93. Hamood, interview.

94. Haragely, interview.

95. C. Alawan, interview, 2005; E. Alawan interview, 2012; Hamood interview, 2007.

96. Sally Howell, "Finding the Straight Path: A Conversation with Mohsen and Lila Amen About Faith, Life, and Family in Dearborn," in *Arab Detroit: From Margin to Mainstream*, ed. Andrew Shryock and Nabeel Abraham (Detroit: Wayne State University Press, 2000), 241–277.

97. Norton, *Hezbollah*. The Movement of Hope, a Lebanese political movement established in 1974 as the "Movement of the Dispossessed," becoming a powerful Shi'i militia during the Lebanese Civil War and later a major Lebanese political party

98. Norton, *Hezbollah*. The Party of God, a Lebanese militia and eventual political party that spun off from Amal (officially) in 1985 and represented the more militant South Lebanese.

99. Walbridge, *Without Forgetting the Imam*; E. Alawan, interview, 2012.

100. Many of the Sunni members did not embrace Khomeini as Chirri did, nor did they appreciate the Shi'i nationalism or the Iranian-influenced aesthetics and religious traditions now expressed at the ICA. C. Alawan, interview, 2005.

101. After the Israeli invasions of Lebanon in 1978 and 1982, Chirri switched much of his political energy toward opposing the occupation and lecturing in support of the new Islamist movements in South Lebanon and in opposition to communism.

102. Margaret Miller, "'Shah Was Worse Than Hitler,'" *Detroit News*, September 25, 1980.

103. Miller, "'Shah Was Worse Than Hitler.'"

104. Imam Mohammad Jawad Chirri, "Mailgram to Honorable Doctor Sadiq Ghutbzadah Foreign Minister of Iran," November 29, 1979, Mohammad Jawad Chirri Collection, Box 7, Bentley Historical Library.

105. Adnan Chirri, interview by Sally Howell, Dearborn, MI, 2005; C. Alawan, interview, 2005. Because the publically accessible pages of Imam Chirri's FBI file do not begin until 1981, I cannot document the impression his trip made on federal authorities. He was investigated repeatedly in the 1980s for suspected support of various pro-Iranian and anti-Israel "terrorist" groups, but cleared of inappropriate activities. In 1986 and 1987 Chirri was vetted as a possible negotiator for the Americans held hostage in Lebanon. The Bureau suspected that Hizbullah operatives would find him "too Americanized" to be trusted. Memorandum, FM Detroit to Director, re. LEBNAB, November 4, 1986; FM New York to Director, re. LEBNAB, November 13, 1986; New York Teletype to Director, February 12, 1987.

106. Chirri, "A Press Release."

107. Chirri, "A Press Release."

108. Shaykh Mohammad Jawad Chirri, "Soviet Union No Match for Islam!," 2011, video of lecture available at http://www.youtube.com/watch?v=CXLlycMtwmw&featur e=youtube_gdata_player. The video also reveals that the occasion of this lecture was a Muharram gathering, and the decorations of the hall clearly depict new Iranian and Iraqi influences.

109. Albanians were classed as Europeans and thus not subjected to changes in immigration law that affected other Muslims. In fact, as political dissidents, they had privileged access to green cards outside the quota system. See Trix, *Albanians in Michigan*.

110. Ismail, interview.

111. Ismail, interview.

112. Curtis, *Muslims in America*.

113. Elkholy, *The Arab Moslems in the United States*.

114. Haragely, interview.

115. Walbridge, *Without Forgetting the Imam*, 112.

Chapter 8

1. Mishawaka Indiana was indeed home to a small mosque in this period, but Kahf (personal communication, January 11, 2014) sees this mosque more as a conflation of the mosques her family knew in Ross, North Dakota, Cedar Rapids, Iowa, and Michigan City, Indiana. Each of these has close historical ties to Detroit's first imams and mosques.

2. Muqtedar Khan, *American Muslims: Bridging Faith and Freedom* (Beltsville, MD: Amana, 2002); Zaid Shakir, *Scattered Pictures: Reflections of An American Muslim* (Hayward, CA: Zaytuna Institute, 2005); Mucahit Bilici, *Finding Mecca in America: How Islam Is Becoming an American Religion* (Chicago: University of Chicago Press, 2012); McCloud, *Transnational Muslims*.

3. Sally Howell, "Muslims as Moving Targets: External Scrutiny and Internal Critique in Detroit's Mosque," in *Arab Detroit 9/11: Life in the Terror Decade* (Detroit: Wayne State University Press, 2011), 151–185.

4. Aminah Beverly McCloud, "African American Muslim Women," in *The Muslims of America*, ed. Yvonne Haddad (London: Oxford University Press, 1991), 178.

5. Curtis, *Islam in Black America*; Sherman A. Jackson, *Islam and the Blackamerican*; Manning Marable, *Race, Reform, and Rebellion: The Second Reconstruction and Beyond in Black America, 1945–2006*, 3rd edn (Jackson: University Press of Mississippi, 2007).

6. GhaneaBassiri, *History*, 165.

7. Lincoln and Mamiya, *The Black Church*, 234.

8. Hayden White, *The Content of the Form: Narrative Discourse and Historical Representation* (Baltimore: Johns Hopkins University Press, 2009), 14.

9. Bilici, *Finding Mecca in America*, 95.

10. Bilici, *Finding Mecca in America*, 110.

11. N. Hamed, interview; E. Alawan, interview; "This Is What the Court Observer Had to Say About Our Elections," *Muslim Star*, February 1981.

12. Quoted in Andrew Shryock, "Finding Islam in Detroit: The Multiple Histories, Identities, and Locations of a City and Its Muslims" (Stanford, CA: Stanford University, 2007).

13. This line of argument, applied more to Arab than to Muslim Americans, is developed by Nabeel Abraham, Andrew Shryock, and myself in "The New Order", 381–393.

14. Pew Forum, *Muslim Americans: No Signs of Growth in Alienation or Support for Extremism*; Bilici, *Finding Mecca in America*; McCloud, *Transnational Muslims*.

15. Howell, "The Competition for Muslims, 260.

16. Andrew Shryock, "Attack of the Islamophobes: Religious War (and Peace) in Arab/Muslim Detroit," in *Islamophobia in America*, ed. Carl Enrst (New York: Palgrave MacMillan, 2013), 145–174; William Youmans, "Domestic Foreign Policy: Arab Detroit as an Important Place in the War on Terror," in *Arab Detroit 9/11: Life in the Terror*

Decade, ed. Nabeel Abraham, Sally Howell, and Andrew Shryock (Detroit, MI: Wayne State University Press, 2011); Howell, "Muslims as Moving Targets."

17. Much of it, too, will eventually come to light. Several people I spoke with during the course of this research mentioned archives they have in their possession, or are aware of, that pertain to the history of the city's Albanian, Bengali, Lebanese Shi'a, Lebanese Sunni, and African American congregations. Some of these collections are related to the lives and work of the city's first imams. As these papers are donated to local archives or shared privately with scholars, a richer and larger history may be possible.

BIBLIOGRAPHY

Newspaper and Archival Sources

"400 Syrians Protest Visit of Emir Here." *Detroit Free Press*, January 18, 1927.

Abu Khalil, Najla. "The American Women's Muslim Society Celebrates Its Second Anniversary Since Its Establishment." *Nahdat al-Arab*, February 11, 1949.

"A Dream Fades: Sale of Mosque Finis to Mohammedan Vision." *Detroit Free Press*, July 9, 1927.

Adler, Philip. "Allah Hears Supplication for Doles From Detroit." *Detroit News*, December 30, 1932.

"Albanian Mosque Celebrates Grand Opening." *Muslim Star*, December 1963.

al-Habhab, Kamel Mansour. "Slow Down You Exagerattors (in Arabic)." *Al-Bayan*, June 9, 1921.

Ali, Duse Mohammed. "Leaves from an Active Life." *The Comet* (n.d.).

"'Allah Ho Akbar!' Is Chant in Detroit When City's Moslems Gather for Service." *Detroit News*, April 25, 1926.

"Al-Mumineen Mosque vs. City of Detroit," *Muslim Star* 15, no. 108 (April 1975): 6.

"Al-Mumineen Mosque Welcomes Convention of Muslim Students." *Muslim Star* 6, no. 42 (October 1966): 7.

A Muslim. "My Opinion: On the Esteemed Shaykh Khalil Bazzi Who Is the Prefered Religios Leader of the Immigrants." *Nahdat al-Arab*, December 13, 1949.

Aossey, Bill Yahya. *The Role of the Islamic Center and Its Necessity in the Development of Muslim Communities in North America*. Naff Arab American Collection (NAAC), National Museum of American History, 1978.

"Arabian Colony." *Detroit Journal*, July 21, 1897.

"Arabian Colony Holds Mortgage-Burning Rites." *Detroit News*, November 13, 1939.

"Articles of Association. America-Asia Society." Michigan Department of Energy, Labor, and Economic Growth, March 12, 1926.

"Articles of Association of the Arabian-American Society." State of Michigan, County of Wayne, March 23, 1916. Collection of Kamel Bazzy.

"Articles of Association, Hajj Sammsan Abdullah Mosque (Islamic Mission)." Michigan Corporation and Securities Commission, November 18, 1952. Michigan Department of Liscensing and Regulatory Affairs.

"Articles of Association (Ecclesiastical Corporation)." Universal Islamic Society. State of Michigan, Department of Commerce, October 12, 1925.

"Articles of Incorporation of American Moselm Society," 1942. Essie Abraham Collection, Box 1, American Moslem Society Articles of Incorporation Folder. Bentley Historical Library.

"Articles of Incorporation, Universal Consolidation of Islam, Holy Mosque." Michigan Corporation and Securities Commission, October 16, 1964. Michigan Department of Liscensing and Regulatory Affairs.

"Brotherhood of Nations Picnic a Success." *Highland Parker*, September 2, 1926.

Cameron, Charles. "A Street of All Nations." *Detroit Saturday Night*, June 12, 1926.

———. "Detroit Druses Watch Revolt." *Detroit Saturday Night*, May 22, 1926.

"Certificate of Amendment to the Articles of Incorpporation, Hajj Sammsan Abdullah Mosque." Michigan Corporation and Securities Commission, August 17, 1966. Michigan Department of Liscensing and Regulatory Affairs.

Chirri, Mohammad Jawad. "A Press Release." Islamic Center of Detroit, unknown. Mohammad Jawad Chirri Collection, Box x. Bentley Historical Library.

———. "Mailgram to Honorable Doctor Sadiq Ghutbzadah Foreign Minister of Iran." November 29, 1979. Mohammad Jawad Chirri Collection, Box x. Bentley Historical Library.

———. "New School to Open at Islamic Mosque in Dearborn." *Nahdat al-Arab*, June 24, 1949.

———. "Soviet Union No Match for Islam!," http://www.youtube.com/watch?v=CXLlyc Mtwmw&feature=youtube_gdata_player.2011.

Devlin, John. "Mosque: Its Builders." *Detroit News*, January 21, 1921.

"Federation of Islamic Associations Second Annual Islamic Mid-Year Seminar." *Muslim Star* 18, no. 133 (October 1977): 11.

Ferris, Ryan, and Andrew Shryock, trans. "The Future of the New Generation." *Nahdat al-Arab*, May 5, 1949.

"FIA-A Catalyst Organization." *Muslim Star* 18, no. 130 (July 1977): 5.

"Gold the Root; Death the Bud." *Detroit News*, July 24, 1924.

Hassen, Mohammed. "General Invitation to My Muslim Brothers in Detroit and Windsor, Canada." Translated by Ryan Ferris. *Nahdat al-Arab*, October 5, 1948.

"Highland Park Mosque Still Houses 'Faithful.'" *Detroit News*, August 20, 1922.

"Hussein Abbas Murdered in His Sleep." *The Highland Parker*, March 14, 1924.

"Is Head of Detroit Moslem Association." *Detroit Free Press*, September 28, 1916.

"Karoub Freed in Killing Case." *Detroit News*, December 24, 1924.

Karoub, Michael. "Golden Jubilee Celebration Marks Fifty Years of Service to Ara-Americans an Islam." *Golden Jubilee Celebration of the Reverend Imam Hussien Adeeb Karoub* (1962): 7–8.

Karoub, Mohammed. "3,000 Riyal will be Paid to Anyone who can Prove that there is no Mosque in Detroit." *Al-Bayan*, June 9, 1921.

———. "al-ihtifal al-kabir bi-'id al-fitr al-mubarik." *Al-Bayan*, June 14, 1921.

Majid, Satti. "al-Islam fi-Amrika." *Al-Balagh*, 1935.

Makled, Hussein. "The Founding of the Islamic Center of America." Translated by Saja Alasry. Hussein Makled Collection. Bentley Historical Library. 1990.

Mashike, Sidney. "Historical Perspective on the Federation of Islamic Associations in the U.S. and Canada." *Muslim Star* 18, no. 130, July 1977.

"Michigan Articles of Association (Eccliastical Corporation) of Moslem Mosque of Highland Park." Michigan Corporation and Securities Commission, April 4, 1958.

"Michigan Articles of Incorporation of Progressive Arabian Hashmie Society." Michigan Corporation and Securities Commission, July 20, 1936.

Miller, Margaret. " 'Shah Was Worse Than Hitler.' " *Detroit News*, September 25, 1980.

"Minutes of Special Meeting of Minarat al-Hoda." February 20, 1939. Essie Abraham Collection, Box 1, Islamic Organizations Folder. Bentley Historical Library.

"Mohammedans Get Their Own Soup Kitchen." *Detroit Free Press*, January 12, 1933.

"Mohammedans to Celebrate Feast." *Detroit Free Press*, September 28, 1916.

"Moslems Answer Miriani Rebuff: Convention a Religious Party, Acting Mayor Is Informed." *Detroit News*, August 3, 1957.

"Moslems Avow Loyalty to U.S.: Laud Religious Freedom at Oriental Dinner to Highland Park Notables." *Detroit Free Press*, February 12, 1921.

"Moslems Celebrate Feast of Id-Ul-Fitr." *Detroit Free Press*, June 9, 1921.

"Moslems Dedicate Temple to Fulfill a 20-Year Dream: Detroit Syrian Colony Conducts Ceremonies; Building to Be Church and School." *Detroit News*, May 31, 1937.

"Moslems Here Build Mosque." *Detroit Free Press*, January 21, 1921.

"Moslems Here End Month of Fasting." *Detroit News*, August 7, 1948.

"Moslems in Detroit Mark Turk's Victory." *Detroit Free Press*, September 9, 1922.

"Moslems to Open Dearborn Temple: Will Dedicate First One in Detroit Area Sunday." *Detroit Free Press*, May 29, 1937.

"Mosque, Empty, Will Be Razed: Highland Park Will Lose Picturesque Shrine to Islam's Faith Soon." *Detroit News*, August 9, 1922.

"Mosque Sheik Quits, Works as Watchman." *Detroit Free Press*, November 11, 1922.

"Mountain in Mohammed's Path." *Detroit News*, December 9, 1924.

Muhammad, Wallace Deen. "The Destruction of the Devil." *Muhammad Speaks*, July 11, 1975.

Muller, Carl. "Faith of Islam Withers in Detroit Atmosphere." *Detroit Free Press*, April 20, 1924.

Najduch, John. "Moslem Holy Day Observed: Pakistan Group Here Prays for Peace." *Detroit News*, October 14, 1948.

"Opening Ceremony of the Islamic Mosque in Dearborn, Michigan." *Nahdat al-Arab*, June 6, 1949.

"Religion Bars 400 from Soup Lines: Mohammadans Can't Eat Relief Food." *Detroit Free Press*, December 12, 1932.

Richards, William. "Moslem Mufti Seeks to Make Detroit Islam." *Detroit Free Press*, February 13, 1921.

Sadiq, Mufti Mohammed. "Arabian Hospitality." *Moslem Sunrise* 1, July 21, 1921.

———. "Brief Report of the Work in America." *Moslem Sunrise* 2, (October 1921): 112.

———. "Brief Report of the Work in America." *Moslem Sunrise*, II, 1, 1923.

———. "My Advice to the Muhammadans in America." *Moslem Sunrise* 2, October 1921.

———. "One Year's Moslem Missionary Work in America." *Moslem Sunrise* 1 (July 1921): 12–13.

———. "Thee Only Solution of Color Prejudice." *Moslem Sunrise* 2 (October 1921): 41–42.

———. "Untitled." *Moslem Sunrise* 2, October 1921.

"Seeds of Islam, Find no Root." *Detroit Free Press*, September 24, 1922.

Shahid, Dhost Muhammad. "Mufti Muhammad Sadiq: Founder of Ahmadiyya Muslim Mission in the United States of America." *Muslim Sunrise*, July 31, 2013.

Smith, Faye Elizabeth. "Bits of the Old World in Detroit—Armenia." *Detroit Saturday Night*, March 18, 1922.

———. "Bits of the Old World in Detroit—China." *Detroit Saturday Night*, March 4, 1922.

———. "Bits of the Old World in Detroit: The Turks." *Detroit Saturday Night*, April 22, 1922.

"Snub by Miriani Incenses Moslems: Mayor Candidate Refuses to Greet Delegates at Party." *Detroit Free Press*, August 3, 1957.

"Syrian Emir Heads to Detroit." *New York Times*, March 28, 1924.

"The Al-Mumineen Mosque, Inc., Will Remain Open." *Muslim Star* 18, no. 128 (May 1977).

"The Big Party." *Al-Daleel* 3, no. 9 (July 1945).

"Theater Notices." *Detroit Free Press*, October 29, 1926.

"This Is What the Court Observer Had to Say About Our Elections." *Muslim Star*, 19: 158, February 1981.

"Turk Confesses Murder for Love, Death of Hussein Abbas, Wealthy Syrian Grocer, Attributed to Wife's Plotting." *The Highland Parker*, March 26, 1924.

"United Syrian Citizen's Society Celebrates 'Independence Day.'" *Highland Parker*, July 8, 1926.

"Urges Turk Negro Colony." *New York Times*, June 30, 1930.

"U. S. Citizenship and Immigration Services FOIA/PA Request Regarding Mohamad Jawad Chirri," April 5, 2011.

"Woodsmen of the World to Get Mohammedan Mosque." *The Highland Parker*, July 7, 1927.

Interviews

Abraham Family. Interview by Sally Howell. Dearborn Heights, 2006.

Abraham, Robert (Sy). Interview by Sally Howell. Dearborn Heights, MI, 2006.

Alasry, Abdo. Interview by Sally Howell. Dearborn, MI, 2008.

Alawan, Charles Khalil (Hajj Chuck). Interview by Sally Howell. Dearborn, MI, 2005.

———. Interview by Sally Howell. Farmington, MI, August 9, 2010.

Alawan, Eide. Interview by Sally Howell. Dearborn, MI, 2005.

———. Interview by Sally Howell. Dearborn, MI, 2012.

Alcodray, Mike. Interview by Sally Howell. Dearborn, MI, 2005.

Ali, Derrick. Interview by Robert Dannin. August 29, 1989.

Alwan, Mazen. Interview by Sally Howell. West Bloomfield, MI, 2007.

Amen, Ronald Interview by Sally Howell. Dearborn Heights, MI, August 12, 2010.

Atwel, Helen Okdie. Interview by Sally Howell. Dearborn, MI, December 2, 2000.

Balooly, Alex. Interview by Sally Howell. Dearborn Heights, MI, 2008.

Bazzi, Najah. Interview by Sally Howell. Plymouth, 2006.

Bazzy, Shaykh Khalil. Interview by Alixa Naff. Detroit, MI, 1962. Series 4/C. NAAC. National Museum of American History.

Begg, Ghaleb. Interview by Sally Howell. Bloomfield Hills, MI, 2001.

Berry, Michael. Interview by Sally Howell. Dearborn, MI, 2007.

Bomourad, Fatme. Interview by Sally Howell. Dearborn, MI, 2005.

Caurdy, Joseph. Interview by Sally Howell. Saline, MI, 2005.

Chirri, Adnan. Interview by Sally Howell. Dearborn, MI, 2005.

Clarke, Hansen. Interview by Sally Howell. Lansing, MI, 2006.

Ecie, Alex. Interview by Alixa Naff. Detroit, MI, 1962. Series 4/C. NAAC. National Museum of American History.

Ecie, Gladys. Interview by Sally Howell. Dearborn, MI, 2005.

El-Amin, Shedrick. Interview by Sally Howell. Dearborn, MI, July 10, 2012.

El Haje, Fatima. Interview by Sally Howell. Dearborn, MI, 2005.

El Haje, Hussein. Interview by Sally Howell. Dearborn, MI, 2005.

Fahd, Akil. Phone interview by Sally Howell. August 19, 2012.

Gutman, Halimah Akhtar. Interview by Sally Howell. Long Island, New York, May 26, 2010.

Hai, Mahmood. Interview by Sally Howell. Canton, MI, May 24, 2012.

Hamed, Aida Karoub. Interview by Sally Howell. Farmington Hills, MI, 2005.

———. Interview by Sally Howell. Farmington Hills, MI, 2007.

Hamed, Nihad. Interview by Sally Howell. Farmington Hills, MI, 2005.

Haragely, Julia. Interview by Sally Howell. Dearborn, MI, 2007.

Hamood, Hussein. Interview by Sally Howell. Madison Heights, MI, 2007.

Hassen, Marilynn. Interview by Sally Howell. Dearborn Heights, MI, 2006.

Hogue, Benjamin. Interview by Sally Howell. July 10, 2012.

Igram, Abdullah. Interview by Alixa Naff. Cedar Rapids, IA, 1980. Series 4/C. NAAC. National Museum of American History.

Ismail, Vehbi. Interview by Sally Howell. Harper Woods, MI, 2005.

Jabara, Ardella and Julia. Interview by Sally Howell. Romulus, MI, 2007.

Karoub, Mohammed. Interview by Alixa Naff. Detroit, MI, 1980. Series 4/C. NAAC. National Museum of American History.

Karoub, Alice. Interview by Sally Howell. Northville, MI, 2005.

Karoub, Carl H. Interview by Sally Howell. Livonia, MI, 2005.

Karoub, Carl M. Interview by Sally Howell. Farmington Hills, MI, 2005.

Karoub, Jeff. Interview by Sally Howell. Livonia, MI, 2005.

Khalid, Saleem. Interview by Sally Howell. Detroit, MI, 2008.

Khalid, Tahira Hassanein. Interview by Sally Howell. Detroit, MI, 2008.

Maeh, Azira. Interviw by Sally Howell. Detroit, 2005.

Makled, Hussein. Interview by Sally Howell. Dearborn Heights, MI, 2005.

Mardini, Mohammad. Interview by Sally Howell. n.d.

Quader, Ather Abdul, Ghaus Malik, Sharif Gindy, and Shah Ali Akbar. Interview by Sally Howell and Akil Fahd. Rochester Hills, MI, May 20, 2011.

Rahmann, Saleem, and Gary al-Kassab. Interview by Sally Howell and Andrew Shryock. Detroit, MI, 2005.

Restum, William. Interview by Sally Howell. August 17, 2014.

Sabree, Eric. Interview by Robert Dannin. Detroit, MI, August 30, 1990.

Sharieff, Hatima. Interview by Sally Howell. Clarkston, MI, 2008.

Yusuf, Selim, and Kifani Cece. Interview by Sally Howell. Dearborn, MI, July 7, 2011.

Ziyad, Catherine. Interview by Sally Howell. Detroit, MI, 2008.

Select Bibliography

Abdullah, Zain. "Narrating Muslim Masculinities: The Fruit of Islam and the Quest for Black Redemption." *Spectrum* 1, no. 1 (August 2012): 141–178.

Abiva, Hussein. "Baba Rexheb: A Sufi Saint for America." In *First Symposium on Bektashi-Alevism at Suleyman Demirel University*, 2005.

Abraham, Nabeel. "Anti-Arab Racism and Violence in the United States." In *The Development of Arab-American Identity*. Ann Arbor: University of Michigan Press, 1994.

———. "Arab Detroit's 'American' Mosque." In *Arab Detroit: From Margin to Mainstream*. Edited by Nabeel Abraham and Andrew Shryock, 629. Detroit: Wayne State University Press, 2000.

———. "National and Local Politics: A Study of Political Conflict in the Yemeni Immigrant Community of Detroit, Michigan." University of Michigan, 1978.

Abraham, Nabeel, and Andrew Shryock. *Arab Detroit: From Margin to Mainstream*. Edited by Abraham Nabeel and Andrew Shryock. Detroit: Great Lakes Books, 2000.

Abraham, Nabeel, Sally Howell, and Andrew Shryock. *Arab Detroit 9/11: Life in the Terror Decade*. Detroit: Wayne State University Press, 2011.

Abu-Lughod, Lila. *Remaking Women: Feminism and Modernity in the Middle East*. Berkeley: University of California Press, 1998.

Abusharaf, Rogia. *Wanderings: Sudanese Migrants and Exiles in North America*. Ithaca, NY: Cornell University Press, 2002.

Abu-Lughod, Ibrahim. *The Transformation of Palestine: Essays on the Origin and Development of the Arab-Israeli Conflict*. Evanston, IL: Northwestern University Press, 1921.

Ahmed, G. M. "Muslim American Organizations." In *The Muslims of America*. Edited by Yvonne Haddad. New York: Oxford University Press, 1991.

Aidi, Hisham. "Let Us Be Moors: Islam, Race and 'Connected Histories.'" *Middle East Report* 7, no. 229 (2003): 42–53.

Alawan, Raad. *Oldest Mosque in Michigan Celebrates 70 Years*. Dearborn, MI, 2009.

Alford, Terry. *Prince Among Slaves: The True Story of an African Prince Sold Into Slavery in the American South*. New York: Oxford University Press, 1986.

Ali, Duse Mohamed. *In the Land of the Pharaohs*. New York: Appleton and Co., 1911.

Allen, Christopher. *Islamophobia*. London: Ashgate, 2011.

Alsultany, Evelyn. "The Changing Profile of Race in the United States: Media Representations and Racialization of Arab- and Muslim-Americans Post-9/11." Ph.D. dissertation: Stanford University, 2005.

Asad, Talal. *The Idea of an Anthropology of Islam*. Washington, DC: Center for Contemporary Arab Studies, 1986.

Aswad, Barbara. "The Southeast Dearborn Arab Community Struggles for Survival Against Urban 'Renewal.'" In *Arabic-Speaking Communities in American Cities*. Edited by Barbara C Aswad, 53–84. New York: Center for Migration Studies, 1974.

Bagby, Ihsan. *A Portrait of Detroit Mosques: Muslim Views on Policy, Politics and Religion*. Clinton Township: Institute for Social Policy and Understanding, 2004.

Bakalian, Anny, and Medhi Bozorgmehr. *Backlash 9/11: Middle Eastern and Muslim Americans Respond*. Berkeley: University of California Press, 2009.

Baker, Wayne, Sally Howell, Amaney Jamal, Ann Chih Lin, Andrew Shryock, Ronald Stockton, and Mark Tessler. *Detroit Arab American Study DAAS, 2003*. Ann Arbor, MI: Institute for Social Research, 2006.

Bald, Vivek. *Bengali Harlem: And the Lost Histories of South Asian Americans*. Boston: Harvard University Press, 2013.

——. "Overlapping Diasporas, Multiracial Lives: South Asian Muslims in U.S. Communities of Color, 1880–1950." *Souls* 8, no. 4 (December 2006): 3–18.

Bali, Rifat. "From Anatolia to the New World." In *Turkish Migration to the United States*. Edited by A. Deniz Balgamis and Kemal Karpat. Madison: University of Wisconsin Press, 2008.

Barrett, James. "Americanization from the Bottom Up: Immigration and the Remaking of the Working Class in the United States, 1880–1930." *Journal of American History* 79, no. 3 (1992): 996–1020.

Barrow, Heather. "'The American Disease of Growth': Henry Ford and the Metropolitanization of Detroit, 1920–1940." In *Manufacturing Suburbs: Building Work and Home on the Manufacturing Fringe*. Edited by Robert Lewis. Philadelphia: Temple University Press, 2004.

Bazzy, Kamal, and Yehia Shamy. *Shaykh Khalil Bazzy: 75 Years in Religious and Immigration Services*. Beirut, Lebanon: Dar Al-Mahajaj, 2012.

Berg, Herbert. *Elijah Muhammad and Islam*. New York: New York University Press, 2009.

Berger, Peter. "The Global Picture." *Journal of Democracy* 15, no. 2 (2004): 76–80.

——. *The Sacred Canopy: Elements of a Sociological Theory of Religion*. New York: Doubleday, 1969.

Beynon, Erdmann Doane. "The Voodoo Cult Among Negro Migrants in Detroit." *American Journal of Sociology* 43, no. 6 (May 1938): 894–907.

Bilge, Barbara. "Voluntary Associations in the Old Turkish Community of Metropolitan Detroit." In *Muslim Communities in North America*. New York: State University of New York Press, 1994.

Bilici, Mucahit. "Being Targeted, Being Recognized: The Impact of 9/11 on Arab and Muslim Americans." *Contemporary Sociology: A Journal of Reviews* 40, no. 2 (March 2011): 133–137.

——. *Finding Mecca in America: How Islam is Becoming an American Religion*. Chicago: University of Chicago Press, 2012.

Bodnar, John. *The Transplanted: A History of Immigrants in Urban America*. Bloomington: Indiana University Press, 1985.

Boosahda, Elizabeth. *Arab-American Faces and Voices: The Origins of an Immigrant Community*. Austin: University of Texas Press, 2003.

Bowen, Patrick D. "Satti Majid: A Sudanese Founder of American Islam." *Journal of Africana Religion* 1, no. 2 (2013): 194–209.

Boyle, Kevin. *Arc of Justice: A Saga of Race, Civil Rights, and Murder in the Jazz Age*. New York: Henry Holt, 2004.

Brünner, Rainer. *Islamic Ecumenism in the 20th Century: The Azhar and Shiism Between Rapprochement And Restraint*. Leiden: Brill, 2004.

Bryan, Ford R. *Henry's Lieutenants*. Detroit: Wayne State University Press, 1993.

Buck, Christopher. *Religious Myths and Visions of America: How Minority Faiths Redefined America's World Role*. Santa Barbara, CA: ABC-CLIO, 2009.

Building Islam in Detroit. "Featured Mosques," n.d. http://biid.lsa.umich.edu/.

Bukhari, Zahid, Sulayman Nyang, Mumtaz Ahmad, and John Esposito, eds. *Muslims' Place in the American Public Square: Hopes, Fears, and Aspirations*. New York: AltaMira Press, 2004.

Cainkar, Louise A. *Homeland Insecurity: The Arab American and Muslim American Experience After 9/11*. New York: Russell Sage Foundation Publications, 2011.

Carby, Hazel V. *Race Men*. Cambridge, MA: Harvard University Press, 2000.

Cesari, Jocelyne, ed. *Encyclopedia of Islam in the United States [2 Volumes]*. Westport, CT: Greenwood, 2007.

———. *When Islam and Democracy Meet: Muslims in Europe and in the United States*. New York: Palgrave Macmillan, 2006.

Chirri, Mohammad Jawad. *Inquiries About Islam*. Detroit: Islamic Center of America, 1962.

———. *The Shiites Under Attack*. Detroit: Islamic Center of America, 1986.

Chopra, Karen McBeth. "A Forgotten Minority: Historical and Current Discrimination Against Asians from the Indian Subcontinent." *Detroit College of Law Review* (Winter 1995): 1269.

Clegg, Claude Andrew. *An Original Man: The Life and Times of Elijah Muhammad*. New York: St. Martin's Griffin, 1998.

Curtis, Edward E. IV. *Black Muslim Religion in the Nation of Islam, 1960–1975*. Chapel Hill: University of North Carolina Press, 2006.

———, ed. *The Columbia Sourcebook of Muslims in the United States*. New York: Columbia University Press, 2009.

———. *Encyclopedia of Muslim-American History, 2-Volume Set*. 1st ed. New York: Facts on File, Inc., 2010.

———. *Islam in Black America*. Albany: State University of New York Press, 2002.

———. "Islamism and Its African American Muslim Critics: Black Muslims in the Era of the Arab Cold War." *American Quarterly* 593 (2007): 683–710.

———. *Muslims in America: A Short History*. New York: Oxford University Press, 2009.

Curtis, R. M. "Urban Muslims: The Formation of the Dar ul-Islam Movement." In *Muslim Communities in North America*. Edited by Yvonne Haddad and Jane Idleman Smith. New York: State University of New York Press, 1994.

Dannin, Robert. *Black Pilgrimage to Islam*. New York: Oxford University Press, 2002.

Darden, Joe, Richard Hill, June Thomas, and Richard Thomas. *Detroit: Race and Uneven Development*. Philadelphia: Temple University Press, 1987.

Davidson, Lawrence. "Debating Palestine: Arab-American Challenges to Zionism 1917–1932." In *Arabs in America: Building a New Future*. Edited by Michael Suleiman. Philadelphia: Temple University Press, 1999.

Davidson, Roderic. "The Image of Turkey in the West: In Historical Perspective." *The Turkish Studies Association* no. 5 (1981): 1–6.

Deeb, Lara. *An Enchanted Modern: Gender and Public Piety in Shi'i Lebanon*. Princeton, NJ: Princeton University Press, 2006.

Dillard, Angela Denise. *Faith in the City: Preaching Radical Social Change in Detroit*. Ann Arbor: University of Michigan Press, 2007.

Diouf, Sylviane. *Servants of Allah: African Muslims Enslaved in the Americas*. New York: New York University Press, 1998.

Dorman, Jacob. "'A True Moslem Is a True Spiritualist': Black Orientalism and Black Gods of the Metropolis." In *The New Black Gods: Arthur Huff Fauset and the Study of African American Religions*. Edited by Edward E. Curtis IV and Danielle Brune Sigler, 116–144. Bloomington: Indiana University Press, 2009.

Duffield, Ian. "American Influences of Duse Mohamed Ali." In *Pan-African Biography*. Edited by Robert A. Hill, 11–56. Los Angeles: University of California Press, 1987.

Ehrenreich, John. *The Altruistic Imagination: A History of Social Work and Social Policy in the United States*. Ithaca, NY: Cornell University Press, 1985.

Eickelman, Dale F. "Islam and the Languages of Modernity." *Daedalus (Boston)* 129, no. 1 (2000): 119–135.

———. "Mass Higher Education and the Religious Imagination in Contemporary Arab Societies." *American Ethnologist* 19, no. 4 (1992): 643–655.

Eickelman, Dale F., and James Piscatori. *Muslim Politics*. Princeton, NJ: Princeton University Press, 2004.

Elkholy, Abdo A. *The Arab Moslems in the United States: Religion and Assimilation*. New Haven, CT: College & University Press, 1966.

Ellis, Mark. *Race, War, and Surveillance: African Americans and the United States*. Bloomington: Indiana University Press, 2001.

Ellwood, Robert S. *1950: Crossroads of American Religious Life*. Louisville: Westminster John Knox Press, 2000.

Eschen, Penny M. Von. *Race Against Empire: Black Americans and Anticolonialism, 1937–1957*. Ithaca, NY: Cornell University Press, 1997.

Espiritu, Yen Le. "Gender and Labor in Asian Immigrant Families." In *Gender and U.S. Immigration: Contemporary Trends*. Edited by Pierrette Sondagneu-Sotelo. New York: Sage Publications, 1999.

Esposito, John, and Ibrahim Kalin. *Islamophobia: The Challenge of Pluralism in the 21st Century*. New York: Oxford University Press, 2011.

Essien-Udom, Essien U. *Black Nationalism: A Search for an Identity in America*. Chicago: University of Chicago Press, 1962.

Etienne, Le Roy. "Les Musulmans et Le Pouvoir En Afrique Noir." *Journal of Legal Pluralism and Unofficial Law* (1984): 143–145.

Evanzz, Karl. *The Messenger: The Rise and Fall of Elijah Muhammad*. New York: Vintage, 1999.

Farley, Reynolds, Sheldon Danzinger, and Harry Holzer. *Detroit Divided*. New York: Russell Sage Foundation Publications, 2000.

Fessenden, Tracy. *Culture and Redemption: Religion, the Secular, and American Literature*. Princeton, NJ: Princeton University Press, 2007.

Fischer, Michael M. J., and Mehdi Abedi. *Debating Muslims: Cultural Dialogues in Postmodernity and Tradition*. Madison: University of Wisconsin Press, 1990.

Georgakas, Dan. *Detroit, I Do Mind Dying*. 1st ed. Cambridge, MA: South End Press, 1998.

GhaneaBassiri, Kambiz. *A History of Islam in America*. Cambridge: Cambridge University Press, 2010.

Giffin, Susan. *Michael Berry*. Bloomington, IN: AuthorHouse, 2007.

Gilkes, Sheryl. *Saints in Exile*. Oxford: Oxford University Press, 1995.

Gomez, Michael A. *Black Crescent: The Experience and Legacy of African Muslims in the Americas*. Cambridge: Cambridge University Press, 2005.

Good, David L. *Orvie: The Dictator of Dearborn: The Rise and Reign of Orville L. Hubbard*. Detroit: Wayne State University Press, 1989.

Grabar, Oleg. "Symbols and Signs in Islamic Architecture." In *Architecture and Community Building in the Islamic World Today*. Millerton: Aperture, 1983

Gregory, Derek. *The Colonial Present: Afghanistan, Palestine, and Iraq*. Malden, MA: Blackwell Publishing, 2004.

Gregory, James. *The Southern Diaspora: How the Great Migration of Black and White Southerners Transformed America*. Chapel Hill: University of North Carolina press, 2005.

Gross, Ariela. *What Blood Won't Tell: A History of Race on Trial in America*. Cambridge, MA: Harvard University Press, 2008.

Gualtieri, Sarah. "Becoming 'White': Race, Religion and the Foundations of Syrian/ Lebanese Ethnicity in the United States." *Journal of American Ethnic History* 20, no. 4 (2001): 29–58.

———. *Between Arab and White: Race and Ethnicity in the Early Syrian American Diaspora*. Berkeley: University of California Press, 2009.

Haddad, Yvonne Yazbeck. "Arab Muslims and Islamic Institutions in America: Adaptation and Reform." In *Arabs in the New World: Studies on Arab-American Communities*. Edited by Sameer Abraham and Nabeel Abraham, 209. Detroit: Wayne State University, Center for Urban Studies, 1983.

———. *A Century of Islam in America*. Washington, DC: American Institute for Islamic Affairs, 1986.

———. "The Dynamics of Islamic Identity in North America." In *Muslims on the Americanization Path?* Edited by Yvonne Yazbeck Haddad and John Esposito. Atlanta: Scholars Press, 1998.

———. "Maintaining the Faith of the Fathers: Dilemmas of Religious Identity in the Christian and Muslim Arab-American Communities." In *The Development of Arab-American Identity*. Edited by Ernest McCarus. Ann Arbor: University of Michigan Press, 1994.

Haddad, Yvonne Yazbeck, and Jane Idleman Smith. "The Ahmadiyya Community of North America." In *Mission to America: Five Islamic Sectarian Communities in North America*, 49–78. Gainesville: University Press of Florida, 1993.

———. *Muslim Communities in North America*. Albany: State University of New York Press, 1994.

Handlin, Oscar. *The Uprooted*. 2nd ed. Boston: Little, Brown, 1973.

Hardy, Clarence. "Fauset's (Missing) Pentecostals: Church Mothers, Remaking Respectability, and Religious Modernism." In *The New Black Gods: Arthur Huff Fauset and the Study of African American Religions*. Edited by Edward E. Curtis IV and Danielle Brune Sigler, 15–30. Bloomington: Indiana University Press, 2009.

Herberg, W. *Protestant, Catholic, Jew: An Essay in American Religious Sociology*. Garden City, NJ: Anchor Books, 1960.

Hitti, P. K. *The Syrians in America.* New York: George H. Doran, 1924.

Howell, Sally. "The Competition for Muslims: New Strategies for Urban Renewal in Detroit." In *Islamophobia/Islamophilia: Beyond the Politics of Enemy and Friend.* Edited by Andrew Shryock, 260. Bloomington: Indiana University Press, 2010.

———. "Finding the Straight Path: A Conversation with Mohsen and Lila Amen About Faith, Life, and Family in Dearborn." In *Arab Detroit 9/11: Life in the Terror Decade.* Edited by Andrew Shryock and Nabeel Abraham, 241–277. Detroit: Wayne State University Press, 2000.

———. "Muslims as Moving Targets: External Scrutiny and Internal Critique in Detroit's Mosque." In *Arab Detroit 9/11: Life in the Terror Decade*, 151–185. Detroit: Wayne State University Press, 2011.

Howell, Sally, and Amaney Jamal. "Belief and Belonging." In *Citizenship and Crisis: Arab Detroit after 9/11.* Edited by DAAS Team. New York: Russell Sage Foundation, 2009.

Howell, Sally, and Andrew Shryock. "Cracking Down on Diaspora: Arab Detroit and America's 'War on Terror.'" *Anthropological Quarterly* no. 763 (2003): 443.

Ismail, Vehbi. "Islam and the Federation." *The Moslem Life* VI, no. 3 (1958): 22–33.

Jackson, Sherman A. *Islam and the Blackamerican: Looking Toward the Third Resurrection.* New York: Oxford University Press, 2005.

Johnson, Steve. "The Muslims of Indianapolis." In *Muslim Communities in North America.* Edited by Yvonne Yazbeck Haddad. New York: State University of New York Press, 1994.

Johnson, Sylvester. "Religion Proper and Proper Religion: Arthur Fauset and the Study of African American Religions." In *The New Black Gods: Arthur Huff Fauset and the Study of African American Religions.* Edited by Edward E. Curtis IV and Danielle Brune Sigler, 145–170. Bloomington: Indiana University Press, 2009.

———. "The Rise of Black Ethnics: The Ethnic Turn in African American Religions, 1916–1945." *Religion and American Culture: A Journal of Interpretation* 20, no. 2 (July 1, 2010): 125–163.

Kahera, Akel Ismail. "Urban Enclaves, Muslim Identity and the Urban Mosque in America." *Journal of Muslim Minority Affairs* 22, no. 2 (2002): 369–380.

Karpat, Kemal. "The Ottoman Emigration to America, 1860–1914." *International Journal of Middle East Studies* 17, no. 2 (1985): 175–209.

———. "The Turks in America." *Turcs d'Europełdots et d'Ailleurs, Les Annales de L'Autre Islam* 3 (1995): 232–233.

Khan, Dada Amir Haider. *Chains to Lose: Life and Struggles of a Revolutionary Memoirs of Dada Amir Haidar Khan.* Edited by Hasan Ghardezi. 2 vols. Karachi, Pakistan: Pakistan Study Center, 2007.

Khan, Muqtedar. *American Muslims: Bridging Faith and Freedom.* Beltsville, MD: Amana, 2002.

———. "Living on Borderlines: Islam Beyond the Clash and Dialogue of Civilizations." In *Muslims' Place in the American Public Square.* Edited by Zahid H. Bukhari, Sulayman S. Nyang, Mumtaz Ahmad, and John L. Esposito. Walnut Creek, CA: AltaMira Press, 2004.

Khater, Akram F. *Inventing Home: Emigration, Gender, and the Middle Class in Lebanon, 1870–1920.* Berkeley: University of California Press, 2001.

Khattak, Shahin Kuli Khan. *Islam and the Victorians: Nineteenth Century Perceptions of Muslim Practices and Beliefs*. New York: Tauris Academic Studies, 2008.

Kuran, Timur. "The Provision of Public Goods Under Islamic Law: Origins, Impact, and Limitations of the Waqf System." *Law Society Review* 35, no. 4 (2001): 841–897.

Leach, William R. *Land of Desire: Merchants, Power, and the Rise of a New American Culture*. New York: Vintage, 1994.

Leonard, Karen I. *Making Ethnic Choices: California's Punjabi Mexican Americans*. Philadelphia: Temple University Press, 1992.

———. *Muslims in the United States: The State of Research*. New York: Russell Sage Foundation, 2003.

———. *The South Asian Americans*. Westport, CT: Greenwood Press, 1997.

Leveau, Robert. "The Islamic Presence in France." In *The New Islamic Presence in Western Europe*. Edited by T. Gerholm and Y. G. Lithman, 107–122. New York: Mansell, 1988.

Lincoln, C. Eric. *The Black Muslims in America*. Boston: Beacon Press, 1961.

Little, Douglas. *American Orientalism: The United States and the Middle East Since 1945*. Chapel Hill: University of North Carolina Press, 2002.

Lincoln, C. Eric, and Lawrence H. Mamiya. *The Black Church in the African American Experience*. Durham, NC: Duke University Press, 1990.

Lipset, Seymour M. *American Pluralism and the Jewish Community*. New Brunswick, CT: Transaction Publishers, 1990.

Little, Douglas. *American Orientalism: The United States and the Middle East Since 1945*. Chapel Hill: University of North Carolina Press, 2002.

Loewen, James W. *Sundown Towns: A Hidden Dimension of American Racism*. New York: Touchstone, 2006.

Majaj, Lisa Suhier. "Arab American Ethnicity: Locations, Coalitions and Cultural Negotiations." In *Arabs in America: Building a New Future*. Edited by Michael Suleiman. Philadelphia: Temple University Press, 1999.

Majid, Anouar. *We Are All Moors: Ending Centuries of Crusades Against Muslims and Other Minorities*. St. Paul: University of Minnesota Press, 2012.

Makdisi, Ussama. *Artillery of Heaven: American Missionaries and the Failed Conversion of the Middle East* (Google eBook). New York: Cornell University Press, 2009.

———. *The Culture of Sectarianism: Community History and Violence in Nineteenth Century Ottoman Lebanon*. Berkeley: University of California Press, 2001.

Malik, Iftikhar. *Islam and Modernity: Muslims in Europe and the United States*. Sterling, VA: Pluto Press, 2004.

Mandaville, Peter. *Transnational Muslim Politics: Reimagining the Umma*. New York: Routledge, 2001.

Mandaville, Jon E. "Usurious Piety: The Cash Waqf Controversy in the Ottoman Empire." *International Journal of Middle East Studies* 10, no. 3 (1979): 289–308.

Marable, Manning. *Race, Reform, and Rebellion: The Second Reconstruction and Beyond in Black America, 1945–2006*. 3rd ed. Jackson: University Press of Mississippi, 2007.

Marr, Timothy. *The Cultural Roots of American Islamicism. The Cultural Roots of American Islamicism*. Cambridge: Cambridge University Press, 2006.

Marsh, Clifton E. "The Nation of Islam and the World Community of Al-Islam in the West 1965–1980." In *The Lost-Found Nation of Islam in America*, 67–78. Lanham, MD: Scarecrow Press, 2000.

May, Martha. "The Historical Problem of the Family Wage: The Ford Motor Company and the Five Dollar Day." *Feminist Studies* 8, no. 2 (1982): 399–424.

McAlister, Melanie. *Epic Encounters: Culture, Media, and U.S. Interests in the Middle East Since 1945*. Berkeley: University of California Press, 2001.

McCloud, Aminah Beverly. *African American Islam*. New York: Routledge, 1995.

_____."African American Muslim Women." In *The Muslims of America*. Edited by Yvonne Haddad, 177–187. London: Oxford University Press, 1991.

_____. *Transnational Muslims in American Society*. 1st ed. Gainesville: University Press of Florida, 2006.

Metcalf, Barbara. *Making Muslim Space in North America and Europe*. Berkeley: University of California Press, 1996.

Mitchell, Timothy. *Questions Of Modernity*. Minneapolis: University of Minnesota Press, 2000.

Moore, R. Laurence. *Religious Outsiders and the Making of Americans*. New York: Oxford University Press, 1986.

Munger, Elizabeth. *Michigan City's First One Hundred Years. Bygone Places Along the "Hoosier Line": The Monon Railroad Line Third Subdivision*. 1969.

Naber, Nadine. "Ambiguous Insiders: An Investigation of Arab American Invisibility." *Ethnic and Racial Studies* 23, no. 1 (2000): 37–61.

———. "Introduction: Arab Americans and U.S. Racial Formation." In *Race and Arab Americans Before and After 9/11: From Invisible Citizens to Visible Subjects*. Edited by Nadine Naber and Amaney Jamal. Syracuse: Syracuse University Press, 2008.

Naff, Alixa. *Becoming American: The Early Arab Immigrant Experience*. Carbondale: Southern Illinois University Press, 1985.

"The Arabic-Language Press," in The Ethnic Press in the United States, ed. Sally Miller (New York: Greenwood Press, 1987).

Nagi, Dennis. *The Albanian-American Odyssey: A Pilot Study of the Albanian Community of Boston, Massachusetts*. Carbondale: Southern Illinois University Press, 1989.

Nance, Susan. "Respectability and Representation: The Moorish Science Temple, Morocco, and Black Public Culture in 1920s Chicago." *American Quarterly* 54, no. 4 (2002): 623–659

Nielsen, Jorgen S. *Towards A European Islam (Migration, Minorities and Citizenship)*. New York: St. Martin's Press, 1999.

Nash, M. Naeem. "Muhammad Ezaldeen (1866–1957) Founder of the Addeynu Allahe Universal Arabic Association." In *Encyclopedia of Muslim American History*. Edited by Edward Curtis IV, 175–176. New York: Facts on File, 2010.

Norton, A. R. *Hezbollah: A Short History*. Princeton, NJ: Princeton University Press, 2009.

Orfalea, Gregory. *The Arab Americans: A History*. New York: Olive Branch Press, 2006.

Peters, Emryrs. "Aspects of Rank and Status Among Muslims in a Lebanese Village." In *People and Culture of the Middle East*. Edited by L. E. Sweet. Garden City, NY: Natural History Press, 1970.

Pew Forum on Religion and Public Life. *Muslim Americans: Middle Class and Mostly Mainstream*. Washington, DC: Pew Research Center, 2007.

Pew Forum on Religion in Public Life. *Muslim Americans: No Signs of Growth in Alienation or Support for Extremism*. Washington, DC: Pew Research Center, August 2011. Available at http://www.people-press.org/2011/08/30/muslim-americans-no-signs-of-growth-in-alienation-or-support-for-extremism/.

Poston, Larry. *Islamic Da`wah in the West: Muslim Missionary Activity and the Dynamics of Conversion to Islam*. New York: Oxford University Press, 1992.

Portes, Alejandro, and Ruben Rumbaut. *Immigrant America*. 2nd ed. Berkeley: University of California Press, 1996.

Portes, Alejandro, and Min Zhou. "The New Second Generation: Segmened Assimilation and Its Variants." *Annals of the American Academy of Political and Social Science* 530, no. 1 (1993): 74–96.

Prashad, Vijay. *Everybody Was Kung Fu Fighting: Afro-Asian Connections and the Myth of Cultural Purity*. Boston: Beacon Press, 2001.

——. *The Karma of Brown Folk*. Minneapolis: University of Minnesota Press, 2000.

Qureshi, Regula. "Transcending Space: Recitation and Community Among South Asian Muslims in Canada." In *Making Muslim Space in North American and Europe*. Edited by Barbara Metcalf, 46–64. Berkeley: University of California Press, 1996.

Qutb, Said. *Amrika Allati Ra'ayt Fi Mizan Al-insaniyya*. Cairo: Al-Rasala, 1951.

——. *Ma'alim Fi al-Tariq*. Cairo: Dar al-Shuruq, 1992.

Rahman, Ahmed. "Story by Ahmed Abdul Rahman." *Transformations*. n.d.

Razack, Sherene. *Casting Out: The Eviction of Muslims from Western Law and Politics*. Toronto: University of Toronto Press, 2008.

Rouse, Carolyn Moxley. *Engaged Surrender: African American Women and Islam*. 1st ed. Berkeley: University of California Press, 2004.

Said, Edward W. *Orientalism*. New York: Vintage, 1978.

Saliba, Therese. "Resisting Invisibility: Arab Americans in Academia and Activism." In *Arabs in America: Building a New Future*. Edited by Michael Suleiman. Philadelphia: Temple University Press, 1999.

Salvatore, Armando. *Islam and the Political Discourse of Modernity*. Ithaca, NY: Ithaca Press, 1999.

Samhan, Helen. "Not Quite White: Racial Classification and the Arab-American Experience." In *Arabs in America: Building a New Future*. Edited by Michael Suleiman. Philadelphia: Temple University Press, 1999.

Schopmeyer, Kim. "Arab Detroit after 9/11: A Demographic Portrait." In *Arab Detroit 9/11: Life in the Terror Decade*. Edited by Nabeel Abraham, Sally Howell, and Andrew Shryock, 29–65. Detroit: Wayne State University Press, 2011.

"Shah Jahan Mosque—Britain's First Purpose-built Mosque Est. 1889," n.d. http://www.shahjahanmosque.org.uk/.

Shaheen, Jack. *Arab and Muslim Stereotyping in American Popular Culture*. Washington, DC: Center for Muslim-Christian Understanding, History and International Affairs, Edmund A. Walsh School of Foreign Service, Georgetown University, 1997.

Shakir, Zaid. *Scattered Pictures: Reflections Of An American Muslim*. Hayward, CA: Zaytuna Institute, 2005.

Sheba, George. "Caroling with the Keralites: The Negotiation of Gendered Space in an Indian Immigrant Church." In *Gatherings in Diaspora: Religious Communities and the New Immigration*. Edited by R. Stephen Warner and Judith G. Wittner, 265–294. Philadelphia: Temple University Press, 1998.

Sheehi, Stephen. *Islamophobia: The Ideological Campaign Against Muslims*. Atlanta: Clarity Press, 2011.

Shouk, Ahmed Abu, J. O. Hunwick, and R. S. O'Fahey. "A Sudanese Missionary to the United States: Satti Majid, 'Shaykh al-Islam in North America,' and His Encounter with Noble Drew Ali, Prophet of the Moorish Science Temple Movement." *Sudanic Africa* 8 (1997): 137–191.

Shryock, Andrew. "Attack of the Islamophobes: Religious War (and Peace) in Arab/Muslim Detroit." In *Islamophobia in America*. Edited by Carl Enrst, 145–174. New York: Palgrave MacMillan, 2013.

———. "Finding Islam in Detroit: The Multiple Histories, Identities, and Locations of a City and Its Muslims." Stanford, CA: Stanford University, 2007.

———. *Islamophobia/Islamophilia: Beyond the Politics of Enemy and Friend*. Bloomington: Indiana University Press, 2010.

Shryock, Andrew, and Ann Chih Lin. "Arab American Identities in Question." In *Citizenship and Crisis: Arab Detroit after 9/11*. Edited by DAAS Team, 35–68. New York: Russell Sage Foundation, 2009.

Shryock, Andrew, Sally Howell, and Nabeel Abraham. "The New Order and Its Forgotten Histories." In *Arab Detroit 9/11: Life in the Terror Decade*. Edited by Andrew Shryock, Sally Howell, and Nabeel Abraham, 381–393. Detroit: Wayne State University Press, 2011.

Smart, Ninian. *Dimensions of the Sacred: An Anatomy of the World's Beliefs*. 1st ed. Berkeley: University of California Press, 1999.

Smith, Timothy. "New Approaches to the History of Immigration in Twentieth-Century America." *American Historical Review* 71 (July 1966): 1265–1279.

Starrett, Gregory. *Putting Islam to Work: Education, Politics, and Religious Transformation in Egypt*. Berkeley: University of California Press, 1998.

Stenhouse, T. B. H. *The Rocky Mountain Saints*. New York: Appleton and Company, 1873.

Stout, Daniel, and Judith Buddenbaum. *Religion and Mass Media: Audiences and Adaptations*. Edited by Daniel A. Stout and Judith M. Buddenbaum. Thousand Oaks: Sage Publications, 1996.

Suad, Joseph. "Against the Grain of the Nation." In *Arabs in America: Building a New Future*. Edited by Michael Suleiman. Philadelphia: Temple University Press, 1999.

Sugrue, Thomas. *The Origins of Urban Crisis: Race and Inequality in Postwar Detroit*. Princeton, NJ: Princeton University Press, 1996.

Suleiman, Michael. "A History of Arab-American Political Participation." In *American Arabs and Political Participation*. Edited by Philippa Strum, 155. Washington, DC: Woodrow Wilson Center, 2006.

———. "'I Come to Bury Ceasar, Not to Praise Him': An Assessment of the AAUG as an Example of an Activist Arab-American Organization." *Arab Studies Quarterly* 9, no. 3, 4 (2007): 75–95.

Swanson, Jon. "Sojourners and Settlers in Yemen and America." In *Sojourners and Settlers: The Yemeni Immigrant Experience*. Edited by Jonathon Friedlander. Provo: University Press of Utah, 1988.

Terry, Janice. "Community and Political Activism Among Arab Americans in Detroit." In *Arabs in America: Building a New Future*. Edited by Michael Suleiman. Philadelphia: Temple University Press, 1999.

Trix, Frances. *Albanians in Michigan – A Proud People from Southeast Europe*. East Lansing: Michigan State University Press, 2001.

———. Trix, F. "The Bektashi Tekke and the Sunni Mosque of Albanian Muslims in America." In *Muslim Communities in North America*. Edited by Yvonne Haddad and Jane Smith. New York: State University of New York Press, 1994.

———. *Spiritual Discourse: Learning with an Islamic Master*. Philadelphia: University of Pennsylvania Press, 1993.

Turner, Richard Brent. *Islam in the African-American Experience*. Bloomington: Indiana University Press, 1997.

Vincent, Theodore G. *Black Power and the Garvey Movement*. Berkeley: Ramparts, 1971.

Walbridge, Linda. "The Shi'a Mosques and Their Congregations in Dearborn." In *Muslim Communities in North America*. Edited by Yvonne Yazbeck Haddad and Jane Idleman Smith. New York: State University of New York Press, 1994.

———. *Without Forgetting the Imam: Lebanese Shiism in an American Community*. Detroit: Wayne State University Press, 1997.

Warner, R. Stephen. *A Church of Our Own: Disestablishment and Diversity in American Religion*. New Brunswick, NJ: Rutgers University Press, 2005.

———. "Work in Progress: Toward a New Paradigm for the Sociological Study of Religion in the United States." *The American Journal of Sociology* 98, no. 5 (1993): 1044–1093.

Warner, R. Stephen, and J. G. Wittner. *Gatherings in Diaspora: Religious Communities and the New Immigration*. Philadelphia: Temple University Press, 1998.

Wasfi, Atif. *An Islamic-Lebanese Community in U.S.A: a Study in Cultural Anthropology*. Beirut: Beirut Arab University, 1971.

Waters, Mary. *Black Identities: West Indian Immigrant Dreams and American Realities*. New York: Russell Sage Foundation, 1999.

———. *Ethnic Options: Choosing Identities in America*. Berkeley: University of California Press, 1990.

Weiner, Isaac. *Religion Out Loud: Religious Sound, Public Spaces, and American Pluralism*. New York: New York University Press, 2013.

Weisenfeld, Judith. *Hollywood Be Thy Name: African American Religion in American Film, 1929–1949*. Berkeley: University of California Press, 2007.

Werbner, Pnina. *Imagined Diasporas Among Manchester Muslims: The Public Performance of Pakistani Transnational Identity Politics*. Oxford: James Currey, 2002.

White, Hayden. *The Content of the Form: Narrative Discourse and Historical Representation*. Baltimore: John Hopkins University Press, 2009.

Whitman, Sidney. *Turkish Memories*. New York: Charles Scribner's Sons, 1914.

Williams, Raymond. *Religions of Immigrants from India and Pakistan: New Threads in the American Tapestry*. Cambridge: Cambridge University Press, 1988.

Wolf, C. Umhau. "Muslims in the Midwest." *The Muslim World* no. 50 (1960): 39–48.

Wuthnow, Robert. *Between States and Markets: The Voluntary Sector in Comparative Perspective*. Princeton, NJ: Princeton University Press, 1991.

Youmans, William. "Domestic Foreign Policy: Arab Detroit as an Important Place in the War on Terror." In *Arab Detroit 9/11: Life in the Terror Decade*. Edited by Nabeel Abraham, Sally Howell, and Andrew Shryock. Detroit: Wayne State University Press, 2011.

Younis, Adele, and Philip Kayal. *Coming of the Arabic Speaking People to the United States*. Staten Island: Center For Migration Studies, 1995.

Younis, Mohammed. *Muslim Americans Exemplify Diversity, Potential: Key Findings from a New Report*. Washinton: Gallup Center for Muslim Studies, 2009.

INDEX

Note: Page numbers in *italics* indicate photographs and illustrations.

abaya, 45

Abbas, Hussein, 40, 43, 48, 58–59, 298n121

Abbas, Muneera, 58–59, 65–66

Abdullah, Zain, 222

Abraham, Elias Mohammed, 79

Abraham, Essie, 110, 216

Abraham, Nabeel, 183–84, 186, 258, 259

Abraham, Robert (Sy), 110, 129, 183, 212–13

Abrahamic tradition, 52

Abushakra, Abbas, 87, 88

Addeynu Allahe Universal Arabic Association (AAUAA), 85

adhan (call to prayer), 30, 212, 239

Afghani, Jamal Al-Din, 169

Afghan Muslims, 42, 93

African American Muslims
and archival materials, 326n17
and conversions to Islam, 80–85
and countercultural Islam, 240, 246, 248
and demographic shifts in American Islam, 9
and Islamic reform and revivalism, 236
and scholarly focus on Nation of Islam, 274
and social tensions, 190

See also Ahmadiyya Movement; Masjid al-Mu'mineen; Masjid al-Salam; Masjid Wali Muhammad; Nation of Islam (NOI)

African slaves, 11, 22, 31, 274, 292n3

African Times and Orient Review, 76–77

Ahl al-Bayt, 117, 162, 167, 308n59

Ahmad, Mirza Ghulam, 52, 84

Ahmadiyya Movement
and African American converts, 82–84, 274
and African American liberation, 85
and Dearborn's first mosques, 119
and discrimination against American Muslims, 49
as focus of scholarship, 1
and the Karoub family, 91–92
and the Moslem Mosque of Highland Park, 52–55, 59
and scholarly focus on American Islam, 1
and transcommunal Islam, 188
and the Woking Mosque, 76

Ahmed, A. M., 72

Ahmed, Ghulam, 91

Aiddora, Mohammad, 72

Akhtar, Jamil, 71

Akram, Wali, 82

Alasry, Abdo, 7, 208, 210–14, 277–78

Alawan, Charles Kalil (Hajj Chuck)
  and Dearborn's first mosques, 119–20, 122
  family background, 308n57
  and the FIA, 157–58
  on Hashmie Hall, 127–29
  and the Islamic Center of America (Detroit), 161, 162, *164*
  and midcentury Muslim immigrants, 141–42
  and mosques of Dearborn, 132
  and Sunni-Shiʿa conflict, 116–18

Alawan, Eide, 218, 219, 265

ʿAlawis, 47

Albanian American Moslem Society (AAMS), 142, 145, 148–49, *149*, 155, 168

Albanian American Moslem Youth Club, 155

Albanian Islamic Center (AIC), *170*
  and Cold War pressures on American Islam, 27
  and Islamic orthodoxy, 258
  and Islamic reform and revivalism, 219
  and Islamic revolutions, 268
  and midcentury Muslim immigrants, 167–73
  and mosque construction, 185
  and origin of American Muslim community, 286

The Albanian Moslem Life, 150, 152, 168

Albanian Moslem Society of Detroit, 142

Albanian Muslims
  and archival materials, 326n17
  demographic impact on American Islam, 214
  and ethnic divisions, 294n37
  and immigration patterns, 314n106
  and immigration policy in the US, 324n105
  and independence movements, 64
  and Islamic revolutions, 268
  and Muslim identity formation, 93
  and new generations of Muslim clerics, 134
  and race issues, 70, 79

and return immigration, 306n23
  and sectarian divisions, 42, 291n49
  and Vehbi Ismail, 144–50

Albanian Women's Association, 171

Alcodray, Mike, 181

alcohol consumption, 146, 182, 195, 196–97, 209

Ali, Derrick, 225

Ali, Duse Mohamed
  and the Central Islamic Society, 301n36
  and Muslim identity formation, 96
  and pan-Africanism, 85
  and race issues, 75–80
  and the Universal Islamic Society, 71–72, *72*, 80

Ali, Noble Drew (Timothy Drew), 82, 83–84, 85, 240

Ali, Zainab, 142

Alli, Jack, 170

All India Brotherhood, 93

Alwan, Mazen, *228*
  and countercultural Islam, 241, 245
  on divine revelation, 322n41
  and gender issues in Islam, 250–51, 253
  and Islamic revivalism, 220, 226–27, 229, 234–35, 236–40
  and Islamic revolutions, 261, 268
  and the Muslim World League, 322n38
  and Warith Deen Mohammad, 234–38
  See also Masjid Wali Muhammad

Al-Alwani, Taha Jabir, 24

Amen, Lila, 262, 264

Amen, Mohsen, 262, 264

America-Asia Society, 77–78

American African Orient-Trading Company, 77, 78

Americanization, 4, 154, 173, 180, 281, 299n13

American Mohammedan Society, 32

American Moslem Society (AMS), *131*, *177*, *178*
  and the Albanian Islamic Center, 168, 170
  and Albanian Muslims, 148
  and al-Mu'mineen Mosque, 199
  American-born Muslim leaders, 175–76

anniversary celebration, 4–8
and archival materials, 9
and countercultural Islam, 242–43
and cross-cultural mutuality, 312n47
and Dearborn's first mosques, 127–32
and the Federation of Islamic
    Associations, 277–78
founding families, 108
and gender issues in Islam, 257
and Islamic orthodoxy, 23–24
and Islamic reform and revivalism, 219
and Islamic revolutions, 259, 262
and midcentury Muslim immigrants,
    135, 142–43, 173
and midcentury transnational Islam,
    154–55
and mosques of Dearborn, 97, 110,
    120, *121*, 122, 123–24, 130–31
origin of, 98
reconstruction of, 286
and Sunni tradition, 308n54
and transcommunal Islam, 188, 193
and transitional conflicts in American
    mosques, 208–12, 215–16
and transnational pressures on
    American Islam, 28
and visibility of American Islam,
    124–25
and women's auxiliaries, 182–87
and the Young Pakistan Association,
    312n46
American Moslem Women's Society
    (AMWS), *121*, 130, 131–32, 155,
    182–87, 210, 213, 216
American Muslim Bekaa Center, 110,
    216, 278
al-Amin, Jamil (H. Rap Brown), 241
al-Ansari, Jameat Zaid Ibn Thabit, 234
antebellum period, 22
anticolonialism, 27, 66, 71, 76–77, 79,
    85–89, 86
anticommunism
    and Albanian Muslims, 144–46, 148,
        150, 168, 169–70, 172
    and Chirri, 267–68, 324n101
    and Islamic revolutions, 267–68
    and Lebanese politics, 309n4

and midcentury Muslim immigrants,
    136–37
and Middle East politics, 172
and Muslim Student Association, 202
and Nasser, 318n74
and transcommunal Islam, 191
anti-immigrant sentiment, 65–68, 275
anti-Muslim sentiment, 65–68, 69–70,
    74–75, 87–88, 207
anti-Semitism, 221
anti-war movement, 241
Antwerp, Eugene Von, 148
The Arab (1915), 66
Arab American Message, 179
Arab American Muslims, 9. *See also*
    American Moslem Society (AMS);
    Islamic Center of America (ICA)
Arabian-American Society, 36
Arab Israeli War (1967), 20, 281
Arab Israeli War (1973), 252
The Arab Moslems in the United States
    (Elkholy), 291n49
Arab nationalism, 48, 157, 158
Arab Oil Embargo, 205, 207, 221
Arab Revolt, 43, 66, 87
archival materials, 8–9, 326n17
Armenian Crisis/genocide, 34, 61, 65–68,
    75, 89
Arslan, Shakib, 88
asabiyah, 113
Asad, Talal, 182
al-Aseer, Adil, *178*, 204, 206–7,
    234, 252
Ashura, 41, 147, 166–67, 266, 314n90,
    316n90
Asiatic Barred Zone Act of 1917, 35
Asmar, George, 88–89
Assad, Dawud, 204
Asser El Jadeed Arabian Islamic Society
    of Michigan City, 32, 144, 153
assimilationism, 5, 6, 9, 11
Atatürk, Mustapha Kemal, 84
automobile industry, 70, 94, 104,
    207. *See also* Ford Motor
    Company
Al-Azhar University, 83–84, 145, 152,
    159, *160*, 181, 186, 202

Badawi, Jamal, 5
Bader Elmoneer Society, 32, 311n34
Bagram, Dervish, 170
al-Balagh, 37, 295n45
Balkans, 42
Balkan Wars, 37
Balooly, Hassan, 130
Bangladeshi Muslims, 35, 36, 42, 70–71,
    92–95, 214, 318n70, 326n17. *See
    also* Maeh, Acir Udin
al-Banna, Hassan, 202
al-Barakani, Imam, 212
Barton, Elizabeth, 53
Al-Bayan, 54–55, 89
Bayt al-Qureish, 246
Bazzy, Kalil, *72*
    and the Albanian Islamic Center, 170
    and Albanian Muslims, 148–49
    and the American Moslem Society,
        181, 182
    and Chirri, 142–44
    and civic life, 125
    and critiques of American Islam, 278
    education, 39–41, 311n29
    and Hashmie Hall, 102, 111, 115–16,
        125, *127,* 132–33, 142
    and Highland Park, 39–41, 42
    and Islamic Center of America (ICA),
        166
    and Islamic revolutions, 265
    and the Moslem Mosque of Highland
        Park, 50, *51,* 55, 61–62
    and Muslim identity formation, 96, 102
    and new generations of Muslim clerics,
        138
    and Qur'an recitation, 306n13
    refusal of salary, 143, 311n27
    and religious education, 102
    and role of imam, 39–41, 115–16
    and social practices of Muslim
        community, 37, 173
    and Sunni-Shi'a conflict, 39–43, 58,
        115–16
    and Syrian nationalism, 88, 89
    and the Universal Islamic Society,
        71–72, *72, 74*

and weddings, 295n62
Bednell, Robert, 53
Begum, Sultan Shahjehan, 44
Bekaa Valley immigrants, 42, 47, 90, 98,
    106, 122, 124, 187
Bektashi Sufis, 142, 145, 147, 168,
    170–71, 291n49, 311n24
Bengali Muslims. *See* Bangladeshi
    Muslims
Berry, Abdel Latif, 264–65, 267, 271
Berry, Joseph, 142
Berry, Michael, 107–8, 304n107
Berry, Mohammad, 142
Bey, Furuq Z., 242
the Beys, 241–47, 249, 253
Bilalian Muslims, 229, 238
The Bilalian News, 234
Bilge, Barbara, 34, 94
Bilici, Mucahit, 277
Bimm, Frank, 314n103
Bint Ijbayl immigrants, 34, 39–40, 106,
    143
Blackamericans, 218, 234. *See also*
    African American Muslims
Black Bottom neighborhood, 70, 73, 194
Black Panthers, 191
Black Power Movement, 20, 27–28, 225,
    240–41, 244, 274
black separatism, 15, 85
Bonnie Brook Social Club, 264, 265
British Empire, 32, 86
Brown, H. Rap, 241
Buffalo Moslem Welfare Society, 32
burial practices, 37, 39, 41, 92–93, 120,
    151. *See also* funeral services

Cairo University, 159
caliphate, 308n59
calligraphy, 36
Cameron, Charles, 88, 272–73
Carby, Hazel, 75–76
Carter, Jimmy, 266
Catholics, 86, 108, 220, 303n76
Cece, Kilani, 244
Cedar Rapids Muslim Community, 151
Cesari, Jocelyn, 16

Drew, Timothy (Noble Drew Ali), 82
Druze community, 54, 86–89
dubkeh, 207, 262
Duffield, Ian, 78, 300n36

Eastman, Carl, *263*
Eastman, Miriam, *263*
Ecie, Alex, 36, 56
Ecie, Gladys, 108, 109, 123
ecumenicalism, 160, 168, 188, 246, 284
education
    and Adil al-Aseer, 206–7
    and the Albanian Islamic Center, 168
    and American-born Muslim leaders, 183
    and Federation of Islamic Associations
        (FIA), 152, 168, 186
    and Hashmie Hall, 141
    and the Islamic Center of America, 167
    and mosques of Dearborn, 98, 101,
        183, 212–13
    training of imams, 129
    and transnational Islam, 196
egalitarianism, 74
Egypt, 158, 202–3, 313n83
Egyptian Supreme Council of Islamic
    Affairs, 204
Eickelman, Dale, 21–22, 101, 102
Eid al-Adha, 55, 131, 147, 211, 312n46,
    314n46
Eid al-Fitr, 48, 147, 312n46
Eid al-Mawlid. *See mawlids* (birthday
    services in praise of the Prophet and
    his family)
Eisenhower, Dwight, 169, 170
Eissa, Ali, 131
El-Amin, Shedrick, 226, 233
El-Bokka League, 121–23
El Haje, Fatima, 107–8
El Haje, Hussein, 7, 107–8, 123
Elkholy, Abdo
    on Albanian Muslims, 147
    and the American Moslem Society,
        181, 182
    arrival in the US, 26
    on ethnic isolationism, 18
    and the Federation of Islamic
        Associations, 151–52, 158

on sectarianism, 291n49
and source materials, 23
and Sunni-Shi'a conflict, 307n49
on women's contributions, 270
Ellwood, Robert, 136
Emergency Quota Act, 61
endowments for mosques, 44–45, 149
Enlightenment, 69
Espritu, Yen Le, 259
ethnicity issues
    and the Albanian Islamic Center, 171
    ancestry categories, 288n13
    and demographic shifts in American
        Islam, 9–10
    ethnic cleansing, 66
    ethnic clubs, 32, 103
    ethnic isolationism, 18–20
    ethnic neighborhoods and enclaves, 63
    ethnonational associations, 36, 90
    ethnoracial identities, 81
    ethnoreligious identity, 103
    founding of ethnically particular
        organizations, 122
    interethnic relations, 28–29
    in midcentury American mosques,
        281–82
    and mosques of Dearborn, 99–100
    and religious identity, 60–61
    social reproduction of ethnic
        communities, 185
evangelical movements, 137, 220
Ezaldeen, Mohammed (James Lomax),
    84–85

factionalism, 283–84, 308n55
Fadlallah, Al-Sayyad Mohammed
    Hussein, 264, 265
Fahd, Akil, 190, 244
Faisal, Daoud Ahmed, 192
Faisal I of Syria, 49
Faisal of Saudi Arabia, 92, 171
Fard (Muhammad), Wallace D., 82–83,
    219, 229–30, 235, 317n46
Farooqi, Ismail, 24
Farouk I of Egypt, 145
Farrakhan, Louis, 232
al-Faruqi, Ismail, 169

and demographic pressures on
American Islam, 215–16, 216–17
and the Federation of Islamic
Associations, 204
and gender issues in Islam, 257
and Islamic education, 90–91
and Islamic reform and revivalism, 234,
239, 270, 271, 277–78
and transcommunal Islam, 191–93
Karoub, Osman, 41, 54
Karoub Printing, 179
"Keiriat Island Moslem" group, 37–38
Khairat ul-Umma, 32, 37
Khalid, Saleem, 200, 208–9, 248, 250,
255–56
Khalid, Tahira Hassanein
and al-Mu'mineen Mosque, *199*, 200,
201, 205–7
on conversions to Islam, 194
and countercultural Islam, 244, 247–48
and gender issues in Islam, 252–53,
257
on Hassanein's conversion, 195–97
and Islamic reform and revivalism, 271
and transcommunal Islam, 192
Khalid of Saudi Arabia, 314n104
Khan, Dada Amir Haider, 36, 70, 73–75,
78–79, 302n58
Khan, Hassan, 71
Khater, Akram F., 306n23
Khomeini, Ruhollah, 260, 261, 262, 266,
268
King, Martin Luther, Jr., 197
Kizilay (Red Crescent Society), 37–38, 72
Korhonen, Sharon Abraham, 110, 129,
212, 213
Kurdish Muslims, 34, 35, 36, 42
Kurds, 64

labor unions, 126–27
laffi (Iranian-style turban), 267
Lateef, Yusuf, 242
Leach, William, 66–67
Lebanese civil war, 20, 139, 220
Lebanese Muslims, 4, 7, 24, 25, 104,
209, 214, 307n38, 326n17. *See also*
Syrian Muslims

Lebanon, 107, 309n4, 310n6, 324n105
"legacy Muslims," 8
Levy Asphalt, 209
Lincoln, Eric, 276
linguistic divisions, 10
literacy, 101
Little, Douglas, 66
Lomax, James (Mohammed Ezaldeen), 84

madhhab, 159–60
Maeh, Acir Udin, 35, 42, 70, 96, 102
Maeh, Azira, 92, 93, 95, 205
Maghrib, 243
al-Mahayssin, Mohammed, 48
the Mahdi, 260
Majid, Satti, 37–38, 80, 84, 102
Majma' (The Islamic Institute of
Knowledge), 271
Makled, Hussein
and Chirri, 154–55, 313n68
and Hashmie Hall, 142
and the Islamic Center of America,
161
and midcentury Muslim immigrants,
139–40, 141–42
and United Syrian Citizens Society,
139–41
Mamiya, Lawrence, 276
Mandate Palestine, 151
Mandaville, Peter, 12–13
Mardini, Mohammad, 278, 320n114
Marj al Angar, 41
marja'(spiritual guide), 41, 260
Maronites, 69, 86, 89
Marr, Timothy, 14
marriage practices, 11, 34–35, 311n29
masbaha (prayer beads), 45, 110
Mashike, Sidney, 162
masjid, 19, 120, 122–24, 213, 226, 236,
247, 251
Masjid al-'am (Mosque for All Muslims),
177, 188, 190, 215, 216
Masjid al-Asr, 253, 255
Masjid al-Haqq, 255
al-masjid al-Islami, 120. *See also*
American Moslem Society
(AMS)

Muslim World League (*Cont.*)
  and the Muslim Student Association,
    204–5
  and salaries of religious leaders,
    235–36, 268, 319n80
mutual aid societies, 32, 36, 190

nadi (club), 18, 24, 126, 132–33
Nadi al-Arabi al-Hashmie (the Hashemite
    Arab Club). *See* Progressive Arabian
    Hashmie Society (Hashmie Hall)
Naff, Alixa, 36–37, 40, 55, 91, 132–33,
    180, 306n23
Naggar, Abdel Halim, 170
Nahdat al-Arab, 135, 141, 143–44, 148,
    152–53, 310n21
Najaf, 41
Nasr, Seyyed Hossein, 24
Nasser, Gamel Abdel, 157–59, 160,
    185–86, 202, *203,* 313n83, 318n74
nationalism, 20, 32, 150, 202
Nationality Act of 1790, 68
national origins, 4
Nation of Islam (NOI)
  and African American converts, 81
  and African American liberation, 85
  and anti-American rhetoric, 317n46
  and business practices, 321n32
  and countercultural Islam, 240, 244,
    245, 249
  and cultural assimilation of
    Muslims, 12
  and ethnic isolationism, 18–19
  as focus of scholarship, 1–3
  and gender issues in Islam, 251, 255
  and the *hajj,* 171
  and Islamic orthodoxy, 22, 25–26
  and Islamic reform and revivalism,
    28, 219, 221–26, 229–30, 231–34,
    234–38, 274–75, 321n28
  and missionary efforts, 274–75
  and new generations of Muslim
    clerics, 137
  and Orientalism, 15
  origins of, 27
  and Pakistani Muslims, 312n60

and race/class issues, 76, 78, 82–83,
    174–75
  and recruitment of American Muslims,
    205
  and transcommunal Islam, 188,
    190–91, 223–26
nativism, 12, 61, 63, 64, 68
Negritude, 15
Negro World, 77, 81, 302n65
New Baghdad Café, 58
New Oriental Hall, 72–73, *74*
New Syria Party (NSP), 87–89, 89–90
"noble savage," 14
North American Islamic Trust, 218

objectification, 21–22, 101
oil embargo, 205, 207, 221
O'Reilly, Jack, 5
Organization of Arab Students, 202
Oriental Association, 80
Orientalism
  and Ahmadiyya converts, 82
  and citizenship issues, 27
  and Dearborn's first mosques, 125
  and European colonialism, 13–16
  and failure of first mosque, 57
  and Muslim American identity, 2
  and polygamy, 65–68
  and race issues, 68–71, 76–80
  and Syrian nationalism, 89
  and the Universal Islamic Society,
    63–65, 75
Osseiran, Adil, 137–38, 310n7, 311n29
"Otherness," 14–15
Ottoman Empire
  and the Armenian Crisis, 66
  early Muslim immigrants, 31–32,
    34–35
  fez popularity, 79
  and independence movements, 66
  and midcentury Muslim immigrants,
    138
  millet administrative regime, 69
  and mosque endowments, 45
  and sectarian divisions, 299n22
  and Sunni-Shi'a conflict, 42

and Syrian nationalism, 86
and World War I, 43, 61, 285, 310n15
See also Turkey

Pakistan Association of Detroit, 312n46
Pakistani Muslims, 172, 174, 192,
   197–98, 214, 312n60
Palestine, 86–87, 126, 137–38, 151, 157,
   174, 212
Palestine War, 20
Palestinian Muslims, 209, 214, 259
Palestinian War (1948), 158
pan-Africanism, 15, 27, 64, 75, 81, 82, 85
pan-Arabism, 64, 86, 202
pan-Islamism, 10, 27, 64
Paradise Valley, 105
Pasha, Djemal, 88
Pasha, Kemal, 88
"people of the book," 102
pilgrimage, 38
Piscatori, James, 21–22
pluralism, 10–13, 281–82
plural marriage. *See* polygamy
political issues and activism, 20–21, 126,
   135, 143, 276, 285
polygamy
   and citizenship issues, 65, 67–68,
      313n68
   and countercultural Islam, 248
   and gender issues in Islam, 253–54
   and immigration policy, 49
   and media depictions of Islam, 65–68
   and Mormonism, 299n16
Poole, Elijah. *See* Muhammad, Elijah
positive integration, 5
Prashad, Vijay, 75
Progressive Arabian Hashmie Society
   (Hashmie Hall) *(Nadi al-Arabi
   al-Hashmie), 118*
   and civic life, 125–26
   and Dearborn's first mosques, 120, 122
   and the Federation of Islamic
      Associations, 155
   finances of, 132
   and gender issues in Islam, 257
   incorporation of, 121

and the Islamic Center of America, 97
and Islamic reform and revivalism, 278,
   280
and midcentury Muslim immigrants,
   137–43
opening day ceremonies, 125
origin in, 117–19
and Osseiran visit, 137–38
prayer services, *162*
reopening of, 142
and social function of early mosques, 18
and Sunday school, 154
and visibility of American Islam,
   124–25
proselytizing, 108–9, 246. *See also*
   missionaries
Protestant Christianity, 137

qibla, 46–47, 54, 120, 140, 171, 226,
   296n78
Queraishi, Shair Mohamed, 78, 302n57
Qur'an
   and the Albanian Islamic Center, 170
   and alcohol prohibition, 146
   and early American mosques, 59
   and Islamic orthodoxy, 22, 262
   and mawlids, 111
   and Muslim identity formation, 91
   Qur'anic recitation, 38, 103, 162, 262,
      306n13
Quraysh tribe, 308n59
Qutb, Said, 202–3

race issues
   and African American converts to
      Islam, 84
   and American foreign policy, 7–8
   and changing role of American
      mosques, 282
   and citizenship, 68–71
   and class issues in Islam, 192
   and demographic shifts in American
      Islam, 10
   and Duse Mohamed Ali, 75–80
   and the Federation of Islamic
      Associations, 204

and Hassanein's conversion, 195
and transcommunal Islam, 188, 191–93
and *zakat,* 318n64
Saudi Arabia, 171–72, 204, 208, 233,
    314n104, 321n28
Sayegh, Fayez, 157
scarves and head coverings. *See hijab*
schisms, 40–41
second-wave feminism, 220
sectarian divisions and conflict, 39–43,
    57–59, 291n49, 299n22. *See also*
    Shiʿa Islam; Sunni Islam
segregation, 18–20, 216, 267, 269, 303n76
September 11 terrorist attacks, 4, 6, 15,
    17, 20–21, 279
settlement houses, 299n13
Shahbander, Abdul Rahman, 86–87
Shaltout, Mahmoud, 159, *160*
Shariʿa law, 204, 285
Sharieff, Haitama, 198, *203*, 249, 253–55,
    257, 317n42
Sharieff, Haleem, *203*, 257
Shaykh (honorific), 40
The Sheik (1921), 66
Shiʿa Islam
    and the American Moslem Society, 177
    and America's first imams, 39–43
    and archival materials, 326n17
    arrival in US, 307n51, 307n53
    and Dearborn's first mosques, 118
    and early Muslim immigrants, 34
    and ethnic divisions, 294n37
    and the FIA, 155, 159
    and funeral practices, 127
    and the *hajj,* 137
    in Indiana, 311n34
    and the Islamic Center of America, 167
    and Islamic orthodoxy, 24, 25
    and Islamic reform and revivalism, 220,
        222, 223, 274–75
    and Islamic revolutions, 259, 265
    and Lebanese politics, 309n4, 310n6
    and midcentury Muslim immigrants, 138
    and the Moslem Mosque of Highland
        Park, 47, 61
    and mosques of Dearborn, 97, 127,
        132–33, 307n49

and Muslim identity formation, 90
and Orientalism, 15–16
and professionalization of imam role,
    143
Sunni-Shiʿa conflict, 20, 55–56, 58–59,
    72, 83, 119–20, 308n55
and Syrian culture, 308n57
and Syrian nationalism, 88
Shura Council, 211
Sierra Leone, 313n83
Sister Clara Muhammad University, 225
slavery, 11, 22, 31, 274, 292n3
Smith, Faye Elizabeth, 65, 68, 94
Smith, Joseph, 299n16
Smith, Timothy, 290n43
social clubs, 36, 97, 126, 132–33, 185,
    190, 214, 283. *See also* Progressive
    Arabian Hashmie Society
Society for the Development of Our Own,
    317n46
South Asian Muslims. *See also* Afghan
    Muslims; Indian Muslims; Pakistani
    Muslims
Southend neighborhood (Dearborn),
    97, 98, 104, 139, 177, 209–10,
    309n83
Southern Christian Leadership
    Conference, 191
South Lebanon, 174
Soviet Union, 267
Spanish conquistadors, 31
Stabenow, Debbie, 5
Starrett, Gregory, 21, 104
State Street Mosque, 62, 192, 242
Stenhouse, T. B. H., 299n16
stereotypes, 7–8, 21
St. George's Antiochian Orthodox
    Church, 39
St. Maron's Catholic Church, 39, 88
stock market crash of 1929, 94, 96
St. Thomas Orthodox Church, 144, 168
suburbanization, 104–6, 136, 255–56
Suez Crisis, 157
Sufi orders, 142, 220, 241, 245, 291n49
Sugrue, Thomas, 190
Suleimaniyyah Mosque, 41
Sunday prayer, 211

Sunday school
  and the Albanian Islamic Center, 168
  and al-Mu'mineen Mosque, 199
  and the American Moslem Society, 7,
    182–83, 212–13
  American Moslem Women's Society,
    185–86
  and changes in American mosques, 17
  and Chirri, 154
  and Christian churches in Dearborn,
    108
  and Dearborn's first mosques, 119,
    127–30
  and the Islamic Center of America, 162
  and Islamic reform and revivalism, 173,
    259
  and midcentury Muslim immigrants,
    144
  and the Moslem Mosque of Highland
    Park, 62
  and social function of early mosques, 19
Sunna, 248, 291n49
Sunni Islam
  and African American converts, 84, 218
  and Albanian Muslims, 145, 147, 168
  and American-born Muslim leaders,
    182–83
  and the American Moslem Society,
    177, 308n54
  and America's first imams, 39–43
  and archival materials, 326n17
  and countercultural Islam, 245
  and early Muslim immigrants, 34
  and ethnic divisions, 294n37
  and the FIA, 155, 159
  and gender issues in Islam, 316n24
  and Islamic orthodoxy, 23–24, 25
  and Islamic reform and revivalism,
    222–23, 224, 225, 274–75
  and Lebanese politics, 310n6
  and *mawlid* tradition, 307n38
  and the Moslem Mosque of Highland
    Park, 47
  and mosques of Dearborn, 97, 127,
    130, 132–33, 307n49
  and Muslim identity formation, 90

and the Nation of Islam, 28, 238, 240
and race issues, 82, 85
and social clubs, 126
Sunni-Shi'a conflict, 20, 55–56, 58–59,
  72, 83, 119–20, 307n49, 307n51,
  308n55
and Syrian culture, 308n57
and Syrian nationalism, 88
and transcommunal Islam, 190
Supreme Council of Islamic Affairs, 204
Swanson, Jon, 106
Sykes-Picot Agreement, 86
syncretism, 12, 22, 25
Syria, 64, 79, 106, 149
Syrian Christians, 294n23
Syrian Mohammaden Lodge, 33
Syrian Muslims, *228*
  and the American Moslem Society, 7,
    176
  and demographic shifts in American
    Islam, 4
  and early Muslim immigrants, 32–33,
    34, 35, 36
  and immigration policy, 61, 68–69,
    299n27
  and immigration records, 299n20
  and the Moslem Mosque of Highland
    Park, 48, 54–55, 56, 59
  and mosques of Dearborn, 97–98, 104,
    106, 109, 112, 114–15, 117, 119–20,
    122–24, 124–26, 132–33
  and Muslim identity formation, 38–39
  and new generations of Muslim
    clerics, 134, 147–48, 151, 153,
    154, 157
  and race issues, 69–70
  and return immigration, 306n23
  and Sunni-Shi'a conflict, 120
  and Syrian nationalism, 85–89
  and US citizenship, 106

Tablighi Jama'at
  and al-Mu'mineen Mosque, 198, 201
  and American-born Muslim leaders,
    175–76
  and the American Moslem Society, 210